DATE DUE

DE 5 '98		

DEMCO 38-296

Discrete Mathematics

MIKE PIFF

Discrete Mathematics

An introduction for software engineers

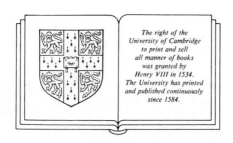

The right of the
University of Cambridge
to print and sell
all manner of books
was granted by
Henry VIII in 1534.
The University has printed
and published continuously
since 1584.

CAMBRIDGE UNIVERSITY PRESS

Cambridge

New York   Port Chester

Melbourne   Sydney

Published by the Press Syndicate of the University of Cambridge
The Pitt Building, Trumpington Street, Cambridge CB2 1RP
40 West 20th Street, New York, NY 10011, USA
10 Stamford Road, Oakleigh, Melbourne 3166, Australia

© Cambridge University Press 1991

First published 1991

Printed in Great Britain at the University Press, Cambridge

Library of Congress cataloguing in publication data available

British Library cataloguing in publication data available

ISBN 0 521 38475 3 hardback
ISBN 0 521 38622 5 paperback

CONTENTS

Appendices

PREFACE

Computing was historically taught as a branch of mathematics, usually of applied mathematics if a distinction was made. This family union came to an end when computer science diverged from mere numerical calculations towards more general objects such as data records, parse trees, and also the theory of how a computer works. The emphasis has recently become more mathematical, but with a different sort of mathematics. Also, computer science has itself spawned its own offspring, in the shape of software engineering and information technology.

Mathematics departments accustomed to teaching first year single honours mathematics undergraduates normally teach them a course in continuous mathematics and one on abstract algebra, or linear algebra, or both. Computer scientists have been pressing for their first year to be taught mathematics which is more relevant to the current needs of that discipline, and, in particular, some discrete mathematics. The content of discrete mathematics is broadly similar to what used to be known as *combinatorics*, but also includes topics from the foundations of mathematics, such as logic and set theory.

This book is designed as a course in discrete mathematics for first year computer scientists or software engineers in universities and colleges of further education. The book should form the basis of a full, one year option of two lectures a week, either as a subsidiary course to computer science, or as part of a mathematics first year option, say replacing part or all of the algebra normally taught there. At the University of Sheffield, any students taking computing courses are taught most of the material in this book, together with a full course in analysis and a short course in the methods of linear algebra.

In Chapter 2 we lay the foundations of mathematical logic. The ideas will probably be familiar to the student from elementary programming, but introduced in terms of 0's and 1's rather than truth values. The simplification of logical expressions will almost certainly be new, as will predicate calculus and program verification.

Chapter 3 introduces the algebra of set theory, and the important idea of a cartesian product, which is essential to the definition of relations and mappings in Chapters 4 and 5. The approach to these two topics has been unified, since the calculation of compositions and inverses of *finite* relations and mappings, which is only of peripheral interest to mathematicians, is central to the applications in computing. Chapter 5 also includes an introduction to the infinite, and to diagonal arguments, which are used to show that certain calculations are impossible. It concludes with applications to relational databases and relational normalization.

Chapter 6 defines the mathematical objects called graphs and digraphs, although they will be familiar to the reader by this time, since they will have been used in several other chapters. In Chapter 7, we meet some of the graphical algorithms which every student of computing should know about.

Chapter 8 treats the way axiom systems are built, and introduces the ideas of semigroups and formal languages, with applications to stacks and the syntax of grammars.

The book concludes with implementations in *Modula-2* of many of the algorithms introduced in previous chapters. These are to illustrate how the mathematics can be turned into concrete calculations.

It is expected that the student will be familiar with some programming language such as *Pascal, Ada* or *Modula-2*, to appreciate some of the examples, and the algorithms in Chapter 7. Which language he is familiar with is immaterial, since there are only trivial differences in their syntax at the level at which we shall be using them.

It cannot be stressed too strongly that this core of discrete mathematics comprises some of the essential tools for today's applications in computing, and is the basic language which every student of computing should take pride in mastering, as essential to him as fluency in his favourite programming language. Each new idea presented must be thoroughly assimilated, until it determines the way he tackles any new situation. As each new idea is digested, it is essential that he carefully reads the examples presented at that point, and attempts all the exercises. These exercises serve the important purpose of getting the student to think in precise terms about new ideas. For this reason, hints or solutions to many of the exercises are given in the appendices. Many of the exercises are purely mathematical in content; a mathematical problem extracts the essential difficulty of a subject far better than a verbose discussion of a real-life application can. Some of the exercises are deliberately open ended, to encourage the student to think of more original applications. It is hoped that thinking about these will provide the student with some entertainment.

This book is not a course on formal methods in computer science, it is a mathematics textbook. On the other hand, I have tried to include enough of the applications of discrete mathematics to make the student realize that mathematics has many and varied uses in both the theory and practicalities of computing. I hope I have avoided the failings of many of the other books in this field, which pretend to be a mathematics course, are written like a computing course, but turn out to be neither. I have wasted much time attempting to find just one suitable recommended book for my students in the past. The many students who have commented on my course have contributed immeasurably to my appreciation of what they expect from such a course, what they find difficult, and how to minimize those difficulties. I hope this book amply reflects their comments.

This textbook was typeset in Donald E. Knuth's typesetting language TeX, using the macro package LaTeX developed by Leslie Lamport. Any errors remaining are entirely my own fault. First reports of any remaining errors will be gratefully acknowledged.

I would particularly like to thank John Pym for the original idea of writing this book, and David Tranah and Alan Harvey of Cambridge University Press for their help and encouragement during the last year of its preparation, when everything from building works to the failure of the university network seemed to conspire against my finishing on time. Finally, I should like to thank my wife Shelagh and daughters Emily and Dulcie for their unending patience and support whilst I was writing it; without them it would not have been possible.

Mike Piff
University of Sheffield
December 21, 1990

1

Introduction

1.1   Discrete mathematics

Discrete mathematics is the study of those parts of mathematics which do not require any knowledge of *limits, convergence, differentiation,* and so on. It encompasses most of the foundations of mathematics, such as logic, set theory, relations, and also graph theory, formal language theory and an indeterminate chunk of abstract algebra.

The boundaries are necessarily vague, as they are in any subject, and we can never be sure, as our study progresses, that we will not need some result from another area. Anyone studying the time complexity of sorting algorithms would find it difficult not to use some ideas from the calculus; both logic and formal languages subsume the whole of mathematics; the study of finite error correcting codes leads into some sophisticated uses of matrices and polynomial algebras.

Mathematics provides us with a way of describing the so called 'real world' in an accurate, concise and unambiguous way. We extract the properties which we wish to describe, write down a few mathematical relations, and then work algebraically with those relations. As long as the mathematics and the object of our study have those common properties, any deduction we make in the mathematical model can be translated back to the real world.

It does not matter whether the mathematical description is close to the way a task is implemented. A common mistake is to think in terms of concrete realizations rather than properties. The implementation might use either arrays or pointers; sets or arrays of boolean values; data in memory or in files. The mathematical description should be divorced from these minor details, and should concentrate on the common properties of all such implementations. Then, if a change has to be made to the way the data is stored, it is only the interface between that data and the rest of the program that needs to be changed.

1

The mathematical model contains no more and no less than what has been put into it by the formulator. Careful thought at this stage is worth years of rewriting a program at a later date.

There are few mathematical prerequisites for a course in discrete mathematics. Some Greek letters are used in this book. The full Greek alphabet is included in the index, where the name of each letter is followed by the upper and lower case forms of that letter.

1.2 Numbers

The *natural* numbers are defined as the numbers 1, 2, 3, ..., whilst the *cardinal* numbers are 0, 1, 2, etc. The *integers* consist of all zero, positive and negative whole numbers 0, 1, −1, 2, −2, etc. The *rational* numbers are the fractions p/q, where p and q are integers, and $q \neq 0$, for example, 2/3, −27/13 and $2\frac{1}{2}$. All rational numbers have a decimal expansion which repeats indefinitely, or recurs, such as $\frac{1}{7} = 0.1428571428571\cdots$. Finally, the *real* numbers consist of all rational numbers, and also all numbers such as e, π, and $\sqrt{2}$ that have non-recurring decimal expansions.

In Section 3.2, we shall introduce the notations $\mathbb{N}$, $\mathbb{Z}^+$, $\mathbb{Z}$, $\mathbb{Q}$ and $\mathbb{R}$ for these sets of numbers. The distinction between naturals and cardinals is important, and the two are often confused.

A notation which we shall occasionally need is the *factorial* notation

$$n! = n \times (n - 1) \times (n - 2) \times \cdots \times 2 \times 1,$$

where n is a natural number. This notation is extended to cardinal numbers by putting $0! = 1$. The factorial is known to enumerate the *permutations* of a collection of n objects, that is, the number of ways of ordering those objects. It is also used in defining the *binomial coefficients*

$$\binom{n}{r} = \frac{n!}{(n-r)!r!},$$

called n *choose* r. These enumerate the different ways of selecting an unordered collection of r objects from a total collection of n objects.

•*Exercise 1.1* Prove the two assertions above.

1.3   Mathematical induction

There is an important method of proof, called *mathematical induction*, which is used several times in this book, and which needs to be fully understood. Suppose we have a statement regarding the natural number n, and we know that the statement is true when $n \leqslant l$, for some fixed l, usually with $l = 1$. Suppose also that we can prove that its truth for all $n \leqslant m$, the *inductive hypothesis*, implies its truth for $n = m + 1$, for each $m \geqslant l$. Then it is true for all natural numbers n. This is because we know it is true for $n \leqslant l$, and so can prove it is true for $n = l + 1$. But now it is true for $n \leqslant l + 1$, so it is true for $n = l + 2$. And so the argument continues.

> **Example 1.2** We show that $2n^3 + 3n^2 + n$ is always divisible by 6, where n is a natural number. We choose $l = 1$, and check that when $n = l = 1$ we have $2 + 3 + 1 = 6$, so the result is true for $n = 1$. Next we assume that the result is true whenever $n \leqslant m$, and look at the result when $n = m + 1$:
>
> $$
> \begin{aligned}
> 2(m+1)^3 \quad + \quad & 3(m+1)^2 + (m+1) \\
> = \quad & 2(m^3 + 3m^2 + 3m + 1) + 3(m^2 + 2m + 1) + (m+1) \\
> = \quad & (2m^3 + 3m^2 + m) + (6m^2 + 12m + 6) \\
> = \quad & (2m^3 + 3m^2 + m) + 6(m^2 + 2m + 1),
> \end{aligned}
> $$
>
> and we see a sum of two terms, both divisible by 6. Hence the result is true for $n = m + 1$. Thus, by induction, it is true for all n.

The reader of this book should look up *induction* in the index to see just how important this method of proof is.

- **Exercise 1.3** Show that $9^n + 7$ is always divisible by 8.

- **Exercise 1.4** Show that $9^n - 8n - 1$ is always divisible by 64.

- **Exercise 1.5** Show by induction that the sum s_n of the first n natural numbers equals $n(n+1)/2$.

- **Exercise 1.6** Show that the sum S_n of the squares of the first n natural numbers equals $n(n+1)(2n+1)/6$.

2

Logic

2.1 Introduction

Mathematics is the science of inference. It starts from axioms describing the world, and makes deductions from those axioms according to the accepted rules of reason.

It became apparent in the nineteenth century and early in the twentieth century that these rules of inference themselves could be made the subject of mathematical investigation, and thus there was a possibility that the whole logical process could be mechanized. One could write down the initial assumptions, and then merely turn a handle to obtain the conclusion. These investigations resulted in what is known as *symbolic logic*. Although the original goal may have eluded us, because of certain profound discoveries concerning the process of proof, what remains is a powerful notation for expressing ideas in a precise form, and an elegant mathematical theory of logic which we shall be studying in this chapter.

Let us first look at a few places where mathematical logic is used.

Example 2.1 Whenever control branches in a computer program, a logical condition has been evaluated, and the program has branched accordingly. In higher level languages such conditions are expressed in terms of *boolean* values, returned whenever arithmetical comparisons such as (a<b) are evaluated. These values are combined using *connectives* such as AND and OR and the operation NOT, together with comparisons such as (a=b)>(c<d) working directly on the boolean values. Making such a condition work efficiently is usually synonymous with making its statement as short as possible.

Example 2.2 Suppose that a body of facts has been assembled by a police force, recording all incidents in their area, together with details of known criminals, suspicious sightings, and so on. A new

4

incident occurs, and they want to obtain information on any *related* incidents, where *related* means different things according to the type of incident. Thus the definition of *related* might read '*if* burglary *then* (same mode of entry *or* recent car theft) *else if* car theft *then* (rowdiness in pub nearby *or* same make of car *or* accident reported) *else* ...'. Any program to sift information is going to have to be able to make logical deductions.

Example 2.3 When a new microchip is being produced, its circuits are designed in such a way that it performs any switching as efficiently as possible. The pathways through the chip's circuitry are interrupted by *gates*, where logical operations are performed on one or more pathways, and other pathways are subsequently opened or closed. The numbers of these gates generally determine the efficiency of the chip. In the logical design stage, given a specification of the chip, the goal is to achieve this specification with as few gates as possible.

Example 2.4 In *program verification*, a fragment of program is tested to see if it achieves its desired results. Usually there will be conditions on the values of its variables when it is entered, and a condition to be satisfied when it is exited. We would like to prove that it meets these conditions. It could then be certified as free of bugs.

Example 2.5 In *formal specification*, the objective is, not to verify an existing program, but to write down a mathematical specification of a system so that it can be generated mechanically, or, at least, so that it is internally consistent and fulfills the needs of the customer! We might also wish to write or generate a *prototype* version of the system, to test on the customer, to see if the specification lives up to expectations.

One of the major faults of ordinary language is that it is too vague. It works very well provided the logical content is not too high, but above a certain threshold it fails completely to convey the right message. Even in the cases when it does convey the right message, the user has to be extremely careful with the order of his words, as the slightest change may alter the meaning.

Example 2.6 Consider the statements 'he answered the wrong questions' and 'he answered the questions wrong'. Viewed as describing the performance of a candidate in an examination, the former presumably means that he failed, whereas the latter leaves him the possibility of scraping enough marks to pass.

2.2   Propositions

In symbolic logic we are only concerned with statements which are either true or false.

> **Definition** A **proposition** is a statement which is either true or false.

> **Example 2.7** The following are all propositions.
>   (i) Blue is a colour.
> (ii) $1 + 1 = 2$.
> (iii) $1 + 1 = 3$.
> (iv) All computer scientists have dark hair.
>   (v) Any two natural numbers have a unique highest common factor.
> The following are *not* propositions.
> (vi) Are you going out somewhere?
> (vii) $2 + 3$.
> (viii) Sheffield.
> (ix) Noisy yellow derivatives eat cucumber sandwiches.

> •**Exercise 2.8** Are the following propositions?
>   (i) The sky is always green.
> (ii) $(2 > 3)$ and I am a Dutchman.
> (iii) Everyone has two ears.
> (iv) Every integer n satisfies $n < n + 1$.
>   (v) This is Chapter 2.
> (vi) This sentence is false.

2.3   Propositional variables

To simplify the handling of the collection of all propositions, and the combination of these propositions, we introduce the idea of propositional variables and truth values.

> **Definition** A **propositional** or **boolean variable** is a variable which can only take one of the values **T** or **F**, representing the **truth values true** and **false** respectively.

Thus a propositional variable is simpler than a real variable, which can take infinitely many values. If P is a propositional variable, then either we have $P = \mathbf{T}$ or $P = \mathbf{F}$. Also, since any proposition is either true or false, we can set a propositional variable equal to a proposition, and then it takes on the truth value of that proposition.

> ***Example 2.9*** If P is a propositional variable, then setting P equal to the proposition '$2 < 3$' gives P the value $\mathbf{T}$. Setting it equal to 'I am a ten-legged dog' gives it the value $\mathbf{F}$.

Boolean variables, named after the mathematician Boole, occur explicitly in *Ada*, *Modula-2* and *Pascal*. In these languages, we can set such variables equal to conditions such as (a<b) or (x IN s). Also, a procedure is allowed to return a boolean value, enabling the construction of quite complicated propositions.

If we look at the representation of the values $\mathbf{T}$ and $\mathbf{F}$ used in computing languages, we find there are two conventions. In the first, represented by the languages *Pascal*, *Ada* and *Modula-2*, $\mathbf{F} = 0$ and $\mathbf{T} = 1$. In the second, represented by *BASIC*, $\mathbf{F} = 0$ and $\mathbf{T} = -1$. Whereas *Modula-2* might check the least significant bit of a boolean variable to decide whether it is true or false, *BASIC* might check the sign bit, that is, the most significant bit of the variable.

> •***Exercise 2.10*** Discuss the different behaviour of the fragment
> $$\texttt{UNTIL (a=b)<(c=d)}$$
> in *Modula-2* and *BASIC*.

2.4 Predicates

Predicates are statements involving variables, which become propositions as soon as the variables are assigned values. Before we can get anywhere with predicates, we need to specify what values the variables are allowed to take. This is usually handled by saying that a *universe of discourse* has been specified, and any variables in a predicate take values in this universe. We generally use lower case letters for variables and upper case letters for predicates, so we can readily tell which is which.

> ***Example 2.11*** If the universe of discourse is chosen to be the natural numbers, then x will denote a natural number, and $P(x)$ might denote the statement 'x is prime'. The predicate $G(x, y)$ might mean '$x < y$'.

Example 2.12 Equally well, we might wish to take the universe to be the collection of customers at a certain bank. Then x would represent a customer, and $O(x)$ might mean 'x is overdrawn'.

Definition A **predicate** is a statement $P(x_1, \ldots, x_n)$ which has n **variables** or **places** $x_1, \ldots, x_n$, and which becomes a proposition as soon as specific objects from the universe of discourse are substituted for the variables $x_1, \ldots, x_n$.

●***Exercise 2.13*** Think of a three-place predicate.

●***Exercise 2.14*** Think of a ten-place predicate.

The predicates we most often meet are 1- and 2-place predicates. The former are related to sets, and the latter to relations, the subjects of Chapters 3 and 4. We can regard propositions as 0-place predicates, in that no variables have to be assigned values before we can decide whether or not they are true.

Example 2.15 If the universe of discourse is the natural numbers, then
$$P(x, y) \iff x^2 = y$$
is a predicate in two variables, and $P(2, 4)$ is a proposition which is true, since $2^2 = 4$; $P(1, 2)$ is false.

We shall return later to the study of predicates. For the time being, we shall only use them as a way of generating propositions to use in examples. Most useful propositions are obtained from some predicate by assigning values to all its variables. Thus, for instance, the statement 'I am thirsty' can be considered as derived from a predicate $T(x)$ on substitution of 'I' for x. The statement 'He gave her a book' is a substitution in a predicate $Gave(s, o, i)$, where the variables s, o and i are the subject, object and indirect object respectively. The assignment is $s = $ 'he', $o = $ 'a book' and $i = $ 'her'.

●***Exercise 2.16*** Rephrase the following in predicate notation. Assume an appropriate universe of discourse in each case.

  (i) x is a parent of y.

  (ii) x is a real number.

  (iii) Twice x equals three times y.

  (iv) $x < y \leqslant z$.

  (v) $m = \frac{1}{2}(x + y)$.

  (vi) Job x has higher priority than job y, and will therefore run before job y.

(vii) $x \leqslant x$.

(viii) Variable x is of type t.

2.5 Truth tables

Let us investigate how we can determine when a complicated expression is true, given the truth or falsity of each of its propositional variables. Assuming it is built from only a finite number of these variables, the answer is easily found by listing all the possible combinations of truth values.

Definition Let P, Q, R, ..., be propositional variables. Suppose we have some formula $W(P, Q, R, ...)$, involving the propositional variables, which is such that, whenever these variables are replaced by truth values, W becomes a proposition. Then W is called a **well-formed formula**, or **wff** for short.

Suppose we have some wff $W(P, Q, R)$. We can draw up a *truth table* for W in the following way. We list all the possible combinations of values for P, Q and R, and next to them list the truth value of W, as in Figure 2.1

Fig. 2.1 **A truth table**

P	Q	R	W
T	T	T	T
T	T	F	F
T	F	T	F
T	F	F	F
F	T	T	F
F	T	F	T
F	F	T	T
F	F	F	F

The number of rows in the truth table depends on the number of variables there are. With n variables, there will be 2^n rows to the table. Twenty variables would give over a million rows. For such a modest number of variables, there has to be a better way of deducing what the truth value of the wff is, and we shall see later that the most efficient solution is usually to partially simplify the wff according to well-defined rules, and then use the simplified version to *calculate* any line of the table we might need.

> *Definition* The **truth table** of the wff $W(P_1, \ldots, P_n)$ is a table with 2^n rows and $n + 1$ columns, each row listing a different combination of truth values of the propositions $P_1, \ldots, P_n$, followed by the corresponding truth value of W.

From such a truth table, we can deduce what happens if $P_1, \ldots, P_n$ are replaced by concrete propositions. In Figure 2.1 we can deduce that if P is false, Q is true and R is true, then W is false.

The reader will probably be familiar with this technique, which is used in manuals on programming languages to describe how the various logical operations work. Many of these use the numbers 0 and 1 instead of **F** and **T**. We shall regard this practice as illiterate!

As far as truth tables are concerned, the interesting cases occur, as we shall see, when the whole of the last column consists of either **T**s or **F**s. In these cases, the wff is always true or always false, and it expresses a logical theorem

> •*Exercise 2.17* What is the truth table of P?

> •*Exercise 2.18* How do you think we could define the truth table of a 1-place *predicate*?

2.6 Negation

The simplest way to obtain a new wff from an old one is to take the opposite of its meaning.

> *Definition* Let W be a wff. The **negation** of W is the wff $\neg W$, read as 'not W', which is true if and only if W is false.

This is best described in terms of a single propositional variable P, when we can form the truth table for $\neg P$, as in Figure 2.2. To obtain the truth table of the negation of a more general wff W from that of W, we change every **T** in the last column to **F**, and every **F** to **T**.

> •*Exercise 2.19* Find the truth table for the negation of W in Figure 2.1.

Fig. 2.2 Negation

P	$\neg P$
T	F
F	T

Several different symbols are used for the negation of a wff. The commonly used ones are $\neg W$, $\bar{W}$, W', $-W$, $\sim W$, and NOT W. In programming languages, the last few are ordinarily used, because of the restricted character sets of most keyboards.

- •*Exercise 2.20* How does the mathematical notation for negation differ fundamentally from the usual grammatical use of the word 'not' in English?

- •*Exercise 2.21* In the following, indicate whether or not the one statement is the negation of the other. Assume the obvious universe of discourse.
  - (i) $x < y$; $x \geqslant y$.
  - (ii) x is a parent of y; x is a son of y.
  - (iii) All sheep are white; all sheep are not white.
  - (iv) I am lucky; I am unlucky.

2.7 Conjunction

The proposition formed from two other propositions, which is true only when they are both true, is called the *conjunction* of the two propositions.

Example 2.22 From 'I wrote that program' and 'I did it quickly' we could form 'I wrote that program quickly', or 'I wrote that program and I did it quickly' or 'I quickly wrote that program'. All these say the same thing.

Definition Let W_1 and W_2 be two wffs. The **conjunction** $W_1 \wedge W_2$ of W_1 and W_2 is the wff which is true only when W_1 and W_2 are both true.

We again have competing notations for the conjunction, the common ones being $W_1 \wedge W_2$, $W_1 \& W_2$, $W_1.W_2$, and (W_1 AND W_2), the last three being most common in programming languages.

● *Exercise 2.23* Let P ='I solved this problem', Q ='It was done quickly', R ='It was wrong', S ='I got no marks for it', T ='I gave a silly answer'. Rewrite the following in ordinary English.

(i) $P \wedge \neg Q$.   (ii) $(\neg S) \wedge (\neg T)$.

(iii) $P \wedge (\neg(Q \wedge \neg R)) \wedge \neg(S \wedge T)$.

If P and Q are propositional variables, we form the truth table of $P \wedge Q$ as in Figure 2.3. It would be less circular to define the conjunction directly from this truth table, rather than the definition we originally gave.

Fig. 2.3 **Conjunction**

P	Q	$P \wedge Q$
T	T	T
T	F	F
F	T	F
F	F	F

Unlike the negation operation, which acts on a single wff, the conjunction joins two wffs into a single wff. It is an example of what are known as *connectives*. We shall meet several instances of these connectives in the following pages. We could also envisage ways of joining *more than* two propositions together, but it turns out that this can always be done by using only connectives which join two at a time. Thus such higher-order connectives need never be used.

One of the most fundamental conventions of mathematics, and also computing, is that if we have an ambiguous expression, such as $a - b \times c$ for instance, we use brackets to force its evaluation in a certain order, such as $a-(b \times c)$ or $(a-b) \times c$. We do just this in logic, and the convention is that if a connective appears between bracketed expressions, then we must evaluate the bracketed expressions first, and *then* combine them. Of course, the brackets must all match correctly, and all the connectives must link two expressions together, and a negation cannot immediately precede a closing bracket. These sort of rules are the reason why a wff is described as *well-formed*.

● *Exercise 2.24* Find the truth tables of each of

(i) $P \wedge P$;   (ii) $P \wedge \neg P$;   (iii) $\neg(P \wedge P)$;
(iv) $\neg(P \wedge \neg P)$;   (v) $(P \wedge Q) \wedge R$.

● *Exercise 2.25* Phrase the following in terms of predicates.

  (i) x is a real number greater than π.
  (ii) The file f is both copy and delete protected, but not archived.
  (iii) $x < y < z$.
  (iv) x is a common ancestor of y and z.
  (v) Terminal x is connected directly to computer c, but terminal y is not.

2.8 Disjunction

When we wish to state that at least one of two propositions is true, we are using the *disjunction* of the propositions.

Definition Let W_1 and W_2 be wffs. The **disjunction** $W_1 \vee W_2$ of W_1 and W_2 is true if and only if at least one of W_1 and W_2 is true.

When P and Q are propositional variables, the disjunction has the truth table as in Figure 2.4.

Fig. 2.4 Disjunction

P	Q	$P \vee Q$
T	T	T
T	F	T
F	T	T
F	F	F

The usual notations for disjunction are $W_1 \vee W_2$, $W_1 \mid W_2$, $W_1 + W_2$, and (W_1 OR W_2). The disjunction, like conjunction, is a connective. It is loosely expressed in English as 'Either...or...', but there is a possible confusion here, in that this construction is also used to express the mutual exclusion of two possibilities, that is, either P or Q *but not both*. The mathematical notation, however, is completely unambiguous.

Example 2.26 Consider the statement 'a proposition is either true or false'. This expresses the fact that a proposition cannot be both true *and* false, and so is an example of an *exclusive or* operation.

Now consider the statement 'most flags contain the colour red or the colour blue'. This time, we are not saying that a flag containing both red and blue is rare; we *are* saying that one which contains *neither* is rare.

•**Exercise 2.27** Let P ='I bank with Floyds Bank', Q ='I am in credit', R ='I use a credit card', S ='I write a cheque', T ='I pay a bill'. Rewrite the following in ordinary English.

(i) $S \vee R$.   (ii) $P \wedge ((\neg Q) \vee S)$.   (iii) $R \vee S$.
(iv) $(Q \vee \neg T)$.   (v) $(\neg T) \vee (Q \wedge S) \vee ((\neg Q) \wedge R)$.

We are now in a position to write down the truth tables of wffs of unlimited complexity, just by following the rules for the constituent connectives. The rest of propositional calculus is concerned solely with the different ways a wff can be rewritten, possibly with a view to simplifying it.

Example 2.28 The truth table of $\neg((\neg P) \wedge (\neg Q))$ appears in Figure 2.5. We have included any extra columns we might need to cal-

Fig. 2.5 Truth table of $\neg((\neg P) \wedge (\neg Q))$

P	Q	$\neg P$	$\neg Q$	$(\neg P) \wedge (\neg Q)$	$\neg((\neg P) \wedge (\neg Q))$
T	T	F	F	F	T
T	F	F	T	F	T
F	T	T	F	F	T
F	F	T	T	T	F

culate intermediate results. This is good practice, since trying to do too much at once only ends in grief!

•**Exercise 2.29** Find the truth tables of
(i) $(P \wedge Q) \vee R$;   (ii) $(P \vee R) \wedge (Q \vee R)$.

•**Exercise 2.30** Write the following in terms of predicates.
(i) If f is a userfile, it cannot be both copy and write protected.
(ii) If x and y are files, and they have the same filename, they are identical.
(iii) x is a terminal, and is either on a direct or a network line.
(iv) The message m came from x or y.

2.9 Other connectives

The next connective we shall introduce is usually called the *implication* connective, though we must be careful to distinguish it from *logical implication*, to be introduced in Section 2.10.

> **Definition** Let W_1 and W_2 be wffs. The **implication** of W_2 by W_1, written $W_1 \to W_2$, is false only when W_1 is true but W_2 is false. An alternative way of defining $W_1 \to W_2$ is as $(\neg W_1) \vee W_2$, and we say 'W_1 implies W_2.'

We are not suggesting in this definition that there is any sort of causal link between W_1 and W_2, in that the truth of W_1 somehow lets us *deduce* the truth of W_2. The statement $W_1 \to W_2$ is true or false in the same sort of impartial way that $W_1 \wedge W_2$ or $W_1 \vee W_2$ can be. Thus, '$(2 > 3) \to$ "London is the capital of Great Britain"' is true, even though the two statements appear to have nothing in common. And, certainly, $2 > 3$ does not *force* London to be a capital; the statement '$(2 > 3) \to$ "London is not the capital of Great Britain"' is equally true. For $\neg(2 > 3) \vee X$ is true regardless of the meaning of X.

The truth table of implication is given in Figure 2.6.

Fig. 2.6 Implication

P	Q	$P \to Q$
T	T	T
T	F	F
F	T	T
F	F	T

Example 2.31 Let $P =$'I am a politician', $Q =$'Politicians are dishonest', $R =$'I am dishonest'. Then $P \to R$ is true provided I am not an honest politician. Thus if I am a mathematician, it is true. If I am dishonest, it is true. If I am a dishonest politician, it is true.

If we look at $R \to P$, this is true provided I am not a dishonest non-politician. If I am an honest politician it is true; in fact, it is true whenever I am honest. If I am a politician it is true. If I am a dishonest politician, it is true. But if I am a dishonest mathematician, it is false, though you might not believe me in that case!

Now consider $(P \wedge Q) \to R$. This is true whatever I am, and an honest mathematician should be able to prove that it is true. By the time we have studied quantifiers we will have the tools to do so.

• **Exercise 2.32** Let $P =$'I am a student', $Q =$'I work hard', $R =$'I am poor', $S =$'I am intelligent', $T =$'I am hungry'. Rewrite the following in ordinary English.

(i) $(P \vee S) \to Q$.   (ii) $(P \wedge R) \to T$.

(iii) $S \to \neg P$.

The implication connective suggests a sort of ordering of the truth values of two wffs, and this is reflected in its representation in programming languages. In *Modula-2*, FALSE<TRUE, so $P \to Q$ is expressed by P<=Q. Unfortunately, the arrow appears to be pointing in the wrong direction! In *BASIC*, usually TRUE=-1, FALSE=0, so we need P>=Q.

• **Exercise 2.33** Rephrase the following in terms of predicates, using the connective →.

(i) If x is an integer, then it is a real number.

(ii) If f is a user file, it is either write or copy protected.

(iii) If x divides y then it does not exceed y.

(iv) If x has system priority 6, he can access filestore f.

The analogue of equality of two boolean variables in a program is given in the next definition.

Definition Let W_1 and W_2 be wffs. The **biconditional** or **equivalence** of W_1 and W_2, written $W_1 \leftrightarrow W_2$, is false only when W_1 is true but W_2 is false, or W_1 is false but W_2 is true.

The biconditional is true only when W_1 and W_2 have the same truth value. The truth table is given in Figure 2.7.

Fig. 2.7 Biconditional

P	Q	$P \leftrightarrow Q$
T	T	T
T	F	F
F	T	F
F	F	T

In *Modula-2* the biconditional is expressed by P=Q.

•*Exercise 2.34* Write the following in terms of predicates, using the connective $\leftrightarrow$. Some of them are ambiguous, but do your best to interpret them as biconditionals. The fault is in everyday language, and we have to be careful to translate it into mathematical language, guessing at what the writer *really* intended.

  (i) x has access to file f if and only if his priority is 7.

  (ii) x will only be charged interest if he is overdrawn on an ordinary account, or is overdrawn by more than the limit y on a special account.

  (iii) The car c runs fine, provided you don't overrev it.

  (iv) The bird b is a puffin if it is a seagoing bird, and it either has a parrot-like bill, or else it shows a pronounced white facial patch.

There are two more connectives, which are of considerable use in the design of electronic circuits.

Definition The **nand** operation W_1 nand W_2 is false precisely when $W_1 \wedge W_2$ is true.

    The **exclusive or** operation W_1 xor W_2 is true only when W_1 and W_2 have opposite truth values.

The nand operation is true provided its operands are not both true. The exclusive or operation is the exact opposite of the biconditional.

The sorts of conditions we meet in loop control are of the form which can be handled in terms of what we have so far covered.

Example 2.35 Suppose that a REPEAT...UNTIL loop should terminate if $a = 0$, or if b and c are both 0, or if $a < 0$ and $b < c$. The condition is

       `(a=0) OR ((b=0)AND(c=0)) OR ((a<0)and(b<c))`.

Alternatively, we could use the condition

       `(a<>0) <= (((b<>0)<(c=0)) OR ((a>=0)<(b<c)))`.

There are many other equivalent conditions for termination which we could use, and which one we choose depends on the relative efficiency of their evaluation, and how much effort it is worth devoting to finding the most efficient.

•*Exercise 2.36* Write terminating conditions for a REPEAT...UNTIL loop which match the following verbal descriptions. Assume that the mathematical variable a coincides with the variable a in the loop, and so on.

  (i) Terminate if $a < b \leqslant c$.

 (ii) Terminate if $a > b$ and either $a > c$ or $b - a > c$.

(iii) Terminate as soon as a, b and c have different values.

(iv) Terminate as soon as a and b have the same sign.

 (v) Terminate when a and $b - c$ have opposite signs, neither being zero.

•*Exercise 2.37* Consider the loop

```
REPEAT

    . . .

UNTIL ((a-b)<=c)<=((NOT((a=0)AND(b=1)))
              AND(((a+c)<b)OR((a-c)>3)));
```

in which the variables are all of type `INTEGER`. Find out whether it will terminate when the variables have the following values.

(i)   a=0, b=1, c=2.   (ii)   a=0, b=1, c=-2.

(iii)   a=14, b=1, c=10.   (iv)   a=0, b=2, c=-1.

2.10   Logical equivalence and logical implication

Our purpose in this section is to discover why we can move from one line of a mathematical argument to another. There are certain fundamental laws of logical reasoning, which permit us to say that from one statement being true, we can deduce that another statement is true. The simplest cases of this happen when, for example, the second statement is in some sense *weaker* than the first. The truth of P ought to imply the truth of $P \vee Q$.

It might seem strange that such an implication could ever be useful, but consider the following.

Example 2.38 Nat Paticlur phones the booking offices of Icarus Airlines, and asks for a flight to Athens on either Friday or Saturday. Gladys Ërvu takes the call, and taps the request into the booking computer. As it happens, there *is* a flight on Saturday. The computer flashes up the message 'Request accepted', and gives the details of the flight.

During the design stages, a green systems analyst decided that a request for a flight should specify a single day only, and that any request for a range of days should result in 'Error 267: incorrect date format— please retype' being flashed upon the screen. After some prompting from Icarus Airlines, who claimed that this sort of request was quite common, and that one customer was in the habit of asking for a flight 'in the Spring, I'm not fussy when—just find me a flight', the analyst modified the prototype so that it would accept any set of dates. The message "Of course it's obvious that if there is a flight on *Saturday* then there is a flight on *either Friday or Saturday*—anybody can see that!" was deemed inappropriate!

Thus we see that it might be a quite useful sort of deduction for a computer to make, to derive $P \lor Q$ from P. We must be careful to ensure that the deduction $P \land Q$ is not made from P with equal abandon. The deduction of P or Q from $P \land Q$ would be perfectly correct. It is not clear which deductions are legal and which are not.

Consider Example 2.28, where we showed that the truth table of $\neg((\neg P) \land (\neg Q))$ is identical to that of $P \lor Q$. This property of having the same truth table is described as *logical equivalence*. In this case, we can deduce either expression from the other.

Definition Let W_1 and W_2 be two wffs, involving the same propositional variables $P, Q, R, \ldots$. Suppose that, for given truth values of the propositional variables, W_1 and W_2 are always either simultaneously true or simultaneously false. Then W_1 and W_2 are said to be **logically equivalent**, written $W_1 \iff W_2$.

When W_1 and W_2 are logically equivalent, it does not matter logically which of the two we use. There may be reasons of simplicity or expedience which would decide us to prefer one expression to the other.

Alternative notations for logical equivalence are $W_1 \equiv W_2$ and $W_1 \iff W_2$.

• **Exercise 2.39** Prove the following logical equivalences, by calculating the truth tables of the two wffs.

(i) $P \iff \neg\neg P$.   (ii) $P \land Q \iff \neg(\neg P \lor \neg Q)$.

(iii) $(P \lor Q) \land \neg P \iff Q \land \neg P$.

(iv) $\neg(P \to Q) \iff P \land \neg Q$.

(v) $P \leftrightarrow Q \iff \neg P \leftrightarrow \neg Q$.

(vi) $P \to (Q \lor R) \iff (P \land \neg Q) \to R$.

(vii) $P \to Q \iff (P \lor Q) \leftrightarrow Q$.

(viii) $P \to (Q \to R) \iff (P \land Q) \to R$.

(ix) $P \to (Q \to R) \iff Q \to (P \to R)$.

(x) $(P \land Q) \to R \iff (P \to R) \lor (Q \to R)$.

This handles the exact equivalence of two wffs, but we also need something weaker to handle one-way implications. If we look at logical equivalence, we see that a **T** in a certain position in the truth table of one wff corresponds to a **T** in the same position in the other truth table, and *vice versa*. Drop the '*vice versa*' and we have what we want.

Definition If W_1 and W_2 are wffs, we say that W_1 **logically implies** W_2 if any assignment of truth values to the propositional variables which makes W_1 true also makes W_2 true. We then write $W_1 \implies W_2$.

Alternative notations for logical implication are $W_1 \implies W_2$ and $W_1 \vdash W_2$.

Example 2.40 $(P \wedge Q) \vee (Q \wedge \neg R) \implies (Q \vee R)$, as we easily see from its truth table in Figure 2.8. Whenever there is a **T** in column 4,

Fig. 2.8 Logical implication

P	Q	R	$(P \wedge Q) \vee (Q \wedge \neg R)$	$Q \vee R$
T	T	T	T	T
T	T	F	T	T
T	F	T	F	T
T	F	F	F	F
F	T	T	F	T
F	T	F	T	T
F	F	T	F	T
F	F	F	F	F

there is also a **T** in column 5.

● **Exercise 2.41** Prove the following logical implications, by means of truth tables.

(i) $P \implies P \vee Q$.   (ii) $P \wedge Q \implies P$.

(iii) $Q \implies P \rightarrow Q$.   (iv) $P \wedge \neg P \implies Q$.

(v) $P \leftrightarrow Q \implies P \rightarrow Q$.

(vi) $P \rightarrow Q \implies (P \vee R) \rightarrow (Q \vee R)$.

(vii) $(P \leftrightarrow Q) \wedge (Q \leftrightarrow R) \implies P \leftrightarrow R)$.

(viii) $(P \rightarrow Q) \wedge (Q \rightarrow R) \implies (P \rightarrow R)$.

(ix) $(P \rightarrow Q) \wedge (R \rightarrow S) \implies (P \vee R) \rightarrow (Q \vee S)$.

2.11   Tautologies and contradictions

Certain wffs are true for all values of the constituent variables. This shows when the last column of the truth table consists entirely of **T** values. These wffs are theorems of mathematical logic.

Definition A wff is called a **tautology** if it is true no matter what the truth values of its propositional variables.

Example 2.42 The wff $W = (P \to Q) \to ((P \vee R) \to (Q \vee R))$ is a tautology. Its truth table is given in Figure 2.9.

Fig. 2.9   A tautology

P	Q	R	$P \to Q$	$P \vee R$	$Q \vee R$	$(P \vee R) \to (Q \vee R)$	W
T	T	T	T	T	T	T	T
T	T	F	T	T	T	T	T
T	F	T	F	T	T	T	T
T	F	F	F	T	F	F	T
F	T	T	T	T	T	T	T
F	T	F	T	F	T	T	T
F	F	T	T	T	T	T	T
F	F	F	T	F	F	T	T

Example 2.43 $B \vee \neg B$ is a famous Shakespearian tautology!

Indeed, whenever W_1 and W_2 are logically equivalent, it is clear that $W_1 \leftrightarrow W_2$ will be a tautology, and *vice versa*. Thus one way of checking logical equivalence is to check the corresponding biconditional, and see if it is a tautology.

• **Exercise 2.44** Rework Exercise 2.39 by proving that a certain expression is a tautology.

Similarly, $W_1 \implies W_2$ if and only if $W_1 \to W_2$ is a tautology. The only way that $W_1 \implies W_2$ differs from $W_1 \to W_2$ is that the former is written at a higher level than the latter. In $W_1 \to W_2$, we have a wff which is waiting for the truth values to be substituted, when it will become either true or false. In $W_1 \implies W_2$, we are stating that $W_1 \to W_2$ will turn out true *whatever* values we substitute for its propositional variables. This is a very subtle distinction.

A tautology W is often written as $\vdash W$ or $\implies W$. This expresses
the fact that it is logically implied by 'nothing at all'; we can deduce it
without making any initial assumptions.

• **Exercise 2.45** Rework Exercise 2.41, but prove the logical implications by showing that a certain expression is a tautology.

• **Exercise 2.46** Show that the following are tautologies.

(i) $Q \to (P \leftrightarrow (P \wedge Q))$.

(ii) $[(P \to Q) \wedge (R \to S) \wedge (P \vee R)] \to (Q \vee S)$.

(iii) $[(P \vee Q) \wedge (P \to R) \wedge (Q \to \neg R)] \to (P \,\text{xor}\, Q)$.

(iv) $[(P \vee Q) \wedge (P \to R) \wedge (Q \to \neg R) \wedge R] \to P$.

(v) $[\neg(P \leftrightarrow Q)] \leftrightarrow [(P \vee Q) \wedge (\neg P \vee \neg Q)]$.

The opposite of a tautology is something that is always false.

Definition A wff is called a **contradiction** if it is false no matter
what the truth values of its propositional variables.

Example 2.47 $B \wedge \neg B$ is a contradiction.

For every tautology, there is an equal and opposite contradiction. If
W is a tautology, $\neg W$ will be a contradiction, and *vice versa*. Also,
W_1 and W_2 will be logically equivalent precisely when $W_1 \,\text{xor}\, W_2$ is a
contradiction.

• **Exercise 2.48** Show that the following are contradictions.

(i) $P \to \neg P$.   (ii) $P \leftrightarrow \neg P$.

(iii) $(P \wedge Q) \,\text{xor}\, (P \wedge (Q \vee \neg P))$.

(iv) $(P \to Q) \wedge (Q \to R) \wedge P \wedge \neg R$.

(v) $(P \vee \neg P) \,\text{nand}\, (P \to (P \vee Q))$.

(vi) $(P \to (Q \wedge R)) \,\text{xor}\, ((P \to Q) \wedge (P \to R))$.

(vii) $(P \to Q) \,\text{xor}\, (P \to (P \wedge Q))$.

2.12 Modus ponens

Consider the tautology $W_1 \wedge (W_1 \to W_2) \to W_2$. This enables us to
make the logical implication $W_1 \wedge (W_1 \to W_2) \implies W_2$. If both W_1 and
$W_1 \to W_2$ are both *known* to be true, or are *assumed* to be true in some
theory, then we can deduce that W_2 is also true.

Example 2.49 From 'I am an Englishman' and 'Mad dogs and
Englishmen go out in the midday sun' we can logically deduce that
'I go out in the midday sun'.

The sort of reasoning above is called *modus ponens*, and is the most basic of all steps in logical reasoning. All it really says is that if P is true, and Q is true whenever P is true, then Q is true. This seems so obvious to us that you might wonder why we even state it. However, all mathematical theories are built around propositions called *axioms*, which are assumed to be true, and a mathematical deduction will end by asserting that some non-axiomatic proposition is true. The method of deduction will usually be *modus ponens*.

•*Exercise 2.50* Make a deduction from the following axioms, where x denotes an animal which is standing on your foot.

A_1: Any long-nosed mammal is either an ant-eater or elephant.

A_2: Elephants are huge.

A_3: Ant-eaters are small.

A_4: Indian elephants are small-eared.

A_5: Nairobi is in Africa.

A_6: Any non-Indian elephant is African.

A_7: x has a long nose.

A_8: x lives in Nairobi.

A_9: x is a mammal.

A_{10}: x is huge.

A_{11}: x has large ears.

•*Exercise 2.51* Sylvia Warbler is a keen computer scientist and ornithologist. When she learnt to identify birds herself, she did it from identification guides. These gave lists of the characteristic features of all the birds she might encounter, and she just had to read all of the descriptions until she found one which matched the bird she had seen. Thus, 'medium-sized, black' would not identify a bird uniquely, but 'medium-sized, black, with red, curved bill' would.

Explain how Sylvia could make life easier for others by writing a computer program to do the identification.

2.13   Proof by contradiction

Consider the tautology $(W_1 \rightarrow W_2) \leftrightarrow [(W_1 \wedge \neg W_2) \rightarrow \mathbf{F}]$. This simple statement gives us a powerful means of proof, called *proof by contradiction*. It works as follows. Suppose we know, or assume, W_1 to be true. We wish to deduce that W_2 is true. First, $W_1 \rightarrow W_2$ is logically equivalent to $(W_1 \wedge \neg W_2) \rightarrow \mathbf{F}$. We start as though W_1 and W_2 were true and false respectively, and try to obtain a series of deductions ending in $\mathbf{F}$. If we succeed, we have verified that $(W_1 \wedge \neg W_2) \to \mathbf{F}$ is a tautology, and so have proved $W_1 \to W_2$. This allows us to deduce W_2.

This might sound strange, but often it gives us a quicker proof of W_2, since we have more to work from when we assume both W_1 and $\neg W_2$ than when we just assume W_1.

A special case of proof by contradiction is that, to prove W, we show that $\neg W \implies \mathbf{F}$. This corresponds to the assignment $W_1 = \mathbf{T}$ and $W_2 = W$ in the general proof by contradiction.

Example 2.52 We prove by contradiction that there are infinitely many primes. Assume that there are only finitely many, say $p_1, \ldots, p_n$ for some $n \in \mathbf{N}$. Look at the number $p = p_1 p_2 \cdots p_{n-1} p_n + 1$. Evidently p is too large to be prime, being larger than any of $p_1, p_2, \ldots, p_n$. Also, it leaves a remainder 1 on division by any of $p_1, p_2, \ldots, p_n$, so is not divisible by any of them. Thus we have a contradiction, since either p is prime, or it has prime factors, and neither hypothesis works.

Compare this with a direct proof, where we would have to construct an infinite sequence of primes!

This technique of proof by contradiction can be used to demonstrate that a certain situation can never arise in a program. We assume that it has arisen, and then obtain a contradiction.

Example 2.53 Let us show that a loop
```
REPEAT
    . . .
UNTIL (a<0) AND
      ((a>1) OR (((b>2) OR (a<0))<=(a>3)));
```
will never terminate, where a and b are integer variables. We assume that it does terminate, so that the condition is true for some a and b. Then $a < 0$, and also $(a > 1) \vee (((b > 2) \vee (a < 0)) \to (a > 3))$. Since $a > 1$ is false, we must have $((b > 2) \vee (a < 0)) \to (a > 3)$. The condition $a < 0$ forces $(b > 2) \vee (a < 0)$ to be true, but $a > 3$ is false, a contradiction, so the loop can never terminate.

The importance of proof by contradiction will become apparent to the reader if he looks up *contradiction* in the index.

• **Exercise 2.54** Show that the following loop can never terminate, where the variables are of type INTEGER.

```
REPEAT
...
UNTIL (i>(j+k)) AND ((i*i+j*j)=(k*k))
          AND (j>i) AND (j<0);
```

2.14 Basic identities

We collect in this section a list of basic logical equivalences, which should be verified and memorized by the reader. Most of these have already been introduced in previous sections, or have very short proofs using truth tables. They are all stated in terms of propositional variables P, Q and R, but any wffs can be substituted for these.

Negation: $\neg T \iff F, \neg F \iff T, \neg\neg P \iff P$.

Domination: $P \wedge T \iff P, P \wedge F \iff F, P \vee T \iff T$,
$\quad P \vee F \iff P$.

Idempotent: $P \wedge P \iff P, P \vee P \iff P$.

Distributive: $P \wedge (Q \vee R) \iff (P \wedge Q) \vee (P \wedge R)$,
$\quad P \vee (Q \wedge R) \iff (P \vee Q) \wedge (P \vee R)$.

Commutative: $P \vee Q \iff Q \vee P, P \wedge Q \iff Q \wedge P$.

Associative: $P \wedge (Q \wedge R) \iff (P \wedge Q) \wedge R$,
$\quad P \vee (Q \vee R) \iff (P \vee Q) \vee R$.

Excluded middle: $P \vee \neg P \iff T, P \wedge \neg P \iff F$.

Trivial Implication: $P \to T \iff T, P \to F \iff \neg P$,
$\quad T \to P \iff P, F \to P \iff T$.

de Morgan's Laws: $\neg(P \vee Q) \iff (\neg P) \wedge (\neg Q)$,
$\quad \neg(P \wedge Q) \iff (\neg P) \vee (\neg Q)$.

Absorption: $P \vee (P \wedge Q) \iff P, P \wedge (P \vee Q) \iff P$.

Contrapositive Implication: $P \to Q \iff \neg Q \to \neg P$.

Definitions: $P \to Q \iff (\neg P) \vee Q$,
$\quad P \leftrightarrow Q \iff (P \wedge Q) \vee (\neg P \wedge \neg Q)$,
$\quad P \text{ nand } Q \iff \neg(P \wedge Q)$,
$\quad P \text{ xor } Q \iff (P \wedge \neg Q) \vee (\neg P \wedge Q) \iff (P \vee Q) \wedge \neg(P \wedge Q)$.

• **Exercise 2.55** Prove all of the above by means of truth tables.

• **Exercise 2.56** The *nor* operator is defined by $P!Q \iff \neg(P \vee Q)$. Prove the following.
(i) $P!P \iff \neg P$.   (ii) $(P!P)!P \iff F$.
(iii) $[(P!P)!P]![(P!P)!P] \iff T$.
(iv) $(P!Q)!(P!Q) \iff P \vee Q$.

(v) $(P!P)!(Q!Q) \iff P \wedge Q$.

(vi) $[(P!P)!Q]![(P!P)!Q] \iff P \rightarrow Q$.

Hence any logical connective can be written in terms of the nor operation.

● **Exercise 2.57** Find similar expressions to the above, but this time using the *nand* operation.

2.15   Simplification of wffs

Which of $\neg(P \wedge Q)$ and $\neg P \vee \neg Q$ is simpler is merely a matter of taste. However, most people would agree that **T** is simpler than

$$[(P \rightarrow Q) \wedge (Q \rightarrow R)] \rightarrow (P \rightarrow R),$$

although perhaps not quite so expressive! What we are going to do in this section and the next is look at one criterion of simplicity. When you study the logical design of circuits, you will discover that this is not the end of the matter, and that there are other criteria too. A familiarity with the techniques here is the absolute minimum prerequisite for understanding these other criteria.

The first thing we shall require of a 'simple' wff is that it should only involve disjunction, conjunction and negation. We could do away with either conjunction or disjunction as well, but this would stop us proceeding to the next goal.

● **Exercise 2.58** Why could we do without conjunction?

We can use the definitional identities of Section 2.14 to get rid of any other connectives.

Example 2.59 We can rewrite

$$
\begin{aligned}
W &= (P \rightarrow Q) \rightarrow R \\
&\iff (\neg P \vee Q) \rightarrow R \\
&\iff \neg(\neg P \vee Q) \vee R
\end{aligned}
$$

● **Exercise 2.60** Get rid of all symbols except propositional variables and the symbols $\neg$, $\wedge$ and $\vee$ in the following wffs.

(i) $[(P \rightarrow Q) \wedge (Q \rightarrow R)] \rightarrow (P \leftrightarrow R)$.

(ii) $(P \operatorname{xor} Q) \rightarrow (Q \operatorname{xor} P)$.

(iii) $(P \operatorname{nand} Q) \operatorname{nand} (P \operatorname{xor} (Q \rightarrow P))$.

Our second requirement will be that $\neg$ symbols should appear only immediately adjacent to propositional variables. This step can be accomplished by means of de Morgan's laws and the rule that $\neg\neg$ can be dropped. These rules are the logical analogues of the rules $-(a + b) = (-a) + (-b)$ and $- - a = a$ in ordinary arithmetic, except that the first is somewhat distorted. It is this distortion which makes all the difference between mathematical logic and arithmetic. The best we can do to approximate the rules in arithmetic is to think of them as rules like $-(a + b) = (-a)(-b)$ and $-(ab) = (-a) + (-b)$, but neither of these are true for ordinary numbers.

After this simplification, a $\neg$ will never immediately precede a bracket.

Example 2.61
$$\neg(\neg P \vee Q) \vee R \quad \Longleftrightarrow \quad ([\neg\neg P] \wedge \neg Q) \vee R$$
$$\Longleftrightarrow \quad (P \wedge \neg Q) \vee R$$

Example 2.62
$$\neg[\neg(P \vee Q) \vee (Q \vee R)] \quad \Longleftrightarrow \quad \neg\neg(P \vee Q) \wedge \neg(Q \vee R)$$
$$\Longleftrightarrow \quad (P \vee Q) \wedge (\neg Q \wedge \neg R)$$

• **Exercise 2.63** Simplify the following so that $\neg$ connectives do not appear outside any brackets.

(i) $\neg(P \wedge Q \wedge R)$.   (ii) $\neg((P \wedge Q) \vee (Q \wedge R))$.

(iii) $\neg(\neg(P \wedge Q) \wedge (Q \vee \neg(R \wedge P)))$.

Our third requirement will be that a bracketed expression should not be immediately preceded or followed by an $\wedge$ connective, except when that expression is just a propositional variable or the negation of a propositional variable. In these two cases, it is the convention to drop the brackets anyway, so that, for instance, $P \wedge (\neg Q)$ would be written $P \wedge \neg Q$, whilst $\neg P \wedge Q$ means $(\neg P) \wedge Q$.

What we are saying is that the only factors we are allowing to enter into a conjunction are things of the form P or $\neg P$. To see the rationale for this simplification, consider the arithmetic expression

$$a \times (b + c \times (d + e)).$$

We would simplify this by multiplying out the brackets to obtain

$$a \times (b + c \times (d + e)) = (a \times b) + a \times c \times (d + e)$$
$$= a \times b + a \times c \times d + a \times c \times e,$$

where we have used the fact that multiplication and addition are associative to keep down the number of brackets involved. Think of $\wedge$ as multiplication, ∨ as addition, and quantities such as P or $\neg P$ as indivisible entities like $a, b, c, \ldots$ above. Also, use the normal conventions of arithmetic that $a \times b + c \times d$ will not need bracketing.

The observant reader will wonder why we did not identify ∧ with + and ∨ with × above. This is a very valid point, and, indeed, it is perfectly permissible to simplify logical expressions in this way. What we obtain is a wff in which ∨ never appears outside a bracket. This leads to an alternative, parallel simplification of a wff, the early stages of which are identical to those above.

Example 2.64 $P \wedge (Q \vee P) \iff (P \wedge Q) \vee (P \wedge P)$.

Example 2.65 We simplify

$$
\begin{aligned}
W &= ((\neg P) \vee Q) \wedge ((\neg Q) \vee R) \\
&\iff ((\neg P) \wedge (\neg Q)) \vee ((\neg P) \wedge R) \vee (Q \wedge (\neg Q)) \vee (Q \wedge R) \\
&\iff (\neg P \wedge \neg Q) \vee (\neg P \wedge R) \vee (Q \wedge \neg Q) \vee (Q \wedge R).
\end{aligned}
$$

In the last example, we could use the *priority* of the operators ¬, ∧ and ∨, from strongest to weakest. Hence ¬ applies to the next available complete expression; then ∧ joins together the nearest pair of expressions; finally, ∨ gets what is left. Because of the associative laws, our wff would not need any brackets. In practice, a long expression is clearer if brackets are inserted round each conjunction. An alternative is to leave more space round ∨ symbols than we leave round ∧ symbols.

 • **Exercise 2.66** Simplify the following wff so that a ∧ symbol never precedes a bracketed expression:

$$P \wedge (Q \vee R \vee (\neg S \wedge (T \vee U))).$$

2.16   Disjunctive form

The simplification we have been following has lead us from our original wff, containing a combination of all the possible connectives, to a logically equivalent wff which is of a very special form. In it, there is a main disjunction of *terms*, each term being a conjunction of *factors*, and each factor being of the form P or $\neg P$. Thus a perfectly general expression has been transformed into one with a very rigid format.

Definition We say that a wff is in **disjunctive form** if it is just **T** or **F**, or is a single disjunction of **terms** W_i,

$$W_1 \vee W_2 \vee \cdots \vee W_n,$$

where each of the terms W_i is a conjunction of **factors** F_k,
$$W_i = F_1 \wedge F_2 \wedge \ldots \wedge F_p,$$
each factor F_k is either of the form P_k or $\neg P_k$, for some propositional variable P_k, and the variables P_k appearing in each term W_i are all distinct.

Theorem 2.1 Any wff is logically equivalent to a disjunctive form. This form will not necessarily be unique.

Proof We have previously shown that we can reduce any wff other than **T** or **F** to a disjunction of conjunctions. Suppose a term in the disjunction is
$$W_i = F_1 \wedge F_2 \wedge \ldots \wedge F_p,$$
and suppose that $F_1 = P$, $F_2 = \neg P$. Then $W_i \iff$ **F**. On the other hand, if $F_1 = F_2 = P$ then F_2 can be dropped from W_i. Thus, if a propositional variable is repeated in some term, either the repetition can be dropped, or the whole term is false, and the term can be dropped from the disjunction, except in just one case. If all terms give **F** then the original wff is **F**. Thus we always arrive at a disjunctive form.

This form is not necessarily unique, since we see that P, $P \vee (P \wedge Q)$, and $(P \wedge Q) \vee (P \wedge \neg Q)$ are all in disjunctive form, and any of them might have resulted from simplifying $P \wedge (P \vee Q)$. $\qquad\square$

The disjunctive form produced above often has many redundancies in it, which we shall try to remove in the next section. However, it generally gives a simpler expression than the original wff.

Example 2.67 We simplify the disjuncion of conjunctions
$$
\begin{aligned}
W \quad &= \quad (\neg P \wedge \neg Q) \vee (\neg P \wedge R) \vee (Q \wedge \neg Q) \vee (Q \wedge R) \\
&\iff \quad (\neg P \wedge \neg Q) \vee (\neg P \wedge R) \vee (Q \wedge R),
\end{aligned}
$$
since $Q \wedge \neg Q \iff$ **F**.

Example 2.68 We reduce W to disjunctive form, where
$$
\begin{aligned}
W \quad &= \quad \neg(P \vee Q) \vee (P \wedge \neg(\neg P \vee R)) \\
&\iff \quad (\neg P \wedge \neg Q) \vee (P \wedge (\neg\neg P \wedge \neg R)) \\
&\iff \quad (\neg P \wedge \neg Q) \vee (P \wedge (P \wedge \neg R)) \\
&\iff \quad (\neg P \wedge \neg Q) \vee (P \wedge P \wedge \neg R) \\
&\iff \quad (\neg P \wedge \neg Q) \vee (P \wedge \neg R).
\end{aligned}
$$

•**Exercise 2.69** Reduce the following wffs to disjunctive form.
(i) $\neg(P \rightarrow (P \wedge Q))$.
(ii) $[(P \rightarrow Q) \wedge (Q \rightarrow R)] \rightarrow [P \rightarrow R]$.

(iii) $[\neg(P \to \neg R)] \wedge \neg[\neg P \to Q]$.   (iv) $(P \text{ nand } Q) \leftrightarrow P$.

(v) $(P \text{ nand } Q) \wedge \neg(P \text{ xor } Q)$.

● **Exercise 2.70** Put the following into disjunctive form.

(i) $(P \text{ nand } Q) \text{ xor } R$.   (ii) $(P \to Q) \leftrightarrow (P \to R)$.

(iii) $(P \leftrightarrow Q) \leftrightarrow ((P \leftrightarrow (Q \text{ xor } R)))$.

(iv) $(P \text{ xor } Q) \text{ xor } R$.

2.17   Disjunctive normal form and truth tables

The next stage in our simplification is to expand some of the terms of a disjunctive form, so that every propositional variable appears in every term. The cost might be that we obtain an exponentially large number of terms in our expansion. With n variables, there could be up to 2^n terms. There is an upper bound on the number of terms which can be produced in a general disjunctive form, of $3^n - 1$. This is because in each term, a variable P appears as P, $\neg P$, or not at all. Hence, there may still be some advantage in the expansion if we have a very large number of terms anyway.

Example 2.71 Let us look at

$$
\begin{aligned}
W \quad &= \quad (\neg P \wedge \neg Q) \vee (P \wedge \neg R) \\
&\Longleftrightarrow \quad (\neg P \wedge \neg Q \wedge R) \vee (\neg P \wedge \neg Q \wedge \neg R) \\
&\qquad \vee (P \wedge Q \wedge \neg R) \vee (P \wedge \neg Q \wedge \neg R).
\end{aligned}
$$

Whenever a term T does not use the variable P, we expand it using

$$ T \iff T \wedge \mathbf{T} \iff T \wedge (P \vee \neg P) \iff (T \wedge P) \vee (T \wedge \neg P). $$

This process is repeated until every term involves every variable. At this stage, some complication of our expression will generally have occurred. However, some terms may now be duplicated, and such duplicates can be dropped. If all 2^n possible conjunctions occur, the whole expression can be replaced by $\mathbf{T}$.

Definition A wff W is said to be in **disjunctive normal form** or **DNF** if W is in disjunctive form, no terms are duplicated, and each term explicitly involves every one of the propositional variables.

The term *normal form* is applied in mathematics to any situation where a mathematical object is transformed into an essentially unique new form by some well-defined rules.

Theorem 2.2 Every wff is logically equivalent to a disjunctive normal form, which is unique, apart from the ordering of the terms, and the ordering of the factors in each term.

Proof We have seen above that it is possible to put every wff into DNF. To show uniqueness, we only have to show that if we have two DNFs, then any term which appears in one also appears in the other. However, the 2^n different terms are mutually exclusive, in that, for instance, $P \land Q \land \neg R$ is true only when P and Q are true and R is false. No DNF which does not include this term will be true under these circumstances, so we see that the DNF is determined by the *truth table* of the wff. The terms correspond with the **T** values in the last column of the truth table, and the number of terms equals the number of **T**s. If there are 2^n **T**s, the DNF is **T**, and if there are none, it is **F**. □

What we have shown is that by algebraically calculating the DNF of W, we have calculated its truth table, and that from the truth table we can deduce the DNF.

Example 2.72 Figure 2.1 has DNF
$$(P \land Q \land R) \lor (\neg P \land Q \land \neg R) \lor (\neg P \land \neg Q \land R).$$

Example 2.73 The wff $P \lor Q$ has DNF
$$(P \land Q) \lor (P \land \neg Q) \lor (\neg P \land Q).$$

• **Exercise 2.74** Find the DNF of each of the wffs in Exercise 2.69.

• **Exercise 2.75** Find the DNF of each of the wffs in Exercise 2.70.

2.18 Design and simplification of circuits

Consider Figure 2.10, representing a wire running from A to B. We are also given a proposition P. There is a switch on the wire, which is closed when P is true and open when P is false. If the wire had been labelled with $\neg P$, we would have assumed that the switch was open if P was true, and closed if P was false.

Fig. 2.10 A wire circuit

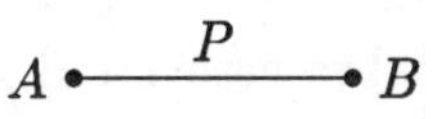

$$A \bullet \!\!\!-\!\!\!-\!\!\!\overset{P}{-\!\!\!-\!\!\!-}\!\!\!-\!\!\! \bullet B$$

Suppose next that there is some complicated network of wires between A and B, and that these wires are labelled with the names of propositional variables. Any assignment of truth values to these variables will either make or break the circuit between A and B.

Two special cases deserve attention. The circuit in Figure 2.11 represents a permanently closed circuit, and corresponds to **T**. On the other hand, the circuit of Figure 2.12 represents **F**.

Fig. 2.11 Closed circuit

$A \bullet\!\!\!\!\!-\!\!\!-\!\!\!-\!\!\!-\!\!\!-\!\!\!-\!\!\!-\!\!\!-\!\!\!\bullet B$

Fig. 2.12 Open circuit

$A \bullet \qquad\qquad \bullet B$

Let us see what happens when we combine two switches together. First, look at Figure 2.13, in which the two switches P and Q are in

Fig. 2.13 Conjunction

series. There will only be a closed circuit between A and B when P and Q are both true, namely, when $P \land Q$ is true. Thus we have formed a 'conjunction' circuit. If P and Q are in parallel, as in Figure 2.14, then the circuit closes if either P or Q is closed, that is, when $P \lor Q$ is true. This is a 'disjunction' circuit.

•*Exercise 2.76* Form an 'implication' circuit.

If a propositional variable appears more than once in a diagram, we assume that all the switches associated with it move in unison. A special case is the standard two-way switch of Figure 2.15, which can

Fig. 2.14 **Disjunction**

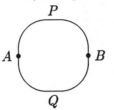

be represented by a pivoted bar which moves up and down to make a circuit from A to B or from A to C, as in Figure 2.16.

Fig. 2.15 **Two-way switch...**

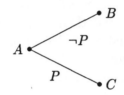

Fig. 2.16 **...and its physical counterpart**

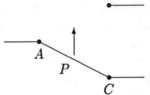

It is clear that, given any wff, we can write it in disjunctive form and thus find a circuit which reproduces it. It is not even necessary to go this far, since all we want is that a $\neg$ should not appear outside a bracketed expression.

Example 2.77 We design a circuit for $(P \vee Q) \to R$. We have
$$(P \vee Q) \to R \iff \neg(P \vee Q) \vee R$$
$$\iff (\neg P \wedge \neg Q) \vee R$$
so the circuit is as given in Figure 2.17.

• *Exercise 2.78* Design circuits for the following wffs.

(i) $(P \vee Q) \leftrightarrow R$.   (ii) $(P \to Q) \vee [R \wedge \neg(P \wedge R)]$.

(iii) $(P \text{ xor } Q) \text{ nand } R$.

Fig. 2.17 **Circuit design**

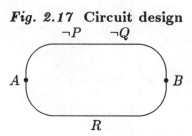

●*Exercise 2.79* Design circuits for the following.

(i) $(P \text{ nand } Q) \leftrightarrow (P \text{ xor } Q)$.

(ii) $(P \leftrightarrow Q) \to (P \to [Q \leftrightarrow R])$.

(iii) $[(P \to Q) \to (P \to R)] \leftrightarrow (Q \leftrightarrow R)$.

Our methods also enable us to take a circuit, write down a logical expression for that circuit, and then design another circuit which is equivalent to the original, and hopefully simpler. The reader might like to experiment with this technique. There are no rigid rules to follow in this task, just rules which tend to work fairly well, or *heuristics*, as they are called.

2.19   Quantifiers

Mathematics is chiefly concerned with general statements, that is, statements which are true for all values of some variable. We have at present no method of specifying this sort of statement, apart from an exhaustive list of all the possible cases. This list would have to include all values of all variables over the whole universe of discourse, and is prohibitive in most instances. We need a notation which will express the fact that $P(x)$ is true for all x. This is precisely what quantifiers do.

A similar thing happens in an existential statement, where something is true for at least one value of a variable. If this statement is very particular, and just involves one variable, such as the statement *Smallest*(x) applied to the natural numbers, then we can say something like *Smallest*(1), which means that 1 is the smallest natural number. If the statement is general, and has many variables, then we might know that the statement is true for at least one value of x, without necessarily being able to pin down any definite value.

Example 2.80 We might know that in a certain computer network, each node has been given a priority for access to the filestore. It is difficult to express the fact that node n_0 has a priority p_0 in the predicate calculus. We could say *Priority*(n_0, p_0), but then we would need a statement like this for every node in the network.

Thus far we have been informal in our Examples when we used the predicate notation, regarding how general the statements were. Henceforth, we shall try to be fastidious. It is of the utmost importance that when you specify the requirements of a system, you should spell out details of this sort. There is the world of difference between saying 'every customer is given a credit card' and 'some customers are given a credit card'. If you just say 'customers are given credit cards with a limit determined on the basis of a security check initiated by Central Office', it is not clear which you mean. If the programmer assumes that every customer has a card, and an operator tries to find the credit limit of a customer who does not have one, an expensive system crash may ensue.

The incorporation of 'for all' and 'there exists' into our symbolism only involves the introduction of two symbols, which look odd because they are A and E *upside down*! Fortunately, our logical symbolism will then be complete.

Definition Let $P(x_1, \ldots, x_n)$ be an n-place predicate and let i be a subscript with $1 \leqslant i \leqslant n$. The $(n-1)$-place predicate $\forall x_i \, P(x_1, \ldots, x_n)$ is the predicate

$$Q(x_1, \ldots, x_{i-1}, x_{i+1}, \ldots, x_n)$$

which is true for given values $a_1, \ldots, a_{i-1}, a_{i+1}, \ldots, a_n$ of its variables only if

$$P(a_1, \ldots, a_{i-1}, x_i, a_{i+1}, \ldots, a_n)$$

is true for *all* values of x_i. The symbol $\forall$ is called the **universal quantifier**.

The main complication in the above definition is the number of variables involved, so we shall look at some Examples where the number of variables is small. In the following, the universe of discourse will be the natural numbers, unless otherwise stated.

Example 2.81 Let us look at a trivial case, where the variable quantified does not appear explicitly in the predicate: $\forall x \, (a = b)$ is true if $a = b$ and false if $a \neq b$. The universal quantifier has no effect. The form of this Example is $\forall x \, P(a, b)$, where P is a 2-place predicate masquerading as a 3-place predicate. The whole expression, complete with quantifier, is a 2-place predicate, and is identical to $P(a, b)$.

Example 2.82 The statement $\forall x \, (x^2 > 12)$ is false, since $1^2 < 12$. It is a proposition, or 0-place predicate, of the form $\forall x \, P(x)$.

Example 2.83 The statement $\forall y \, (x \leqslant y)$ is a predicate in x, and it is true if $x = 1$, false otherwise. This time we form a 1-place predicate $\forall x \, P(x, y)$.

Example 2.84 The statement $\forall x \forall y \, (x^2 + y^2 \geqslant 2)$ is true. First, the 1-place predicate $\forall y \, (x^2 + y^2 \geqslant 2)$ is formed, then the proposition $\forall x \forall y \, (x^2 + y^2 \geqslant 2)$ is formed from it. This proposition is of the form $\forall x \forall y \, P(x, y)$. We shorten this to $\forall x, y \, P(x, y)$.

Example 2.85 Let the universe of discourse be the collection of all firms in some industry. Let $P(x, y)$ be the predicate 'x supplies parts to y'. Then $\forall y \, P(x, y)$ is true of x if x supplies parts to all firms, including x! It is a 1-place predicate.

Example 2.86 Consider the statement 'any natural number is the sum of two squares'. Let $P(a, b, c)$ stand for $c^2 = a^2 + b^2$. Then $\neg P(a, b, c)$ expresses the fact that $c^2 \neq a^2 + b^2$, and $\forall a, b \, \neg P(a, b, c)$ says that c^2 *never* equals $a^2 + b^2$ for any a or b. The negation of this says that $c^2 = a^2 + b^2$ for some a and b, so our statement is
$$\forall c \, (\neg \forall a, b \, \neg P(a, b, c)).$$
This is clumsy, and the existential quantifier will make it less so.

• ***Exercise 2.87*** State the following in terms of universal quantifiers, assuming a suitable universe of discourse.

   (i) All the customers are in credit.

   (ii) Every prime number other than 2 is odd.

   (iii) All suppliers of part p reside in Birmingham.

   (iv) Any stainless steel knife made in Sheffield is guaranteed for life.

   (v) Given any integer, there exists a larger one.

   (vi) A request for personal records must be handled within 14 days.

• ***Exercise 2.88*** Use quantifiers to rephrase the following.

   (i) The sum of any two odd integers is even.

   (ii) Little boys are made from slugs and snails and puppy dogs' tails, but little girls are made from sugar and spice and all things nice.

   (iii) A request for data was not acknowledged on Friday.

Definition Let $P(x_1, \ldots, x_n)$ be an n-place predicate, and let i be a subscript with $1 \leqslant i \leqslant n$. The $(n-1)$-place predicate $\exists x_i \, P(x_1, \ldots, x_n)$ is the predicate
$$Q(x_1, \ldots, x_{i-1}, x_{i+1}, \ldots, x_n)$$
which is true for given values $a_1, \ldots, a_{i-1}, a_{i+1}, \ldots, a_n$ of its variables only if
$$P(a_1, \ldots, a_{i-1}, x_i, a_{i+1}, \ldots, a_n)$$
is true for *at least one* value of x_i. The symbol $\exists$ is called the **existential quantifier.**

The existential quantifier just states the existence of at least one value of its variable which makes the predicate true, whereas the universal quantifier states that the predicate must be true for all values of its variable.

Example 2.89 The statement $\exists x \, (x^3 - 1000x^2 - 1 > 1000000)$ is true, since
$$1001^3 - 1000(1001)^2 - 1 = 1002000 > 1000000.$$

Example 2.90 The statement
$$\exists p \, (p \text{ is prime and } p > 10^{10^{10}})$$
is true, and we proved it in Example 2.52. We gave an *existential proof* of the fact that the collection of primes was infinite.

Example 2.91 The proposition $\forall x \exists y \, (x < y)$ is true. We first examine $\exists y \, (x < y)$. Given any individual x, this is certainly true, as we only need to take $y = x + 1$. Thus the result is true for all x as required.

Example 2.92 On the other hand, $\exists y \forall x \, (x < y)$ is false. The predicate $\forall x \, (x < y)$ is false for every value of y, since $x < y$ fails when $x = y$. Hence, there exists no y to make it true, and the result is false.

This indicates that we need to be careful with the order in which we write our quantifiers, as the statement of a predicate can be completely changed by a simple transposition of two quantifiers.

Example 2.93 In Example 2.86, we mentioned that the translation would be easier if we used the existential quantifier. Well, here it is:
$$\forall c \, \exists a, b \, P(a, b, c).$$

● **Exercise 2.94** Translate the following into predicates and quantifiers.

(i) Any file is associated with a *username*.

(ii) If there is a request to copy a file from one disk to a second, and the file already exists on the second, then a warning message is issued concerning the transfer.

(iii) No two files can have the same name and extension.

(iv) Every constituency has a representative in the Parliament.

We again see a certain amount of arbitrariness in the information included in the mathematical formulation. This is just a matter of judgement; inevitably, we are sure to include either too much or too little detail in our specification, and so will have to go back at some stage and modify it. Mathematics provides no solution to that problem; all it can do is ensure that what we *do* include is unambiguous.

2.20   Predicate calculus

Let us now permit our wffs to involve predicates as well as propositional variables. Each predicate acts like a proposition, in that when its variables are given values, it becomes a proposition. We can combine predicates using any of the connectives we met in earlier sections. We can also quantify any variables universally or existentially. We obtain what is known as the *predicate calculus*. This gives us our most powerful tool for making statements in symbolic logic.

Example 2.95 We wish to make statements about manufacturers of parts in some industry. The predicate we wish to form is

$$Q(m, p) = \text{'}m \text{ manufactures } p\text{'}.$$

Our only problem is in deciding on a universe of discourse, and the problem arises since we must include both manufacturers *and* parts. If we include both, we get nonsense substitutions such as 'Jones Bros. manufactures Jones Bros.' or 'nuts manufactures bolts'.

The solution to the above is to let our predicate implicitly include two predicates $M(x) = \text{'}x$ is a manufacturer' and $P(x) = \text{'}x$ is a part'. Our *real* predicate is

$$R(m, p) = M(m) \land P(p) \land Q(m, p),$$

which is automatically false if m is a part or p is a supplier. We say that the variables have a *type*, and this gives us far more freedom of expression in predicates, although nothing new can be done which could not have been done without these types. The methods of Chapter 3 are more convenient for our purposes, and are the accepted way of handling 1-place predicates such as M and P. We would normally write something like $\exists m \in M$ or $\forall p \in P$ to indicate that m is a manufacturer and p is a part.

Again, for 2-place predicates, the methods of Chapter 4 are more convenient, allowing us to write $x < y$ rather than $L(x, y)$. The difference between the two notations is that in the former, the relational operator appears *between* its operands, whereas in the latter the predicate appears *before* its operands. The former is called *infix* and the latter *prefix*. The infix notation is preferred by mathematicians; all of the mathematical symbols $+$, $-$, $\times$ and $/$ of arithmetic are infix. Unfortunately, although most programming languages include these standard operations, very few of them let you define your own.

●*Exercise 2.96* Name two that do.

Let us look at some identities satisfied by predicates and quantifiers.

- $\forall x \forall y \, P(x, y) \iff \forall y \forall x \, P(x, y)$.
- $\exists x \, P(x) \iff \neg \forall x \, \neg P(x)$.
- $\forall x \, P(x) \iff \neg \exists x \, \neg P(x)$.
- $\exists x \, P(x) \iff \exists y \, P(y)$.
- $\forall x \, P(x) \iff \forall y \, P(y)$.
- $\exists x \, [P(x) \vee Q(x)] \iff [\exists x \, P(x)] \vee [\exists y \, Q(y)]$.
- $\exists x \, [P(x) \vee Q(x)] \iff \exists x \exists y \, [P(x) \vee Q(y)]$.
- $\forall x \, [P(x) \wedge Q(x)] \iff [\forall x \, P(x)] \wedge [\forall y \, Q(y)]$.
- $\forall x \, [P(x) \wedge Q(x)] \iff \forall x, y \, [P(x) \wedge Q(y)]$.
- $\exists x \, [P(x) \wedge Q(x)] \implies [\exists x \, P(x)] \wedge [\exists y \, Q(y)]$.
- $[\exists x \, P(x)] \wedge [\exists y \, Q(y)] \iff \exists x, y \, [P(x) \wedge Q(y)]$.
- $[\forall x \, P(x)] \vee [\forall y \, Q(y)] \iff \forall x, y \, [P(x) \vee Q(y)]$.
- $\forall x, y \, [P(x) \vee Q(y)] \implies \forall x \, [P(x) \vee Q(x)]$.

●*Exercise 2.97* Convince yourself of the truth of the above results.

As a consequence, we can change the name of a quantified variable, but only if we do not choose an existing name. We cannot change $P(x, y)$ into $P(y, y)$ without a change in meaning.

Our main use for the predicate calculus in the remainder of this book will be in the concise statement of mathematical ideas, rather than as a rigorous method of proof. If we wish to use the predicate calculus all the time, there exist real barriers to our understanding, because of its complex notations. It is always there if ever we need to write some specification with absolute rigour. To see just how complicated this might be, let us look at a trivial mathematical property, that of being a common factor of two numbers.

Example 2.98 We shall state the result that h is the highest common factor of the natural numbers a and b, in terms of the predicate $D(x, y)$, meaning 'x divides y' and the predicate $G(x, y)$, meaning 'x is greater than or equal to y'.

We take our universe of discourse to be the natural numbers. The first property h must have is that it should divide both a and b, that is $D(h, a) \wedge D(h, b)$. Next, it should be true that any common factor f of a and b must be at least as large as h, so $(D(f, a) \wedge D(f, b)) \rightarrow G(f, h)$, for all f. Thus the predicate $Hcf(h, a, b)$ is logically defined as

$$D(h, a) \wedge D(h, b) \wedge \forall f \ [(D(f, a) \wedge D(f, b)) \rightarrow G(f, h)].$$

Since this is a mess, it would be better to define a common factor predicate $C(x, y, z)$ to mean $D(x, y) \wedge D(x, z)$. Then

$$Hcf(h, a, b) \iff C(h, a, b) \wedge \forall f \ C(f, a, b) \rightarrow G(f, h).$$

• **Exercise 2.99** Express the fact that any two natural numbers have a highest common factor.

• **Exercise 2.100** If a and b are natural numbers, then there exist *integers* c and d such that the highest common factor h of a and b equals $ac + bd$. Express this result in terms of predicate calculus.

2.21   Formal verification

Suppose we wish to verify that a fragment of a program does the job for which it was designed. We need a faithful logical specification of what its objective is before we can do our verification. We shall assume that this is given as a logical condition on the variables in the fragment. It is called the *postcondition*. There will also need to be restrictions on the variables, perhaps that they are all non-zero, or that one of them is positive. Such conditions are called *preconditions*. The aim is to show that the preconditions before executing the fragment imply the postconditions afterwards.

Definition We shall write $P\{\mathtt{F}\}Q$ if P and Q are two predicates in the variables of the program fragment $\mathtt{F}$, and the truth of P before $\mathtt{F}$ is executed implies the truth of Q afterwards. We then say that $\mathtt{F}$ is **correct** with respect to the **precondition** P and **postcondition** Q.

Example 2.101 $n \geqslant 0\{\mathtt{n:=n+1}\}n \geqslant 1$. If $n \geqslant 0$ before $\mathtt{n:=n+1}$, then $n \geqslant 1$ afterwards.

Example 2.102 $P\{\}P$ for any predicate P. The empty fragment changes nothing in the program, so if P is true beforehand, it is still true afterwards.

If we wish to find the circumstances under which a fragment will work correctly, that is, will satisfy the postconditions after execution, then we are involved in calculating necessary preconditions for the correctness of the fragment.

Definition The **weakest precondition** for a fragment F and predicate Q is the weakest predicate $P = \mathcal{WP}(\mathtt{F}, Q)$ such that $P\{\mathtt{F}\}Q$.

It is weakest in the sense that it encompasses all values of the variables which make Q true after F has executed.

Example 2.103 $\mathcal{WP}(, P) = P$. If P is true after executing the empty fragment, then it must have been true beforehand.

Example 2.104 $\mathcal{WP}(\mathtt{F;G}, P) = \mathcal{WP}(\mathtt{F}, \mathcal{WP}(\mathtt{G}, P))$. If P is to be true after executing F and then G, then $\mathcal{WP}(\mathtt{G}, P)$ must have been true before executing G, and so this is the postcondition for executing F.

Example 2.105 $\mathcal{WP}(\mathtt{IF\ L\ THEN\ F\ ELSE\ G\ END}, P)$ is
$$(L \to \mathcal{WP}(\mathtt{F}, P)) \wedge (\neg L \to \mathcal{WP}(\mathtt{G}, P)).$$
This is because, if P is to be true after the conditional, and L was true before, then F was executed, so we must have had $X = \mathcal{WP}(\mathtt{F}, P)$ true beforehand. So, if L was true beforehand, X must also have been true, and this is the same as saying that $L \to X$ was true beforehand. The other half is similar.

•***Exercise 2.106*** Complete the argument.

Example 2.107 In the above examples, the variables were irrelevant, but in an assignment we need to mention them explicitly. We need to calculate
$$\mathcal{WP}(\mathtt{x:=f(x,y,z,\ldots)}, P(x,y,z,\ldots)).$$
This is $P(f(x,y,z,\ldots),y,z,\ldots)$. We must ensure that the assignment *only* changes the single variable x; if there are side effects to the assignment, then the formula above is no longer valid.

The same thing can be done for looping statements and procedure calls, and, with some effort, various datatypes can be considered in the assignments. We shall be content in this simple introduction to look at an example which only uses the fragments considered so far.

Example 2.108 Suppose we have three integer variables a, b and c, and we wish to calculate the largest of them in the variable m. Consider the following fragment of code:

```
IF a>=b THEN m:=a ELSE m:=b; END;
IF m<c THEN m:=c; END;
```

We shall verify mathematically that this correctly calculates the largest value. The postcondition, that m should be the largest of a, b and c, is

$$(m \geqslant a) \wedge (m \geqslant b) \wedge (m \geqslant c) \wedge ((m = a) \vee (m = b) \vee (m = c)).$$

First, consider the postcondition $m \geqslant a$. We note that

$$\mathcal{WP}(\texttt{m:=c}, m \geqslant a) = c \geqslant a,$$

so

$$\begin{aligned} R(m, a, b, c) &= \mathcal{WP}(\texttt{IF m<c THEN m:=c; END}, m \geqslant a) \\ &= ((m < c) \to (c \geqslant a)) \wedge ((m \geqslant c) \to (m \geqslant a)). \end{aligned}$$

This whole expression is the postcondition for the first line. Now

$$\mathcal{WP}(\texttt{m:=a}, R(m, a, b, c)) = R(a, a, b, c)$$

and

$$\mathcal{WP}(\texttt{m:=b}, R(m, a, b, c)) = R(b, a, b, c),$$

so we can finally write down the weakest precondition for $m \geqslant a$:

$$((a \geqslant b) \to R(a, a, b, c)) \wedge ((a < b) \to R(b, a, b, c))$$

$$= ([a \geqslant b] \to [((a < c) \to (c \geqslant a)) \wedge ((a \geqslant c) \to (a \geqslant a))])$$

$$\wedge([a < b] \to [((b < c) \to (c \geqslant a)) \wedge ((b \geqslant c) \to (b \geqslant a))]).$$

But $(a < c) \to (c \geqslant a)$, and $(a \geqslant c) \to \mathbf{T}$ are both true. Next, if $a < b$ and $b < c$ then $c \geqslant a$. Finally, if $a < b$ then $b \geqslant a$, so the final implication will also be true. The weakest precondition is thus $\mathbf{T}$.

In a similar fashion, we can handle $m \geqslant b$ and $m \geqslant c$. It only remains to finally verify that the weakest precondition for $(m = a) \vee (m = b) \vee (m = c)$ is $\mathbf{T}$. This is left as an Exercise.

• **Exercise 2.109** Complete the argument above.

• **Exercise 2.110** Explain why

$$\mathcal{WP}(\mathbf{F}, P \wedge Q) = \mathcal{WP}(\mathbf{F}, P) \wedge \mathcal{WP}(\mathbf{F}, Q).$$

• **Exercise 2.111** Investigate $\mathcal{WP}(\mathbf{F}, P \vee Q)$ and $\mathcal{WP}(\mathbf{F}, \neg P)$ in a similar vein to the last Exercise.

3

Set theory

3.1 Introduction

Suppose that we are using the notations of mathematical logic, as described in Chapter 2. We have some universe of discourse E, and let us suppose that a predicate $R(x)$ is given. We could look at the objects in E in turn, and check for each object whether or not $R(x)$ is true. If we then selected the collection of objects which made $R(x)$ true, we would have what is known as a *set*.

Although the predicate calculus allows us to do anything we desire, it has been found over the last century or so that set notation is far more convenient and natural. A predicate in one variable is thought of as expressing a property of objects in the universe of discourse; a set is the collection of all those objects with that property. Conversely, given a collection of objects in the universe of discourse, we can form a predicate which expresses the property of being in that collection. Sets and one place predicates are completely interchangeable.

> *Example 3.1* A username for an Apostrophe computer consists of a string of six letters and digits. The director of computing services is responsible for informing the Apostrophe which strings are valid usernames. This he does by creating a file of valid usernames. If there are 500 users of the Apostrophe, the file will have 500 lines. The 2,176,782,336 possible usernames have been reduced by a factor of around 4 million.
>
> Think of the 2 billion possibilities as the universe of discourse, and the 500 usernames as those which make a predicate $Valid(n)$ true. There would probably be no other way to express this predicate except in the form of such a list.

Of course, there is more to mathematical logic than just one place predicates. The connectives encountered in Chapter 2 must also be handled, and we shall find that there are parallel operations on sets which achieve the same purpose. We shall regard n-place predicates as the sets of ordered pairs, triples, and so on, which make the predicates true, ready for a more detailed treatment in Chapters 4 and 5.

3.2   Sets and elements

We assume that there is a fixed universe of discourse E, and that we are given a predicate $P(x)$, where x is a variable ranging over E.

Example 3.2 Let E consist of the natural numbers and let $P(x)$ be the predicate 'x is even'. This predicate determines a set of even natural numbers $2, 4, 6, 8, \ldots$.

A predicate determines a set of objects for which that predicate is *true*.

Definition Let $P(x)$ be a one place predicate on the universe of discourse E. The collection of all objects x in E such that $P(x)$ is true is called a **set**. This set is written as

$$\{\, x : P(x)\,\} \quad \text{or} \quad \{\, x | P(x)\,\}.$$

Informally, a set is a collection of objects; given such a collection, it will be defined either as a list or by means of a predicate. In the former case, it is trivial to specify a predicate which defines membership of that list.

Notice the braces or 'curly brackets' used to specify a set. These are used universally in mathematics to denote sets. The use of square brackets to denote sets in *Pascal* dates from the time when { and } were not readily available on all computer terminals. This unfortunate circumstance has been rectified in *Modula-2*.

The notation $\{\, x : P(x)\,\}$ is to be read 'the set of x such that $P(x)$'. If this set is denoted by the symbol A, and if a happens to make $P(a)$ true, then this defines a certain relationship between a and A.

Definition Let $A = \{\, x : P(x)\,\}$, and suppose that $P(a)$ is true. We say that a is an **element** of A, and write $a \in A$.

The notation $a \in A$ is read 'a is in A', 'a is an element of A' or sometimes 'a in A'. The notation is also used before the colon in a set definition, to express a condition satisfied by x. We prefer the notation

$$A = \{\, x \in E : P(x)\,\},$$

as it indicates what the universe of discourse is, if that was not clear from the context. More complicated conditions could be inserted, to

help clarify a complex definition. It is common to see notations such as
$$A = \{\, x \in E : P(x), Q(x), \dots \,\}$$
rather than the alternative
$$A = \{\, x \in E : P(x) \wedge Q(x) \wedge \cdots \,\}.$$
A sequence of predicates separated by commas is read as a conjunction. Sometimes we also meet $\{\, x^2 : x \in X \,\}$ for $\{\, y : y = x^2, x \in X \,\}$.

Another use of the membership notation is in conjunction with quantifiers. The expression $\forall a \in A \;\; Q(a, y)$ has an obvious interpretation, and if A was defined by the predicate $P(x)$, it is equivalent to stating that $\forall a \, (P(a) \rightarrow Q(a, y))$.

If $b \in A$ is false, that is, $P(b)$ is false, then we write $b \notin A$, and say that b is not an element of A. A predicate thus splits E into two parts, A and everything else.

There is also a notation for a 'listed' set. If the definition consists of an enumeration of all the elements of the set, then we list the elements between 'set brackets', and omit the colon and a predicate. Thus $\{\, 1, 2, 3 \,\}$ is a set with elements 1, 2 and 3. In general,
$$\{\, x_1, \dots, x_n \,\} = \{\, x : (x = x_1) \vee (x = x_2) \vee \cdots \vee (x = x_n) \,\}.$$
We can even have an infinite list, but we must take care to specify what we mean. An infinite list such as $\{\, 1, 2, 3, \dots \,\}$ is open to misinterpretation by the malicious, naïve or perceptive mathematician. Although the set of natural numbers was intended, could the rule have been to start with 1 and 2, and then take the sum of the last two numbers? This would give a set which continued $\{\, 1, 2, 3, 5, 8, 13, 21, \dots \,\}$, but even now there are infinitely many different rules for continuing the list of values.

Let us look at the notations used for some of the commonly occurring sets of numbers in mathematics. We could give rigorous mathematical descriptions of these sets, but that would consume far too much valuable time. We shall be content with a brief description of each set, and a list of some of its elements.

Example 3.3 The set $\mathbb{N}$ consists of all *natural numbers*.
$$\mathbb{N} = \{\, 1, 2, 3, 4, 5, 6, 7, 8, 9, 10, \dots \,\}.$$

Example 3.4 The set $\mathbb{Z}$ consists of all integers. The German word *Zahl* means number.
$$\mathbb{Z} = \{\, \dots, -5, -4, -3, -2, -1, 0, 1, 2, 3, 4, 5, \dots \,\}.$$

Example 3.5 Non-negative integers are called *cardinal numbers*.
The notation is
$$\mathbb{Z}^+ = \{\, 0, 1, 2, 3, 4, 5, 6, 7, 8, 9, \ldots \,\}.$$

Example 3.6 The set of numbers used for measurement and
coordinate computations is called the set of *real numbers* $\mathbb{R}$. Non-
negative reals are also written as $\mathbb{R}^+$. There are good theoretical
reasons why the elements of $\mathbb{R}$ have not been written as a list. See
Section 5.9 for an explanation.

Example 3.7 The set of quotients of integers, or fractions, is called
the *rational numbers* $\mathbb{Q}$.
$$\mathbb{Q} = \{\, x \in \mathbb{R} : x = p/q, p \in \mathbb{Z}, q \in \mathbb{N} \,\}.$$
In Section 5.9 we shall write $\mathbb{Q}$ as a list.

When a set is listed, it does not matter in which order its elements
appear. Thus $\{\, 1, 2, 3 \,\}$ and $\{\, 3, 2, 1 \,\}$ are identical. It is also possible to
have $\{\, 1, 2, 3, 2, 1 \,\}$, although this looks strange. It might happen that
this apparent duplication of elements would result from a definition such
as
$$A = \{\, (-1)^n : n \in \mathbb{N} \,\} = \{\, (-1)^1, (-1)^2, (-1)^3, (-1)^4, \ldots \,\}.$$
The duplication is not real—there are only two elements in this set.

If the predicate defining a set is always false, then nothing satisfies
it, and we obtain a set called the *empty set*. This is denoted by one of
the symbols $\{\ \}$ or $\varnothing$.

Example 3.8 The definition
$$A = \{\, x \in \mathbb{R} : x^2 = -1 \,\}$$
defines A as the empty set.

At the other extreme, a predicate which is always true will not remove
anything from the universe of discourse E. The set E is also known as
the *universal set*.

Example 3.9 The definition
$$A = \{\, x \in \mathbb{R} : x^2 = (x - 1)(x + 1) + 1 \,\}$$
defines A as equal to the universal set $\mathbb{R}$.

We introduce a notation for the number of elements in a finite set.

Definition Let A be a finite set. The number of elements in the set
A is called the **size**, **cardinality** or **cardinal** of A, and is written $|A|$.

The vertical bar notation is commonly used to denote the size or length of an object. If A is infinite, say $A = \mathbb{N}$, then we write $|A| = \infty$. If A is finite, then $|A|$ will always be a cardinal number, hence the term *cardinal*.

Example 3.10 $|\{\, 2, 3, 5, 7, 11 \,\}| = 5$, and
$$|\{\, x \in \mathbb{N} : |(x - 10)((x - 10)^2 - 75)| < 100 \,\}| = 7.$$

• **Exercise 3.11** Verify the second assertion in the above Example by drawing the graph of $y = (x - 10)((x - 10)^2 - 75)$ and calculating y for x ranging from 1 to 20.

Example 3.12 *Pascal* and *Modula-2* have a set concept built into the language. If we say

```
TYPE elements=[0..15]; sets=SET OF elements;
VAR  e:elements; s:sets;
```

in *Modula-2*, for instance, then we can test to see whether an element is in a set, by using

```
IF (e IN s) THEN ... END;
```

and we can also assign to a set and test for equality,

```
s:={1,7,11}; IF s={1,11,14} THEN ... END;
```

and do the other operations on sets to be described later.

The main drawback of this limited implementation of sets is that elements usually belong to a very restricted universe, generally something like $\{\, 0, 1, \ldots, 15 \,\}$. Also, it is part of the languages that only certain types of objects can be in sets. We cannot have a set of real numbers, of procedures, or of arrays. There are good implementational reasons why these restrictions are imposed, but no good mathematical ones.

• **Exercise 3.13** Enumerate the following sets.
(i) $\{\, x \in \mathbb{R} : x^2 = 4 \,\}$. (ii) $\{\, x \in \mathbb{R} : x^2 + 3x + 2 = 0 \,\}$.
(iii) $\{\, x \in \mathbb{R} : x^3 + 1 = 0 \,\}$. (iv) $\{\, x \in \mathbb{R} : \sin \pi x = 1 \,\}$.
(v) $\{\, x \in \mathbb{Q} : x^2 = 2 \,\}$. (vi) $\{\, n \in \mathbb{N} : n^n = 2n \,\}$.

• **Exercise 3.14** Enumerate the following sets.
(i) $\{\, x \in \mathbb{R} : x^4 = x^2 \,\}$. (ii) $\{\, x \in \mathbb{R} : \sin x = \sin 2x \,\}$.
(iii) $\{\, n \in \mathbb{Z} : 2^n = 3^n \,\}$. (iv) $\{\, x \in \mathbb{Q} : x^3 = 2 \,\}$.

• **Exercise 3.15** Explain how one of the limitations on sets in *Pascal/Modula-2* can be overcome, by storing arrays of boolean values. Point out some drawbacks to this approach.

3.3   Subsets

Sometimes there is a special relationship between two sets, such that
any element of one is automatically an element of the other.

Definition Let A and B be sets. Suppose that every element $a \in A$
satisfies $a \in B$. We say that A is a **subset** of B, or that B is a
superset of A, and write $A \subseteq B$ or $B \supseteq A$. The condition to be
satisfied is

$$\forall a \, (a \in A \rightarrow a \in B).$$

Example 3.16 We have $\mathbb{N} \subseteq \mathbb{Z}^+ \subseteq \mathbb{Z} \subseteq \mathbb{Q} \subseteq \mathbb{R}$.

Two sets are *equal* if they have the same elements. The predicates
defining them need not be identical.

Definition Let A and B be sets. If $A \subseteq B$ and $B \subseteq A$, we say that
A and B are **equal** or **identical** sets, and write $A = B$.

• **Exercise 3.17** Show that $\{\, x \in \mathbb{R} : |x| < 1 \,\} = \{\, \tan^{-1} x : x \in \mathbb{R} \,\}$.

Occasionally we wish to indicate that one set is a subset of another,
but is strictly smaller.

Definition If A and B are sets, $A \subseteq B$ but $A \neq B$, we say that
A is a **proper subset** of B, or that B is a **proper superset** of A,
and write $A \subset B$ or $B \supset A$.

Example 3.18 The expressions S<=T and S<T express the fact that
S is a subset/proper subset of T, in *Pascal* and *Modula-2*.

Example 3.19 We have $\mathbb{N} \subset \mathbb{Z}^+ \subset \mathbb{Z} \subset \mathbb{Q} \subset \mathbb{R}$.

The relations $\subseteq$ and $\subset$ are called *set inclusions*.

• **Exercise 3.20** Show that $\mathbb{Q} \subset \mathbb{R}$.

• **Exercise 3.21** Either prove or disprove the following set inclusions.
  (i) $\{\, x \in \mathbb{R} : |x| < 1 \,\} \subset \{\, x \in \mathbb{R} : x^2 + 2x < 3 \,\}$.
  (ii) The set of points (x, y) in the plane with $x^2 + y^2 \leqslant 1$ is a proper
       subset of the set of points with $-1 \leqslant x, y \leqslant 1$.

• **Exercise 3.22** Show that the set of points (x, y) with $x^2 + y^2 \leqslant 1$
is a proper subset of the set of points with $|x| + |y| \leqslant 1.5$.

Given a set S, we can form a new set whose *elements* are the subsets
of S.

Definition Let S be a set with elements in the universal set E. The **power set** of S is the set
$$\mathcal{P}(S) = \{\, A \subseteq E : A \subseteq S \,\}.$$
Thus $A \in \mathcal{P}(S)$ if and only if $A \subseteq S$. The introduction of this power set turns a set inclusion into a set membership of a higher order set; such a change of notation is sometimes useful to show that results about membership imply results about inclusion.

Example 3.23 The power set of $S = \{\, 1, 2 \,\}$ is
$$\mathcal{P}(S) = \{\, \varnothing, \{\, 1 \,\}, \{\, 2 \,\}, \{\, 1, 2 \,\} \,\}.$$
We have $\{\, 1 \,\} \in \mathcal{P}(S)$, but $\{\, 2, 3 \,\} \notin \mathcal{P}(S)$.

•***Exercise 3.24*** Show that the power set of a finite set S always consists of $2^{|S|}$ elements, and for $|S| \geqslant 2$, half of these elements have even cardinal and half have odd cardinal.

3.4 Complements and differences

If a set is the result of using a predicate with one variable on the universe of discourse, it seems reasonable to enquire what happens if we negate that predicate. What results is the set of objects which *do not* satisfy $P(x)$.

Definition Let the universal set be E and let A be a subset of E. The **complement** of A is the set
$$A' = \{\, x \in E : x \notin A \,\}.$$
There are several other notations used for complements of sets. The notations $\bar{A}$, A^c and $\mathcal{C}(A)$ are commonly used. Unfortunately, all of these notations make no mention of E, so we must make it clear what the set E is. If $E = \mathbb{Z}$ then $\mathbb{N}'$ has a different meaning to what it has if $E = \mathbb{R}$. It is possible to use the notation $\mathcal{C}_E(A)$ to make the universal set clear. We would then have $0.5 \in \mathcal{C}_{\mathbb{R}}(\mathbb{N})$ but $0.5 \notin \mathcal{C}_{\mathbb{Z}}(\mathbb{N})$.

A more general notation can be used for complements.

Definition Let A and B be two subsets of the universal set E. The **difference** $A \setminus B$ is the set
$$A \setminus B = \{\, x \in E : x \in A, x \notin B \,\}.$$
To see why this is a set, we need only assume that A and B were defined by the predicates $P(x)$ and $Q(x)$. The predicate $P(x) \wedge \neg Q(x)$ defines $A \setminus B$. This notation is read 'A take away B' or 'A minus B' or 'A set

minus B'. It is also written as $A - B$, although some authors only use this notation when $B \subseteq A$, when $A - B$ is called the *complement of B in A*.

Example 3.25 In *Modula-2* and *Pascal*, the notation S-T denotes the difference $S \setminus T$ of two sets.

With this notation, A' can be written $E \setminus A$ or $E - A$, removing the ambiguity we noticed earlier.

Example 3.26 If $A = \{1, 2, 3, 4, 5, 6, 7\}$ and $B = \{1, 3, 5, 7, 9\}$ then $A \setminus B = \{2, 4, 6\}$.

• **Exercise 3.27** Find the values of the following expressions, when $E = \{1, 2, 3, 4, 5, 6\}$ and $A = \{1, 2, 3\}$, $B = \{1, 2\}$, $C = \{1, 4, 5\}$, $D = \{1, 2, 4, 6\}$.

(i) $A \setminus B$.   (ii) A'.   (iii) $(A \setminus C) \setminus D$.
(iv) $A \setminus (C \setminus D)$.   (v) $(A \setminus D)'$.

• **Exercise 3.28** Evaluate the following, with $E = \{1, 2, 3, 4, 5\}$ and $A = \{1, 3, 5\}$, $B = \{1, 3, 4\}$, $C = \{2, 4, 5\}$.

(i) $(A \setminus B)'$.   (ii) $(A \setminus A)'$.   (iii) $A' \setminus B$.
(iv) $(A' \setminus B)' \setminus (A \setminus C)'$.   (v) $((A \setminus B) \setminus A)'$.

3.5   Unions and intersections

Having looked at the negation of a predicate, we should also look at the disjunction and conjunction of two predicates.

Definition Let A and B be two subsets of the universal set E. Their **union** is the set
$$A \cup B = \{x \in E : (x \in A) \vee (x \in B)\},$$
and their **intersection** is the set
$$A \cap B = \{x \in E : (x \in A) \wedge (x \in B)\}.$$

These two operations can be applied to any number of sets, as they are *associative* operations. Thus $A_1 \cup A_2 \cup \cdots \cup A_n$ denotes the set of all elements of E which are in at least one of $A_1, \ldots, A_n$, and $A_1 \cap A_2 \cap \cdots \cap A_n$ is the set of elements common to all of the sets $A_1, \ldots, A_n$. We can also write
$$\bigcup_{i=1}^{n} A_i \quad \text{and} \quad \bigcap_{i=1}^{n} A_i$$
for these unions and intersections.

Example 3.29 $\{1,2,3\} \cup \{2,4,6\} \cup \{3,6,9\} = \{1,2,3,4,6,9\}$.

Example 3.30 $\{1,3,5,7\} \cap \{1,5,9\} \cap \{1,2,3,4,5,6\} = \{1,5\}$.

Example 3.31 $(\{1,2,3\} \cup \{1,4\}) \cap \{1,4,6\} = \{1,4\}$.

• **Exercise 3.32** Find the values of the following expressions, where $E = \{1,2,3,4,5,6\}$ and $A = \{1,2,3\}$, $B = \{1,2,6\}$, $C = \{1,4,5\}$, $D = \{1,4,6\}$.

(i) $A \cap B$.   (ii) $A' \cap (B \cup C)$.   (iii) $(A \cap B) \cup C$.

(iv) $(A \cup B) \cap (A \cup C)$.   (v) $(A \cup D)'$.

(vi) $(A \setminus B) \cap C$.   (vii) $(A \setminus (B \cap (C \setminus D')))'$.

• **Exercise 3.33** Evaluate the following, with $E = \{1,2,3,4,5\}$ and $A = \{1,3,5\}$, $B = \{1,3,4\}$, $C = \{2,4,5\}$.

(i) $(A \cup B')'$.   (ii) $(A \cup B')' \cap (A' \setminus C')'$.

(iii) $((A' \cap B')' \setminus C) \cup A$.

(iv) $(((A \cup C) \setminus (B \cap C))' \setminus (B' \cup D'))'$.

(v) $(A \setminus B) \cup (B \setminus A)$.   (vi) $(A \cup B) - (A \cap B)$.

(vii) $(((A \cup B)' \cup A)' \cup B)'$.

• **Exercise 3.34** Show that if $A, B \subseteq E$ then $A \setminus B = A \cap B'$.

Sometimes two sets have no elements in common.

Definition Let A and B be subsets of the universal set E. If $A \cap B = \emptyset$, we say that A and B are **disjoint**.

The notion of disjointness can be applied to any number of sets.

Example 3.35 A computer program is running, accepting input a character at a time. The program can be described as being in one of a finite set of states $S = \{s_1, \ldots, s_n\}$. According to the state s it is in, and the character being read, it changes to one of a collection A_s of new states. For instance, suppose that the state is supposed to represent the fact that it is analysing a line that the user is typing in, and it is in a state c, representing the fact that it is reading a command. Typing a letter will leave it in state c; a space will put it in state p, meaning read a parameter; and any other character will put it into state e, an error. Thus $A_s = \{c, p, e\}$.

If we look at what happens after a further character has been read, we see that our program could be in one of the states in $A_c \cup A_p \cup A_e$.

We are modelling what is known as a *finite state machine*.

•*Exercise 3.36* Consider the finite state machine which has states a, b, c, d, e, f and g, and with $A_a = \{b, e\}$, $A_b = \{a, g\}$, $A_c = \{c, d, g\}$, $A_d = \{c, d\}$, $A_e = \{f\}$, $A_f = \{b, d\}$ and $A_g = \{g\}$. If it is started in state a, where could it be two steps later?

•*Exercise 3.37* Do Exercise 3.36 for each possible starting state, and advancing three steps.

•*Exercise 3.38* Call a state t *reachable* from a state s if the machine can be in state t some time after it was in state s. Which states are reachable from state d in Exercise 3.36?

•*Exercise 3.39* For each starting state in Exercise 3.36, find all states reachable from that state.

Sometimes we want to take unions and intersections of infinite collections of sets. This is no more difficult than for a finite number; the only problem is to specify the infinite collection in the first place. Consider first the case where we have an infinite sequence of sets $A_1, A_2, A_3, \ldots$. We can write $A_1 \cup A_2 \cup A_3 \cup \cdots$ for the set of elements of at least one of the sets, and $A_1 \cap A_2 \cap A_3 \cap \cdots$ for the set of common elements. This notation is usually contracted into $\bigcup_{i \in \mathbb{N}} A_i$ and $\bigcap_{i \in \mathbb{N}} A_i$, and $\mathbb{N}$ is then called an *index set*. For this index set, we often see the notations $\bigcup_{i=1}^{\infty} A_i$ and $\bigcap_{i=1}^{\infty} A_i$ used.

The notation can be used for any collection of sets, no matter how they are indexed, and we have the notations

$$\bigcup_{i \in I} A_i = \{x \in E : \exists i \in I \, (x \in A_i)\}$$

and

$$\bigcap_{i \in I} A_i = \{x \in E : \forall i \in I \, (x \in A_i)\}.$$

These notations can be used, of course, when I is a finite set.

•*Exercise 3.40* What do you think $\bigcup_{i \in \varnothing} A_i$ and $\bigcap_{i \in \varnothing} A_i$ might give?

•*Exercise 3.41* For each $n \in \mathbb{N}$ define $A_n = \{m \in \mathbb{N} : m > n\}$. Calculate $\bigcup_{n=1}^{\infty} A_n$ and $\bigcap_{n=1}^{\infty} A_n$.

•*Exercise 3.42* Put $S = \mathbb{N} \setminus \{1\}$. For each $n \in S$ define
$$A_n = \{m \in S : m = kn \text{ for some } k \in S\}.$$
Describe $S \setminus \bigcup_{n \in S} A_n$.

3.6   Distributive laws

Corresponding to the distributive laws of logic, there are parallel laws for sets.

> **Example 3.43** Consider the set of customers at the Bank of Iserica who are overdrawn, and also have either a Mister credit card or an Iserican Express card (or possibly both). They are either overdrawn and have a Mister card, or they are overdrawn and have an Iserican Express card, or both.
>
> Consider next the set of customers who are either overdrawn, or have both cards. This set is the set of customers who are overdrawn or have a Mister card, and also are overdrawn or have an Iserican Express card, if you can follow that.

This Example illustrates the following result.

Theorem 3.1 (Distributive Laws) We have the following two results for subsets $A, B, C \subseteq E$:

$$A \cup (B \cap C) = (A \cup B) \cap (A \cup C)$$
$$A \cap (B \cup C) = (A \cap B) \cup (A \cap C).$$

Proof If
$$A = \{\, x \in E : P(x) \,\}, \quad B = \{\, x \in E : Q(x) \,\}, \quad C = \{\, x \in E : R(x) \,\},$$
then
$$B \cap C = \{\, x \in E : Q(x) \wedge R(x) \,\},$$
by definition. Thus

$$
\begin{aligned}
A \cup (B \cap C) &= \{\, x \in E : P(x) \vee (Q(x) \wedge R(x)) \,\} \\
&= \{\, x \in E : (P(x) \vee Q(x)) \wedge (P(x) \vee R(x)) \,\} \\
&= \{\, x \in E : P(x) \vee Q(x) \,\} \cap \{\, x \in E : P(x) \vee R(x) \,\} \\
&= (A \cup B) \cap (A \cup C)
\end{aligned}
$$

as required, using the distributive laws of logic.

The other identity is left as an Exercise. $\square$

• **Exercise 3.44** Prove the other identity in the above Theorem.

In using the distributive laws, we have the same freedom as we have in mathematical logic as to the direction in which we simplify any expression. We can multiply $\cap$ into $\cup$ brackets, or multiply $\cup$ into $\cap$ brackets, or do a combination of both. Without any guiding principles, there is no guarantee that the 'simplified' expression will be simpler than the original.

•*Exercise 3.45* Simplify the following expressions, by means of the distributive laws.

(i) $(A \cup B) \cap (C \cup D)$.   (ii) $(A \cup B \cup C) \cap (D \cup E)$.

(iii) $(A \cup B) \cap (B \cup C) \cap (C \cup A)$.

(iv) $(A \cap B) \cup (B \cap C) \cup (C \cap A)$.

•*Exercise 3.46* Show that $|A \cup B| = |A| + |B| - |A \cap B|$ for all sets A and B. What do you think the formula might be for three sets?

•*Exercise 3.47* Prove the results

$$A \cap \left(\bigcup_{i \in I} B_i \right) = \bigcup_{i \in I} A \cap B_i, \qquad A \cup \left(\bigcap_{i \in I} B_i \right) = \bigcap_{i \in I} A \cup B_i.$$

3.7   de Morgan's Laws

The rules for simplifying complements are similar to those for multiplying negations into brackets in mathematical logic.

Example 3.48 Consider the set of computers which do not use an Outel processor running at 60Mhz. This is the set of computers which either do not use an Outel processor, or do not run at 60Mhz. It is the union of the set of non-Outel computers and the set of non-60Mhz computers.

Example 3.49 If we look at the set of computers which do not have either a hard disk or an optical disk, we are looking at the set of computers which do not have a hard disk and also do not have an optical disk. This is the intersection of the set of computers with no hard disk and the set of computers with no optical disk.

Unions are transformed into intersections and *vice versa*.

Theorem 3.2 (de Morgan's Laws) We have the following two results for subsets $A, B \subseteq E$:

$$(A \cup B)' = A' \cap B'$$
$$(A \cap B)' = A' \cup B'.$$

Proof Consider the first identity. Suppose that $A = \{ x \in E : P(x) \}$ and $B = \{ x \in E : Q(x) \}$. Then

$$A \cup B = \{ x \in E : P(x) \vee Q(x) \},$$

and so

$$(A \cup B)' = \{ x \in E : \neg(P(x) \vee Q(x)) \}$$
$$= \{ x \in E : (\neg P(x)) \wedge (\neg Q(x)) \}$$

$$= \{x \in E : \neg P(x)\} \cap \{x \in E : \neg Q(x)\}$$
$$= A' \cap B'$$

as required, using de Morgan's laws for logic. □

•*Exercise 3.50* Prove the other de Morgan Law.

•*Exercise 3.51* Prove the following two identities.
$$A \setminus (B \cup C) = (A \setminus B) \cap (A \setminus C).$$
$$A \setminus (B \cap C) = (A \setminus B) \cup (A \setminus C).$$

3.8 Proofs of set identities

Consider an equation such as

$$((A \cup B) \setminus (C \cap D)) \cap (B \cap D)' = (A \cap C) \cup (B \cap D'). \qquad (*)$$

There are three different statuses for this identity:

(i) The identity is *true* no matter what sets A, B, C and D we take.
(ii) The identity is *false* no matter what sets A, B, C and D we take.
(iii) The identity is *true* for some choices of A, B, C and D, and *false* for others.

It is only in the first case that we describe the equation as a *set identity*. It is not sufficient to show that for a particular combination of sets the equation is true. All this does is to eliminate the second possibility; it does not distinguish between the first and third. In the case above, if we substitute $A = B = C = D = \emptyset$, we obtain $E = E$, which is true. But this by no means establishes the identity. In fact, it is not an identity at all.

•*Exercise 3.52* Find a combination of sets which makes $(*)$ false.

The recourse to concrete sets in proving identities is a common fault which should be resisted at an early stage. After all, we would not test a program by running it on a couple of sets of data, would we?

•*Exercise 3.53* Give a counter-example to the last statement!

The correct methods of proving set identities are either to rephrase in terms of predicates, or to use some sort of *normal form* for sets. We shall meet two more methods in Sections 3.9 and 3.10.

Let us collect together the basic identities which can easily be proved by means of predicates.

Negation: $E' = \emptyset$, $\emptyset' = E$, $(A')' = A$.

Domination: $A \cap E = A$, $A \cap \emptyset = \emptyset$, $A \cup E = E$, $A \cup \emptyset = A$.

Idempotent: $A \cap A = A$, $A \cup A = A$.

Distributive: $A \cap (B \cup C) = (A \cap B) \cup (A \cap C)$,
$A \cup (B \cap C) = (A \cup B) \cap (A \cup C)$.

Commutative: $A \cup B = B \cup A$, $A \cap B = B \cap A$.

Associative: $A \cap (B \cap C) = (A \cap B) \cap C$,
$A \cup (B \cup C) = (A \cup B) \cup C$.

Exclusion: $A \cup A' = E$, $A \cap A' = \emptyset$.

Trivial Inclusion: $\emptyset \subseteq A \subseteq E$.

de Morgan's Laws: $(A \cup B)' = A' \cap B'$, $(A \cap B)' = A' \cup B'$.

Absorption: $A \cup (A \cap B) = A$, $A \cap (A \cup B) = A$.

Complemented Inclusion: $A \subseteq B \iff B' \subseteq A'$.

Definitions: $A \subseteq B \iff A \cap B' = \emptyset$, $A \setminus B = A \cap B'$,
$A = B \iff (A \cap B) \cup (A' \cap B') = E$.

This list is comparable with that in Section 2.14.

•*Exercise 3.54* Convince yourself of the truth of the identities above.

We have established the relationships which are needed to transform a set expression into a *union of intersections*. The steps are an exact parallel of those given in Chapter 2, and so we will not need to give much in the way of explanation. The stages are:

(i) Rewrite everything in terms of unions, intersections and complements in E.

(ii) Complement into brackets, using de Morgan's laws.

(iii) Multiply intersections into union brackets, using the distributive laws.

(iv) Remove any duplicated intersections.

(v) If required, expand every intersection until it involves every set variable, and remove any duplicated intersections.

The last stage will produce a 'normal form' for the expression, although it is rarely called that.

Example 3.55 We express $A \cap (B \cap C)'$ as a union of intersections.
$$A \cap (B \cap C)' = A \cap (B' \cup C')$$
$$= (A \cap B') \cup (A \cap C').$$
This could be expanded further, if required, to
$$A \cap (B \cap C)' = (A \cap B' \cap C) \cup (A \cap B' \cap C') \cup (A \cap B \cap C').$$

Example 3.56 We simplify $(A \cap B')' \cap (A \cup C)$

$$= (A' \cup B) \cap (A \cup C)$$

$$= ((A' \cup B) \cap A) \cup ((A' \cup B) \cap C)$$

$$= ((A' \cap A) \cup (B \cap A)) \cup ((A' \cap C) \cup (B \cap C))$$

$$= (A \cap B) \cup (A' \cap C) \cup (B \cap C)$$

$$= (A \cap B \cap C) \cup (A \cap B \cap C') \cup (A' \cap B \cap C) \cup (A' \cap B' \cap C)$$
$$\cup (A \cap B \cap C) \cup (A' \cap B \cap C)$$

$$= (A \cap B \cap C) \cup (A \cap B \cap C') \cup (A' \cap B \cap C) \cup (A' \cap B' \cap C).$$

We could stop at the fourth line if we did not require the normal form.

• **Exercise 3.57** Put each of the following into normal form.

(i) $A \cap (B \cup A)$.   (ii) $(A \cup B)' \cap (C \cup A)$.

(iii) $A \cup B$.   (iv) $(B \setminus (A \cup C)) \cap (C \setminus A)$.

(v) $(B \setminus (A \cup C)) \cup (C \setminus A)$.

• **Exercise 3.58** Put each of the following into normal form.

(i) $((A \cup B)' \cap C) \cap (A \cup B \cup C')$.

(ii) $(((A \cup B)' \cap C) \cap (A \cup B \cup C'))'$.

(iii) $(A \cup B) \cap (C \cap (A' \cup B))'$.

(iv) $(A \cup B) \cap (B \cup C) \cap (C \cup D)$.

(v) $(C \cap (A \cap B')')' \cap (A' \cup (B \cap A))$.

(vi) $(A \setminus B) \setminus C)$.

(vii) $(A \setminus (B \setminus (A' \cap C)')')'$.

Once two set expressions are in normal form, it is trivial to verify whether or not they are identical; we simply verify that the same terms occur in both. If they agree, then we have a chain of set equalities relating the two expressions; if they differ, it is easy to find a collection of sets which makes the two expressions different.

Example 3.59 Suppose that we have a set expression which reduces to

$$(A \cap B \cap C) \cup (A' \cap B \cap C')$$

and another which reduces to

$$(A \cap B \cap C) \cup (A' \cap B' \cap C) \cup (A' \cap B' \cap C').$$

The term $(A' \cap B \cap C')$ occurs in the first expression but not in the second. We use it to construct a collection of sets which make the two expressions differ. Take $E = \{1\}$. In fact, we could take E to be any nonempty set. Put $A = \emptyset$, $B = E$ and $C = \emptyset$. The first expression evidently contains 1, because $A' = B = C' = \{1\}$. However each term in the second expression is empty; for instance, in $A' \cap B' \cap C'$, $B' = \emptyset$. Thus the whole of the second expression equals the empty set, and so the two expressions differ.

•*Exercise 3.60* Either prove, or disprove by counter-example, the following identities between subsets A, B and C of the universal set E.

(i) $(A \cap B')' \cup B = A' \cup B.$ (ii) $A \cup (B \cap A) = A.$
(iii) $(A \cup B) \cap (A \cup B') = A.$
(iv) $(A \cup C) \cap [(A \cap B) \cup (C' \cap B)] = A \cap B.$
(v) $[((A \cap C) \cap B) \cup ((A \cap C) \cap B')] \cup (A \cap C)' = A.$

•*Exercise 3.61* Let A, B and C be three sets. If $A \cup B = A \cup C$ and $A \cap B = A \cap C$, show that $B = C$.

3.9   Venn diagrams

There is a way of pictorially exhibiting the relationships between several sets. We draw an oval for each set, and then examine the areas of the diagram which correspond to the sets we have in mind. For instance,

Fig. 3.1 **Venn diagram**

the oval in Figure 3.1 is meant to represent a set S, and an element x is represented by a point of the plane. In this Figure, a is an element of S, but b is not.

The problem with this method is that although it aids the intuition with three or fewer sets, its use is very limited for four or more sets, because we have to draw the sets in 'general position', that is, in as general a relationship to one another as regards intersections as is possible. This is difficult to do with four sets, and almost impossible with five.

To illustrate the technique, suppose that we wish to represent the relationship between three sets A, B and C. We draw ovals to represent these sets in the most general position possible, and these ovals cut the plane into eight elementary regions, representing the eight possible

Fig. 3.2 **Venn diagram for three sets**

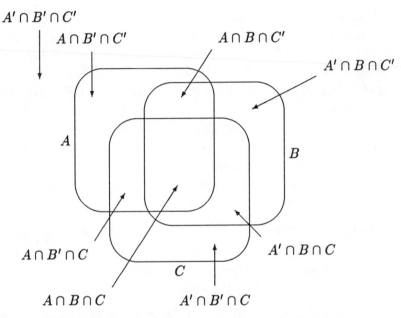

terms in a normal form, as in Figure 3.2. If we examined the region representing $A \cap (B \cup C)$, for instance, we should find that it was given by the union of three elementary regions.

•*Exercise 3.62* Shade these regions in on a diagram.

The proof of set identities is then supposed to proceed by verifying that the two expressions give rise to the same regions. Because most real applications involve a large number of sets, this technique is of little practical importance except in the most trivial cases

•*Exercise 3.63* 'Prove' the distributive laws using a Venn diagram.

3.10   Membership tables

The reader may be surprised by the fact that so far we have not mentioned what happens to truth tables when we move from logic to set theory. After all, if we do not have too many variables, the truth table

is a very effective way of proving tautologies, logical equivalences and
implications. Surely the same technique could be used in set theory.

This is indeed the case. The analogue of a truth table in logic is
called a *membership table*. It is a table listing all the different regions
in the Venn diagram, and so it turns out to be a rigorous equivalent of
the Venn diagram technique.

If A is a subset of E and $x \in E$, we say that the *membership value*
of x in A is **T** if $x \in A$ and **F** otherwise. For two sets A and B, for
instance, there are four possible combinations of membership values for
a given x, namely $x \in A, x \in B$, giving **TT**, $x \in A, x \notin B$ giving **TF**,
$x \notin A, x \in B$ giving **FT**, and $x \notin A, x \notin B$ giving **FF**. These coincide
with the regions of a Venn diagram. In general, for sets $A_1, \ldots, A_n$,
there will be 2^n such membership combinations.

If we take some expression $X(A_1, \ldots, A_n)$ formed by taking unions,
intersections and complements, it is clear that this expression defines
a list consisting of a truth value for each of these 2^n combinations of
membership values.

Definition The **membership table** of the expression
$X(A_1, \ldots, A_n)$ is a table with 2^n rows and $n + 1$ columns,
each row listing a different combination of membership values of
$A_1, \ldots, A_n$, followed by the corresponding membership value of X.

This membership table can be calculated in the same way as the truth
table for a wff. Expressions are then equivalent if and only if their tables
are identical. We thus have a method of proof which corresponds to the
truth table method.

Example 3.64 We show that $A \cap (B \cup C) = (A \cap B) \cup (A \cap C)$ in
Figure 3.3. We see that the appropriate columns are identical, and
so the identity is true.

• **Exercise 3.65** Rework Exercise 3.60, but use membership tables
to verify the equalities, or to show that the identities are false for
some choices of sets.

3.11   Cartesian products

When we started to look at sets, we said that a 1-place predicate $P(x)$
defines a set $A = \{\, x \in E : P(x) \,\}$. We might now ask, what is defined

Fig. 3.3 Membership table

A B C	B∪C	A∩(B∪C)	A∩B	A∩C	(A∩B)∪(A∩C)
T T T	T	T	T	T	T
T T F	T	T	T	F	T
T F T	T	T	F	T	T
T F F	F	F	F	F	F
F T T	T	F	F	F	F
F T F	T	F	F	F	F
F F T	T	F	F	F	F
F F F	F	F	F	F	F

by a 2-place predicate $P(x, y)$? If the object defined is to be a set, then the elements of that set must in some way involve two elements of E.

Example 3.66 Let E be the set of all people, and let $P(x, y)$ mean 'x is a parent of y'. The predicate is true if we select two individuals $a =$ Justin Tyme and $b =$ Annie Tyme, and Justin is Annie's father. Moreover, an ordering of Justin and Annie is implied, as $P(a, b)$ is true, but $P(b, a)$ is false.

Thus a two place predicate defines a set of pairs of individuals, where the order of the two individuals in the pair is important. In mathematics, we call such pairs *ordered pairs*, and write them as (x, y). The object (x, y) and the object (y, x) are regarded as different, unless $x = y$ of course. This bracketed notation is convenient, as it is exactly what follows the predicate identifier P, for instance. A predicate $P(x, y)$ in the elements $x, y \in E$ can also be regarded as a 1-place predicate on a universe F whose elements are the ordered pairs (x, y), as x and y range over E. Strictly, we should use a different symbol $Q(z)$ for the predicate, where a typical $z = (x, y)$, and then we should write $Q((x, y))$ in full. In practice, we are just lazy, and write $P(x, y)$.

A three place predicate will define a set of triples (x, y, z), and an n-place predicate will define n-*tuples* $(x_1, \ldots, x_n)$.

Definition An **ordered pair** of elements of the set A is a pair (x, y) with $x, y \in A$. Two such pairs (x_1, y_1) and (x_2, y_2) are regarded as **equal** only when $x_1 = x_2$ and $y_1 = y_2$.

More generally, for any $n \in \mathbb{N}$, an **ordered n-tuple** of elements of A is an object $(x_1, x_2, x_3, \ldots, x_n)$ with $x_1, \ldots, x_n \in A$. Two such ordered n-tuples $(x_1, \ldots, x_n)$ and $(y_1, \ldots, y_n)$ are regarded as equal only when $x_i = y_i$ for all $i \in \mathbb{N}$ with $1 \leqslant i \leqslant n$.

Example 3.67 If $A = \mathbb{N}$ then $(1,1,1)$, $(1,2,3)$ and $(2, 123456, 87)$ are ordered 3-tuples, or triples, from A.

•**Exercise 3.68** List all of the ordered 5-tuples, or quintuples, from the set $A = \{\, \mathbf{F}, \mathbf{T} \,\}$.

•**Exercise 3.69** What do you think ordered 1-tuples look like?

Given a set A and a fixed $n \in \mathbb{N}$, we can form the set of all n-tuples from A.

Definition Let A be a set, and let $n \in \mathbb{N}$. The **n-th power A^n** of A is defined as the set of all n-tuples from A,

$$A^n = \{\, (x_1, \ldots, x_n) : x_1, \ldots, x_n \in A \,\}.$$

This should be distinguished carefully from the *power set* of A, which consists of all *subsets* of A. A subset $\{\, 1, 3 \,\}$ of $\{\, 1, 2, 3, 4, 5 \,\}$ is not the same as the ordered pair $(1, 3)$. For $\{\, 1, 3 \,\}$ and $\{\, 3, 1 \,\}$ are identical sets, whereas $(1, 3)$ and $(3, 1)$ are definitely regarded as different ordered pairs.

Example 3.70 If $A = \{0, 1\}$ then $A^2 = \{(0, 0), (0, 1), (1, 0), (1, 1)\}$.

We can do the same sort of construction of ordered n-tuples even when the things appearing in an n-tuple come from different sets. When we do this, we obtain what is known as a *cartesian product* of the sets, named after the mathematician Descartes.

Definition Let A and B be two sets. The **cartesian product $A \times B$** is defined as

$$A \times B = \{\, (a, b) : a \in A, b \in B \,\}.$$

Similarly, the cartesian product $A_1 \times A_2 \times \cdots \times A_n$ of n sets is defined as

$$\{\, (a_1, \ldots, a_n) : a_i \in A_i \text{ for all } i \text{ with } 1 \leqslant i \leqslant n \,\}.$$

Example 3.71 Let A be a set of electronic components, and let $B = \mathbb{N}$. Let $P(a, b)$ mean 'a has price b'. We could certainly form $E = A \cup B$ and take E^2 as the set of pairs from which we select the appropriate pair consisting of a component and a price. However, E^2 contains pairs consisting of two components, of two prices, and of a price then a component. It would be more convenient and more meaningful to exclude all such pairs at the start, as they only confuse matters. The set $A \times B$ is more natural.

We notice that $A \times B$ and $B \times A$ are different sets in general, as is clear from the above Examples. If one of the sets in a product is empty then no n-tuples are possible, so the product is empty.

- **Exercise 3.72** Find $A \times B$ and $B \times A$, where $A = \{1, 2, 3\}$ and $B = \{2, 4\}$. Calculate $(A \times B) \cap (B \times A)$.

- **Exercise 3.73** Show that $(A \times B) \cap (B \times A) = (A \cap B)^2$.

4

Relations

4.1 Introduction

This chapter will introduce a far-reaching generalization of the concept of a function. Its definition will reflect the fact that it could be implemented on a computer by a list with two columns, one column with entries from one set, and the other column with entries from a second set. This is a simple example of a *relational database.*

The idea of a cartesian product of two sets introduced in Chapter 3 is a very powerful one, and will enable us to considerably extend the range of applications we can model.

> *Example 4.1* In a *Modula-2* program, several procedures Proc_1, Proc_2, Proc_3, ..., are defined. In the definition of Proc_1, there are calls to both Proc_2 and Proc_1 itself. In Proc_2, there are calls to Proc_1 and Proc_3. In Proc_3, there are calls to Proc_2, and Proc_5, and so on. It is required to find the exact dependency of each procedure on any others, both directly and indirectly.

If we can tabulate the direct dependencies, then we can find all of the indirect ones too, by chasing through chains of direct calls. To find the effect of a call of any procedure, we merely need to create a *list* or *database* of pairs of procedure names, listing (Proc_i, Proc_j) whenever Proc_i calls Proc_j. The list is as in Figure 4.1.

This list could also be written as a mathematical subset of P^2, where $P = \{$ Proc_1, Proc_2, Proc_3, ... $\}$. The subset is

$$\{ (\text{Proc\_1}, \text{Proc\_1}), (\text{Proc\_1}, \text{Proc\_2}), (\text{Proc\_2}, \text{Proc\_1}), \dots \}.$$

Another way of specifying the fact that Proc_i calls Proc_j would be to use some symbol such as Proc_i $\prec$ Proc_j. Yet another way would be to invent a predicate

$$Procedurecall(\text{Proc\_i}, \text{Proc\_j})$$

Fig. 4.1 Table of procedure calls

Proc_1	Proc_1
Proc_1	Proc_2
Proc_2	Proc_1
Proc_2	Proc_3
Proc_3	Proc_2
Proc_3	Proc_5
⋮	⋮

which would accomplish the same effect in a more verbose manner. Finally, we could draw a *graph* of the relationships, where each procedure is represented by a dot, and i is linked to j if `Proc_i` calls `Proc_j`, as in Figure 4.2.

Fig. 4.2 Graph of procedure calls

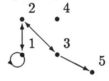

Example 4.2 A vendor of PCs wishes to prepare a list consisting of the registration number of each PC sold by him, and the name of its owner. This time, we take a subset of $R \times O$, where R is the set of registration numbers (say, $R = \mathbb{N}$), and O is the set of owners' names. Symbolically, we could write $r \triangleleft o$ for 'the PC with registration number r is owned by o', or we could use a predicate $Owner(r, o)$.

As a final illustration, consider the set S defined as

$$S = \left\{ (x, y) \in \mathbb{R}^2 : x = y^2 \right\}.$$

This can loosely be described as the set of points on the graph of the many-valued partial function $y = \sqrt{x}$. It is an example to illustrate the close connection between the *relations* we have been discussing, and the mathematical concept of a *function* or *mapping*. We shall explain later why it is described as being a *partial* function.

4.2   Relations or Correspondences

We have met several instances of a list of pairs of objects (a, b), and need a definition which is general enough to cover all the cases we are likely to meet in which this situation arises. We should like to express the fact that the object a might be of a completely different *type* from b, and so we include enough generality to cover this fact.

Definition Let A, B be two sets. A **relation** or **correspondence** between A and B is a subset $R \subseteq A \times B$.

Notice that there is an implied *order* of the two sets A and B in this definition. This is indicated both by the way we describe the relation as *between A and B*, and also in the mathematical definition in terms of *ordered pairs* (a, b).

A relation is, loosely speaking, a sort of 'function' from A to B, which is not necessarily defined for all $a \in A$, and which takes the 'value' b at a if $(a, b) \in R$. The problem is that this 'value' is not uniquely defined, so what we really have is a 'many-valued, not-everywhere-defined' function.

Example 4.3 Let $A = \{0, 1, 2\}, B = \{3, 4, 5\}$. Then
$$R = \{(0, 3), (0, 4), (1, 4)\}$$
is a relation between A and B. Its *graph* is the diagram in Figure 4.3.

Fig. 4.3 A relation

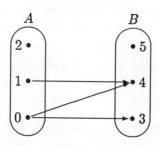

The notion of a graph of a relation is a useful aid to understanding its nature. We draw an arrow from a to b if (a, b) is in the relation.

If R is a relation between A and B, then we usually write $a\,R\,b$ if $(a, b) \in R$. In Example 4.3, we could write $0\,R\,3$, $0\,R\,4$, and so on. We are already used to several relations which are written this way.

Example 4.4 The relation between $\mathbb{R}$ and $\mathbb{R}$ given by
$$\{(x,y) \in \mathbb{R}^2 : x < y\}$$
is just the relation $<$.

In theoretical examples, there might be some easy way to calculate whether a relationship is true or false, but in the chaos of the real world, the *only* way to describe a relation might be as a physical list of pairs. We shall show in Section 5.9 that it is impossible to write the relation $<$ of Example 4.4 as a list of ordered pairs.

Example 4.5 A certain bureaucratic firm keeps a file in which are listed each of its employees' names, together with the name of his immediate superior. The top men in the firm are considered as being subordinate only to themselves, so are distinguished by appearing as pairs of the form (t, t). This is illustrated in Figure 4.4. This relation

Fig. 4.4 **Pecking order**

Smith	Jones
Ford	Austin
Austin	Popple
Popple	Popple
Morris	Popple
Camberwell	Morris
Jones	Ford
⋮	⋮

could be written as $a \leftarrow b$. Popple notes that Smith parked in Popple's parking place this morning, and so has a word with Austin. Do you see why?

We *could* extend our file so that (x, y) appeared whenever x was subordinate to y, but this would really be unnecessary, as the relevant information is contained in the above list, ready for the computer to calculate. What we have here is an example of the *transitive closure* of a relation. The relation we store is a fairly compact one, but the one we are interested in is its transitive closure.

Another way of expressing $a \, R \, b$ is to write $R(a, b)$, where this time R is regarded as a predicate, the interpretation being that $R(a, b)$ is true only when $(a, b) \in R$. That brings to three the number of different ways we are using the symbol R for a relation. If we wished to be more pedantic, we would use different notations for them, such as $(a, b) \in S_R$, $a \, R \, b$ or $P_R(a, b)$ to distinguish the set of pairs, the operator and the predicate. It is difficult to confuse the three uses of R, since the context will indicate which one is being used.

Often A and B are the same set.

Definition A **binary relation** on the set A is a subset $R \subseteq A^2$. The binary relation $\imath_A$ on A defined by $a \, \imath_A \, a$ for all $a \in A$ is called the **identity relation** on A.

•**Exercise 4.6** Draw the graph of the binary relation $\leqslant$ on $A = \{0, 1, 2, 3\}$.

•**Exercise 4.7** Draw the graph of the binary relation R on $A = \{2, 3, \ldots, 8\}$ where $a \, R \, b$ means that a is a proper divisor of b, that is, b/a is an integer, not equal to unity.

•**Exercise 4.8** Draw the graph of the part of the binary relation that is visible in Figure 4.4.

4.3   Domain and Range

Consider the following Example.

Example 4.9 The Madland Bank keeps a file in which it lists account numbers, followed by the name of one of the account holders. Its account numbers are always positive integers of at most eight decimal digits.

Mathematically, this must correspond to some sort of relation $R \subseteq A \times B$, but what are the two sets A and B?

We could say that A is the set of those numbers which are account numbers of customers, but then what do we do when a new customer wants to bank with Madland Bank? Do we change the set A to include a new account number. Similarly, when a customer deserts Madland Bank, do we remove his account number from A? It is far simpler to choose A in the first place to be a set large enough to encompass any possible additions or deletions of account numbers. We could take $A = \mathbb{N}$.

For similar reasons, we could conceptually take B as the set of all human beings, alive or yet to live, and that would solve the problem of new and old customers at a stroke.

The important lesson to learn from the above is that *A and B can both be chosen as larger sets than they need to be.* When we look at the minimal sets which will work for our relation, assuming that it is static, then we must assume that they could be smaller than A and B. There is no absolute rule which will tell us what to take for A or B, and in the above Example, we could have taken $A = \mathbb{Z}$ or $A = \mathbb{R}$ just as well, although these choices would have concealed the fact that Madland Bank always chooses a positive integer for its account numbers. Another choice would have been the set $A = \{\, n \in \mathbb{N} : n < 10^8 \,\}$.

Whatever the choice of A and B, there are at least two sets which we can define unambiguously, namely, the set of all used Madland Bank account numbers, and the set of all Madland Bank customers.

Definition If R is a relation between A and B, then we define the **domain** of R as the set of all $a \in A$ such that $(a, y) \in R$ for at least one $y \in B$, that is, the set
$$\{\, a \in A : \exists y \in B \,(a\,R\,y) \,\}.$$
Similarly the **range** is defined as
$$\{\, b \in B : \exists x \in A \,(x\,R\,b) \,\}.$$

In Example 4.3, the domain is $\{\, 0, 1 \,\}$ and the range is $\{\, 3, 4 \,\}$. In Example 4.4, the domain and range both equal $\mathbb{R}$.

•**Exercise 4.10** What is the significance of the range of the relation in Example 4.1?

•**Exercise 4.11** What are the domain and range of the relation in Exercise 4.6?

•**Exercise 4.12** What are the domain and range of the relation in Exercise 4.7?

4.4   Inverses of relations

When we first defined a relation, we decided that we needed two sets A and B and a set of *ordered* pairs from $A \times B$ to describe it. In Example 4.9, we have pairs (a, c) representing an account number a and customer c. But why do we have pairs (a, c) rather than pairs (c, a)?

Surely the Madland Bank could produce its file with the order of the
two columns reversed, and it would serve the same purpose?

In fact, the choice of taking $A \times B$ or $B \times A$ is arbitrary.

Definition If $R \subseteq A \times B$ is a relation between A and B, then the
inverse relation $R^{-1} \subseteq B \times A$ is defined as the relation between B
and A given by

$$b \, R^{-1} \, a \iff a \, R \, b.$$

Alternatively,

$$R^{-1} = \{ (b, a) \in B \times A : (a, b) \in R \}.$$

We shall see that there is a good reason for using the term *inverse* to
describe the connection between R and R^{-1}. It is to do with what
happens when one of the relations describes a *function*, and we shall
investigate this further in Chapter 5.

Example 4.13 The relation in Example 4.3 has inverse the relation
on $B \times A$ with a graph as in Figure 4.5.

Example 4.14 Let R be the relation between $\mathbb{Z}$ and $\mathbb{Z}^+$ defined by
$m \, R \, n \iff m^2 = n$. Thus

$$R = \{ (m, n) : m \in \mathbb{Z}, n \in \mathbb{Z}^+, m^2 = n \}.$$

Then

$$R^{-1} = \{ (n, m) : m \in \mathbb{Z}, n \in \mathbb{Z}^+, m^2 = n \}.$$

We thus find that $-2 \, R \, 4$, $0 \, R \, 0$, $16 \, R^{-1} \, 4$, $25 \, R^{-1} \, -5$, and so on.

•**Exercise 4.15** Consider the following argument:
$$2 = \sqrt{4} = \sqrt{(-2) \times (-2)} = -2.$$
Refute it by describing what is happening in terms of relations.

Fig. 4.5 **Inverse relation**

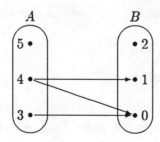

4.5 Composition of relations

Consider the following situation.

> ***Example 4.16*** A library has a file in which is kept the serial num-
> ber s of each of its books, together with details of the author a of
> each book. In a second file it keeps the library card number c of
> its borrowers, and the serial numbers s of any books they have bor-
> rowed. It wishes to issue a reminder to its borrowers of the authors
> of all books currently on loan to them.

If the first file is represented symbolically by the relation $s \to a$ and the
second file by $c \triangleright s$, then what we need is to convert this information
somehow into a relation of the form $c \Rightarrow a$.

> ***Definition*** Let $R \subseteq A \times B$ and $S \subseteq B \times C$ be two relations. The
> relation $S \circ R \subseteq A \times C$ is defined by
> $$S \circ R = \{ (a, c) : a \in A, c \in C, \exists b \in B \, ([a \, R \, b] \wedge [b \, S \, c]) \},$$
> and is called the **composition** of S with R.

We are free to choose *either* order for the composition of relations. This
author has chosen to reverse the order, despite the fact that the notation $a \, R \, b \, S \, c$ suggests the order $R \circ S$. Each choice has its plus and
minus points, but the link with functions is much easier to see when the
order is reversed. Such reversal is quite common in mathematics, and
appears whenever objects are combined according to a 'function of a
function' definition, such as in mathematical symmetries and permutations. Reversals are also seen when inverses of compositions are formed,
so we must get used to this 'looking glass' world of relations, and learn
to read our products from right to left. We shall resume this discussion
in Chapter 5.

> ***Example 4.17*** Let $A = \{a, b, c\}$, $B = \{d, e, f\}$, $C = \{g, h, i\}$.
> Let R and S be relations from A to B and from B to C respectively,
> such that $a \, R \, d$, $a \, R \, f$, $b \, R \, d$, $c \, R \, e$, $d \, S \, h$, $d \, S \, i$, $e \, S \, g$ and $e \, S \, h$.
> We draw the graphs of R and S to obtain the graph of $S \circ R$, as in
> Figure 4.6. To obtain the relationship $S \circ R$, we choose $x \in A$ and
> $y \in C$, and see if there is a route from x to y in the graph. If there
> is, we join x to y in $S \circ R$, as in Figure 4.7.

> •***Exercise 4.18*** Find $S \circ R$, where R is a relation between $A = \{a, b, c, d\}$ and $B = \{e, f, g\}$, and S is a relation between B and

Fig. 4.6 Composition

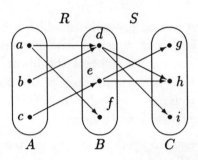

Fig. 4.7 Composition completed

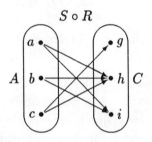

$C = \{ h, i, j, k \}$, and
$$R = \{ (a, e), (b, e), (b, g), (c, e), (d, f) \}$$
whilst
$$S = \{ (e, h), (e, k), (f, j), (f, k), (g, h) \}.$$

• **Exercise 4.19** Let S and F be binary relations on $\mathbb{Z}$ given by the formulae
$$S = \{ (a^2, a) : a \in \mathbb{Z} \}, \quad F = \{ (a^4, a) : a \in \mathbb{Z} \}.$$
Find $S \circ F$.

• **Exercise 4.20** Let R and S be binary relations on $\mathbb{R}$ given by
$$R = \{ (x, y) \in \mathbb{R}^2 : x^2 + y^2 = 20 \},$$
$$S = \{ (x^2, x) : x \in \mathbb{R} \}.$$
Show that $R \circ S$ and $S \circ R$ are different relations.

If $R \subseteq A \times B$ is a relation on A, it is easy to see that $R^{-1} \circ R \neq \imath_A$ in general. Indeed, in Example 4.14, 2 R 4 and 4 R^{-1} -2 but we do not, of course, have $2\ \iota_A\ -2$. Also, in Example 4.9, R links an account number to a customer, and R^{-1} links a customer to an account number. Suppose that Mr. R. Aving-Lunet has two accounts with Madland Bank, with account numbers 00112345 and 00112346. Then

$$(00112345, \text{R. Aving-Lunet}) \in R$$

and

$$(00112346, \text{R. Aving-Lunet}) \in R$$

so

$$(\text{R. Aving-Lunet}, 00112346) \in R^{-1}$$

and finally

$$(00112345, 00112346) \in R^{-1} \circ R.$$

This is not looking like a good candidate for the name ι_A!

If we are to interpret relations as generalized functions, then we must expect things to go wrong somewhere. It is for this reason that the accepted definition of a function is so much more restrictive than that of a relation. See Exercise 4.15 for an example of what can go wrong if we think of a relation as a function. However, we do have the following result.

Theorem 4.1 (Associativity) Let $R \subseteq A \times B$, $S \subseteq B \times C$, and $T \subseteq C \times D$ be relations. Then $T \circ (S \circ R) = (T \circ S) \circ R$.

Proof Consider $(a, d) \in (T \circ S) \circ R$. This happens if and only if there exists a $b \in B$ such that $(a, b) \in R$ and $(b, d) \in (T \circ S)$. But then the last condition happens if and only if there exists a $c \in C$ such that $(b, c) \in S$ and $(c, d) \in T$. It is easy to see that the other relation leads to the same condition. Thus they must be identical relations. □

To see the significance of this result, we shall need three relations we can string together.

Example 4.21 The WhatNext Bank keeps several files to monitor the day-to-day activities of its customers. The first is a list of account holders and account numbers, which we shall view as relation R. The second is a file which lists the day's transactions by attaching a number to each transaction, and listing the account and transaction number. This is relation S. It also keeps several files which list each transaction number, with the amount, type, time, and so on. We shall pick one of these only, the one which gives the time of each transaction, and call the relation T.

Let us discover what the associative law means in this situation. First, we can combine S with T, to form $T \circ S$, a list of account numbers *versus* times of transactions. This can be combined with R to give $(T \circ S) \circ R$, or account holders *versus* times of transactions. Equally well, we can combine R with S to form $S \circ R$, or account holders *versus* transaction numbers. This combined with T gives the relation $T \circ (S \circ R)$, and the associative law means that this is the same relation as we calculated previously.

The Theorem is thus not so mysterious after all. We do not need to bracket $T \circ S \circ R$ at all, as the meaning is clear without brackets.

4.6   Binary relations

We recall that a *binary relation* on A is a relation between A and A. Such a relation can always be composed with itself, and also its inverse is a binary relation on the same set.

It might be thought that a binary relation is a very special case of a general relation, but *any* relation can be made artificially into a binary relation by the following trick. If $R \subseteq A \times B$ is a relation, put $C = A \cup B$, and define $R' \subseteq C^2$ by the set equality $R' = R$. Thus R' consists of the same pairs as R. Then R' is a binary relation which in a sense is equivalent to R. The disadvantage of this transformation is solely in the practical inconvenience of forming the union of A and B. We might end up with a set consisting of account numbers mixed with customers, or of cheque numbers mixed with times, which we would prefer to keep separate. We saw the same problems with predicates in Chapter 2.

If R is a binary relation on A, then it is normal to write $R^2 = R \circ R$, $R^3 = (R \circ R) \circ R$, and so on. We also write $R^0 = \imath_A$, $R^1 = R$. We can also form $R^{-2} = R^{-1} \circ R^{-1}$, and any negative powers of R.

Example 4.22 Let P be the set of all people, and let R be the binary relation expressed by saying that $(a, b) \in R$ means a is a parent of b. Then R^2 is the grandparent relation on P, and R^3 is the great-grandparent relation. The relation R^{-1} is the child relation, where $a\,R^{-1}\,b$ means a is a child of b, so R^{-2} will be the grandchild relation, and so on.

Example 4.23 We calculate R^2, where R is the binary relation on $A = \{\, a, b, c \,\}$ given by
$$R = \{\, (a, b), (b, a), (b, c) \,\}.$$

This relation can be represented by the graph of Figure 4.8. We

Fig. 4.8 R

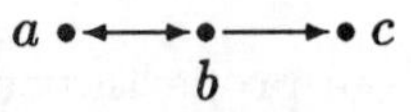

$$a \bullet\longleftrightarrow\bullet\longrightarrow\bullet\, c$$
$$b$$

draw two copies of the set A, and draw an arrow from x in the first copy to y in the second copy to denote the fact that $(x, y) \in R$, as in Figure 4.9. To form R^2, we lay together two copies of R, and follow

Fig. 4.9 R expanded

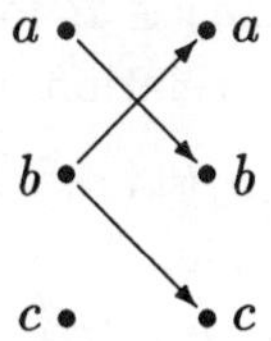

the routes through the diagram, as in Figure 4.10. Thus R^2 is the relation

$$R^2 = \{(a, a), (b, b), (a, c)\}.$$

Fig. 4.10 Calculation of R^2

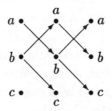

• **Exercise 4.24** Calculate R^2 for the relation $R \subseteq \mathbb{Z}^2$ given by
$$R = \{(n^2, n^4) : n \in \mathbb{Z}^+\}.$$

• **Exercise 4.25** Calculate R^2 for the relation $R \subseteq \mathbb{Z}^2$ given by
$$R = \{(n^6, n^{10}) : n \in \mathbb{Z}^+\}.$$

4.7 Properties of binary relations

We shall look at some general properties which may or may not be possessed by a binary relation. These all correspond to simple properties of the graph of the relation, and can all be defined in terms of the powers of the relation.

A relation has the first of our properties only if each element possesses an edge looping round on itself, a *loop*, in the terminology of graph theory.

Definition If $R^0 \subseteq R$ we say that R is **reflexive**. This is equivalent to saying that $a \, R \, a$ for all $a \in A$.

The statement that $R^0 \subseteq R$ means that R includes all pairs in R^0. But $R^0 = \imath_A$ by definition, and the pairs included in $\imath_A$ are all those of the form (a, a). This means that $(a, a) \in R$ for all $a \in A$, so $a \, R \, a$ for all $a \in A$. An example of a reflexive relation is $\imath_A$.

Example 4.26 Consider $\{(a, b) : a, b \in \mathbb{R}, a \leqslant b\}$. This is just the relation $a \leqslant b$, and it is reflexive.

Example 4.27 The relation $R \subseteq P^2$ between people, where $a \, R \, b$ means that a and b use the same bank, is reflexive.

Example 4.28 The computer typesetting program TEX used to produce this book uses *control words* to do the sort of job done by procedures in *Modula-2*. It has *definitions*, like the declarations of procedures, and *expansions*, which are like procedure calls. The control words always start with the 'backslash' character \, for example, \cwone, \cwtwo.

The definition of a control word will usually include references to other control words, and it is not required that these other control words should be defined at that stage. This situation is different to that of *Modula-2* procedure declarations. However, when a control word is eventually expanded, it is required that those control words used in its definition *must* make sense at that time. For instance, we might have \def\doubleu{\u\u} at one place in the manuscript, and further on, we could have \def\u{u}. Any previous attempt to expand \doubleu would lead to an error. After the second definition, the control word \doubleu will be expanded to \u\u, which will in turn expand to uu. A later definition \def\u{you} would cause subsequent occurrences of \doubleu to expand to youyou.

Define a binary relation on the control words used in this book, by saying that \cwone>\cwtwo means that the expansion of \cwone requires that \cwtwo should already be defined. This relation is reflexive, since, to expand \cwone, it itself must have been defined somewhere.

Example 4.29 The relation of Figure 4.11 is reflexive.

Fig. 4.11 A reflexive relation

$$a \qquad b \qquad c$$

•*Exercise 4.30* Show that the binary relation R on $\mathbb{R}$ given by

$$R = \left\{ (a, b) \in \mathbb{R}^2 : a^2 + b^3 \text{ is even} \right\}$$

is reflexive.

The notion of *symmetry* applied to a relation describes the situation where a being related to b is synonymous with b being related to a.

Definition If $R = R^{-1}$ then R is **symmetric**. Equivalently, $a \, R \, b$ if and only if $b \, R \, a$.

We *could* get away with the abbreviated definition $R^{-1} \subseteq R$ for symmetry, as this implies $R^{-1} = R$.

•*Exercise 4.31* Verify the above assertion.

The graph of a symmetric relation will show, for every arrow from a to b, an opposite arrow from b to a.

Both reflexivity and symmetry of a relation are useful properties to check for, especially if the relation is being stored as a list on a computer. Reflexivity means that none of the pairs (a, a) need be explicitly stored, provided a note is kept somewhere of the fact that this property holds. If $|A| = n$, this could save in storage by an amount proportional to n. Symmetry will mean that only one of (a, b) and (b, a) need be stored, and could save storage by a factor of a half, or an amount proportional to $\frac{1}{2}n(n - 1)$ at the very best.

Example 4.32 The relation of Figure 4.12 is symmetric.

Example 4.33 Consider the set P of all people, and write $a \, M \, b$ if a is married to b. Then M is a symmetric relation on P. It is not

Fig. 4.12 **A symmetric relation**

reflexive. A file recording marriages should store only one pair for each couple, perhaps the (husband, wife) pair.

•*Exercise 4.34* Show that the relation in Exercise 4.30 is symmetric.

The next property is typical of what are called *order* relations. In these, if a is related to b, with $a \neq b$, then b is *definitely not* related to a. Thus $1 < 2$ but $2 \not< 1$. Also, 5 divides 30, but 30 does not divide 5.

Definition If $R \cap R^{-1} \subseteq R^0$ then R is **anti-symmetric**.

The requirement is that $a\,R\,b$ and $b\,R\,a$ can only happen simultaneously when $a = b$; it is not required that $a\,R\,a$ should be true for all a.

In Example 4.4 we have an anti-symmetric relation, since $a < b$ and $b < a$ *never* happen simultaneously. Example 4.26 is also anti-symmetric, since $a \leqslant b$ and $b \leqslant a$ together force $a = b$.

Example 4.35 In a non-recursive programming language, such as *Fortran*, a procedure or subroutine cannot call itself, directly or indirectly. It follows that if SUB_1 calls SUB_2, then SUB_2 cannot call SUB_1. Thus the relationship defined by one subroutine calling another is anti-symmetric.

In recursive languages, such as *Pascal, Modula-2* and *Ada*, this anti-symmetry is relaxed, at the expense of a more complicated calling mechanism. Whereas *Fortran* stores the return address from a subroutine at a fixed location in memory, and similarly, allocates any variable space needed by the routine statically, *Modula-2* would be implemented by keeping the return address and local variables on a *stack*, which can expand arbitrarily in size.

Example 4.36 The *block structured* programming languages, *Pascal, Modula-2* and *Ada*, allow one procedure to be local to another. The declaration of Proc_1 might include a declaration of Proc_2, which itself includes a declaration of Proc_3, and so on. The property of one procedure of being local to another is an anti-symmetric relation. The local procedure can access all variables local to the containing procedure, but not *vice versa*. We thus have a parallel relation between procedures, defined as whether one procedure can access the local variables of another.

• *Exercise 4.37* Discuss the nesting of *local modules* in *Modula-2*.

Example 4.38 The relation of Figure 4.13 is anti-symmetric.

Fig. 4.13 An anti-symmetric relation

$$a \quad b \quad c$$

• *Exercise 4.39* Show that the binary relation R on $\mathbb{Z}$ given by
$$R = \left\{ (n^2, n) : n \in \mathbb{Z} \right\}$$
is anti-symmetric.

Our final property for a binary relation is the *transitive* property. The easiest way to think of this property is in terms of the graph of the relation. Suppose that there exists a way of moving from a to b by following the arrows in the graph. For a transitive relation, we will always find that there was an arrow directly from a to b which we could have followed instead.

It turns out that we can provide a simple inductive proof to show that if $a\,R\,b$ and $b\,R\,c$ always imply $a\,R\,c$, then the binary relation is transitive in the above sense.

• *Exercise 4.40* Verify the above assertion.

Definition If $R^2 \subseteq R$ then R is **transitive**. Equivalently, we require that if $a\,R\,b$ and $b\,R\,c$, then $a\,R\,c$.

The phrasing in terms of R^2 is equivalent to what we have said above, because $a\,R^2\,c$ means that there exists a b with $a\,R\,b$ and $b\,R\,c$. These two conditions should imply that $(a, c) \in R^2 \subseteq R$, and *vice versa*.

A transitive relation should have a compact representation as a file, as we can see if we compare a list for the order relation $a < b$ on the set $\{1, \ldots, 10\}$ with the abbreviated list
$$1 < 2 < 3 < 4 < 5 < 6 < 7 < 8 < 9 < 10.$$

The 36 possible true relationships have been condensed into just 9 basic ones. A similar collapsing should be possible for any transitive relation. Figure 4.13 is not transitive, since $a\,R\,b$ and $b\,R\,c$, but we do not have $a\,R\,c$.

Example 4.41 Procedure nesting is a transitive relation, as is module nesting.

Example 4.42 Indirect procedure calling is a transitive relation. If `Proc_1` calls `Proc_2`, and `Proc_2` calls `Proc_3`, then `Proc_1` calls `Proc_3`.

Example 4.43 The relation of Figure 4.14 is transitive.

Fig. 4.14 A transitive relation

• ***Exercise 4.44*** Consider the syntax of your favourite programming language. This defines some syntactic structure, such as a ⟨*whilestatement*⟩, in terms of ⟨*expression*⟩ and ⟨*statement*⟩, plus the two reserved words `WHILE` and `DO`.

Define a relation on the syntactic structures used in your language, such that one structure is related to another if the definition of the first uses the name of the second. Try to guess what properties are possessed by this relation. Then examine the syntax carefully to see if you were correct.

Find a book on another programming language, and check whether your findings still hold.

Example 4.45 Let P be the set of all people who have ever lived. Define $a \to b$ to mean that a is an ancestor of b. Then $\to$ is transitive, but not symmetric or reflexive.

Example 4.46 Let $|$ be the relation on $\mathbb{Z}$ defined as
$$| = \{ (p, q) : p, q \in \mathbb{Z}, \exists k \in \mathbb{Z} \, (q = kp) \}.$$
We read $p|q$ as 'p divides q'. Then $|$ is reflexive and transitive but not symmetric.

• ***Exercise 4.47*** Show that the relation R defined on $\mathbb{N}$ by
$$a \, R \, b \iff ab \text{ is even}$$
is not transitive.

• ***Exercise 4.48*** Let A be a set of students taking the same examination papers. For $a, b \in A$, write $a \leqslant b$ if b did at least as well as a on every paper. If $B \subseteq A$, define
$$\underline{B} = \{ a \in A : a \leqslant b \text{ for all } b \in B \}$$

and
$$\overline{B} = \{\, a \in A : b \leqslant a \text{ for all } b \in B \,\}.$$
Thus $\underline{B}$ consists of all students who did no better on any paper than anyone in B, and $\overline{B}$ consists of all students who did at least as well on every paper as everyone in B. Either set might happen to be empty. We have the convention that $\overline{\varnothing} = \underline{\varnothing} = A$.

Show that $B \subseteq \overline{(\underline{B})}$.

● **Exercise 4.49** In the original definition of the language *Pascal*, there was the restriction that if a type T_2 was defined in terms of a type T_1, then T_1 must previously have been declared, except that T_2=^T_1 was allowed before T_1 was declared, so long as T_1 was declared later in the same block. This was essential if dynamic lists were to be programmable, the usual example being where T_2 points to a record type T_1, where one of the fields of this record type is of type T_2.

Formulate a relation between types, and explain which property has been relaxed.

Someone then noticed that there was a conflict in the following:

```
type T_1=real;
procedure funnyproc;
    type T_2=^T_1;
        T_1=integer;
```

Is T_2 a pointer to a real or to an integer? Find out what was done about this error. Why do you think the error was not spotted immediately?

● **Exercise 4.50** For each of the following relations on the given set, say whether it is *reflexive*, *symmetric*, *anti-symmetric* or *transitive*.

(i) $\mathbb{Q}$, $x \sim y \iff |x| \leqslant |y|$.

(ii) $\mathbb{Z}$, $x \sim y \iff 7$ divides $(x + y)$.

(iii) $\mathbb{Z}$, $x \sim y \iff 2$ divides $(x + y)$.

(iv) $\mathbb{N}$, $x \sim y \iff x^2 y$ is even.

(v) $\mathbb{N}$, $x \sim y \iff x^2 y^3$ is odd.

● **Exercise 4.51** Think of 8 binary relations on some finite set having each of the 8 possible combinations of the properties *reflexive*, *symmetric*, *transitive*.

What combinations are possible with *anti-symmetric*?

•**Exercise 4.52** Let $\sim$ be any relation on S. For $A \subseteq S$, define
$$\sim A = \{\, x \in S : \forall a \in A \,(x \sim a)\,\}$$
$$A\sim = \{\, x \in S : \forall a \in A \,(a \sim x)\,\}.$$
Show that if $A \subseteq B \subseteq S$ then $\sim B \subseteq \sim A$, $B\sim \subseteq A\sim$. Show also that $A \subseteq (\sim A)\sim$, $A \subseteq \sim(A\sim)$.

•**Exercise 4.53** Let $\sim$, $\equiv$ be two relations on S. Define $\cong$, $\approx$ by
$$x \cong y \quad \Longleftrightarrow \quad (x \sim y) \vee (x \equiv y),$$
$$x \approx y \quad \Longleftrightarrow \quad \exists z \in S[(x \sim z)\&(z \equiv y)].$$
Investigate whether *reflexivity* of both of $\sim$, $\equiv$ implies reflexivity of $\cong$ and $\approx$. Do the same for *symmetry, antisymmetry* and *transitivity*.

This Exercise is here to discourage you from the temptation of trying to mix together several relations, all with the same property, and then assuming that the resulting relation will have this same property.

4.8   Transitive closure

In several previous Examples, we have seen that it might be possible to write down a 'skeleton' relation which is much simpler than the one we are studying. In Example 4.5, *immediate subordinate* was a simpler relation than *subordinate*, and in the ordering of integers, the pairs $(i, i+1)$ form the simpler relation. For procedure calls, direct call is easier to handle than indirect call.

In general, if R is a binary relation on A, and if $a, b \in A$ are such that there exist $c_1, c_2, \ldots, c_n \in A$ with
$$a \, R \, c_1, \; c_1 \, R \, c_2, \; \ldots \; , \; c_n \, R \, b,$$
then we say that $a \, R^+ \, b$, and call R^+ the *transitve closure* of R. It is clear that $a \, R^+ \, b$ if and only if $a \, R^n \, b$ for some $n > 0$.

Definition Let R be a binary relation on A. We define the **transitive closure** R^+ of R by
$$R^+ = \bigcup_{n=1}^{\infty} R^n,$$
and the **reflexive transitive closure** R^* by
$$R^* = \bigcup_{n=0}^{\infty} R^n.$$
We include all pairs (a, a) in the reflexive transitive closure.

Example 4.54 We shall calculate the transitive closures of the relation R on A given in Figure 4.8. We have previously calculated R^2, and a similar calculation of R^3 gives
$$R^3 = \{\,(a,b),(b,a),(b,c)\,\}.$$
We do not need to continue the calculation any further, since it is clear that any chain $u\,R\,v\,R\,w\,R\cdots R\,z$ with four or more Rs must contain repetitions of some of $v,w,\ldots,z$, and so we can collapse any relationship in R^4 to one in R, R^2 or R^3. Thus
$$R^+ = R \cup R^2 \cup R^3 = \{\,(a,a),(b,b),(a,b),(b,a),(b,c),(a,c)\,\}$$
and
$$R^* = R^0 \cup R^+ = \{\,(a,a),(b,b),(c,c),(a,b),(b,a),(b,c),(a,c)\,\}$$

The trick which we used in the preceding Example works for any finite set A, where we have
$$R^+ = \bigcup_{n=1}^{|A|} R^n, \quad \text{and} \quad R^* = \bigcup_{n=0}^{|A|} R^n.$$

•***Exercise 4.55*** Prove the above assertion, using induction on $|A|$.

Example 4.56 The relation S on $\mathbb{Z}$ given by
$$S = \{\,(m,m+1) : m \in \mathbb{Z}\,\}$$
has transitive closure $<$ and reflexive transitive closure $\leqslant$. R is called the *successor* relation.

•***Exercise 4.57*** Define a *symmetric* closure of a binary relation.

•***Exercise 4.58*** Could you define the *reflexive, symmetric, transitive* closure $R^\#$ of a binary relation? What does this do to the *parent* relation '*a is a parent of b*'?

•***Exercise 4.59*** What about the *anti-symmetric*, transitive closure?

•***Exercise 4.60*** Show that if R is a symmetric binary relation on A, then R^+ and R^* are both symmetric.

4.9 Warshall's algorithm

Suppose we have a finite set A with n elements. We can represent a binary relation R on A by means of an n by n table, where we index the rows and columns by the elements of A, and we put a 1 in row a and column b if $a\,R\,b$, otherwise we put a 0.

Definition Let $A = \{a_1, \ldots, a_n\}$. The **matrix** of the binary relation R on A is the 2-dimensional array M_R of numbers $a_{i,j}$, with $1 \leqslant i, j \leqslant n$, such that

$$a_{i,j} = \begin{cases} 1 & \text{if } a_i \ R \ a_j \\ 0 & \text{otherwise} \end{cases}.$$

We can alternatively use boolean values **T** and **F** instead of 0 and 1.

Matrices are written as rectangular arrays within round or square brackets. The matrix is uniquely defined once an order is imposed upon the elements.

Example 4.61 The matrix of Figure 4.7, with the elements written in the order a, b, c, is $\begin{bmatrix} 0 & 1 & 0 \\ 1 & 0 & 1 \\ 0 & 0 & 0 \end{bmatrix}$.

Storing a relation as such a matrix is not efficient unless most elements happen to be related to most other elements.

Let us look at a few properties of our matrix, which reflect properties of the relation.

Theorem 4.2 Let R be a binary relation with matrix entries $a_{i,j}$.

(i) R is reflexive if and only if $a_{i,i} = 1$ for all i.

(ii) R is symmetric if and only if $a_{i,j} = a_{j,i}$ for all i and j.

(iii) R is anti-symmetric if and only if $a_{i,j} = 1 - a_{j,i}$ for all i and j.

Proof These are all immediate consequences of the definitions.   □

•***Exercise 4.62*** Rephrase the Theorem assuming that M_R is boolean.

There is a notable absence of transitivity from the above Theorem. The reason is that it is quite difficult to spot this property from the matrix. However, the matrix does let us calculate the powers of a binary relation fairly efficiently. The calculation is done by a sort of truncated arithmetic, where we are only interested in whether a number is zero or greater than zero.

Example 4.63 For the relation of Figure 4.7, to find out if b is related to c in R^2, we see if at least one of $a_{2,1}a_{1,3}$, $a_{2,2}a_{2,3}$ or $a_{2,3}a_{3,3}$ is nonzero. In this case, all are zero, so we put a 0 in our matrix.

The calculation of R^k from R^{k-1} and R will take time of order n^3, so calculating R^n will take time $n \times n^3 = n^4$, and the final addition of all the matrices to produce the transitive closure will take time $n \times n^2 = n^3$.

Fig. 4.15 **Warshall's algorithm**
FOR $i := 1$ **TO** n **DO**
  FOR $j := 1$ **TO** n **DO**
    IF $a[j, i] = 1$ **THEN**
      FOR $k := 1$ **TO** n **DO**
        IF $a[i, k] = 1$ **THEN**
          $a[j, k] := 1;$
        END;
      END;
    END;
  END;
END;

Thus the time to calculate a transitive closure appears to be of order n^4 for large n. There is a way to shorten the calculation to an n^3 process, by combining all the stages together. The algorithm to do this is due to *Warshall*, and is presented in Figure 4.15. This algorithm replaces the matrix by its transitive closure. Let us prove this fact.

Theorem 4.3 Warshall's algorithm correctly calculates the transitive closure.

Proof Let $A = \{a_1, \ldots, a_n\}$. Any entries of M_R which are changed to 1s are so changed correctly. The only question is, are enough entries changed? Suppose that we can find a chain of $k > 2$ elements

$$s_1 \ R \ s_2 \ R \ s_3 \ R \cdots R \ s_k$$

in A. We shall see how the algorithm shortens this chain by modifying R. We can assume that no element is immediately repeated in the chain.

Suppose a_1 appears as s_p, with $1 < p < n$. The relationships $s_{p-1} \ R$ $a_1 \ R \ s_{p+1}$ will be converted at the first stage of the algorithm into $s_{p-1} \ R \ s_{p+1}$, and a_1 will be eliminated from the chain, except when it appears at the endpoints.

Normalize the chain again, by ignoring immediate repetitions of any element. If $k = 2$ we are done, otherwise, repeat the last step with a_2 replacing a_1, then a_3, and so on up to a_n. It is clear that everything will be eliminated from the chain apart from the endpoints, and so the endpoints are indeed related in the modified relation.   □

An implementation of Warshall's algorithm is given in the appendices.

4.10   Equivalence relations

Even though two objects are not strictly identical, we sometimes see that they are similar enough for us to be able to ignore any differences between them. The degree of identification depends on the context. Jones and Postlethwaite are definitely different people, but as far as the Inland Revenue is concerned, they might as well be identical if they have the same income and marital status. A name engraver might, on the other hand, decide they are completely different. A judge will regard them as equivalent in the law, but their favourite football teams might notice a distinct difference in their behaviour!

Definition A binary relation R on the set A is called an **equivalence relation** if it is reflexive, symmetric and transitive.

Example 4.64 Consider the following definition:

Two types T_1 *and* T_2 *are said to be* compatible types *if they are identical, they are declared to be equal, by* T_1=T_2, *if one is declared as a subrange of the other, or if they are both declared as subranges of another type* T_3.

The above looks very plausible, until we try to verify that compatibility is an equivalence relation, or try to write a program to recognize compatibility, such as a compiler. We notice that T_3 might be declared equal to T_2, which was itself declared as a subrange of T_1. T_3 and T_1 should now be compatible, but they are not, as we can see by examining the definition. T_3 is neither declared equal to, nor as a subrange of T_1. Nevertheless, *implicitly*, T_3 is a subrange of T_1. Thus there *is* some sense in the definition, but what is it?

The answer lies in a confusion between a relation and its closure. The *correct* definition of compatibility is:

Define the relation R *between types, by saying that* T_1 *and* T_2 *are related under* R *if either* T_1 *is declared to be equal to* T_2, *or* T_1 *is declared to be a subrange of* T_2. compatibility *of two types is defined as being*

related under the reflexive, symmetric, transitive closure
$R^{\#}$ of R.

See Exercise 4.58 for a definition of $R^{\#}$.

We have a definition which is in accordance with what we intended; also, the muddle of subranges has collapsed into a single case.

Example 4.65 The first stage of a compiler is called a *lexical analyser*. It breaks the program into objects called *tokens*, typical of which are the following: BEGIN, END, :=, MyIdentifier.

The lexical analyser attaches a class to each token, and the tokens are henceforth indivisible objects. Thus BEGIN would be a *reserved word*, := would be an *operator*, and MyIdentifier would be an *identifier*.

As far as the lexical analyser is concerned, all reserved words are regarded as equivalent in its classification.

• **Exercise 4.66** Regard two variables in a program as equivalent if they both address the same portion of memory. If var_1 and var_2 are equivalent, and we execute var_1:=c, then after the assignment, the value of var_2 will also equal c.

Are such variables possible in *Pascal*? *Modula-2*?

Example 4.67 The relation in Figure 4.16 is an equivalence relation.

Fig. 4.16 An equivalence relation

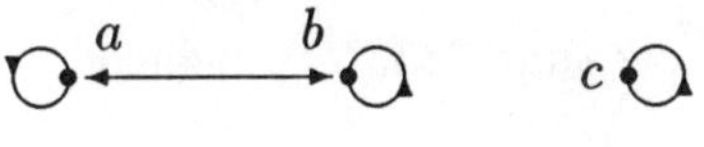

Equivalence relations are almost invariably written using the symbols $\sim$ or $\equiv$.

Example 4.68 Let $n \geqslant 2$ be a fixed integer. Consider the relation $\equiv$ defined on $\mathbb{Z}$ as

$$\{\, (p, q) : p, q \in \mathbb{Z}, n | (q - p) \,\},$$

where $|$ denotes the relation defined in Example 4.46. We shall show that $\equiv$ is an equivalence relation on $\mathbb{Z}$.

Reflexive Clearly $n | (p - p)$ for any $p \in \mathbb{Z}$, so $p \equiv p$ for all $p \in \mathbb{Z}$.

Symmetric If $p \equiv q$, so $n | (q - p)$, say $q - p = kn$, $k \in \mathbb{Z}$, then $p - q = (-k)n$, so $q \equiv p$.

Transitive If $p \equiv q$, $q \equiv r$, then $q - p = kn$, $r - q = jn$, where $j, k \in \mathbb{Z}$, and thus $r - p = (r - q) + (q - p) = (j + k)n$, hence $p \equiv r$.

Thus $\equiv$ is an equivalence relation on $\mathbb{Z}$. We commonly see the notation

$$p \equiv q \;(\text{mod } n)$$

to represent this relation.

Definition If $p \equiv q$ (mod n), then we say that p and q are **congruent modulo** n.

Example 4.69 $5 \equiv 17$ (mod 12), $2^{55555} \equiv 2$ (mod 3). The first is obvious. The second follows from the following Exercise.

•**Exercise 4.70** If $a \equiv b$ (mod n) and $c \equiv d$ (mod n), show that $ac \equiv bd$ (mod n).

•**Exercise 4.71** Prove the second assertion in Example 4.69.

•**Exercise 4.72** In each of the following, find an x which is positive and as small as possible, satisfying the congruence.
(i) $2135 \equiv x$ (mod 19)   (ii) $5^2 + 6^2 \equiv x$ (mod 2)
(iii) $2 \times 3 \times 4 \times 5 \times \cdots \times 20 \equiv x$ (mod 10000)
(iv) $2 \times 3 \times 4 \times 5 \times \cdots \times 20 \equiv x$ (mod 23)
(v) $24x \equiv 1$ (mod 17)

•**Exercise 4.73** Find all solutions of the congruence $x^2 \equiv 1$ (mod 11).

•**Exercise 4.74** Solve $x^2 \equiv 1$ (mod 12) completely.

•**Exercise 4.75** Show that $3333^{4444} + 4444^{3333}$ is divisible by 5.

4.11   Partitions

Equivalence relations play an important rôle in mathematics, in that they *partition* the underlying set in the following way.

Definition Let A be a finite set, and let $A_1, \ldots, A_m$ be subsets of A such that $A_i \neq \varnothing$ for all i, $A_i \cap A_j = \varnothing$ if $i \neq j$, and

$$A = \bigcup_{i=1}^{m} A_i = A_1 \cup A_2 \cup \cdots \cup A_m.$$

We say that the sets A_i **partition** the set A, and call these sets the **blocks** or **classes** of the partition.

If A is infinite, we say that the family of sets A_i, with i in the possibly infinite index set I, partitions A if $A_i \neq \emptyset$ for all i, $A_i \cap A_j = \emptyset$ if $i \neq j$, and

$$A = \bigcup_{i \in I} A_i.$$

A partition consists of a family of mutually disjoint subsets of A, none of them empty, whose union equals A.

Example 4.76 The set $\mathbb{Z}$ is partitioned into the two classes $\mathcal{E}$ and $\mathcal{O}$ of *even* and *odd* integers respectively.

Example 4.77 The transactions on a bank statement are partitioned into *credits* and *debits*.

Example 4.78 People are partitioned into the classes *male* and *female*.

Example 4.79 Statements in *Pascal* are partitioned into the following eleven classes:

(i)   Assignments   (ii)   Procedure calls
(iii)   `begin...end` blocks   (iv)   `if` statements
(v)   `case` statements   (vi)   `while` statements
(vii)   `repeat` statements   (viii)   `for` statements
(ix)   `with` statements   (x)   `goto` statements
(xi)   Null statements

The recognition of the partition class of a statement is one of the primary rôles of a compiler. We can think of the compiler as deciding that S starts with `repeat`, say, and so is of type (vii). It calls a procedure to handle a `repeat` statement, which processes all statements until it meets an unmatched `until`, at which point it calls a procedure to read an expression, before terminating.

The same is true of any other class of structures in a compiled language, a simpler example being of a parameter declaration in *Pascal*, which can be of four different types. (See also Chapter 8.)

• **Exercise 4.80** Give a corresponding partition of statements in the programming language *Modula-2*.

• **Exercise 4.81** Partition *types* in *Pascal* and *Modula-2*.

• **Exercise 4.82** Do the same for *operators*. (This is too easy!)

Given any partition of A, we can trivially define an equivalence relation $\sim$ on A by taking $a \sim b$ if and only if a and b are in the same class.

Conversely, given an equivalence relation $\sim$ on A, we can construct a partition of A.

Definition Let $\sim$ be an equivalence relation on A. For each $a \in A$, let $\bar{a}$ be defined as

$$\bar{a} = \{\, x \in A : a \sim x \,\}.$$

This set is called the **equivalence class** of a.

Thus the equivalence class $\bar{a}$ is a set, identified by an element $a \in \bar{a}$.

Example 4.83 The equivalence classes under modulo n arithmetic are $\bar{0}, \bar{1}, \ldots, \overline{n-1}$. These can informally be identified with the numbers $0, 1, \ldots, n-1$.

If $n = 2$, we have binary arithmetic, where $0 + 0 = 0$, $0 + 1 = 1$, and $1 + 1 = 0$. The equivalence classes are $\bar{0}$ and $\bar{1}$; $\bar{0}$ contains all even numbers and $\bar{1}$ all odd numbers. It so happens that we have the rules

$$
\begin{array}{rcccl}
\text{even} & + & \text{even} & = & \text{even} \\
\text{even} & + & \text{odd} & = & \text{odd} \\
\text{odd} & + & \text{even} & = & \text{odd} \\
\text{odd} & + & \text{odd} & = & \text{even},
\end{array}
$$

which allow us to write $\bar{0} + \bar{0} = \bar{0}$, $\bar{0} + \bar{1} = \bar{1}$, and so on. The sum of any element of $\bar{1}$ with any element of $\bar{1}$ gives an element of $\bar{0}$.

Theorem 4.4 The equivalence classes of an equivalence relation on A partition A.

Proof Any two of these equivalence classes are easily shown to be either *identical* or *disjoint* from one another. If multiple copies of any such class are discarded, we end up with a partition of A. □

●**Exercise 4.84** Verify the assertion in the above Proof.

Example 4.85 Two wffs are logically equivalent if they have the same truth table. This is an equivalence relation on wffs, and the equivalence classes consist of all those wffs which have the same disjunctive normal form.

●**Exercise 4.86** Why would disjunctive forms, rather than disjunctive normal forms, not provide a very good means of classifying wffs?

In the appendices, we shall present a program to find the equivalence classes of an equivalence relation.

To test our understanding of the duality between equivalence relations and partitions, we shall look at one of the most fundamental methods of construction used in the foundations of mathematics. It is a technique which allows us to extend the natural numbers into the integers, by constructing a set which behaves in a way indistinguishable from the integers.

Example 4.87 Let $A = \mathbb{N}^2$ and for $a, b \in A$, $a = (a_1, a_2)$, $b = (b_1, b_2)$, put $a \equiv b$ if $a_1 + b_2 = b_1 + a_2$. Then $\equiv$ is an equivalence relation on A, as we demonstrate:

Reflexive $a_1 + a_2 = a_1 + a_2$ so $a \equiv a$ for all $a \in A$.

Symmetric The defining relation is symmetric in a and b, so $a \equiv b$ implies $b \equiv a$.

Transitive Suppose $a \equiv b$ and $b \equiv c$. Then
$$a_1 + b_2 = b_1 + a_2$$
and
$$b_1 + c_2 = c_1 + b_2.$$
Thus
$$a_1 + b_2 + b_1 + c_2 = b_1 + a_2 + c_1 + b_2$$
from which we obtain
$$a_1 + c_2 = c_1 + a_2,$$
that is, $a \equiv c$.

The equivalence classes of $\equiv$ can be regarded as *integers*, by identifying the class $\overline{(a_1, a_2)}$ with the integer $a_1 - a_2$. One can easily verify that a consistent arithmetic can be set up on the equivalence classes, and so we can 'construct' the integers from the natural numbers. Such constructions are extremely important in the foundations of mathematics, where we are showing that a more complicated mathematical object can be defined in terms of a simpler mathematical object, and so the number of assumptions we need to make are considerably reduced. In view of Example 4.56, the whole of integer arithmetic follows from the properties of the successor relation in the natural numbers. The following Exercise will extend this tower even further.

•**Exercise 4.88** Let $A = \mathbb{Z} \times \mathbb{N}$, and define $\equiv$ on A by taking $a \equiv b$, $a = (a_1, a_2)$, $b = (b_1, b_2)$, to mean $a_1 b_2 = b_1 a_2$. Show that this gives an equivalence relation. What do you think the equivalence classes represent?

4.12   Partial orders

We next look at another combination of properties which produce an
object of considerable interest. The definition only differs slightly from
that for an equivalence relation, yet the structure it produces could
hardly be more different.

> *Definition* A binary relation R on the set A is called a **partial
> order relation** if it is reflexive, anti-symmetric and transitive. The
> set A with this ordering is called a **partially ordered set** or **poset**.
> A partial order which has the additional property that for any $a, b \in$
> A we have at least one of $a\,R\,b$ or $b\,R\,a$ is called a **total order**.

When the relational symbol is used in its *infix* position, the normal
symbol used is $\leqslant$. One convention followed is that if $a \leqslant b$ we also write
$b \geqslant a$, and if $a \leqslant b$ and $a \neq b$, we write $a < b$ or $b > a$.

An anti-symmetric, transitive relation is easily transformed into a
partial order, by making it reflexive, that is, by extending it by all pairs
(a, a) in the usual way. We generally write such a relation as $a < b$, and
its extension as $a \leqslant b$. We can therefore define a poset with or without
reflexivity.

> *Example 4.89* The set $\mathbb{Z}$ with the relation $\leqslant$ forms a poset. It has
> the property that for any $a, b \in \mathbb{Z}$ we have either $a \leqslant b$ or $b \leqslant a$.
> Thus the order is total.

> •*Exercise 4.90* Does $\subseteq$ give a partial order relation on the subsets
> of a fixed universal set E? If so, is it *total*?

> •*Exercise 4.91* If R is an anti-symmetric relation, is R^* a partial
> order?

To motivate the rest of this section, we present an Example.

> *Example 4.92* Suppose we have a calculation to perform which is
> split into several operations, some of which need other operations
> to have terminated before they can commence. An example would
> be where one operation uses the results of another operation as its
> data. This is an example of a *sequencing* problem, and the 'having
> to precede' relation is a partial order on the set of operations to be
> performed, or, at least, it is if the initial restrictions are consistent!
>   An example would be where there are ten operations a to j, and
> the ordering is $c < j$, $a < i$, $j < i$, $b < a$, $c < d$, $d < e$, $a < f$, $e < f$,

$b < c$, $d < g$, $g < h$, and any other relationships transitively implied by these.

It is something of a surprise to discover that any finite partially ordered set can be sorted into a total order which respects the original ordering. In Example 4.92, suppose we wished to execute the operations a to j sequentially. We would have to find a total ordering in which b preceded a, d preceded e, and so on. It so happens that such an order exists. This total order is a superset, as a relation, of the original order.

Theorem 4.5 Let $<$ be a partial order relation on A. There exists a total order $\prec$ on A such that if $a < b$ then $a \prec b$. Thus any poset can be *totally ordered*.

Proof If A only has one element, the result is trivial. Suppose we can always totally order a poset of n or fewer elements, and suppose A has $n + 1$ elements, $A = \{ a_1, \ldots, a_{n+1} \}$. We produce the first element of our total order by the following process.

First, assume the first element is $b = a_1$. If $a_2 < b$, choose $b = a_2$ instead. If $a_3 < b$, choose $b = a_3$, and so on, and finally, if $a_{n+1} < b$, take $b = a_{n+1}$. The element b is a *minimal element* of the poset, in the sense that it is not *greater* than any other element, although it is not necessarily *smaller* than *every* other element.

We put b first in our total order, and write $b \prec x$ for all $x \neq b$. We then totally order the rest of A to complete our ordering. $\qquad \square$

The above proof is an inductive proof, but it is of the sort that readily transforms into an algorithm to totally order a set. An implementation is given in the appendices.

• **Exercise 4.93** Totally sequence the operations in Example 4.92.

• **Exercise 4.94** In the following list, the letters represent processes, and $x < y$ means that x must precede y. Totally order the processes.
$$m < h < j < o < f < k$$
$$i < e < d < p$$
$$m < g < e < n < o < d < c$$
$$i < g < b < e < a < j$$

• **Exercise 4.95** Sequence the arithmetic operations performed in the calculation of
$$(c - d/e) \times (a + (b + a)(c - (a - b)/d)).$$

4.13 n-ary relations

In the applications of relations to relational databases, it is more common to find the data represented as n-tuples rather than ordered pairs.

Example 4.96 The file of orders placed with a firm might be regarded as a subset of $P \times D \times N \times O \times X$, where the sets P and D are sets of strings of a fixed size, N and O are equal to $\mathbb{Z}^+$, and X equals $\mathbb{R}$. The quintuple (p, d, n, o, x) represents the fact that in order number o, n of part p, described by d, have been ordered at a unit price of x per part. Typical entries in the file might look like

QFC1001	5/8in. nut	3000	10812	00.13
CBK3544	flanged sprogget	1500	10839	00.27
QFC1001	5/8in. nut	27000	10839	00.13

The theory of relational databases is concerned with the unravelling of horrors like the above, where the logical structure of the data has not been respected in the database. If the unit price changed to 00.14, every line containing QFC1001 would have to be altered.

The only difference between the above Example and an ordinary relation is that the file has more than two columns. Instead of ordered pairs we must take ordered n-tuples to represent this kind of relation.

Definition Let $A_1, \ldots, A_n$ be sets. An n-**ary relation** is defined as a subset R of $A_1 \times A_2 \times \cdots \times A_n$.

Because more than two objects are involved in an n-ary relation, it is impossible to use the *infix* notation $a \, R \, b$, since we would not know whether to put R between a and b, or b and c, in a ternary relation. However, the predicate form of a relation is always available to us, and we can write $R(a_1, \ldots, a_n)$, for $(a_1, \ldots, a_n) \in R$.

If $1 \leqslant r \leqslant n - 1$, then an n-ary relation can be regarded as a relation between $A_1 \times A_2 \times \cdots \times A_n$ and $A_1 \times A_2 \times \cdots \times A_r$. The n-tuple $(a_1, \ldots, a_n)$ is related to the r-tuple $(a_1, \ldots, a_r)$. The split need not reflect the ordering of the original sets, and we could equally well define $N = \{1, 2, \ldots, n\}$ take $X \subset N$, and view our n-ary relation as a relation between $\prod_{n \in N} A_n$ and $\prod_{r \in X} A_r$. In the inverse relation, an r-tuple is related to any n-tuple which contains it.

Now we are familiar with what happens with ordinary relations, the details of n-ary relations will present few obstacles, since the manipulation of the latter is mainly to do with regarding them as split into ordinary relations. Thus the *join* of two n-ary relations is just their composition as ordinary relations, for a suitable splitting of the component sets of the two n-ary relations, as described above. To form the join, we must choose identifiable ranges X in each relation.

Example 4.97 Suppose that we have two relations R and S, with $R \subseteq A \times B \times C \times D$ and $S \subseteq A \times B \times E \times F \times G$. We regard R as relating (a, b, c, d) to (a, b) and S as relating (a, b) to (a, b, e, f, g). The composition relates (a, b, c, d) to (a, b, e, f, g), and so consists of 9-tuples $(a, b, c, d, a, b, e, f, g)$. By convention, we choose not to duplicate a and b, and define the join as consisting of 7-tuples (a, b, c, d, e, f, g).

We shall return to the idea of an n-ary relation in Chapter 5, when we look at the structure of *relational databases*. There are a few new ideas we need before we can give a fuller description of these, and so we postpone their discussion for the time being.

• **Exercise 4.98** A supplier of parts keeps two databases concerning the parts he supplies. Each part has a part number which is unique to it. The first database contains triples consisting of a part number, the quantity supplied, and a unit price. The second database consists of pairs consisting of a part number and a description. How could he produce a list which gives a description of each part, the quantity supplied, and a unit price?

5

Mappings

5.1 Introduction

In this chapter, we shall investigate the important class of relations known as *mappings* or *functions*. These are relations between two sets such that every possible element of the first set appears in one and only one ordered pair. We can regard the relation as a list, with the first column listing the elements in the domain, and the second listing the values of the function. A mapping is usually specified either by giving a rule for which y appears in each pair (x, y), or, for finite sets, by listing the value of the mapping for each value of x.

Example 5.1 The relation $R = \{(n, n^2) : n \in \mathbb{Z}\}$ is a mapping, and the 'rule' is to form the pair containing n as first component, square n and take the result as second component.

Example 5.2 Consider the *Modula-2* declaration

$$f : \texttt{ARRAY[1..n] OF INTEGER}.$$

This produces n integers $f[1]$, $f[2]$, ..., $f[n]$. These can be regarded as the values of a function $f(m)$ which is only defined when $1 \leqslant m \leqslant n$, and this function is represented in the computer by a list f of its values. If n is the number of employees in a firm, m is a payroll number, and $f(m)$ is the salary of employee m, this representation of the salary function would be necessary if there were no obvious formula relating m to $f(m)$.

We shall study the properties of mappings, and will then investigate the question 'how big is an infinite set?' Our answer will lead us to the conclusion that certain mappings are effectively non-computable, in the sense that nobody could ever write a procedure in a programming language to calculate them, although, given any element of their domain, one could certainly write a procedure to calculate the value at that element.

We shall finally close the chapter by looking at the class of objects called *relational databases*. These are the current norm for the storage and retrieval of information. We shall be able to investigate the properties of these databases, and formulate some mathematical descriptions of the operations we perform on them and the properties of interdependence of the data they contain.

5.2   Partial mappings

If we are to regard relations as generalizations of functions, we must elucidate the correct definition of a function. There is an intermediate stage, somewhere between a general relation and a function, which is of some importance in the theory of computations.

Definition Let R be a relation between A and B. Suppose that $a \, R \, b_1$ and $a \, R \, b_2$ never happen together, with $b_1 \neq b_2$. Then we call R a **partial mapping** or **partial function** from A to B.

Fig. 5.1 **A partial mapping**

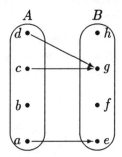

The import of this definition is that, for any given $a \in A$, either there are no pairs $(a, y) \in R$ or there is just one such pair. Provided a is in the domain of R, a unique element b of B is determined such that $(a, b) \in R$. The element b is regarded as the *value* of the partial mapping at a. If a is *not* in the domain of R, there is *no* pair $(a, b) \in R$. We interpret this as saying that the partial mapping does not take a value at a. Thus the partial mapping only takes values on part of A.

Example 5.3 Figure 5.1 represents a partial mapping of $A = \{a, b, c, d\}$ to $B = \{e, f, g, h\}$.

Example 5.4 Take $R = \{(x, 1/x) : x \in \mathbb{R}, x \neq 0\} \subset \mathbb{R}^2$. Then R is a binary relation on $\mathbb{R}$, and it is a partial mapping, since when $x = 0$ there are no pairs $(0, y)$, and for $x \neq 0$ there is only one pair $(x, 1/x)$.

Example 5.5 Take $R = \{(x^2 + 1, 2x + 3) : x \in \mathbb{R}\}$. In this case, we do not have a partial mapping, since on putting $x = 1$ we obtain the pair $(2, 5)$, and putting $x = -1$ we obtain $(2, 1)$, so two pairs start with the same value 2.

To specify a partial mapping from A to B we would normally
 (i) Choose a subset D of A to be the domain of the relation;
 (ii) Choose some rule which, given $x \in D$, returns a value $y \in B$ and then put the pair (x, y) in R.
This vague idea of a 'rule' is the working definition of a partial mapping, and is the way we generally regard such an object. In Example 5.4 we choose $D = \mathbb{R} \setminus \{0\}$ and the rule $f(x) = 1/x$ to insert the pair $(x, f(x))$ in R.

Example 5.6 A motorist notices that the amount of tyre tread depth left on his rear tyres after covering a distance d equals $9 - e^{0.0001d}$, whilst the amount of tread depth on his front tyres equals $9 - e^{0.001d}$. Both formulae only apply until the depth becomes zero.

We show that he can work out how much tread is left on his front tyres by measuring the tread on his rear tyres, up to the point when the front tyres need replacing.

Consider the relation
$$R = \{(9 - e^{0.0001d}, 9 - e^{0.001d}) : d \in \mathbb{R}, d \geqslant 0, 9 - e^{0.001d} \geqslant 0\}.$$
This defines a partial mapping $R \subseteq \mathbb{R}^2$, because the rear tread depth is a decreasing function of distance, so no two pairs in R have the same first component. It is thus possible to deduce what the front tread depth is given the rear depth.

In this case, we can find a formula relating front tread depth f to rear depth r. From $r = 9 - e^{0.0001d}$ and $f = 9 - e^{0.001d}$ we deduce that $(9 - r)^{10} = 9 - f$, giving $f = 9 - (9 - r)^{10}$, provided this is non-negative.

•**Exercise 5.7** Does $R \subseteq \mathbb{R}^2$ given by
$$R = \{(e^n + n, n^2 + \sin n) : n \in \mathbb{Z}\}$$

define a partial mapping?

A partial mapping is a function which is not defined everywhere on the given set, only on its domain. The set B is called the *codomain*, and A is called the *carrier* or *source* for the partial mapping.

It is true that in most cases, once the domain D and range E are known, we can dispense with A and B entirely, and think of R as a *function* from D to E. Despite this, it is still theoretically essential to keep A and B in some situations.

Example 5.8 Let P be a program which has one natural number as its input, and which, for some input values will never terminate. Suppose that, if it does terminate, it prints a single real result and halts. Then P can be regarded as a partial mapping from $\mathbb{N}$ to $\mathbb{R}$. Without any further information, it is impossible to surmise what its domain and range are.

As an example, suppose that the program calculates, for any n, the decimal expansion of π up to the point at which n appears explicitly amongst the digits. Thus $n = 1$ would produce 3.1, $n = 15$ would produce 3.1415, and so on. Do you know whether the program will ever terminate if we input $n = 12345$?

One can think of many numerical programs which are of the above sort. Without the concept of a partial mapping, we have no hope of a mathematical model for them. Our objective should be to ensure that when a program is given a valid input, it should terminate with some sort of output, which is either the result of the calculation we hoped for, or, at worst, an error message. We specify a set A of valid inputs, which can be as complex a set as we like, and a set B of valid outputs. We would like the program to return a value in B no matter where we start it in A. The set B will usually consist of useful results, and also error messages. If the program represents a partial mapping, and is not defined at some $a \in A$, we regard it as erroneous, and it probably contains an infinite loop which we did not foresee.

• **Exercise 5.9** Consider a simple program which is supposed to read the natural number n, and then calculate and print its square. Try to think of what we should take as the sets A and B for the partial mapping it defines.

• **Exercise 5.10** Sometimes the 'output' of a program can be of a more subtle type. Suppose we have written a text editor, which obeys a number of commands. The editor is called by typing `edit filename`, and starts in edit mode. In this mode we can issue the commands

input Go into input mode;

find *string* Search for specified string;

change/*string1***/***string2***/** Change all occurrences of first string to second string;

top Go to top of file;

delete Delete current line;

line *n* Go to line *n*;

quit Exit edit, and leave file unchanged;

file File and exit editor.

In input mode, the editor accepts any text typed until the user hits the ⟨*escape*⟩ key, when it returns to edit mode.

What do you think would be meaningful definitions of A and B for this program?

●*Exercise 5.11* Your editor seems to be working alright, but one day you try to `file` and it gives a warning message 'not enough room on this floppy disk'. You don't have any more formatted disks. What has gone wrong?

●*Exercise 5.12* So you finally got your master program working perfectly! Then, one day, just as you were in the middle of a long calculation, someone accidentally pulled the plug on the computer. What went wrong? No output is returned! But surely the mathematical model was OK, so do you have to think again?

●*Exercise 5.13* The country of Freedonia has an electoral system in which it is illegal to stand in an election as a candidate in more than one constituency. Think of a partial mapping which encapsulates this rule.

5.3   Mappings

Continuing with our quest for the true definition of a function, we impose the restriction that the source and domain of our relation should be identical sets.

Definition Let $R \subseteq A \times B$ be a relation between A and B. Suppose that for each $a \in A$ there is just one pair $(a, b) \in R$. Then R is called a **mapping** or **function** from A to B.

Example 5.14 Figure 5.2 represents a mapping from $A = \{a, b, c, d\}$ to $B = \{e, f, g, h\}$.

Fig. 5.2 **A mapping**

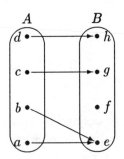

Since the function notation rather than relation notation is the one we invariably use for mappings, henceforth, if f is a relation between A and B which defines a mapping, and $(a, b) \in f$, we shall write $b = f(a)$. For example, in the case of $\imath_A$, we write $\imath_A(a) = a$ for all $a \in A$. There is no question of confusion here, since the predicate and infix notations $f(a, b)$ and $a \, f \, b$ are rarely used for mappings. We write $f : A \to B$ to express the fact that f is a mapping *from A to B*, and we read this notation as 'f maps A to B' or 'f is a mapping of A to B'.

For any $a \in A$, we also write $a \mapsto f(a)$, which reads 'a maps to $f(a)$'. This is to be regarded as the 'text' version of the arrow which appears in the graph of a mapping.

Example 5.15 Let $f : \mathbb{R} \to \mathbb{R}$ be defined by $f(x) = x^2$ for all $x \in \mathbb{R}$. Thus $1 \mapsto 1$, $-2 \mapsto 4$, and so on.

Example 5.16 Let P be the set of all people. Let $S = \{\text{Male}, \text{Female}\}$. Define $s : P \to S$ by taking $s(p)$ to be the sex of p.

Example 5.17 Let U be a finite set, and let P denote the set whose elements are the subsets of U. Thus P is the *power set* $\mathcal{P}(U)$ of U. Define $c : P \to \mathbb{Z}^+$ by $c(S) = |S|$, for any $S \in P$, that is, $S \subseteq U$, and

$|S|$ denotes the number of elements in S. The mapping c maps each subset of U to its *cardinal*.

There is a corresponding notation for partial mappings from A to B. If f is such a partial mapping, we sometimes write $f : A \nrightarrow B$ to express this fact. The 'function' notation is also used for partial mappings, but care must then be taken to ensure that we do not try to manipulate $f(a)$ when a is outside the domain of f. One other thing to note is that the *range* of a mapping or partial mapping $f : A \nrightarrow B$ is equal to the set

$$\{\, b \in B : b = f(a) \text{ for some } a \in A \,\}.$$

This is because saying that $b = f(a)$ is the same as saying that $(a, b) \in f$. Thus the range of a mapping equals the set of values taken by the mapping on its domain.

A mapping is regarded as defined by a set A, a set B, and a subset of $A \times B$. Change B and you have a different mapping, even if you only remove or add a redundant element.

Definition The mappings $f : A \to B$ and $g : X \to Y$ are regarded as **identical** only if $A = X$, $B = Y$, and $f(a) = g(a)$ for all $a \in A$.

Example 5.18 The mappings $f : \mathbb{Z} \to \mathbb{Z}$, $g : \mathbb{Z} \to \mathbb{Z}^+$ and $h : \mathbb{Z}^+ \to \mathbb{Z}^+$ given by the rules $f(n) = g(n) = h(n) = |n|$ are not identical, even though the rules have an identical statement in each case.

The above definition is a little pedantic, and we usually regard two mappings f and g as equivalent if they have a common domain and they take identical values on that domain.

•**Exercise 5.19** Let S, T have m, n elements respectively. How many different mappings are there from S to T?

At first sight, it might seem that our definitions only apply to functions of one variable. However, our definitions have enough generality in them to cope with any number of variables, by using cartesian products. A real function of two real variables is a mapping $f : \mathbb{R}^2 \to \mathbb{R}$, and a function of an integer variable and four real variables, resulting in a cardinal number, is of the form $g : \mathbb{Z} \times \mathbb{R}^4 \to \mathbb{Z}^+$. We might then write

$$g(-7, \pi, \pi, e, \sqrt{2}) = 411.$$

Notice that when we have several variables, it is customary to write $f(x, y)$ rather than the more strictly correct $f((x, y))$. If $f(a, b) = c$ then in terms of relations we have $(a, b)\, f\, c$, or alternatively $((a, b), c) \in f$.

There is no reason why a mapping should not return an ordered n-tuple as its value, an example being the mapping $f : \mathbb{R}^2 \to \mathbb{R}^2$ such that

$$(x, y) \mapsto (x \cos \theta - y \sin \theta, x \sin \theta + y \cos \theta),$$

for some fixed $\theta \in \mathbb{R}$. This maps (x, y) to the same point, but rotated round the origin through an angle θ. Again, we would write $f(x, y)$ in preference to $f((x, y))$.

The definition will also cope with infinities of variables, with a little care in defining infinite products of sets.

Example 5.20 Let $\mathbb{R}^\infty$ denote the set of all infinite-tuples $(a_1, a_2, a_3, \ldots)$, or, in other words, infinite sequences of real numbers. Consider

$$s : \mathbb{R}^\infty \to \{ E \} \cup \mathbb{R},$$

which sums the numbers in the sequence if that is possible, and otherwise returns the value E. Here, E denotes some non-number, which represents an error. Thus

$$s(a_1, a_2, a_3, \ldots) = \sum_{n=1}^{\infty} a_n,$$

if the sum is defined. Then s is a function of an infinite number of variables. We have

$$s(1, 1, 1, 1, \ldots) = E, \quad s(1, \frac{1}{2}, \frac{1}{4}, \frac{1}{8}, \ldots) = 2.$$

Much of *analysis* is concerned with evaluating s.

Example 5.21 Let B be the set of all valid conditions in *Pascal* and let S be the set of *Pascal* statements. The construction IF...THEN...ELSE... is a mapping $f : B \times S \times S \to S$. For example,

$$f(\texttt{a>0}, \texttt{a:=b}, \texttt{a:=c}) = \texttt{IF a>0 THEN a:=b ELSE a:=c}.$$

As far as a compiler is concerned, the procedure which handles an IF statement is all tensed up ready to read a logical expression, terminated by the reserved word THEN, and then a statement. If the statement is not terminated with ELSE, the second statement is taken to be null, otherwise the second statement is read from the program.

The compiler then regards the condition and two statements as a unit, and generates code as though for a single statement. It will have a rule for translating an IF statement, given the translations of the expression evaluation and two subsidiary statements, and this rule describes its mapping.

Thus the mathematical model of a mapping mirrors what the compiler is doing. As an example, suppose that in some processor logical evaluation results in a *zero* flag being set if the result is true, and cleared otherwise. Suppose that the translation of the expression evaluation and two statements are E, S_1 and S_2 respectively. The compiler might transform the triple (E, S_1, S_2) into the 'statement'

```
    E
    BEQ    false
    S_1
    BRA    end
false
    S_2
end
```

• **Exercise 5.22** Do the same for WHILE...DO... in *Pascal*.

• **Exercise 5.23** Does the *Modula-2* expression a MOD b represent a mapping $f : \mathbb{Z}^2 \to \mathbb{Z}$?

• **Exercise 5.24** The Ghetno-Hansar Company produces an internal phone list for its employees. The list consists of two columns; an initial and surname of an employee, and his/her phone number. Each employee has one phone number. When Arthur Minit tries to phone Irmine Gage, he finds two entries for the name I. Gage. Ian Gage answers the phone. What two relations have been confused by the compilers of the directory, and how can the problem be rectified?

5.4   Composition of mappings

The naïve treatment of functions encourages us to take 'functions of functions', such as $\exp(\cos x)$ or 2^{2^x}.

Definition Let $f : A \to B$, $g : B \to C$ be two mappings. The **composition** $g \circ f : A \to C$ of g and f is defined as the mapping given by $g \circ f(a) = g(f(a))$ for all $a \in A$.

An examination of the definition will convince the reader that g and f have been composed as relations. If $f(a) = b$ then $(a, b) \in f$. If $g(b) = c$ then $(b, c) \in g$. Thus according to the definition of composition of relations, $(a, c) \in g \circ f$, in other words, $g \circ f(a) = c$. It is clear that $g \circ f$ will be a mapping, because given a, b is uniquely defined, and thus so is c. Otherwise, the composition of mappings might only be a relation.

Now we see why it is better to write the composition of relations in reverse order. It is because when the relations are mappings, the notation $g \circ f$ matches the notation $g(f(a))$ better. After all, we are regarding a relation as a generalization of a function, so to have one order for functions and the other for relations would be unnecessarily perverse.

Example 5.25 Suppose that a manufacturer has a list of all the parts which are supplied to him, together with the supplier's name. He also has a list of suppliers' names, together with the suppliers' addresses. To obtain the address from which to order a given part, he composes two mappings $s : P \to S$ and $a : S \to A$ to obtain $a \circ s : P \to A$; $a(s(p))$ represents the address of the supplier of part p.

Example 5.26 Let a and b be real numbers. Consider the mapping $f : \mathbb{R}^2 \to \mathbb{R}^2$ such that
$$f(x,y) = (x^2 - y^2 + a, 2xy + b). \qquad (M)$$
We can think of this mapping as 'moving' the point (x, y) to a new position $f(x, y)$. Suppose that we wish to move the new point according to the same rule. We take $f(f(x, y)) = f \circ f(x, y)$. A third move will result in the point $f \circ f \circ f(x, y)$, and so on.

This simple function of two variables is the basis of the patterns called *Mandelbröt* and *Julia* sets. We look at the Mandelbröt set M here. Start with the origin $(0, 0)$, and look at the sequence of points
$$f(0,0), f \circ f(0,0), f \circ f \circ f(0,0), \dots . \qquad (M^*)$$
If all these points lie within a fixed finite distance of the origin, we say that $(a, b) \in M$. Evidently each point is a finite distance from $(0, 0)$, but what we are requiring is the existence of a number K such that the distances are *all* less than this K.

Put $T = \{\, \mathbf{F}, \mathbf{T} \,\}$, and define the mapping $g : \mathbb{R}^2 \to T$ by the condition that $g(a, b) = \mathbf{T}$ if $(a, b) \in M$ and $\mathbf{F}$ otherwise. Then g gives us a logical picture of the set M.

● ***Exercise 5.27*** It can be shown that if one of the points in (M^*) is at distance more than 2 from the origin, then $(a, b) \notin M$. Conversely, if $(a, b) \notin M$ then the terms cannot all be bounded in distance by 2, so the condition is necessary and sufficient. Under the assumption that as far as the resolution of your screen is concerned, if the terms of (M^*) are going to exceed the distance 2, then they will do it within 100 iterations of f, write a program to plot the Mandelbröt

set. You will, of course, only need to plot the range $-2 \leqslant a, b \leqslant 2$.
Also, it is quicker to check that one of the components x and y of
$f \circ f \circ \cdots \circ f(0,0) = (x, y)$ exceeds 2 than to check that $(x^2 + y^2) > 4$.

• *Exercise 5.28* Closely related to the Mandelbröt set are the Julia
sets, which are obtained from the same iterative process. The only
difference is that there is a Julia set $J_{(a,b)}$ for each choice of (a, b).

Fix a and b, and examine the sequence
$$f(x, y), f \circ f(x, y), f \circ f \circ f(x, y), \ldots. \qquad (J^*)$$
for each point (x, y) to see whether it remains bounded. If so, then
$(x, y) \in J_{(a,b)}$.

Write a program to plot the Julia set of (a, b). The interesting
cases occur when (a, b) is near the boundary of M.

It should come as no surprise to us to learn that composition of
mappings is associative, since it is just a special case of the result for
relations.

Theorem 5.1 (Associativity) Let $f : A \to B$, $g : B \to C$, and
$h : C \to D$ be three mappings. Then $h \circ (g \circ f) = (h \circ g) \circ f$.

Proof Either invoke the corresponding Theorem 4.1 for relations, or
notice that both sides mean $h(g(f(a)))$.   □

However, we must not change the *order* of f and g in the composition.

Example 5.29 Let $f, g : \mathbb{R} \to \mathbb{R}$ be defined by $f(x) = 1 - x$,
$g(x) = x^2$ for all $x \in \mathbb{R}$. Then
$$f \circ g(x) = f(g(x)) = f(x^2) = 1 - x^2$$
whilst
$$g \circ f(x) = g(f(x)) = g(1 - x) = (1 - x)^2,$$
and we can see that $f \circ g(2) = 1 - 2^2 = -3$, whilst $g \circ f(2) = (1 - 2)^2 = 1$. Thus $f \circ g$ and $g \circ f$ are different mappings. We express
this fact by saying that *composition of mappings is not commutative*.

• *Exercise 5.30* Is it possible for R to be a mapping, with $R = S \circ T$,
where S and T are relations, neither being mappings?

• *Exercise 5.31* Nave and Gauche PLC have just invested in a new
computer system to keep records of all their customers. The first
stage in their computerization is to empty out several filing cabinets
full of invoices, and transfer the customers' names and addresses onto
disk. They initially produce a file with two columns, listing a name
and address. After a thousand names have been transferred, they

suddenly decide to scrap their original idea and to produce *two* files. The first file has a list consisting of a natural number and a name; the second file has a natural number and an address. Why do you think they did this?

5.5 Surjective and injective

In Example 5.18, the mapping f differed from g and h in that its codomain was larger than it needed to be. The mappings g and h had equal codomains and ranges, and so any reduction in the size of their codomains would be impossible.

> **Definition** A mapping $f : A \to B$ is a **surjection**, or is **surjective** if its range and codomain are identical sets. In other words, given any $b \in B$ there must exist at least one $a \in A$ such that $f(a) = b$.

This is equivalent to saying that the domain of the inverse of the underlying relation of f equals the codomain of f; for the inverse has $b \in B$ in its domain if and only if $(a, b) \in R$ for some $a \in A$, and this happens if and only if b is in the range of R.

> **Example 5.32** Figure 5.3 represents a surjection from $A = \{a, b, c, d\}$ to $B = \{e, f, g\}$.

Fig. 5.3 A surjection

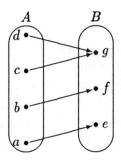

Example 5.33 The Major Motor Company is launching a new model in two weeks' time. It decides to invite all its existing customers to receptions throughout the country to mark the occasion.

It has records of all cars sold over the past years, together with the name and address of the owner. It uses these records to mail the owner of each car.

The mapping $f : C \to O$ of cars to owners is a surjective mapping. We notice that some customers may receive several invitations, if they happen to own several Major motorcars.

•**Exercise 5.34** The Fort Motor Company wishes to get its customers to display a sticker in the rear windscreens of their cars proclaiming 'Fort Cars are Environmentally Friendly'. It sends a sticker to each of its customers. What mistake has it made?

Example 5.35 Let $f : \mathbb{R} \to \mathbb{R}$ be defined by $f(x) = x^5 - 1000x^4$. Then f is known to be surjective for analytical reasons, by a theorem called the *intermediate value theorem*. Thus f takes all possible values in $\mathbb{R}$.

Example 5.36 Let $f : \mathbb{R} \to \mathbb{R}$ be defined by
$$f(x) = \begin{cases} (x^2 - 1)/x & \text{if } x \neq 0 \\ 0 & \text{otherwise.} \end{cases}$$
We shall show that f is surjective by showing that every $y \in \mathbb{R}$ is a value of f. First, if $y = 0$ then we take $x = 0$, since $f(0) = 0$. If $y \neq 0$, we try to find an x with $f(x) = y$. For this to be possible, we must have $(x^2 - 1)/x = y$, or $x^2 - yx - 1 = 0$, which gives us $x = \frac{1}{2}(y \pm \sqrt{y^2 + 4})$, and thus two values of x which map to y. Thus f must be surjective.

Example 5.37 A *symbol table* is being constructed by a compiler. The identifiers in a program are being read and inserted into a table with 1000 spaces, labelled 0 to 999. The rule followed is that for each identifier i, the number of characters in i is cubed, and then taken modulo 1000, and the identifier is inserted in that position. For the identifier `averyverylongidentifier`, the length is 23 characters, and $23^3 = 12167$, so it is inserted in position 167.

Let J be the set of all possible identifiers, and let $N = \{0, 1, \ldots, 999\}$. We can write our mapping $f : J \to N$ as $f(i) = |i|^3 \pmod{1000}$. Such a mapping is called a *hash function*. It is not surjective. We postpone the proof of this until Example 5.41.

Often we impose the restriction that the values which a mapping takes on its domain should not be taken more than once.

Definition The mapping $f : A \to B$ is an **injection**, or is **injective** if $f(x_1) = f(x_2)$ only when $x_1 = x_2$. This is sometimes written $f : A \rightarrowtail B$.

Alternatively, an injective mapping is required to take any value *at most once* on the domain. An equivalent formulation is that the inverse relation of the underlying relation of f must be a partial mapping. This is because the inverse fails to be a partial mapping precisely when $(b, a_1), (b, a_2) \in f^{-1}$, and this happens when $f(a_1) = f(a_2) = b$.

Example 5.38 Figure 5.4 represents an injection from $A = \{a, b, c\}$ to $B = \{e, f, g, h\}$.

Fig. 5.4 An injection

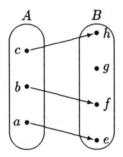

• **Exercise 5.39** Let S, T have m, n elements respectively. How many injections are there from S to T?

• **Exercise 5.40** Let A and B be two finite sets, with $|A| = |B|$. Suppose that $f : A \to B$ is a mapping. Show that f is injective if and only if it is surjective.

Example 5.41 Example 5.37 is not injective, since the identifiers identifier and that obtained by taking ten consecutive copies of it both map to 0. Also, any two identifiers of the same length are mapped to the same position. We can show that f is not surjective either. Indeed, any identifier of length k and one of length $1000 + k$ will both map to the same slot in the table, so we only need consider lengths from 1 to 1000. However, we know that lengths of 10 and

100 go to slot 0, so somewhere or other there must be a vacant slot which can *never* be a value of f. See also Exercise 5.40.

Example 5.42 The mapping $f : \mathbb{R} \to \mathbb{R}$ given by $f(x) = x^3 - 6x^2$ is not injective, since $f(0) = f(6) = 0$.

Let us look at a more substantial example, which illustrates the kind of calculation we have to perform when there is a mathematical formula for our mapping, and we need to know whether it is injective.

Example 5.43 Let $f : \mathbb{R} \to \mathbb{R}$ be defined by $f(x) = x + \sqrt{x^2 + 1}$. We shall show that f is injective. Suppose $f(x_1) = f(x_2)$, that is,

$$x_1 + \sqrt{x_1^2 + 1} = x_2 + \sqrt{x_2^2 + 1}.$$

Then

$$x_1 - x_2 = \sqrt{x_2^2 + 1} - \sqrt{x_1^2 + 1}$$

and so, on squaring, we obtain

$$x_1^2 + x_2^2 - 2x_1x_2 = (x_2^2 + 1) + (x_1^2 + 1) - 2\sqrt{(x_1^2 + 1)(x_2^2 + 1)}$$

which gives, after some cancellation,

$$\sqrt{(x_1^2 + 1)(x_2^2 + 1)} = 1 + x_1x_2.$$

We square again to obtain

$$x_1^2 + x_2^2 + 1 + x_1^2x_2^2 = 1 + x_1^2x_2^2 + 2x_1x_2$$

and this is equivalent to $(x_1 - x_2)^2 = 0$, so we are forced to have $x_1 = x_2$. Hence $f(x_1) = f(x_2)$ implies $x_1 = x_2$, and f is injective.

•***Exercise 5.44*** Let A, B and T be sets, and suppose we are given two mappings $f : T \to A$ and $g : T \to B$, such that f is injective.

Define the relation R between A and B by

$$R = \{ (f(t), g(t)) : t \in T \}.$$

Show that R is a partial mapping.

•***Exercise 5.45*** On a certain multi-user computer, there is a charge for time used, and a penalty for running excessively long programs according to the following rules. First, if the computer time used by the program is t, the charge is given by the formula $t + \log_2 t$. Second, the program is given lower and lower priority the longer it runs, so that in a multi-user situation the elapsed time from submission to completion is $10t + 2^t$. Discover whether the charge is a function of the elapsed time.

•***Exercise 5.46*** Find all mappings $\phi : S_1 \to S_2$ and $\psi : S_2 \to S_1$, where $S_1 = \{ a, b \}$, $S_2 = \{ A, B, C \}$.

Which are *injective*, and which are *surjective*?

•*Exercise 5.47* A certain program accesses an n-dimensional array. It is calculated that its running time, as a function of n, is given by the formula

$$f(n) = \lfloor \log_2 n! \rfloor + 1,$$

where $n! = 1 \times 2 \times \cdots \times n$, and $\lfloor x \rfloor$ denotes the integer part of x, TRUNC(x) in *Modula-2*. Are there any two values of n for which the program has the same running time?

Is the running time an increasing function of n? Are there any positive integer values which are not taken by $f(n)$?

•*Exercise 5.48* Let $f : A \to B$ be a mapping. Show that there exists a set C and an injection $h : C \to B$ and surjection $g : A \to C$, with $f = h \circ g$.

•*Exercise 5.49* A random number generator is called by the function random(n), where $n > 1$ is a natural number, and it is meant to return a random number in the range $0 \ldots (n-1)$, provided n is not too large. On the first call, it returns the system time modulo n. Thereafter, if the last call produced the value k then the next call produces the value $(71773k + 31011) \bmod n$.

What is wrong with this random number generator?

•*Exercise 5.50* Find an injection $f : \mathbb{N}^2 \to \mathbb{N}$.

•*Exercise 5.51* Let $g : A \to B$ and $f : B \to C$. Prove or give counter-examples to the following results.
 (i) $f \circ g$ injective $\implies$ f injective.
 (ii) $f \circ g$ injective $\implies$ g injective.
 (iii) $f \circ g$ surjective $\implies$ f surjective.
 (iv) $f \circ g$ surjective $\implies$ g surjective.

•*Exercise 5.52* In Exercise 5.13, interpret the conditions that the relation is
 (i) a mapping; (ii) injective; (iii) surjective.

5.6 Bijective mappings

A mapping which is both injective and surjective is particularly simple mathematically, being the sort of mapping whose inverse as a relation is also a mapping.

Definition The mapping $f : A \to B$ is a **bijection** or is **bijective** if it is both injective and surjective. For each $b \in B$ there must exist a unique $a \in A$ with $b = f(a)$.

The bijective mapping sets up what is known as a *one-to-one correspondence* between A and B. Each element of A is paired off with one element of B.

Example 5.53 Figure 5.5 represents a bijection from $A = \{\, a, b, c, d \,\}$ to $B = \{\, e, f, g, h \,\}$.

Fig. 5.5 A bijection

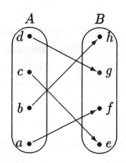

Example 5.54 $\imath_A$ is a bijection from A to A.

Example 5.55 Suppose we have the simple declarations

```
CONST m=20; n=2*maxrow;
TYPE  row=[1..m]; col=[1..n];
      matrix=ARRAY row,col OF INTEGER;
VAR   a:matrix
```

in a *Modula-2* program. The declarations in *Pascal* or *Ada* will only be slightly different. Space for mn integers is set aside by the compiler, starting at some address which we can denote by the symbol a. Suppose that one integer takes up $k = 4$ bytes of storage. Then kmn bytes are used overall.

The array a is commonly stored in row order, that is, first all the entries in row 1 are stored, namely

```
a[1,1], a[1,2], ... ,a[1,n]
```

and then all the entries of row two,

a[2,1], a[2,2], ... ,a[2,n]

and so on, until finally we have the entries of row m,

a[m,1], a[m,2], ... ,a[m,n]

to complete the linear list of entries.

The problem is, when the compiler meets the expression a[5,12], where does it look for this entry?

Entry a[1,1] starts at memory location a. Suppose we want the memory location of the start of a[i,j]. We know that $i-1$ complete rows precede it, and then another $j-1$ entries of row i. These occupy $k(n(i-1)+j-1)$ bytes, so the correct address is $a+k((n(i-1)+j-1)$. We shall check this formula for a[1,1]. We obtain $a+k((n(1-1)+1-1)=a$, which is correct. Try a[m,n]. The address is $a+k((n(m-1)+n-1)=a+k(mn-1)$ which is again correct.

Put $M=\{1,\ldots,m\}$, $N=\{1,\ldots,n\}$ and
$$T=\{0,\ldots,mn-1\}.$$
The mapping $f:M\times N\to T$ given by
$$f(i,j)=n(i-1)+j-1$$
is a bijective mapping.

● **Exercise 5.56** Verify the assertion at the end of the last Example.

● **Exercise 5.57** The mapping $f(m,n)=m(j-1)+i-1$ is also a bijection. Investigate what it does to the ordering of the elements of a two-dimensional array.

● **Exercise 5.58** What do you think is the formula for extracting the elements a[p,q,r] of a three dimensional array?

● **Exercise 5.59** Would the formula $f(i,j)=n(m-i)+n-j$ give a suitable way of storing the elements of a two dimensional array? If so, why do you think it is never used?

Example 5.60 Let
$$A=\{-2^{31},-2^{31}+1,\ldots,2^{31}-1\}$$
and
$$B=\{0,1,\ldots,2^{32}-1\}.$$
Define $f:A\to B$ by $f(m)=m+2^{31}$. Then f is a bijection between A and B, and it represents the way that negative integers are handled in a computer as large positive integers. The set B is really $\{\bar{0},\bar{1},\ldots,\overline{2^{32}-1}\}$, the set of equivalence classes of integers modulo 2^{32}.

Thus the *trick* of representing negative numbers in *two's complement* form is really well grounded in mathematical theory. We choose a power 2^m large enough to exceed all integers we are interested in, double it, and then take arithmetic modulo 2^{m+1}, so that negative numbers are represented as large positive numbers.

• *Exercise 5.61* Is there any reason why a power of two is necessary in the above Example rather than 3?

• *Exercise 5.62* Find the representation of the following numbers in a computer which uses sixteen binary digits to store an integer.
(i)   12.   (ii)   −11.   (iii)   −12.   (iv)   −13.
(v)   1000.   (vi)   −10000.

• *Exercise 5.63* Find a bijection of $\{\, x \in \mathbb{R} : 0 < x < \pi \,\}$ onto $\mathbb{R}$.

• *Exercise 5.64* If we think of a *code* as a mapping of unencoded strings of characters to encoded strings of characters, what properties would you expect this mapping to have?

5.7   Invertible mappings

A mapping is a special sort of relation, and a relation *always* has an inverse, but this inverse need not be a mapping. In the last section we saw two properties which must be possessed by a mapping before its inverse will also be a mapping. These turn out to be necessary and sufficient for an inverse mapping to exist.

Definition The mapping $f : A \to B$ is said to be **invertible** if there exists a mapping $g : B \to A$ such that $g \circ f = \imath_A$ and $f \circ g = \imath_B$.

Example 5.65 The mapping $f : \mathbb{N} \to \mathbb{Z}^+$ given by $f(n) = n - 1$ is invertible. Define $g : \mathbb{Z}^+ \to \mathbb{N}$ by $g(c) = c + 1$. For any $n \in \mathbb{N}$,
$$g \circ f(n) = g(f(n)) = g(n - 1) = (n - 1) + 1 = n$$
and for any $c \in \mathbb{Z}^+$,
$$f \circ g(c) = f(g(c)) = f(c + 1) = (c + 1) - 1 = c.$$

In the above example, it was easy to guess what the definition of g would be. In general we may have to do with an *implicit* definition of g. A mapping g, if it exists, is called an *inverse* of f. Before we go any further, we had better verify that

Lemma 5.2 A mapping can have at most one inverse.

Proof Suppose $g_1 \circ f = \iota_A$ and $f \circ g_2 = \iota_B$. By associativity,
$$g_1 = g_1 \circ \iota_B = g_1 \circ (f \circ g_2) = (g_1 \circ f) \circ g_2 = \iota_A \circ g_2 = g_2.$$
Thus if g_1 and g_2 are both inverses of f, they are identical. $\square$

Viewed from the point of view of relations, the above is natural, since an inverse must be an inverse as a relation, and a relation uniquely determines its own inverse.

Definition If $f : A \to B$ is an invertible mapping, then the unique mapping $g : B \to A$ such that $g \circ f = \iota_A$ and $f \circ g = \iota_B$ is called the **inverse mapping** of f, and is written as $g = f^{-1}$. Thus
$$f^{-1} \circ f = \iota_A, \quad f \circ f^{-1} = \iota_B.$$

•**Exercise 5.66** Let $f : \mathbb{R} \to \mathbb{R}$ be defined by $f(x) = (1 + \sinh x)^3$. Find the inverse of f.

•**Exercise 5.67** It is known that a file which lists customers' names and addresses defines a mapping from customers to addresses. State in ordinary language what this means, and also explain what its invertibility would mean?

•**Exercise 5.68** Suppose that $f : \mathbb{R} \to \mathbb{R}$, and
$$f(3) = 1, \quad f(x) = \frac{x-2}{x-3}, \quad \forall x \neq 3.$$
Find f^{-1} if this inverse exists.

•**Exercise 5.69** Put $A = \mathbb{R} \setminus \{0, 1\}$, and define $f : A \to A$ by
$$f(x) = \frac{1}{1-x}, \quad \text{for all } x \in A.$$
Show that $f \circ f \circ f = \iota_A$, and show that f is invertible.

•**Exercise 5.70** The mapping $g : A \to \mathbb{R}$ satisfies the identity
$$g(x) = 4 + xg(f(x)),$$
where A and f are as in Exercise 5.69. Calculate $g(f(x))$ and $g(f(f(x)))$, and hence show that
$$g(x) = 2\left(\frac{1+x-x^2}{1-x}\right).$$

Having satisfied ourselves that any inverse must be unique, that is, that a mapping has either no inverse or one inverse, we shall characterize the invertible mappings completely.

Theorem 5.3 The mapping $f : A \to B$ is invertible if and only if it is bijective.

Proof Assume first that f is invertible. We show that f is injective and surjective:

Injective Suppose $f(x_1) = f(x_2)$. Then $f^{-1} \circ f(x_1) = f^{-1} \circ f(x_2)$, and so $\imath_A(x_1) = \imath_A(x_2)$, forcing $x_1 = x_2$.

Surjective Given $y \in B$, put $x = f^{-1}(y)$. Then $f(x) = f \circ f^{-1}(y) = y$, and so any $y \in B$ is in the range of f.

Conversely, let us suppose that f is bijective. As a relation, this means that for each $a \in A$ there is a unique $b \in B$ with $(a, b) \in f$, and to each $b \in B$ there exists a unique $a \in A$ with $(a, b) \in f$. Define $g : B \to A$ by letting $g(b)$ be the unique $a \in A$ such that $f(a) = b$. Then $g \circ f(a) = a$ and $f \circ g(b) = b$ by definition, for any $a \in A$ and $b \in B$, so g is the inverse of f. □

The importance of this result is that we can use the inverse notation even when we do not know any closed formula for the inverse.

Example 5.71 Let
$$I = \{\, x \in \mathbb{R} : -\pi/2 \leqslant x \leqslant \pi/2 \,\},$$
and
$$J = \{\, x \in \mathbb{R} : -1 \leqslant x \leqslant 1 \,\}.$$
Then $\sin : I \to J$ is well known to be a bijective mapping, being monotonically increasing on the given domain, and so the mapping $\sin^{-1} : J \to I$ exists. We can use the notation $\sin^{-1}$ before we even know a formula for calculating the mapping.

We could expect that the inverse of a composition of mappings would be simply related to the inverses of the individual mappings, but we have to watch the order in which we compose the two inverses.

Theorem 5.4 Let $f : A \to B$ and $g : B \to C$ be invertible mappings. Then $g \circ f$ is invertible, and $(g \circ f)^{-1} = f^{-1} \circ g^{-1}$.

Proof We only need check that if $h = g \circ f$ and $k = f^{-1} \circ g^{-1}$ then $h \circ k = \imath_C$ and $k \circ h = \imath_A$. Using the associative rule,
$$h \circ k = g \circ f \circ f^{-1} \circ g^{-1} = g \circ \imath_B \circ g^{-1} = g \circ g^{-1} = \imath_C$$
and the other result is similar. □

Either by using this result, or independently, we can deduce the following result.

Corollary 5.5 The composition of two bijections is a bijection.

Proof Follows from Theorems 5.4 and 5.3. □

•***Exercise 5.72*** Is the composition of two injections an injection? What about surjections?

• **Exercise 5.73** Find a suitable definition of *injective* and *surjective* for partial mappings. Under what conditions do you think the inverse of a partial mapping will be a partial mapping?

5.8 Permutations

When we are working with a finite set A, we find that for a mapping $f : A \to A$, the properties of being injective, surjective and bijective are all equivalent. For example, if f is not injective, and has range $R \subseteq A$, and $f(x_1) = f(x_2)$ for some $x_1 \neq x_2$, then $|R| < |A|$, so f is not surjective either. The reader is invited to try Exercise 5.40 if she has not already done so.

There is a special term used for bijections of finite sets.

Definition Let A be a nonempty finite set, and let $f : A \to A$ be a bijection. Then f is called a **permutation** of A.

Since any finite set is just the same as any other finite set of the same size, it is usual to consider only permutations of the finite set $N = \{1, 2, \ldots, n\}$, with $n \in \mathbb{N}$. Also, if the task is not too exhausting, it is usual to specify a permutation by listing the values of f as follows:

$$\begin{pmatrix} 1 & 2 & 3 & \ldots & n \\ f(1) & f(2) & f(3) & \ldots & f(n) \end{pmatrix}.$$

Any ordering of the columns is permissible.

Example 5.74 The permutation

$$f = \begin{pmatrix} 1 & 2 & 3 & 4 & 5 & 6 \\ 2 & 3 & 5 & 6 & 1 & 4 \end{pmatrix}$$

is such that $f(3) = 5$, $f(1) = 2$, and so on. It could have been written

$$f = \begin{pmatrix} 6 & 2 & 3 & 5 & 4 & 1 \\ 4 & 3 & 5 & 1 & 6 & 2 \end{pmatrix}.$$

When we take a composition of permutations, it is usual to write this as a *product*, $fg \equiv f \circ g$. To form this product, we use the definition of a function of a function. We can then define $f^2 = ff$, $f^3 = fff = f \circ f \circ f$, and so on. We take f^0 to be the identity function ι_N, and f^{-1} is the inverse function. Composition of the inverse with itself gives negative powers of f.

Example 5.75 If

$$f = \begin{pmatrix} 1 & 2 & 3 & 4 & 5 & 6 \\ 3 & 4 & 1 & 6 & 2 & 5 \end{pmatrix}, \quad g = \begin{pmatrix} 1 & 2 & 3 & 4 & 5 & 6 \\ 6 & 3 & 1 & 4 & 5 & 2 \end{pmatrix},$$

then $fg(1) = f(g(1)) = f(6) = 5$, $fg(2) = f(g(2)) = f(3) = 1$, and so on. We can obtain the product by a simple device. We rewrite f so that its top line looks like the bottom line of g:

$$f = \begin{pmatrix} 6 & 3 & 1 & 4 & 5 & 2 \\ 5 & 1 & 3 & 6 & 2 & 4 \end{pmatrix}.$$

We replace the bottom line of g by the new bottom line of f to obtain the product:

$$fg = \begin{pmatrix} 1 & 2 & 3 & 4 & 5 & 6 \\ 5 & 1 & 3 & 6 & 2 & 4 \end{pmatrix}.$$

We can regard this as coming from striking out the middle row of

$$\begin{pmatrix} 1 & 2 & 3 & 4 & 5 & 6 \\ 6 & 3 & 1 & 4 & 5 & 2 \\ 5 & 1 & 3 & 6 & 2 & 4 \end{pmatrix}.$$

•**Exercise 5.76** Compute gf, and show that $gf \neq fg$.

•**Exercise 5.77** The inverse of f in Example 5.75 is

$$f^{-1} = \begin{pmatrix} 3 & 4 & 1 & 6 & 2 & 5 \\ 1 & 2 & 3 & 4 & 5 & 6 \end{pmatrix} = \begin{pmatrix} 1 & 2 & 3 & 4 & 5 & 6 \\ 3 & 5 & 1 & 2 & 6 & 4 \end{pmatrix}.$$

For a given $n \in \mathbb{N}$, there are $n!$ permutations of $N = \{1, 2, 3, \ldots, n\}$. These permutations are all invertible, being bijections, and the set of all such permutations is called the *symmetric group* S_n.

•**Exercise 5.78** Write down the six permutations in S_3. For each permutation f, find a smallest $k \in \mathbb{N}$ such that $f^k = \imath_N$.

Usually the only thing that is obvious from the tabular form of a permutation is whether $f(i) = i$ for some $i \in N$.

Definition A **fixed point** of the permutation $f \in S_n$ is a number $i \in N$ such that $f(i) = i$.

Fixed points are defined for any mappings of the form $f : A \to A$, but we only need their definition for permutations.

Example 5.79 In Example 5.75, f has no fixed points, and g has fixed points 4 and 5.

Because it is so difficult to visualize a permutation in tabular form, another notation has been invented, dependent on a special class of permutations.

Definition The permutation f is a **cycle** if it can be written

$$f = \begin{pmatrix} i_1 & i_2 & i_3 & \cdots & i_{r-1} & i_r & i_{r+1} & i_{r+2} & \cdots & i_n \\ i_2 & i_3 & i_4 & \cdots & i_r & i_1 & i_{r+1} & i_{r+2} & \cdots & i_n \end{pmatrix},$$

where the last $n - r$ numbers are fixed points. The cycle is said to be of **length** r. It is written $(\,i_1\ i_2\ i_3\ \ldots\ i_{r-1}\ i_r\,)$.

A cycle of length 1 is just ι_N. A cycle of length 2 is called a **transposition**. A cycle of length n is called a **cyclic permutation** of $1, \ldots, n$.

Thus a cycle permutes the numbers in a very special way. Most of the numbers remain where they are, and the rest are shifted one along a sequence, the last in the sequence being shifted back to the start.

• ***Exercise 5.80*** Find the inverse of the cycle
$$(\,2\ 9\ 5\ 4\ 11\ 6\ 13\ 3\ 15\ 12\,) \in S_{15}.$$

Example 5.81 In Example 5.75, g is a cycle. If we observe the effect of g on 1 to 6, we find that
$$1 \mapsto 6 \mapsto 2 \mapsto 3 \mapsto 1,$$
whilst 4 and 5 are fixed points. We thus have the cycle
$$g = (\,1\ 6\ 2\ 3\,).$$
For f, we find
$$1 \mapsto 3 \mapsto 1, \quad 2 \mapsto 4 \mapsto 6 \mapsto 5 \mapsto 2,$$
and f is not a cycle.

Looking at the last Example, we see that although f is not a cycle, it has a structure consisting of two *disjoint cycles* $c_1 = (\,1\ 3\,)$ and $c_2 = (\,2\ 4\ 6\ 5\,)$, which together make up f. In fact, $f = c_1 c_2 = c_2 c_1$, as is readily verified by writing c_1 and c_2 in full before multiplying them. The cycles are called disjoint because the sets of elements of the cycles are disjoint.

Theorem 5.6 Any permutation can be written as a product of disjoint cycles.

Proof The proof is an elementary induction, based on the number of non-fixed points of the permutation f. If this number is zero, then $f = \iota_N$. Assume the result true for fewer than m non-fixed points, and suppose that f has m non-fixed points. We follow a trail $i_1 \mapsto i_2 \mapsto i_3 \ldots$ starting from a non-fixed point i_1, and see what happens. The number i_k is not a fixed point, as this would imply $f(i_{k-1}) = f(i_k) = i_k$, a contradiction of the bijectivity of f. Thus our trail must close on itself somewhere, as it cannot be infinite. If the first repeated number is i_p, then we cannot have $i_p = i_2$, as again we would have a contradiction. Similarly $i_p \neq i_3, \ldots, i_{p-1}$, and so $i_p = i_1$. Our first cycle is (i_1 i_2 ... i_p). We modify f into a new permutation g by converting $i_1, \ldots, i_p$ into fixed points. The resulting permutation satisfies the induction hypothesis, and so is a product of disjoint cycles. These, and the one produced above, give the cycles for f.   □

•**Exercise 5.82** Write the following as products of disjoint cycles.

(i) $\begin{pmatrix} 1 & 2 & 3 & 4 & 5 & 6 & 7 & 8 \\ 3 & 8 & 5 & 6 & 1 & 4 & 7 & 2 \end{pmatrix}$.

(ii) $\begin{pmatrix} 1 & 2 & 3 & 4 & 5 & 6 & 7 & 8 & 9 & 10 \\ 9 & 8 & 2 & 7 & 1 & 3 & 5 & 4 & 6 & 10 \end{pmatrix}$.

•**Exercise 5.83** Write the following permutations as products of disjoint cycles.

(i) $\begin{pmatrix} 1 & 2 & 3 & 4 & 5 & 6 \\ 3 & 6 & 5 & 2 & 1 & 4 \end{pmatrix}$.

(ii) $\begin{pmatrix} 1 & 2 & 3 & 4 & 5 & 6 & 7 & 8 & 9 & 10 \\ 7 & 9 & 4 & 2 & 5 & 8 & 1 & 10 & 3 & 6 \end{pmatrix}$.

The result above always produces disjoint cycles, but when two permutations are multiplied generally, the cycles of the first will not be disjoint from the cycles of the second. It is therefore important to see what happens when we take a general product of cycles.

Example 5.84 We calculate fgh, where
$$f = (1\ 5\ 4\ 2\ 7), \quad g = (2\ 4\ 6\ 7\ 1\ 3\ 8), \quad h = (5\ 7).$$
First, $h(1) = 1$, as 1 is a fixed point of h. Next, $g(1) = 3$, and $f(3) = 3$, since 3 is a fixed point of f. So $fgh(1) = f(g(h(1))) = 3$. To obtain this result, we have evaluated the permutations from right to left, and taken the result of h to feed g, then the result of g to feed f. In a similar fashion, $fgh(3) = f(g(h(3))) = f(g(3)) = f(8) = 8$. Next, $fgh(8) = fg(8) = f(2) = 7$, and so we continue evaluating round the first cycle of fgh. When this is done, we find its other cycles, if any, until N is exhausted. The result we obtain is
$$fgh = (1\ 3\ 8\ 7\ 4\ 6).$$
We notice that $fgh(5) = fg(7) = f(1) = 5$, so 5 is a fixed point.

•**Exercise 5.85** Evaluate the following as a product of disjoint cycles.
$$(7\ 8\ 10)(6\ 7\ 9)(5\ 6\ 8)(4\ 5\ 7)(3\ 4\ 6)(2\ 3\ 5)(1\ 2\ 4).$$

•**Exercise 5.86** Write the following as a product of disjoint cycles.
$$(1\ 2\ 3)(2\ 3\ 4)(3\ 4\ 5)(4\ 5\ 6)(5\ 6\ 7).$$

Finally, we observe that any permutation is a product of transpositions, because each of its cycles is.

Theorem 5.7 Every permutation in S_n either equals $\imath_N$, or is a product of transpositions.

Proof It is sufficient to write the disjoint cycles as products of transpositions. Consider the product
$$(1 \ 2)(2 \ 3)(3 \ 4)\cdots(m - 2 \ m - 1)(m - 1 \ m).$$
It is easily verified that this gives the cycle $(1 \ 2 \ 3 \ \ldots \ m - 1 \ m)$ upon expansion. Any other cycle is handled similarly.   □

•**Exercise 5.87** Write
$$\begin{pmatrix} 1 & 2 & 3 & 4 & 5 & 6 & 7 & 8 & 9 & 10 \\ 10 & 5 & 6 & 2 & 3 & 9 & 7 & 1 & 4 & 8 \end{pmatrix}$$
as a product of transpositions.

A permutation which results in k transpositions is called *even* or *odd* depending on whether or not k is. The two classes of permutations are disjoint, and partition S_n, for $n \geqslant 2$, into two equal classes. These results are elementary, but not of sufficient interest here to warrant proof. The principal applications of permutations are in the theory of *sorting*. This is concerned with the most efficient methods of transforming a sequence of numbers into an increasing sequence. Usually, the measure of efficiency is the number of comparisons we have to do between numbers in the sequence. The sorting is generally done by means of transpositions of two numbers in the sequence. Our result guarantees that transpositions are sufficient for accomplishing any permutation, and hence any sorting job. An example appears in the appendices.

5.9   Countability

We shall be concerned here with when two infinite sets are of the same size. One way of interpreting this is to say that if $X = Y$ then they are of the same size, and if $X \subset Y$ then X is smaller than Y, but this is not sufficient for most purposes. Even in the finite case we can claim that two different sets are of the same size.

Example 5.88 We have two containers, one containing nuts and the other bolts. How do we find out if they each contain the same number? Easy! Take a nut from one, and a bolt from the other, and put them to one side. Repeat until one container is empty. If both are empty, there were the same number of nuts and bolts, otherwise there must have been a different number.

Clear enough, one might think, but consider what happens when we take infinite sets and try to 'pair off' their elements.

Example 5.89 We have two containers (sets?), one containing all the natural numbers and the other containing all the cardinal numbers. We try the experiment above three times. The first time we take the smallest number out of each container, and place them to one side. We repeat this process, and go on forever taking the smallest numbers out of each container, and pairing them off. We have paired off the two sets $\mathbb{N}$ and $\mathbb{Z}^+$ as much as the bolts and nuts were paired off in Example 5.88. Natural number n is paired with cardinal number $n - 1$.

We start again, but this time, whenever the smallest number is chosen from $\mathbb{N}$, we look for the same number in $\mathbb{Z}^+$, and pair them off. This time, n is always paired with n, so 0 is never selected from $\mathbb{Z}^+$, and $\mathbb{Z}^+$ is bigger than $\mathbb{N}$!

Not to be daunted by this contradiction, we start again, but follow the rule of selecting the smallest number c left in $\mathbb{Z}^+$, and then looking for the number $c + 2$ in $\mathbb{N}$, pairing those off. The number 1 in $\mathbb{N}$ will never be paired, so $\mathbb{Z}^+$ is smaller than $\mathbb{N}$!!

If we look mathematically at the above example, what we have are three mappings $f : \mathbb{N} \to \mathbb{Z}^+$, $g : \mathbb{N} \to \mathbb{Z}^+$, and $h : \mathbb{Z}^+ \to \mathbb{N}$, with rules $f(n) = n - 1$, $g(n) = n$, and $h(c) = c + 2$ respectively, and we also have *no contradiction*. The first is bijective, and the others are injective. We are free to define the equality of the size of two infinite sets in any way we choose, and so we take the following as a natural definition.

Definition If X and Y are sets, and there exists a bijection $f : X \to Y$, then we say that X and Y have the same **size** or **cardinality** or **cardinal**.

If there exists a bijection $f : \mathbb{N} \to X$ then we say that X is **countable**. If X is infinite but not countable, we say that it is **uncountable**.

This does *not* mean that we could really 'count' the elements in a countable set, and say how many there are! All it means is that it is theoretically possible to put those elements into an 'infinite list' or *sequence*.

We might expect that this is what being an *infinite set* means; that a finite set has a finite listing, whereas an infinite set has an infinite listing. As we shall see, things couldn't be more different. This teaches us that it is extremely dangerous to use notations such as $\{a_1, a_2, a_3, \dots\}$ to describe infinite sets, unless such a list exists.

Example 5.90 $\mathbb{Z}^+$ is countable. The mapping $f : \mathbb{N} \to \mathbb{Z}^+$ given by $f(n) = n - 1$ is a bijection.

Example 5.91 $\mathbb{Z}$ is countable. For, define the following bijection $f : \mathbb{N} \to \mathbb{Z}$:

$$f(n) = \begin{cases} n/2 & \text{if } n \text{ is even} \\ -(n-1)/2 & \text{if } n \text{ is odd} \end{cases}.$$

We obtain the infinite listing
$$0, 1, -1, 2, -2, 3, -3, 4, -4, \dots$$
of $\mathbb{Z}$.

Once we know that some mathematical object has a certain property, it usually follows that many other objects closely related to it also have the same property.

Theorem 5.8 Any infinite subset of a countable set is countable.

Proof Suppose X is countable, $f : \mathbb{N} \to X$ is a bijection, and put
$$x_1 = f(1), x_2 = f(2), x_3 = f(3), \dots$$
Suppose $Y \subseteq X$ is infinite. Delete from the above sequence all $x_i \in X \setminus Y$, and suppose the resulting subsequence is
$$y_1, y_2, y_3, \dots$$
Define $g : \mathbb{N} \to Y$ by $g(n) = y_n$. Then g is a bijection, and so Y is countable. $\square$

• **Exercise 5.92** Why is the set $P = \{2, 3, 5, 7, 11, 13, 17, 19, 23, \dots\}$ of all prime numbers countable?

Next, we have another construction of a countable set from a countable set. This one is something of a surprise, since at first sight, the constructed set appears to be much bigger than the one we start with. This increase in size is illusory.

Theorem 5.9 $\mathbb{N} \times \mathbb{N}$ is countable

Proof Form the sequence

$$x_1 = (1,1) \quad x_3 = (1,2) \quad x_6 = (1,3) \quad \cdots$$

$$x_2 = (2,1) \quad x_5 = (2,2) \quad x_9 = (2,3) \quad \cdots$$

$$x_4 = (3,1) \quad x_8 = (3,2) \quad x_{13} = (3,3) \quad \cdots$$

$$x_7 = (4,1) \quad x_{12} = (4,2) \quad x_{18} = (4,3) \quad \cdots$$

and define $f : \mathbb{N} \to \mathbb{N}^2$ by $f(n) = x_n$. The rule is to order the elements of the cartesian product 'diagonally'. $\qquad\square$

Corollary 5.10 If X and Y are countable, then so is $X \times Y$.

Corollary 5.11 If $X_1, X_2, \ldots, X_n$ are countable, then so is $X_1 \times X_2 \times \cdots \times X_n$.

It does not look as if we can break the 'countability barrier' by taking finite products of countable sets!

We are ready to prove one of the major results on countability. After the above results, its proof is very simple, but it seems so paradoxical that its statement always astounds.

Theorem 5.12 $\mathbb{Q}$ is countable.

Proof We first make the observation that the rationals can be described as the set of all quotients p/q of integers p and q where

(i) $q > 0$;

(ii) p and q have no positive common factor other than 1.

Thus it is in obvious bijective correspondence with the subset of $\mathbb{Z} \times \mathbb{N}$

$$K = \{ (p,q) : p \in \mathbb{Z}, q \in \mathbb{N}, p \text{ and } q \text{ have no common factors} \}.$$

This set K is an infinite subset of $\mathbb{Z} \times \mathbb{N}$, and so, by Theorem 5.8 and Corollary 5.10, is countable. $\qquad\square$

How amazing that this set $\mathbb{Q}$, which appears to fill the real line without any gaps, should be as small a set as its proper subset $\mathbb{N}$, which barely makes an impression on the real line!

- **Exercise 5.93** Give the start of a complete listing of the positive rational numbers.

- **Exercise 5.94** Give the start of a complete listing of the rational numbers.

One word of warning! Do not make the mistake of thinking that the list of elements of $\mathbb{Q}$ is supposed to respect the *ordering* of $\mathbb{Q}$ in any way. There is certainly no way we could arrange the rational numbers in a total order in the sense of Theorem 4.5.

- **Exercise 5.95** Show that any countable union of countable sets is countable, that is, if $S_1, S_2, S_3, \ldots$ is an infinite sequence of countable sets, then $\bigcup_{m \in \mathbb{N}} S_m$ is countable.

  Show that the same result holds when the S_ms are finite, but their union is infinite.

- **Exercise 5.96** Show that the set of all valid *Pascal* programs is countable.

- **Exercise 5.97** Do the same for *Modula-2* programs. Note that a *Modula-2* program consists of a main module together with a finite collection of imported modules.

- **Exercise 5.98** Show that the set of all mappings $f : \mathbb{N} \to \mathbb{N}$ which can be described by a rule for calculating $f(n)$ is countable.

- **Exercise 5.99** Show that the set of all mathematical proofs is countable. Would an ordering of all proofs be a useful thing to have?

- **Exercise 5.100** Discuss the following definition: an *infinite* set is a set S with the property that there exists a bijection $f : S \to T$, with $T \subset S$.

Thus far, it would seem that every set is countable. We shall dispose of this assertion by proving

Theorem 5.13 $\mathbb{R}$ is uncountable.

Proof It is sufficient, by Theorem 5.8, to show that the interval
$$X = \{\, x \in \mathbb{R} : 0 \leqslant x < 1 \,\}$$
is uncountable, since then $\mathbb{R}$ cannot be countable, otherwise we have a contradiction. We use a method called a *diagonal argument*.

Every number in X has a representation as an infinite decimal expansion
$$x = 0.a_1 a_2 a_3 a_4 a_5 \ldots$$
where the expansion possibly recurs. We can easily add the restriction that there are no recurring 9s, so $0.249999\cdots$ must be written as $0.25000\cdots$. This makes the decimal expansion unique.

We prove by contradiction that X is uncountable. Suppose we could enumerate all the elements of X, by taking a bijection $f : \mathbb{N} \to X$, and putting $f(n) = x_n$. The infinite list

$$x_1 \;=\; 0.a_{1,1}a_{1,2}a_{1,3}a_{1,4}\cdots$$
$$x_2 \;=\; 0.a_{2,1}a_{2,2}a_{2,3}a_{2,4}\cdots$$
$$x_3 \;=\; 0.a_{3,1}a_{3,2}a_{3,3}a_{3,4}\cdots$$
$$x_4 \;=\; 0.a_{4,1}a_{4,2}a_{4,3}a_{4,4}\cdots$$
$$\vdots$$

would include every real number in X. We shall prove that it cannot include all such numbers by demonstrating the existence of just one number which is not in the sequence. Define $x = 0.a_1a_2a_3a_4\cdots$ by taking

$$a_n = \begin{cases} 1 & \text{if } a_{n,n} = 0 \\ 0 & \text{otherwise} \end{cases}.$$

Then x and x_n differ from one another in their n-th decimal place, and so cannot be equal. It follows that x is not in our sequence, a contradiction. $\square$

The above proof must be read with some care. It is not that one number has been omitted from the sequence, but that no matter how we form the sequence, at least one number will be omitted. Infinitely many numbers get left out, with so large an infinity that it dwarfs the number which are included. Even if countably many numbers were omitted, we could still fit them in by rearranging our sequence; but too many numbers will be omitted from *any* listing of $\mathbb{R}$ for us ever to be able to recover them into that listing.

•*Exercise 5.101* Show that the set of all mappings $f : \mathbb{N} \to \{\,0,1\,\}$ is uncountable.

The results of Exercises 5.101 and 5.98 do *not* contradict one another. The theoretical number of all mappings is far larger than the number which could be specified by a *rule*. Most of them will be unstructured collections of ordered pairs, with no tangible pattern.

•*Exercise 5.102* Show that the power set of $\mathbb{N}$ is uncountable.

•*Exercise 5.103* Show that the set of all *finite* subsets of $\mathbb{N}$ is countable.

5.10 Computability

To give the reader some idea of how the above types of argument are applied in the theory of computations, we shall look at a famous example on non-computability of certain functions.

Theorem 5.14 There exists a mapping $f : \mathbb{Z}^+ \to \mathbb{Z}^+$ which is not implementable in *Modula-2*.

Proof We use a *diagonal argument*.

Consider all functions in *Modula-2* of the simple form

```
PROCEDURE f(x:CARDINAL):CARDINAL;
  (*local declarations*)
BEGIN
  (*implementation*)
END f;
```

The set of such functions is enumerable, since it is $\bigcup_{n=8}^{\infty} F_n$, where F_n is the set of all functions implementable in n characters, and the minimum size of an implementation would be RETURN␣0 in 8 symbols.

Let us enumerate all such mappings, and call them f_1, f_2, f_3 and so on. Remember that this sequence includes *all* implementable mappings of the given type. Consider the mapping $f : \mathbb{Z}^+ \to \mathbb{Z}^+$ defined by $f(n) = f_n(n) + 1$ for all $n \in \mathbb{Z}^+$. There is no implementation for this mapping, since if there were, f and f_n would be identical for some n, which they are not by construction, as $f(n) \neq f_n(n)$. We are forced by this contradiction to conclude that our mapping is not computable! □

Notice the similarity of form between this proof and that of Theorem 5.13. Both use the same diagonal argument, though in slightly different ways. There are a number of similar results which show that this is not a peculiarity of *Modula-2*, and that *no* computer, no matter how designed, can calculate certain mappings. There are also related results to do with the *unprovability* of certain theorems in pure mathematics.

5.11 Relational databases

In this section, we shall use the ideas presented in Chapters 4 and 5 to model a database, and the operations we perform on it. A *database* is merely a system for organizing inter-related bits of information, of the sort we have been looking at in the last two chapters. The simplest type would be a list with one column, perhaps a list of candidates for an examination. Next, we might have a two-column list of candidates and marks scored, and this is the sort of relation we have been looking at most of the time until now. Let us go several stages further, and look at a more realistic example.

Example 5.104 A department might wish to organize its information about examination candidates in the following way. First, it associates a number with each candidate, called his ID. Next, a file is prepared which essentially represents a file of student records. The columns list an ID, name, address, telephone number, home address, home telephone number, date of birth, and date admitted to the department.

The department also keeps a file for each examination subject, in which the columns are an ID and a score.

For the examiners' meeting, another file is prepared, which lists an ID, a name, and then one column for every subject examined, in which scores are entered, or the position is left blank if the candidate did not take that examination. The final column is an average mark of all those papers taken.

The job of preparing the final file above should be left to a computer. There is nothing in it which is not recorded in the other files.

A relational database is conceptually just a collection of k-ary relations on a collection of sets. To make life simpler, the term *relation* will mean *k-ary relation, for some k* in this section.

Definition Let $A_1, \ldots, A_n$ be sets. A **relational database** is a collection $R_1, \ldots, R_q$ of relations on sub-collections of $A_1, \ldots, A_n$.

The individual relations will usually be kept as *files* with k columns, one line representing one k-tuple. The sets partaking in a relation are its *fields*.

The objective in the theory of relational databases is to see how information can be extracted from this collection of files, and how we can specify the interdependencies inherent in each file—say that two suppliers will not have the same postal address. Finally, we try to restructure the files so that each file reflects only one interdependency.

First, we look at the operations for extracting information.

Definition The **projection** of an n-ary relation R on $A_1, \ldots, A_n$ onto the fields $A_{i_1}, \ldots, A_{i_m}$ is defined as the m-ary relation R' on

$A_{i_1}, \ldots, A_{i_m}$ formed by taking the range of the mapping $p : R \to A_{i_1} \times \cdots \times A_{i_m}$, where

$$(a_1, \ldots, a_n) \mapsto (a_{i_1}, \ldots, a_{i_m}).$$

This always produces a new relation with at most as many fields as the original one.

Example 5.105 If $A_i = \mathbb{N}$ for $1 \leqslant i \leqslant 5$, and we project onto fields 1, 3 and 4, and if R contains $(1, 2, 4, 6, 8)$, then R' will contain $(1, 4, 6)$, since $p(1, 2, 4, 6, 8) = (1, 4, 6)$.

Definition Let R be an n-ary relation on $A_1, \ldots, A_n$. Let $P(a_1, \ldots, a_n)$ be a predicate, where $a_i \in A_i$ for all $i \in \{1, \ldots, n\}$. The **selection** of R by the predicate P is the set of n-tuples in R which satisfy P.

Since R itself can be considered as a predicate, we are merely strengthening R into $R(a_1, \ldots, a_n) \wedge P(a_1, \ldots, a_n)$.

Example 5.106 If the predicate were $(a_1 < a_2)$ then $(1, 2, 3, 1, 4)$ would be selected, but not $(1, 1, 3, 1, 4)$ or $(2, 1, 1, 2, 4)$.

The number of fields in a selection will be the same as the number in the original, and the number of k-tuples will never increase.

Example 5.107 The condition might be expressed in a set-theoretic form, such as $a_1 \in B$, where B is any given set. Thus we might have $B = \{1, 2, 5, 9, 10\}$, and if R contained $(1, 2, 4)$ and $(3, 2, 4)$ then $(1, 2, 4)$ would be selected, but not $(3, 2, 4)$.

We have looked at the *join* of two relations on given fields, defined as the composition of two relations, in Chapter 4.

We can also do some set operations directly on relations, provided that they consist of n-tuples of the same types.

Definition Let R and S be two n-ary relations on $A_1, \ldots, A_n$. Their **union**, **difference** and **intersection** are specified in the set-theoretic sense, as $R \cup S$, $R \setminus S$ and $R \cap S$.

If the relations are viewed as lists, we can think of their union as putting the two lists together, removing any duplicated lines; the difference involves deleting the entries of one list which appear in a second list; the intersection takes the common parts of two lists

Example 5.108 Suppose

$$R = \{(1, 2, 3), (2, 1, 4), (3, 1, 1), (1, 1, 1)\}$$

and
$$S = \{\,(5,1,3),(1,1,1),(1,2,3),(1,2,1)\,\}.$$
Then
$$R \cup S = \{\,(1,2,3),(2,1,4),(3,1,1),(1,1,1),(5,1,3),(1,2,1)\,\},$$
$$R \setminus S = \{\,(2,1,4),(3,1,1)\,\},$$
$$R \cap S = \{\,(1,2,3),(1,1,1)\,\}.$$

We can also take set-theoretic products of two relations, by stringing together an r-tuple from the first relation with an s-tuple from the second, to obtain an $(r+s)$-tuple.

Definition Let R and S be r-ary and s-ary relations. Their **product** is the $(r+s)$-ary relation $R \times S$, regarding R and S as sets of r- and s-tuples.

Example 5.109 If $(1,2,1) \in R$ and $(3,12) \in S$ then $R \times S$ will contain $(1,2,1,3,12)$.

It should be mentioned that in the above definitions, each position in the relations concerned has a well-defined field set associated with it, and any operations should respect the differences between these fields as though they were incompatible types in *Pascal*, *Modula-2* or *Ada*. If candidates and scores are both represented as integers in a database, it should not be possible to join two relations on the candidate field of one and the score field of another.

5.12   Functional dependence

The interdependencies underlying any one relation are described as *functional dependences*, and our first job in understanding any mass of data is to decide what these are.

Example 5.110 Suppose you go into a bookshop and ask for the price of a book by author a with title t. You would expect that the assistant would reply that the price was x dollars. This would then be a functional dependence, that (a,t) determines x.

However, consider the unlikely situation that a has written two books with the same title; perhaps two authors named a have written books with the same title, or maybe there are two editions of the same book simultaneously in print. This does happen—take Shakespeare, for example. In this case, perhaps if you specify a publisher p

as well then (a, t, p) will determine x, so we have a functional dependence again.

Definition Let R be an n-ary relation on $A_1, \ldots, A_n$. Let $A_{i_1}, \ldots, A_{i_p}$ and $A_{j_1}, \ldots, A_{j_q}$ be subcollections of the fields of the relation. Define a relation

$$(a_{i_1}, \ldots, a_{i_p}) \, S \, (a_{j_1}, \ldots, a_{j_q})$$

if the two -tuples are projections of a common n-tuple in R. We say that $A_{j_1}, \ldots, A_{j_q}$ is **functionally dependent** on $A_{i_1}, \ldots, A_{i_p}$ if this relation S defines a partial mapping from $A_{i_1} \times \cdots \times A_{i_p}$ to $A_{j_1} \times \cdots \times A_{j_q}$. We say there is **full functional dependence** if no subcollection of $A_{i_1}, \ldots, A_{i_p}$ will produce a partial mapping.

The values of the entries in each n-tuple in positions $i_1, \ldots, i_p$ should completely determine the values in positions $j_1, \ldots, j_q$. In full functional dependence, we need to know *all* of the first p values before the other q can be known.

Example 5.111 In a file listing compact disks, we might expect a list containing a catalogue number, performer, title, recording company, and price, (C, P, T, R, p). We could expect (P, T, R, p) to be functionally dependent on C, and maybe expect p to be functionally dependent on (P, T, R). This sort of functional dependence must be ascertained by looking carefully into accepted practices—do recording companies ever release two versions of the same compact disk at different prices? A mistake could lead to a lot of revision of the files for the catalogue.

Our aim is to ensure that the individual relations reflect full functional dependences. This may mean that some relations will have to be dismantled, and replaced by some equivalent relations.

Example 5.112 In Example 4.96, it would be preferable to dismantle the quintuples (p, d, n, o, x) into smaller parts. Suppose that the price of a part is independent of the order number o and the number n ordered. Price is functionally dependent on part number. It would be better to keep a file with triples (p, d, x) and a file with triples (o, p, n). Updating these files following a price rise would be considerably easier.

•**Exercise 5.113** What would be the best organization of the files if prices of parts were banded according to the number ordered, for example, $< 1000, 1000 \ldots 10000, > 10000$?

The process of disentangling a relational database so that in any of its relations the only functional dependences are on fields $A_1, \ldots, A_p$ such that every other field is fully functionally dependent on them, is known as *relational normalization*. The database should be designed in such a way that the problems of updating it and accessing its data are minimal.

Let us look at an example of normalization. We know what it means to say that in the relation R on $A_1, \ldots, A_p$ a collection of fields $A_{j_1}, \ldots, A_{j_q}$ is functionally dependent on $A_1, \ldots, A_p$. It means that in any n-tuple $(a_1, \ldots, a_n)$, the values of $a_1, \ldots, a_p$ *completely determine* the values of $a_{j_1}, \ldots, a_{j_q}$. Also, *full* functional dependence means that we need to know *all* of $a_1, \ldots, a_p$ before these dependent values are determined.

Suppose that the values of $a_1, \ldots, a_p$ determine all of $a_1, \ldots, a_n$. This means that

$$\{ ((a_1, \ldots, a_p), (a_1, \ldots, a_n)) : (a_1, \ldots, a_n) \in R \}$$

determines a *partial mapping*, $(a_1, \ldots, a_p) \mapsto (a_1, \ldots, a_n)$. Of course, we have simplified things by assuming that the determining fields are the first p fields, but in general the determining fields could be in any positions; we just mentally reorder the n-tuples so that the determining fields precede the other fields.

Suppose that in addition the functional dependence is full, so that no smaller collection of fields than $A_1, \ldots, A_p$ will do. A collection of fields like this is called a *key* for the relation. It is any minimal collection of fields which completely determines the values of all other fields.

Example 5.114 In the records of a library catalogue, we could expect that the *succession number*, that is, the number the library attaches to each and every book it buys, will determine the other information. All this means is that book number 1001345 is attached only to I. Manit and U. Schless, *Relations with no fields*, Emptissety Press, 1990. The other copy of this masterpiece is number 1001391, and was bought shortly after acquiring the first when a reader complained that the first copy must be defective, since it had no pages.

We see that the succession number would be a key, but the combination of author and title would not, since it would not determine the record. If the library has a policy of never duplicating books, author and title *are* a key.

Suppose that the library keeps a separate file in which it records the Library of Congress number l, ISBN number i, author a and title t of its books, and suppose that no author ever writes two books of the same title. Then l determines (i, a, t), i determines (l, a, t), and (a, t) determines (i, l), and the dependences are full. Thus we have three keys to this relation.

In Example 4.96, the quintuples (p, d, n, o, x) describing part of an order have (p, o) as a key. We also see that although p does not determine a full quintuple—there would be many orders, we hope, for the same part—it does fully determine both d and x. What we have is a collection of fields which is fully functionally dependent on another collection of fields, the latter not being a key to the relation. This is regarded as an undesirable property of a relation, and one purpose of normalization is to remove it, by the process of *Boyce-Codd normalization*. We project the original relation onto $P \times D \times X$, and remove D and X from the original relation by a second projection.

Definition A relation is in **Boyce-Codd normal form** if any full functional dependence is on a key.

This is an unusually simple example; in general there might be hundreds of combinations of fields which determine other fields, all overlapping one another, and our problem is to decide how to split the original relation without losing any information. If some fields are dropped because they are dependent on other fields, how can we be certain that they were not needed in the key for the original relation?

The result which lets us split a relation into two is the following.

Theorem 5.15 (Heath) Let R be a relation on $A_1, \ldots, A_n$. Suppose that $A_q, \ldots, A_n$ is functionally dependent on $A_p, \ldots, A_{q-1}$, for $1 < p < q < n$. Then R is the join of its projection on $A_1, \ldots, A_{q-1}$ and its projection on $A_p, \ldots, A_n$, joined by the common fields $A_p, \ldots, A_{q-1}$.

Proof We need to show that the set of n-tuples of R is a subset of the given join, and that no new n-tuples are formed when we perform that join.

Suppose that $(a_1, \ldots, a_n) \in R$. This projects to the -tuples $(a_1, \ldots, a_{q-1})$ and $(a_p, \ldots, a_n)$, and the join of these will reproduce $(a_1, \ldots, a_n)$. Thus the join definitely contains R.

To show that the join is no larger than R, suppose that $(a_1, \ldots, a_n)$ is in the join, and was formed by joining $(a_1, \ldots, a_{q-1})$ with $(a_p, \ldots, a_n)$.

There necessarily exist two n-tuples
$$(a_1, \ldots, a_{p-1}, a_p, \ldots, a_{q-1}, b_q, \ldots, b_n) \qquad\qquad (*)$$
and
$$(c_1, \ldots, c_{p-1}, a_p, \ldots, a_{q-1}, a_q, \ldots, a_n)$$
in R. But the assumed functional dependence implies that
$$(b_q, \ldots, b_n) = (a_q, \ldots, a_n),$$
and so $(*)$ equals the original n-tuple, and is in R, as desired.

We have shown that R is equal to the given join. $\qquad\qquad\qquad$ □

This result is just what we need to prove that our normalization is possible. Unfortunately, unless it is used with some caution, it has the effect of shattering a relation into thousands of smaller relations, even when such a fine subdivision is unnecessary. A blind application to Example 4.96 could split R first into its projections on $P \times D$ and $P \times N \times O \times X$, then the latter could be split further into projections on $P \times X$ and $P \times N \times O$. No further decomposition is possible, since none of p, n or o determines one of the others. The 'undesirable' feature is that the part description and price are in separate files now, whereas it might have been possible to have kept them in the same file. We must always look for a non-key determinant, such as P, and then look for the largest group of fields it determines, in this case $D \times X$. This determines the split $O \times N \times P$ and $P \times D \times X$.

> •*Exercise 5.115* A book catalogue records the following information for each book:
>
>
>
> author
> title
> publisher
> publisher's address
> year of publication
> edition
> number of pages
> price in £
> price in $
> Library of Congress number
> ISBN number.
>
>
>
> The assumptions underlying this scheme are
>
> (i) Both the Library of Congress and ISBN numbers are keys to the file;

(ii) Each publisher has just one address;

(iii) The sterling and dollar prices are computed from a fixed exchange rate.

Describe some undesirable features of this scheme, and suggest ways in which they could be avoided.

●**Exercise 5.116** You are organizing an art exhibition. You wish to store the following information:

artist

title

date

size of painting

hall where exhibited

floor on which exhibited

catalogue number

price

medium (oil or watercolour)

brief biography of artist.

The underlying assumptions are

(i) No two artists have the same name;

(ii) No artist has painted two paintings with the same title;

(iii) Each artist is to have all his paintings exhibited on one floor;

(iv) Each painting is given a unique catalogue number;

(v) The price of a painting is determined by its artist and size.

Suggest a way of organizing this information, explaining in detail why you have chosen to do it this way.

●**Exercise 5.117** Design a database for keeping student records. The records should include the usual personal details, and also information about all courses taken by each student, with space for examination marks.

5.13 Posets and normal forms

We close this chapter with a brief look at the connection between functional dependence and the idea of a partially ordered set, introduced in Chapter 4. We shall introduce a notation which will make discussing functional dependences a little easier.

Let $R \subseteq A_1 \times \cdots \times A_k$ be a relation. Let $S = \{ 1, \ldots, k \}$. Suppose that $M, N \subseteq S$. We say that the N fields are functionally dependent upon the M-fields if the collection of fields A_j with $j \in N$ is functionally dependent upon the collection of fields A_i with $i \in M$. It is clear that this happens if and only if the $(M \cup N)$-fields are functionally dependent upon the M-fields, and so it is only ever necessary to look at the situation where $M \subseteq N$.

Let X be the power set of S; thus the elements of X are the subsets of S. We know that there is a natural partial order relation defined on X, given by $M \subseteq N$ for $M, N \in X$. See Exercise 4.90.

We define a new partial order on the set X. For $M, N \in X$, put $M < N$ if $M \subset N$ and the N-fields are fully functionally dependent on the M-fields. We check that this relation is anti-symmetric and transitive.

Anti-symmetric If $M < N$ and $N < M$ then $M \subset N$ and $N \subset M$, and these are contradictory. Thus the relation is anti-symmetric.

Transitive Suppose $M < N < P$. Then $M \subset N \subset P$, but the functional dependence of the P-fields on the M-fields contradicts the *full* functional dependence of the P-fields on the N-fields, so there is transitivity vacuously.

Thus the reflexive closure of $<$ will define a partial order $\leqslant$ on X.

A key will be a set K with $K < S$. The minimality of the key is ensured by the fact that if $K < S$ then the dependence is full.

Lemma 5.16 The fields K constitute a key of the relation R if and only if $K < S$.

We next investigate the connection between this ordering and Boyce-Codd normalization.

Theorem 5.17 The relation R is in Boyce-Codd normal form if and only if the associated ordering satisfies the condition that $M < N$ implies $M < S$.

Proof We first assume that a relation is in Boyce-Codd normal form. Any full functional dependence is on a key, and any key K satisfies $K < S$, so $M < N$ implies that $M < S$.

For the converse, suppose that a relation satisfies the condition. A full functional dependence $M < N$ implies that $M < S$, which in turn implies that M is a key by the Lemma.   □

We thus have a way of recognizing whether or not our relation is in Boyce-Codd normal form, by drawing a diagram of the full functional dependences between subsets of the fields.

• **Exercise 5.118** Define the relation $\prec$ on the set X of all subsets of S by saying $M \prec N$ if N is functionally dependent upon M, and $M \subset N$. Show that this defines a partial ordering of X.

• **Exercise 5.119** What would happen if we omitted the condition $M \subset N$ in the previous Exercise?

6

Graphs

6.1 Introduction

The idea of a *graph* is one of the most elementary and simple in all of mathematics, yet the theory of graphs is remarkably complex, leading to both general theorems and to famous unsolved problems. We have met graphs already, in Chapters 4 and 5, where we used them to illustrate what was happening in a relation or mapping. In fact, we used *directed graphs* there, which are mathematically identical to binary relations.

There are also *undirected* graphs, which we shall meet for the first time in this chapter; they are broadly equivalent to symmetric relations. The structure of undirected graphs is simpler than that of directed graphs, leading to a rich and fruitful theory. There are complications inherent in the asymmetry of directed graphs which lead to a different sort of outlook, and a concentration on different kinds of problems.

6.2 Undirected graphs

The basic idea in an undirected graph is of a set of points called *vertices* joined by lines called *edges*. These points and edges could be thought of as nodes in an electrical network and wires joining them, or as road junctions and stretches of road between junctions. They could also be thought of as symmetric binary relations, where the vertices might be people, and an edge between two vertices might indicate that the people know one another. What is not sanctioned is the merging of two edges, the way two roads or flightpaths between cities might merge. Every intersection of edges must be marked with a vertex.

Each edge is determined by the pair of vertices that it links, so we might as well think of that edge as a set of two vertices. This stream-lines our model somewhat, and the definition we shall give is sometimes described as that of a *simple* graph. The alternative, where several edges can join the same two vertices, and a vertex can be joined to itself, is called a *multigraph* or *pseudograph*, and will not be treated here, except in passing.

We need a preliminary definition before we can proceed.

Definition Let V be a set. We define
$$V_2 = \{ A \subseteq V : |A| = 2 \},$$
and call this the **unordered product** of V by itself.

The set V_2 just consists of all two-element subsets of V, so it is the set of *possible* edges of a graph with vertices V.

Example 6.1 If $V = \{ a, b, c \}$ then
$$V_2 = \{ \{ a, b \}, \{ b, c \}, \{ a, c \} \},$$
so we could write $\{ b, c \} \in V_2$, $\{ a \} \notin V_2$, and so on.

•**Exercise 6.2** Write out V_2 in full where $V = \{ 0, 1, 2, 3 \}$.

Definition Let V be a finite set, and let E be a subset of V_2. The combination of V and E is said to be an **undirected graph** G with **vertex** set V and **edge** set E. We write this graph as $G = (V, E)$.

Whenever we refer to a *graph*, we shall mean an *undirected graph*, unless we explicitly state otherwise.

To specify a graph G we need to specify two sets, V and $E \subseteq V_2$, and this is reflected in the notation $G = (V, E)$. One might think that the specification of just E would suffice, since each element of E is itself a two element set, so we should be able to reconstruct V by taking the union of all these sets, $V = \bigcup_{e \in E} e$. However, it is possible that there are vertices v for which there are no edges e with $v \in e$. Such vertices are called *isolated*. If we do not permit isolated vertices, then our theory becomes less general, and we find ourselves constantly resorting to special trivial cases in our proofs. It is wise not to prohibit such vertices.

There is a further notation which is useful if we want to refer to the vertex and edge set of a graph anonymously. The vertex set of the graph G is referred to as $V(G)$ and its edge set as $E(G)$.

When we draw a graph, we use a blob of ink to represent each vertex, and a freehand line between two vertices to represent each edge. The line between two vertices must not pass through any other vertex, but it can cross other edges at a non-zero angle. Two edges must never merge together. The two diagrams in Figure 6.1 represent the same graph $G = (V, E)$ with $V = \{ a, b, c, d \}$. Figure 6.2 would not be a valid way

Fig. 6.1 **Identical graphs**

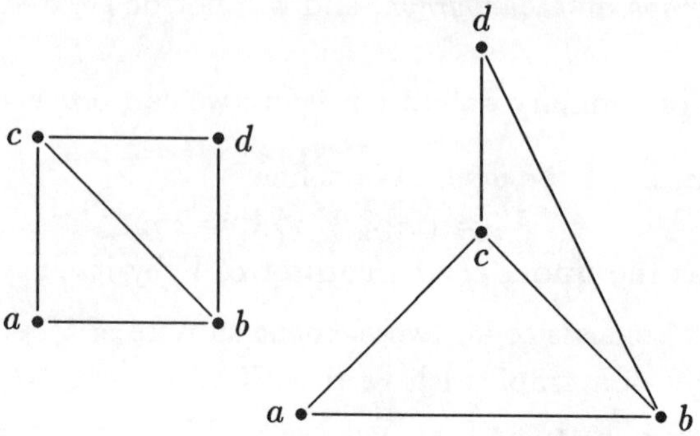

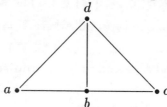

Fig. 6.2 **An incorrect drawing of a graph**

to draw the same graph. The problem here is that the vertex b lies on the edge from a to c. It is impossible to tell from the diagram which of the edges $\{a, b\}$, $\{b, c\}$ and $\{a, c\}$ are supposed to be included in the graph.

• *Exercise 6.3* Draw the graphs whose vertices are the corners, and edges the edges, of a

(i)   Tetrahedron;   (ii)   Cube.

• *Exercise 6.4* There are three other regular solids which can be formed by fitting together congruent regular polygons: two from triangles and one from pentagons. Find out what they are, and draw their graphs.

The notation we are using for edges is cumbersome, and it is preferable to use a simpler notation: henceforth, the edge $\{x, y\}$ will be written as either xy or yx.

6.3   Adjacency and incidence

A graph is characterized by specifying what is joined to what.

Definition Let $G = (V, E)$ be a graph, and suppose $x, y \in V$. We say that x and y are **adjacent** if $xy \in E$, and we also say that the vertices x and y are **incident** to the edge xy.

To describe the relationship of adjacency in a graph, we construct a table, the rows and columns of which are labelled by the vertices, with entries 1 for adjacency and 0 for non-adjacency. What we put on the diagonal is immaterial, but it is conventional to put 0s there, to indicate that a vertex cannot be adjacent to itself.

Example 6.5 Let $V = \{ a, b, c, d, e, f, g \}$ and let
$$E = \{ u = ab, v = cd, w = fg, x = bg, y = af \}.$$
Adjacency can be summarized by the table in Figure 6.3, and the *matrix*

$$\begin{bmatrix} 0 & 1 & 0 & 0 & 0 & 1 & 0 \\ 1 & 0 & 0 & 0 & 0 & 0 & 1 \\ 0 & 0 & 0 & 1 & 0 & 0 & 0 \\ 0 & 0 & 1 & 0 & 0 & 0 & 0 \\ 0 & 0 & 0 & 0 & 0 & 0 & 0 \\ 1 & 0 & 0 & 0 & 0 & 0 & 1 \\ 0 & 1 & 0 & 0 & 0 & 1 & 0 \end{bmatrix}$$

is called the *adjacency matrix* of the graph. Both concepts are relative to the ordering we give to the vertices.

Fig. 6.3 Adjacency table

	a	b	c	d	e	f	g
a	0	1	0	0	0	1	0
b	1	0	0	0	0	0	1
c	0	0	0	1	0	0	0
d	0	0	1	0	0	0	0
e	0	0	0	0	0	0	0
f	1	0	0	0	0	0	1
g	0	1	0	0	0	1	0

Fig. 6.4 **Incidence table**

	u	v	w	x	y
a	1	0	0	0	1
b	1	0	0	1	0
c	0	1	0	0	0
d	0	1	0	0	0
e	0	0	0	0	0
f	0	0	1	0	1
g	0	0	1	1	0

Similarly, we can construct a table describing incidence of edges and vertices, as in Figure 6.4, and a corresponding *incidence matrix*

$$\begin{bmatrix} 1 & 0 & 0 & 0 & 1 \\ 1 & 0 & 0 & 1 & 0 \\ 0 & 1 & 0 & 0 & 0 \\ 0 & 1 & 0 & 0 & 0 \\ 0 & 0 & 0 & 0 & 0 \\ 0 & 0 & 1 & 0 & 1 \\ 0 & 0 & 1 & 1 & 0 \end{bmatrix}.$$

•*Exercise 6.6* Find the adjacency and incidence matrices of the following graphs.

(i) $V = \{\, a, b, c, d, e \,\}$, $E = \{\, ab, bc, ae, cd, bd \,\}$.

(ii) $V = \{\, a, b, c, d, e \,\}$, $E = \{\, ab, bc, cd, de, ae \,\}$.

•*Exercise 6.7* A *multigraph* or *pseudograph* is an object like a graph in which there are vertices and edges, but in which it is possible for several edges to link the same two vertices, or for an edge to link a vertex to itself. Formulate a definition of such an object.

6.4   Isomorphism

In some cases, we can say that two graphs are equivalent, even though their vertex sets are completely different.

Example 6.8 Imagine a graph which represents six university computer nodes connected together as in Figure 6.5. Secondly, imagine six people in a village, called Alf, Ted, Pat, Sam, Pete and George, and suppose that we try to represent the fact that two of them are

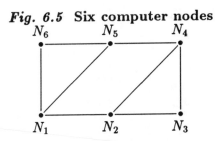

Fig. 6.5 Six computer nodes

very good friends in terms of a graph, where we join two people if they are good friends, as in Figure 6.6. These two graphs are equivalent in some sense, even though they represent completely different situations. We see that we can identify computer nodes with villagers according to the scheme

$$N_1 \mapsto \text{Pat}$$
$$N_2 \mapsto \text{Pete}$$
$$N_3 \mapsto \text{George}$$
$$N_4 \mapsto \text{Sam}$$
$$N_5 \mapsto \text{Alf}$$
$$N_6 \mapsto \text{Ted}$$

and that this identification constitutes a *bijection* between the two vertex sets

$$V = \{ N_1, N_2, N_3, N_4, N_5, N_6 \}$$

and

$$V' = \{ \text{Pat, Pete, George, Sam, Alf, Ted} \}$$

such that two nodes in V are connected if and only if the corresponding two villagers are the best of friends. Adjacency in the first graph coincides with adjacency in the second.

Although the above is an unnatural correspondence—why should village life affect the working of the university computer network?—there are situations where it is essential that we determine whether two models are describing the same graph.

Example 6.9 Suppose that we have two different graphs, representing two complex chemical molecules, the atoms being the vertices and the chemical bonds the edges. We would like to know whether these two molecules are identical.

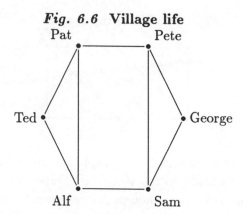

Fig. 6.6 **Village life**

Definition Let $G = (V, E)$ and $G' = (V', E')$ be two graphs. We say that they are **isomorphic** if there exists a bijection $f : V \to V'$ such that for any $u, v \in V$, $uv \in E$ if and only if $f(u)f(v) \in E'$. The mapping f is then called an **isomorphism**.

- **Exercise 6.10** Determine whether or not the two graphs given below are isomorphic.
  - (i) $G = (V, E)$, $V = \{ a, b, c, d, e, f, g \}$ and
    $$E = \{ ab, ad, ae, bd, ce, cf, dg, fg, bf \}.$$
  - (ii) $G = (V, E')$, $V = \{ a, b, c, d, e, f, g \}$ and
    $$E' = \{ ab, bc, cd, de, ef, fg, ga, ac, be \}.$$

- **Exercise 6.11** Suppose we define a *homomorphism* to be a mapping $f : V \to V'$ such that if $uv \in E$ then $f(u)f(v) \in E'$. Think of some examples of such homomorphisms.

- **Exercise 6.12** Define isomorphism for pseudographs.

6.5   Subgraphs

If we take any graph, we can change it into a new graph by removing some of its vertices. If we remove the vertex v, we must also remove any edges incident to v. We can also remove further edges from the graph, and then we obtain the full generality we require.

Definition Let $G = (V, E)$ and $G' = (V', E')$ be two graphs with the property that $V' \subseteq V$ and $E' \subseteq E$. We say that G' is a **subgraph** of G.

Example 6.13 Suppose
$$G = (\{\, a, b, c, d, e, f, g \,\}, \{\, ab, ac, cd, ce, ef, ag, cg, fg \,\})$$
and
$$G' = (\{\, a, c, d, e, g \,\}, \{\, ac, cd, cg \,\}.$$
In G', the two vertices c and e are not adjacent, although in G they were. However, any two vertices which *are* adjacent in G' are certainly so in G.

● ***Exercise 6.14*** Let $G = (\{\, a, b, c \,\}, \{\, ab, bc \,\})$. Find all subgraphs of G.

The subgraphs obtained by vertex deletions alone are the largest possible subgraphs on a given vertex subset.

Definition Let $G = (V, E)$ be a graph, and suppose $V' \subseteq V$. Define
$$E' = \{\, e \in E : e = uv \text{ with } u, v \in V' \,\}.$$
Then $G' = (V', E')$ is called the subgraph **induced** on V' by the graph G, or the **restriction** of G to V', written $G|_{V'}$.

We are stating that $u, v \in V'$ are adjacent in G' if and only if they are adjacent in G.

Example 6.15 In Example 6.13, the induced subgraph on $\{\, a, c, d, e, g \,\}$ has edge set $\{\, ac, cd, ag, cg, ce \,\}$.

For each subset of vertices of a graph, there is one and only one induced subgraph on those vertices. If $G|_{V'}$ has m edges, then there are 2^m corresponding subgraphs on the same vertex set.

● ***Exercise 6.16*** How many induced subgraphs does a graph have?

● ***Exercise 6.17*** Let $G = (V, E)$, $V = \{\, a, b, c, d, e \,\}$, $E = \{\, ab, cd, be, da \,\}$, and $W = \{\, a, c, e \,\}$. Find the subgraph of G induced on W.

6.6 Vertex Degrees

What usually strikes us in a graph is the fact that some vertices have more edges incident to them than others. It might be that one computer node is connected to more nodes than any other, or that one person knows more people than anyone else. The number of vertices adjacent to a given vertex would appear to be a useful concept. Moreover, in deciding whether or not two graphs are isomorphic, it is sensible to compare these numbers first. If they do not tally, then the graphs are not isomorphic.

Definition Let $G = (V, E)$, and let $v \in V$. The number $\deg v$ of distinct edges incident to v is called the **vertex degree** of v,

$$\deg v = |\{\, e \in E : e = vx \text{ for some } x \in V \,\}|.$$

The alternative definition is

$$\deg v = |\{\, u \in V : vu \in E \,\}|,$$

and the two definitions are readily seen to be equivalent.

• **Exercise 6.18** But not for multigraphs! Why? Give a reasonable definition of the degree of a vertex in a multigraph.

Example 6.19 In Figure 6.7, the numbers next to the vertices represent the degrees of the vertices.

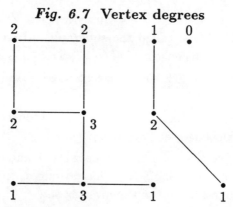

Fig. 6.7 **Vertex degrees**

Some values of the vertex degree are so special that they are picked out as properties of the vertex.

Definition A vertex of degree 0 is called an **isolated** vertex. A vertex of degree 1 is called a **pendant** vertex.

Examination of the set of numbers constituting the degrees of the vertices of any graph will quickly disclose a simple relationship with the number of edges. Add all the degrees together, and you get twice the number of edges.

Theorem 6.1 Let $G = (V, E)$ be a graph. Then

$$\sum_{v \in V} \deg v = 2|E|.$$

Proof This is perhaps so obvious that a proof may seem superfluous. Each edge contributes one to each of two vertex degrees. Hence the result.

A formal proof would go like this. The result is trivial for any graph with no edges, that is, in which every vertex is isolated. Assume as the inductive hypothesis that the result is true for all graphs with n or fewer edges, and suppose $G = (V, E)$ is a graph with $|E| = n + 1$. Choose $e = xy \in E$, and form the graph $G' = (V, E')$ with $E' = E \setminus \{e\}$. Let $\deg' v$ represent the degree of a vertex in G'. Then G' has n edges, so by hypothesis

$$\sum_{v \in V} \deg' v = 2|E'| = 2(|E| - 1).$$

In G' the degrees of x and y are one less than in G. Thus $\deg' x = \deg x - 1$ and $\deg' y = \deg y - 1$, yielding

$$\deg x - 1 + \deg y - 1 + \sum_{\substack{v \in V \\ v \neq x, y}} \deg v = 2|E| - 2,$$

which is what we wished to prove. Hence, by induction, the result is true for all n. □

• *Exercise 6.20* Show that in any graph G the number of vertices of odd degree is even.

• *Exercise 6.21* Either find a graph with the following vertex degrees, or show that no such graph exists.

(i)   3, 2, 2, 2, 1, 1.   (ii)   3, 3, 2, 2, 2, 2.
(iii) 4, 3, 2, 2, 2, 1.   (iv)   4, 4, 2, 2, 2, 2.
(v)   4, 3, 3, 3, 3.   (vi)   5, 5, 5, 5, 3, 3.

• *Exercise 6.22* There are $n \geqslant 2$ people in a room. Show that there exist two people in the room who have the same number of acquaintances in the room.

Some graphs are such that all their vertices have the same degree.

Definition Let $G = (V, E)$ be a graph with the property that every vertex v of G has $\deg v = k$, for some $k \in \mathbb{Z}^+$. We say that G is a **k-regular graph**.

Regular graphs are not difficult to find. The following definition furnishes us with a k-regular graph, for each k.

Definition A graph in which every two vertices are adjacent is called a **complete graph**.

The symbol K_n is used to denote a complete graph with n vertices. What it really represents is a graph which is *isomorphic to* any given complete graph. Being isomorphic is an equivalence relation on the set of all graphs, and K_n is a representative complete graph from the equivalence class of complete graphs with n vertices. Clearly K_n is $(n-1)$-regular, for each $n \geqslant 1$.

The complete graphs are just a special case of a more general sort of graph.

Definition Suppose that $G = (V, E)$ is a graph, and that V is partitioned into disjoint, nonempty components $V = \bigcup_{i=1}^{m} V_i$. Suppose that each edge $e \in E$ is never incident to more than one vertex in any one component. Then G is said to be m-**partite**. When $m = 2$, we call the graph **bipartite**.

In an m-partite graph, every edge crosses from one component to another.

• *Exercise 6.23* Is every graph m-partite, for some value of m?

An m-partite graph might contain all of the possible edges linking its components.

Definition Suppose that $G = (V, E)$ is a graph, and that V is partitioned into disjoint, nonempty components $V = \bigcup_{i=1}^{m} V_i$, and that $|V_i| = a_i$ for each i with $1 \leqslant i \leqslant m$. Suppose also that
$$E = \{ v_i v_j : v_i \in V_i, v_j \in V_j, \text{ for some } i \neq j, 1 \leqslant i, j \leqslant m \}.$$
Then G is said to be a **complete m-partite graph**.

The notation for complete m-partite graphs is $K_{a_1, a_2, \ldots, a_m}$. A *complete bipartite* graph on sets with p and q vertices is then $K_{p,q}$.

• *Exercise 6.24* When are $K_{p,q}$ and $K_{r,s}$ isomorphic?

• *Exercise 6.25* Which graphs are both complete *and* complete bipartite?

There are also many non-complete regular graphs.

Example 6.26 Figure 6.8 is 2-regular. This Example readily gen-

Fig. 6.8 **A 2-regular graph**

eralizes to produce an infinite family of 2-regular graphs.

•*Exercise 6.27* Give an example of a d-regular graph with $2d$ vertices.

6.7   Walks, trails and paths

One of the commonest problems we meet in graph theory is that of deciding whether or not it is possible to get from one vertex to another. For example, in a representation of a computer network, we might need to know if one computer can communicate with another, and, if so, by what route. It sometimes happens that it is possible to show that a link exists without knowing what the optimal communication route is. It may be obvious that every computer is linked to every other computer, yet it may not be easy to say which way to send a message between them. We can distinguish immediately between two different concepts, that of being *connected*, and that of a *shortest path*.

Let us look at another Example to see that we may need to distinguish between three different ways to get from one place to another!

Example 6.28 Consider a man who wishes to get from A to B in a forest. He does not know his way, and he wanders around for some time, often revisiting points where he has been before, and often walking along the same tracks he walked along some hours before, sometimes even retracing his steps. Finally, he reaches B. Most people would say he was *lost* in the forest, but we shall say he has had a *walk*, just to be kind to him.

Next, we meet a young couple who are holding a book called *Forest Trails*. They are walking from A to B for pleasure. The *trail* they follow leads them along an attractive route, which at one point passes some landmark. A short while later, they pass this point again, but are delighted to find that they do not have to retrace the same track—their trail crosses itself cleanly, and sets off in a different direction.

Finally, we have a woman who knows where she is going. She walks from A to B every day. She never revisits the same place on her journey, as time is important to her. She has found her own *path* from A to B, probably the *shortest* path.

In this Example, we see the three main ways we have of moving from one vertex to another in a graph. There are three levels of generality involved, namely, no restrictions at all, then the restriction of not repeating edges, and finally the restriction of not repeating vertices.

> **Definition** Let $G = (V, E)$ be a graph, and let $v_1, \ldots, v_n \in V$ be
> such that $v_i v_{i+1} \in E$ for $1 \leqslant i \leqslant n - 1$. The sequence
>
> $$v_1, \; v_1 v_2, \; v_2, \; v_2 v_3, \; v_3, \ldots, \; v_{n-1}, \; v_{n-1} v_n, \; v_n$$
>
> is said to be a **walk** from v_1 to v_n, and it is usually written as
> $v_1 v_2 v_3 \cdots v_n$ for brevity. If the edges in a walk are all distinct it is
> called a **trail**. If the vertices in a walk are all distinct, apart from
> possibly $v_n = v_1$, it is called a **path**. A walk, trail or path is called
> **closed** if $v_n = v_1$, otherwise it is **open**. Finally, a walk, trail or path
> is called **trivial** if it consists only of a single vertex, otherwise it is
> **nontrivial**.

Thus we see the hierarchy of concepts, depending on whether or not
edges or vertices are repeated. It is clear that if no vertices are repeated,
then no edges can be repeated either—a path is a trail. Moreover, a
closed path with $n > 2$ is a closed trail.

• **Exercise 6.29** Why introduce the restriction $n > 2$?

We should note that, if $v_1, \ldots, v_n \in V$, the notation $v_1 v_2 \cdots v_n$
should only be used when each of the edges $v_i v_{i+1}$ lies in E. As a trivial
case v_1 represents a path from v_1 to v_1, and, if $v_1 v_2 \in E$, $v_1 v_2$ represents
the path $v_1, v_1 v_2, v_2$ from v_1 to v_2.

It is intuitively obvious that if we can find a walk from u to v in a
graph, then we can find a path from u to v. Let us convince ourselves
of this fact before we go any further.

Theorem 6.2 Let $G = (V, E)$ be a graph, and let $W = v_1 v_2 \cdots v_n$ be
a walk from $u = v_1$ to $v = v_n$. There exists a path P from u to v using
only edges of W.

Proof We notice that the result is trivial if $u = v$. Assume that $u \neq v$.

Let G' be the subgraph of G consisting of only the vertices and edges
of W. In G' there still exists the walk W from u to v. Let P be the
shortest walk from u to v in G', in the sense of having the fewest number
of edges. Suppose that $P = w_1 w_2 \cdots w_k$, and assume for a contradiction
that $w_i = w_j$ for some $i < j$. We can omit the part of P between w_i
and w_j to obtain an even shorter walk

$$w_1 w_2 \cdots w_{i-1} w_i w_{j+1} w_{j+2} \cdots w_k$$

from $w_1 = u$ to $w_k = v$, a contradiction of the minimality of P. Thus the result must be true, as assuming otherwise leads to a contradiction. □

To reduce W to a path, we would successively remove redundant sections, like $w_{i+1}w_{i+2}\cdots w_j$ in the proof, until no more existed. This would lead us to a path, but not the *shortest* path, between u and v.

Fig. 6.9 A walk containing a path

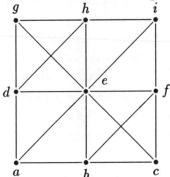

Example 6.30 Take the graph G in Figure 6.9. Then
$$aebfiehgdhedghifc$$
is a walk from a to c. Scanning this from the left, we see that the first repeated vertex is e, so we can shorten it to $aehgdhedghifc$. The vertex e is again repeated, so we can reduce further to $aedghifc$, which is a path from a to c. The original walk also contains the path $aehifc$, which is shorter.

• **Exercise 6.31** We can define the *concatenation* of two walks in the following sense. Let $W_1 = v_1v_2\cdots v_m$, $W_2 = w_1w_2\cdots w_n$, and suppose $v_m = w_1$. The concatenation is the walk
$$W_1W_2 = v_1v_2\cdots v_mw_2w_3\cdots w_n.$$
What difficulties would we encounter in trying to define the same concept for trails and paths?

6.8 Cycles or circuits

The concepts of a closed trail or closed path which passes through more than one vertex are so important that we pick them out as separate definitions.

Definition A nontrivial closed trail is called a **cycle** or **circuit**. A cycle or circuit which is also a closed path is called **simple**.

Thus cycles are not allowed to consist of just a single vertex, or to be of the form u, uv, v, vu, u, for instance, because they are nontrivial, and are also *trails*.

Some authors distinguish between circuits and cycles, reserving one name or the other for what we have called a simple cycle. This is not done uniformly, so we shall use the two words as synonyms.

Our next result is the analogue of Theorem 6.2, except that it is applied to cycles rather than walks. In practice, it makes little difference which vertex of a cycle we take as the initial vertex. Thus we make no distinction between the cycles *abcdefa* and *cdefabc*, for instance, and do not need to describe the first as 'from' a 'to' a.

Theorem 6.3 Let C be a cycle in the graph G. There exists a simple cycle in G using only the edges and vertices of C.

Proof Suppose $C = v_1v_2v_3 \cdots v_n$, where $v_1 = v_n$. As we follow C from v_1 to v_n, some vertices will be visited more than once; for instance, v_1 is visited again as v_n. We define the *gap* between repetitions of such a vertex, as the number of edges of C traversed between two repetitions. This gap is always at least 3, because C is a trail, and the gap is at most $n - 1$.

Choose a repeated vertex for which there is a gap between repetitions which is the least of all such gaps for the whole of C. We have a stretch $C' = v_iv_{i+1} \cdots v_j$ of C which is such that $v_i = v_j$, and $j - i$ is as small as possible, subject to $i < j$. Then C' is a closed trail, and it passes through more than one vertex, because it involves at least 3 distinct edges. Moreover, no vertex is repeated apart from v_i, as otherwise we could find a shorter gap than $j - i$. Thus C' must be a simple cycle. □

The above proof shows that even an apparently obvious result can have quite a subtle proof. The main complication is in excluding the possible triviality of C'.

We shall later study graphs which contain no cycles whatsoever.

Definition A graph is said to be **acyclic** if it contains no cycles. There is no corresponding word to describe a graph which is *not* acyclic!

An acyclic graph contains no simple cycles. Conversely, a graph containing no simple cycles also contains no cycles, by Theorem 6.3. Thus we have

Corollary 6.4 The graph G is acyclic if and only if it contains no simple cycles.

A more subtle result is the following, which is so similar to Theorem 6.3 that its statement should be studied carefully.

Theorem 6.5 Let $G = (V, E)$ be a graph, and let $u, v \in V$, with $u \neq v$. Suppose that there exist two *different* paths from u to v in G. Then G contains a simple cycle.

At first, the existence of the two paths seems to imply the existence of a cycle, by following the first path by the second path in reverse. We soon see that this only produces a closed *walk*, and that is not guaranteed to contain a cycle, as the reader can readily convince himself. It is the fact that the two paths are *different* that we must use.

Fig. 6.10 Two distinct paths determine a cycle

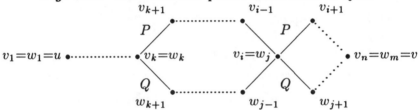

Proof Suppose that $m \leqslant n$, and
$$P = v_1 v_2 \cdots v_{n-1} v_n, \qquad Q = w_1 w_2 \cdots w_{m-1} w_m$$
are different paths from $u = v_1 = w_1$ to $v = v_n = w_m$, with $u \neq v$. Suppose that these paths are identical for the first k vertices, where possibly $k = 1$, and then they differ, either because P has terminated or because $v_{k+1} \neq w_{k+1}$.

If P has terminated, then $k = n$, and $v_k = w_k = v = w_m$. But this forces either the contradiction that $k < m$ but $w_k = w_m$ on Q, or the contradiction that $k = m = n$, and $P = Q$, contrary to assumption.

We therefore deduce that $k < n$, and so $v_{k+1} \neq w_{k+1}$. The stretch $w_{k+1} w_{k+2} \cdots w_{m-1} w_m$ of Q eventually crosses P again at $w_m = v$, and possibly crosses P several times before then. Let w_j be the first vertex of Q after w_k which also lies on P, and suppose $w_j = v_i$, for some i with $k < i \leqslant n$. Then
$$w_k w_{k+1} \cdots w_{j-1} w_j v_{i-1} v_{i-2} \cdots v_{k+1} v_k$$
is a closed walk, and it is certainly nontrivial. It is a path, because, by assumption, the vertices $w_{k+1}, \ldots, w_{j-1}$ are all distinct from the vertices

$v_{k+1}, \ldots, v_{i-1}$. It is thus a simple cycle.   □

There is an immediate consequence of this result which is worth
pointing out.

Corollary 6.6 If G is an acyclic graph and u, v are vertices of G then
either there is no path from u to v in G, or there is a unique path.

- **Exercise 6.32** An *Eulerian circuit* in a connected graph
  $G = (V, E)$ is a circuit which traverses every edge in E once and
  once only. Show that the connected graph G possesses an Eulerian
  circuit if and only if every vertex degree in G is even.

- **Exercise 6.33** When is it possible to find a *walk* in the graph G
  which traverses every edge once and once only?

- **Exercise 6.34** Exhibit an Eulerian circuit in the following if possible.
  (i) The two graphs in Exercise 6.3.
  (ii) K_7.
  (iii) $G = (V, E)$ with $V = \{ a, b, c, d, e, f, g, h, i, j \}$ and
       $E = \{ ab, ac, ae, ag, ah, aj, bd, cd, cg, ci, de, df, eg, ei, fh, gi, ij \}$.

- **Exercise 6.35** When are the following Eulerian for $m, n \geqslant 1$?
  (i) K_n.   (ii) $K_{m,n}$.

6.9   Connectedness and connected components

We have seen that as far as linking two vertices is concerned, we need
only work with paths, since walks automatically contain paths.

Definition A **connected** graph is a graph $G = (V, E)$ in which
there exists a path between any two vertices $u, v \in V$.

Example 6.36 K_n and $K_{m,n}$ are connected graphs for each
$m, n \geqslant 1$.

- **Exercise 6.37** Explain why any complete bipartite graph $K_{m,n}$,
  with $m, n \in \mathbb{N}$, is connected.

- **Exercise 6.38** The graph G has the property that every induced
  subgraph of G is connected. What can be said about G?

When there does exist a path between two vertices, it is possible to
define the *distance* between the two vertices. This is the total length,
measured in numbers of edges, of the *shortest path* between the two

vertices. We only look at paths, since the shortest walk between the vertices will always be a path.

Definition Let $G = (V, E)$ be a graph, $u, v \in V$ vertices of G, and let $v_1 v_2 \cdots v_n$ be a walk from $u = v_1$ to $v = v_n$. We say that this walk has **length** $n - 1$. If we look at all possible walks between u and v, then their lengths give us a set of cardinal numbers. The smallest of these numbers is called the **distance** between the two vertices, and is written $d(u, v)$. If there is no walk from u to v, we put $d(u, v) = \infty$.

The use of the symbol ∞ in the above definition is merely notational. There is no walk of 'infinite' length in this case, there is simply no walk at all!

•**Exercise 6.39** The graph G has minimum vertex degree $\delta(G) = q \geqslant 1$. Show that G contains a path of length q.

We can calculate the distance between any two vertices of a connected graph by an exhaustive search. If $|V| = n$ there are at most $2^{n-2}(n-2)!$ paths in the graph between u and v. For there are at most 2^{n-2} possible subsets of $V \setminus \{u, v\}$ to traverse between u and v, and at most $(n-2)!$ different orderings of each of those subsets. When we look at graph algorithms in Chapter 7, we shall see that there is a much more efficient way of searching for the shortest path.

•**Exercise 6.40** Show that a better bound on the number of paths from u to v is $(n-2)! \, e$.

•**Exercise 6.41** Tabulate the distances $d(x, y)$ between any pair of vertices in the graphs $G = (V, E)$, $V = \{a, b, c, d, e, f\}$, in Figure 6.11.

The distance function has some elementary properties common to all distance functions, which we can easily verify. They are the properties of what is known as a *metric space*.

Theorem 6.7 (Metric properties) In any connected graph $G = (V, E)$, the following properties hold for any vertices $u, v, w \in V$:

(i) **Positive Definiteness:** $d(u, v) \geqslant 0$, with equality if and only if $u = v$;

(ii) **Symmetry:** $d(u, v) = d(v, u)$;

(iii) **Triangle Inequality:** $d(u, v) + d(v, w) \geqslant d(u, w)$.

Fig. 6.11

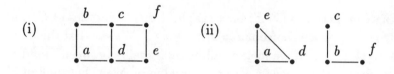

(i)   (ii)

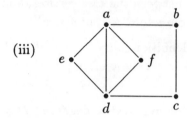

(iii)

Proof   (i) First, $d(u,v)$ is a cardinal number, so $d(u,v) \geqslant 0$. Also, equality only happens if there is a path of length 0 from u to v, which means that $u = v$.

(ii) This is obvious, since a shortest path from u to v must, on reversal, yield a shortest path from v to u.

(iii) Let P be a shortest path from u to v, of length $d(u,v)$. Similarly, let Q be a shortest path from v to w, of length $d(v,w)$. We can form the *walk* $R = PQ$ by concatenating P and Q, that is, by traversing first P and then Q. The length of R is $d(u,v) + d(v,w)$. However, R will not necessarily be the shortest possible route from u to w, so its length is at least $d(u,w)$.

□

The reason for the name *triangle inequality* is that the corresponding property in the plane is that the length of one side of any triangle is at most equal to the sum of the lengths of the other two sides. Distances in the plane are just lengths of straight line segments, thus lengths of sides of triangles.

•*Exercise 6.42* Let v be a vertex of the connected graph $G = (V, E)$. The *eccentricity* $\epsilon(v)$ of G at v is defined as
$$\epsilon(v) = \max_{u \in V} d(u,v).$$
A *centre* of G is a vertex $c \in V$ for which $\epsilon(c)$ is a minimum. The minimum eccentricity is called the *radius* of the graph.

Give an example of a graph with

(i)   only one centre;   (ii)   more than one centre.

●*Exercise 6.43* For each graph in Exercise 6.3, find an open path of longest possible length along its edges. What is your longest length?

Even when a graph is disconnected, we can still study each connected piece of it separately. Let us define a relationship between the vertices of a graph $G = (V, E)$. For $u, v \in V$, we say that v is *reachable* from u if there exists a walk in G from u to v. We can then write $u \triangleright v$, and we have a binary relation on V. It is trivial to check that this relation is an equivalence relation on V. Under this equivalence relation, V is partitioned into disjoint equivalence classes, and these are the sets which determine the connected components of G.

Definition Let $G = (V, E)$ be a graph. We say that $u, v \in V$ are in the same **connected component** if there exists a path from u to v in G. Strictly, a **connected component** is the induced subgraph $G|_X$ on one of the equivalence classes X of the equivalence relation $\triangleright$ introduced above.

Example 6.44 The graph in Figure 6.7 has three connected components.

●*Exercise 6.45* The minimum and maximum vertex degrees of the graph G are denoted by $\delta(G)$, $\Delta(G)$ respectively. The graph G is such that $|V| = n$ and $\delta(G) \geqslant \frac{1}{2}(n - 1)$. Show that G is connected.

6.10   Hamiltonian paths

There is a type of path that is of some interest in graph theory, namely, one which visits every vertex.

Definition Let $G = (V, E)$ be a graph. A **Hamiltonian path** in G is a path which visits every vertex once and once only.

Alternatively, a Hamiltonian path is a path of length $|V| - 1$.

Example 6.46 There is the oft cited example of a *travelling saleswoman* who wishes to fly a circuit of n cities on a continuous route, without visiting any city more than once. If she can find the requisite flights, she has found a Hamiltonian path joining the cities. She may even desire the cheapest such path.

There are several sufficient conditions for the existence of a Hamiltonian path. Here is one of them.

Theorem 6.8 (Ore) Let $G = (V, E)$ be a graph with $|V| = n$, in which $\deg v + \deg w \geqslant n - 1$, for all non-adjacent vertices v and w. Then G possesses a Hamiltonian path.

Proof Suppose that $G' = (V', E')$ and $G'' = (V'', E'')$ are two connected components of G, with $|V'| = p$, $|V''| = q$. Then $p + q \leqslant n$, so if $v \in V'$, $w \in V''$ we have
$$n - 1 \leqslant \deg v + \deg w \leqslant (p - 1) + (q - 1) \leqslant n - 2.$$
Thus we have a contradiction. G must therefore be connected.

Let $P = v_1 v_2 \cdots v_k$ be a path of length $k - 1$ in G, with k as large as possible. Assume that $k < n$. If either v_1 or v_k is adjacent to some vertex not in the path, the path can be extended to length k, and we have a contradiction. Thus v_1 and v_k are *only* adjacent to vertices in the set $\{v_1, \ldots, v_k\}$.

If v_1 and v_k are adjacent, we choose any $u \in V$ with u not on the path. There must be a path from u to v_1, because G is connected. This new path first meets P at some vertex v_i at an edge wv_i. But then
$$wv_i v_{i+1} \cdots v_k v_1 v_2 \cdots v_{i-1}$$
is a path of length k, and again we have a contradiction.

A similar argument holds if v_1 is adjacent to v_j whilst v_{j-1} is adjacent to v_k, for some $j \geqslant 2$. For then we can work on the path
$$v_1 v_2 \cdots v_{j-1} v_k v_{k-1} \cdots v_j$$
instead of P, and derive the same contradiction from the fact that $v_j v_1$ is an edge of G.

Consider $\deg v_1 + \deg v_k$. Every vertex v_j which v_1 is adjacent to stops v_k from being adjacent to v_{j-1}, for $2 \leqslant j \leqslant k-1$. If v_1 is adjacent to r vertices, then v_k is adjacent to at most $k - 1 - r$ vertices, and so
$$\deg v_1 + \deg v_k \leqslant r + k - 1 - r = k - 1 < n - 1,$$
and we still have a contradiction! It is thus wrong to assume that $k < n$. □

• **Exercise 6.47** A chief examiner wishes to timetable twenty mathematics exam papers on twenty consecutive days. Each paper has one examiner. Each examiner invigilates his own papers. It is required that no examiner should invigilate on two consecutive days, and it is known that no examiner is examining more than ten papers. Show that it is possible to construct the timetable.

6.11   Trees and forests

An alternative, more common, and more picturesque name for an acyclic graph is a *forest*. Just as a real forest consists (mainly) of trees, so does our forest consist of trees, which just turn out to be the connected components of the forest.

Definition An acyclic graph is called a **forest**. A connected forest is called a **tree**.

The term *tree* is used in the applications of graphs to *parsing* and *binary searching*, where the tree is drawn in such a way that it *looks* like a real tree, albeit usually upside down, like a *family tree*. Graphical trees are usually more amorphous than real trees, more like trees growing in a weightless environment; they do not generally have the symmetry of real trees.

Example 6.48 Figure 6.12 is a tree.

Fig. 6.12   A tree

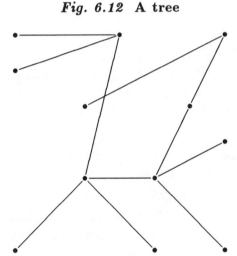

There is an easy consequence of our definitions, which is so immediate that we state it without proof.

Theorem 6.9 Each connected component of a forest is a tree.

When we examined acyclic graphs before, we saw that there was at most one path between any two vertices. We can strengthen this result considerably for a characterization of trees.

Theorem 6.10 A graph G is a tree if and only if for each pair of vertices of G there exists a unique path in G joining those vertices.

Proof Suppose that G is a tree. Then G is connected, so given $u, v \in V(G)$, there exists a path from u to v. But, by Corollary 6.6, there is at most one path because G is acyclic.

Conversely, suppose that the graph G has the property that given any vertices u and v there is a unique path from u to v. Then G is immediately seen to be connected. Suppose it is not acyclic, so there is a simple cycle $C = v_1 v_2 \cdots v_{n-1} v_n$ with $n \geqslant 4$ in G, and $v_n = v_1$. We see that the path $v_2 v_1$ and the path $v_2 v_3 \cdots v_{n-1} v_n$ are distinct paths from $u = v_2$ to $v = v_1$. Thus we have a contradiction, which forces G to be acyclic. It is thus connected and acyclic, so it is a tree. $\square$

In a similar way, we can see that

Theorem 6.11 A graph G is a forest if and only if for each pair of vertices of G there exists at most one path in G joining those vertices.

Proof One direction is equivalent to Corollary 6.6. The other implication follows from Theorem 6.10 applied to each connected component of G. The details are left to the reader. $\square$

The next result on trees could be proved directly, but we prefer to use it to illustrate the power of the apparently innocent Theorem 6.10. In a tree, *every* edge is essential to that tree being connected. Just remove one edge and the tree falls apart. There is a certain minimality in the edges of a tree.

Theorem 6.12 Let $G = (V, E)$ be a tree, and let $e \in E$. Then $G' = (V, E \setminus \{e\})$ is disconnected, and has two components.

Proof If $e = uv$, then in G there is a unique path from u to v, by Theorem 6.10, and this path is uv, of course. It follows that there can be no path from u to v in G', since such a path would also be a second path in G. Thus G' is disconnected.

We need to show that G' has only two components. Since u and v are in different components of G', it is sufficient to show that any other vertex w is connected to either u or v in G'. There exists a path in G from w to u. If this path does not use e, then it is also a path in G', in which case w and u are in the same component of G'. If it does use e, then e must be the very last edge of the path, because u cannot appear twice on the path, so the path is of the form $v_1 v_2 \cdots v_{n-1} v_n$, with

$v_{n-1} = v$ and $v_n = u$. The path $v_1 v_2 \cdots v_{n-1}$ then lies entirely in G', and is a path linking w to v, so w and v are in the same component.

We deduce that G' has only two components. □

There is a notation which is used for the graph obtained by removing the edge e from the edge set of the graph G. It is written $G - e$. It is not a very logical notation, but it does save a bit of writing. Similarly, $G + e$ denotes the graph obtained by adding the new edge e to the graph G.

Theorem 6.12 is concerned with a special sort of edge.

Definition Let $G = (V, E)$ be a graph. An edge $e \in E$ with the property that $G - e$ has more connected components than G is called **a bridge**.

Bridges also exist in graphs that are not forests.

Example 6.49 In Figure 6.13, e, f and g are bridges, but none of the other edges are.

Fig. 6.13 Bridges

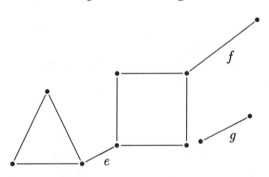

Theorem 6.12 states that every edge in a tree is a bridge.

- **Exercise 6.50** Show that a graph is acyclic *if and only if* each of its edges is a bridge.

- **Exercise 6.51** Show that a connected graph is a tree if and only if each of its edges is a bridge.

- **Exercise 6.52** Find all of the non-isomorphic trees on 7 vertices.

- **Exercise 6.53** Show that every tree with at least two vertices is a bipartite graph.

- **Exercise 6.54** When is $K_{m,n}$ a tree, for $m, n \geqslant 1$?

- **Exercise 6.55** Show that a tree has at most two centres.

6.12   Spanning trees and forests

We have seen that in a sense a tree is a minimal connected graph, so it would seem likely that any connected graph would contain a tree. This result is trivial, since a tree might consist of a single vertex and no edges, and any graph contains such a tree as a subgraph. We must also demand that the tree should have the same vertex set as the original graph.

Definition Let $G = (V, E)$ be a connected graph, and let $T = (V, E')$ be a tree with the same vertex set V as that of G. Then T is called a **spanning tree** for the graph G.

There is also a similar definition which applies to disconnected graphs.

Definition Let $G = (V, E)$ be a graph, and let $F = (V, E')$ be a forest with the same vertex set V as that of G, and such that each tree of F is a spanning tree for one of the connected components of G. Then F is called a **spanning forest** for the graph G.

This definition has to be more complicated to exclude $(V, \emptyset)$ from being a spanning forest of any graph $G = (V, E)$.

To construct a spanning tree for a connected graph, we keep removing edges from it until it is acyclic, subject to never disconnecting it.

Theorem 6.13 Any connected graph G possesses a spanning tree.

Proof If $G = (V, E)$ is acyclic, then it is a tree itself, so we take $T = G$. Thus, suppose that G contains cycles. Consider all connected subgraphs $G' = (V, E')$ of G. The graph G is such a subgraph itself. Choose a subgraph T with $|E'|$ as small as possible. By assumption, T is connected, so it will be a spanning tree if it is acyclic. Assume that T contains a cycle $v_1 v_2 \cdots v_{n-1} v_n$ with $v_1 = v_n$, and $n \geqslant 4$. Put $e = v_2 v_1$.

Suppose we form the graph $T - e$. Then $V(T - e) = V$, and $T - e$ is connected. For, if $u, v \in V$ then there exists a path in T from u to v, say $w_1 w_2 \cdots w_{m-1} w_m$, where $w_1 = u$ and $w_m = v$. If e is not used in this path then u and v are still connected in $T - e$. On the other hand, if $w_k = v_2$ and $w_{k+1} = v_1 = v_n$, with $1 \leqslant k \leqslant m$, then the walk

$$w_1 w_2 \cdots w_{k-1} v_2 v_3 \cdots v_{n-1} v_n w_{k+2} w_{k+3} \cdots w_{m-1} w_m$$

lies in $T - e$, so u and v are still connected in $T - e$. A similar argument also applies if $w_k = v_1$ and $w_{k+1} = v_2$. We thus arrive at a contradiction if we assume that T contains a cycle, so T is the desired spanning tree.   □

This algorithm for finding a spanning tree by searching for cycles and deleting edges will be considerably improved upon in Chapter 7.

Fig. 6.14 A graph...

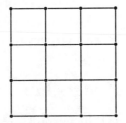

Example 6.56 The graph of Figure 6.14 has a spanning tree as in Figure 6.15.

Fig. 6.15 ...and a spanning tree

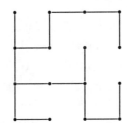

●**Exercise 6.57** Show that any graph has a spanning forest.

Any edge of a connected graph not in a given spanning tree provides a second path between its endpoints, in addition to the unique path within the spanning tree. These two paths determine a simple cycle called the *fundamental cycle* of that edge.

Theorem 6.14 Let $G = (V, E)$ be a connected graph, and let $T = (V, E')$ be a spanning tree of G. Suppose $e \in E \setminus E'$. Then $T + e$ contains a unique cycle, which is simple.

Proof Suppose $e = uv$. The graph $T + e$ contains two distinct paths from u to v, and these paths thus determine a simple cycle in $T + e$, by Theorem 6.5.

The only thing we need to check is that this cycle is unique. Thus, suppose that $T+e$ contains two different cycles C_1 and C_2. Then e must lie on both C_1 and C_2, since otherwise T contains a cycle, which gives a contradiction. The remaining edges of C_1 and C_2 thus determine two paths in T from u to v, and by Theorem 6.5, T contains a cycle, another contradiction. Two different cycles can thus never exist. $\square$

Definition Let T be a spanning tree of the connected graph G, and let $e \in E(G) \setminus E(T)$. The unique cycle in $T + e$ is called the **fundamental cycle** of e with respect to T.

6.13   The number of edges in a tree

The reader who has examined the examples of trees we have seen so far will no doubt have spotted a relationship between the number of edges and vertices in a tree—that $|E| = |V| - 1$. This fact provides us with a simple numerical characterization of trees.

Theorem 6.15 Let $G = (V, E)$ be a connected graph. Then G is a tree if and only if $|E| = |V| - 1$.

Proof We first show that a tree $T = (V, E)$ has this property. Our proof will be an induction on the number $|V|$ of vertices of T.

If $|V| = 1$, then T can have no edges, so the result is trivial.

Suppose the result is true for all trees with n or fewer vertices, for some $n \geqslant 0$, and suppose $|V| = n + 1$. Since the tree T is connected, it follows that E must be nonempty, so choose any edge $e = uv \in E$. Put $G' = T - e$. By Theorem 6.12, G' is disconnected and has two components. Let these two components be $G_1 = (V_1, E_1)$ and $G_2 = (V_2, E_2)$. Then G_1 and G_2 are connected and acyclic, so are both trees. Also, $|V_1|, |V_2| \geqslant 1$, so $|V_1|, |V_2| \leqslant n$, because $|V_1| + |V_2| = |V| = n + 1$. We can therefore use the inductive hypothesis to deduce that $|E_1| = |V_1| - 1$ and $|E_2| = |V_2| - 1$. Finally, as $E = E_1 \cup E_2 \cup \{\, e\, \}$, we conclude that
$$|E| = |E_1| + |E_2| + 1 = (|V_1| - 1) + (|V_2| - 1) + 1 = |V_1| + |V_2| - 1 = |V| - 1$$
as required. Thus the result is true when $|E| = n + 1$, and so, by induction on n, it is true for all trees.

The converse result is that if $G = (V, E)$ is connected and $|E| = |V| - 1$, then G is a tree. By Theorem 6.13, G contains a spanning tree

$T = (V, E')$, with $E' \subseteq E$, and with $|E'| = |V| - 1$, so
$$|V| - 1 = |E| \geqslant |E'| = |V| - 1,$$
forcing $E' = E$. This means that G and T are identical, so G is a tree, as required. □

The 'divide and conquer' technique used above is a powerful tool to use in other applications. It should also be noted that the form of induction used is of the most general kind, from all integers up to and including n, to $n + 1$.

●*Exercise 6.58* Find the sum of the degrees of the vertices of a tree with n vertices, as a function of n.

●*Exercise 6.59* Show that a tree with $n \geqslant 2$ vertices always has a pendant vertex.

●*Exercise 6.60* Modify the above proof so that its inductive step goes from n to $n + 1$ directly.

Our result also leads us to a condition for a forest to be a tree.

Corollary 6.16 A forest $G = (V, E)$ is a tree if and only if $|E| = |V| - 1$.

Proof Suppose that G has r connected components $G_i = (V_i, E_i)$, $1 \leqslant i \leqslant r$. Each component is a tree, and so $|E_i| = |V_i| - 1$, and
$$|E| = \sum_{i=1}^{r} |E_i| = \sum_{i=1}^{r} (|V_i| - 1) = \left(\sum_{i=1}^{r} |V_i| \right) - r = |V| - r,$$
which equals $|V| - 1$ if and only if $r = 1$. □

●*Exercise 6.61* Find a spanning tree for each of the graphs in Exercise 6.3.

●*Exercise 6.62* The tree T has 250 edges. Removal of a certain edge e from T splits T into two disjoint trees T' and T'' such that the number of vertices in T' equals the number of edges in T''. How many vertices and edges do T' and T'' have?

●*Exercise 6.63* Let T be a tree with $n > 1$ vertices. Let d_k denote the number of vertices of T with degree k. Suppose that for all $k > 3$ we have $d_k = 0$. Show that $d_1 = d_3 + 2$. Give an example of such a tree.

6.14   Graph colouring

There is a certain type of scheduling problem which leads to the concept
of a *colouring* of the vertices of a graph.

Example 6.64 It is required to produce a weekly lecturing
timetable for a set of students doing final year options. The students have each chosen a combination of courses which they wish to
pursue, and the timetable must ensure that there are no clashes.
There are also constraints from the fact that lecturers cannot give
two different lectures at the same time, but otherwise we assume
there are no other restrictions.

The model we build is as follows. We regard the lectures as vertices of a
graph, and join two lectures by an edge if they clash with one another,
because either some student wishes to take both, or a lecturer gives
both. We want to put a time at each vertex so that no two *adjacent*
vertices are marked with the same time.

The abstraction we build from this Example is to regard the times
as *colours*.

Definition Let $G = (V, E)$ be a graph, and let C be a finite set,
called the set of **colours**. A **colouring** of G is a mapping $c : V \to C$
such that if $uv \in E$ then $c(u) \neq c(v)$.

Another context in which this idea arises is the following.

Example 6.65 A map is given, and it is required to colour the
regions of this map so that no two adjacent regions are the same
colour. Here the translation is immediate. Each region is represented
by a vertex, and physical adjacency translates directly into graphical
adjacency.

Example 6.66 Figure 6.16 represents a colouring of a graph using
colours a, b, c and d.

•*Exercise 6.67* Explain why the preceding colouring uses as few
colours as possible.

If we want to schedule lectures in the least possible number of times,
then we must colour our graph with as few colours as possible.

Definition The **chromatic number** $\chi(G)$ of a graph G is the least
number of colours needed to colour its vertices.

Fig. 6.16 Graph colouring

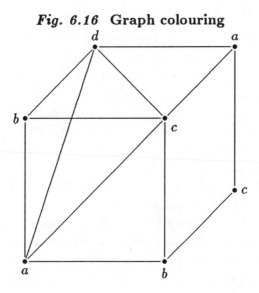

•*Exercise 6.68* Show that $\chi(K_n) = n$ and $\chi(K_{m,n}) = 2$ for all $m, n \geqslant 1$.

A result that is easy to prove, but not necessarily optimal, is the following.

Theorem 6.17 Let $G = (V, E)$ be a graph, and put $\Delta = \Delta(G) = \max_{v \in V} \deg v$. Then $\chi(G) \leqslant \Delta + 1$.

Proof Put $C = \{1, 2, \ldots, \Delta + 1\}$. We shall colour G using C. Arrange the vertices $V = \{v_1, \ldots, v_n\}$ in any order, and successively colour them with the smallest colour that does not lead to a clash. When we get to v_k we might find that it is joined to p vertices which have been coloured, with $p \leqslant \Delta$. At most p colours are thus excluded for this vertex. There will be at least one colour left to colour v_k with, since we have $\Delta + 1 > p$ colours to work with. □

In Chapter 7 we shall implement this result.

•*Exercise 6.69* Suppose that G is connected and *not* regular, and has maximum vertex degree $\Delta(G) = \Delta$. Show that $\chi(G) \leqslant \Delta$. Show that this result need not be true for regular graphs.

6.15   Directed graphs or digraphs

Most of this chapter has been concerned with undirected graphs. For some applications we need to assume that there is a direction associated with each edge. We saw many instances of this in Chapter 4, where there is an asymmetry in a binary relation.

When we redefine a graph so that each edge is directed, what we obtain is just a binary relation on the vertex set, so we are expert in the properties of directed graphs. The only thing that might be new in the rest of this chapter is that we shall define a few terms to be consistent with the terminology of undirected graphs. For instance, the concept of a walk in a directed graph was hardly touched upon in Chapter 4, except as a means of defining the transitive closure. Paths, cycles and distances were not mentioned, because we were interested there in particular types of problems, and these concepts were not relevant. If we are traversing a one-way street network in a city, paths (getting there without any pointless detours) and distances (how long does it take to get there) become more important in our thoughts than transitive closures (it is possible to get there)! Thus it *is* worth revisiting the territory of binary relations, if we can add a new insight into the same mathematical structure.

> **Definition** Let V be a finite set, and let E be a subset of $V^2 = V \times V$. The combination of V and E is said to be a **directed graph** or **digraph**, with **vertex** set V and **edge** set E. We write this graph as $G = (V, E)$.

The only thing we have changed in the definition is that V_2 has become V^2. This is the only difference between directed and undirected graphs.

The notations $V(G)$ and $E(G)$ are used for directed graphs as for undirected graphs. Similarly, we draw a directed graph in the same way as an undirected graph, except that we put an arrow on each edge, so that if $e = (a, b)$ is the edge, the arrow points from a to b. We also use ab to represent the edge (a, b). A new possibility now arises, since it is possible that both ab and ba are edges of G. In that case, we either draw two separate lines, one with an arrow from a to b, and the other from b to a, or we draw one line with both arrows on it. The latter is the practice we shall follow here. It can also happen that $a = b$, when we need an arrow from a to a, looping back on itself. Such an edge aa

is called a *loop*.

Fig. 6.17 A directed graph

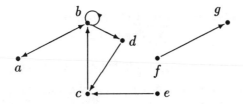

Example 6.70 Figure 6.17 represents the directed graph with vertex set $\{\, a, b, c, d, e, f, g \,\}$ and edge set
$$\{\, ab, ba, bb, bd, dc, cb, ec, fg \,\}.$$

Our intention in this section is merely to indicate what differences there are between the definitions for directed and undirected graphs. The following is a case in point.

Definition Let $G = (V, E)$ be a digraph. We say that u is **adjacent to** v, or v is **adjacent from** u, if $e = (u, v) \in E$. We also say that e is **incident from** u and **incident to** v.

The main complication is that the definitions are not symmetric. In Figure 6.17, b is adjacent to d, but d is not adjacent to b. The edge bd is incident from b to d.

The *adjacency matrix* and *incidence matrix* are defined in the same way as for an undirected graph, except that the incidence matrix must specify the direction of an edge. This is done by inserting $+1$ for the vertex the edge is incident to, and -1 for the vertex the edge is incident from. This leaves the problem of trying to work out what to do for a loop! Well, one answer is just to insert $+1$.

• **Exercise 6.71** Find the
(i)   adjacency,   (ii)   incidence
tables of the digraph in Figure 6.17.

The concepts of an *isomorphism* and a *subgraph* are the same as for undirected graphs. However, we need to make some changes to the definition of vertex degrees.

Definition Let v be a vertex of the digraph $G = (V, E)$. The **indegree** of v is defined as the number of edges incident to v, and the **outdegree** is the number of edges incident from v:

$$\text{indeg}\, v = |\{\, u \in V : uv \in E \,\}|, \quad \text{outdeg}\, v = |\{\, u \in V : vu \in E \,\}|.$$

We notice that a loop vv counts once in both degrees.

• **Exercise 6.72** In an undirected graph, we have

$$\sum_{v \in V} \deg v = 2|E|.$$

What is the corresponding result for a directed graph?

A *complete* digraph is one in which every conceivable edge is present, but the notion is of little importance, as is that of regularity.

• **Exercise 6.73** How many edges does a complete digraph with n vertices have?

One new notion which does have some importance is that of a *tournament*.

Example 6.74 Consider a tournament where n contestants each compete with one another in all of the $n(n-1)/2$ possible pairs. Regard the contestants as the vertices of a graph, and draw an edge from i to j if contestant i beats contestant j.

Our definition is based on *directing* the edges of an undirected complete graph K_n.

Definition Let $G = (V, E)$ be a complete undirected graph. Form a digraph $G' = (V, E')$ from G, by replacing each edge $\{\, u, v \,\} \in E$ by either (u, v) or (v, u), but not both. Then G' is said to be a **tournament**.

That a tournament does not define a *total order* corresponds to the well known but oft ignored fact that the type of tournament described above does not unambiguously determine a *winner*.

Provided we respect the directions on edges, the definitions of a *walk*, *trail* and *path* are the same as for an undirected graph, but for a trail, we must note that if uv and vu are both edges of the graph, then a trail can use both uv and vu. It must not use either more than once. Also, a loop is not permitted in a path.

Any directed walk contains a directed path, and the proof follows the same lines. We can also define *directed cycles* in a digraph, and show that a directed cycle contains a directed simple cycle. A digraph is *acyclic* if it contains no directed cycles. We should note that a, ab, b, ba, a counts as a directed cycle, so cycles can be based on just two vertices in digraphs, unlike the situation in undirected graphs.

> • *Exercise 6.75* If G is a tournament, show that there is a directed path in G which includes every vertex of G.

Trees and forests are not studied in directed graphs, except in that they exist in the underlying undirected graph.

> • *Exercise 6.76* An *isomorphism* of directed graphs is defined in the same way as for undirected graphs, namely a bijection $\phi : V_1 \to V_2$ which is such that $uv \in E_1 \iff \phi(u)\phi(v) \in E_2$. Find all non-isomorphic tournaments on two, three and four vertices.

6.16   Strong components

We see how it is possible to define a path in a digraph from u to v. Given such a path, there is no guarantee that there will be a path from v to u as well. The equivalence relation that decomposed an undirected graph into connected components fails to be symmetric in a digraph. There are two ways round this problem. The first is to look at the underlying undirected graph of our digraph, and define the components there. This is the same as taking the reflexive, symmetric, transitive closure of the relation defining the digraph. The second is to look at the symmetric relationship which exists in the digraph, of *mutual reachability*.

> **Definition** Let G be a digraph, and let $u, v \in V(G)$. We say that v is **reachable** from u if there exists a path from u to v in G. We say that u and v are **mutually reachable** from one another, or are **strongly connected**, if there exists a path from u to v and also a path from v to u in G.

> **Example 6.77** In Figure 6.17, a and c are mutually reachable from one another, because $abdc$ and cba are paths in either direction. Although a is reachable from e, via the path $ecba$, e is not reachable from a.

If $G = (V, E)$ is a digraph, define the binary relation $\diamond$ on V to be that of mutual reachability. As in the undirected case, $\diamond$ is an equivalence relation, and V is partitioned into equivalence classes by $\diamond$.

Definition The **strong components** of a digraph are the equivalence classes of vertices under the binary relation of being mutually reachable. If there is just one component, then the digraph is said to be **strongly connected**.

Example 6.78 The strong components of Figure 6.17 are
$$\{\,a,b,c,d\,\}, \qquad \{\,e\,\}, \qquad \{\,f\,\}, \qquad \{\,g\,\}.$$

• *Exercise 6.79* Find the strong components of the digraphs in Figure 6.18.

Fig. 6.18 Distances in directed graphs

(i)

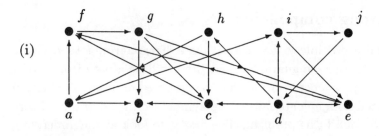

(ii)

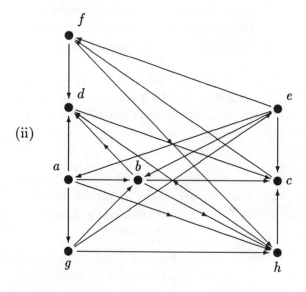

• **Exercise 6.80** Is it possible to form tournaments on n vertices which are:
(i)   acyclic;   (ii)   strongly connected?

• **Exercise 6.81** Show that a directed graph is strongly connected if and only if it has a closed walk which visits every vertex. Exhibit a strongly connected graph which does not have a closed path visiting every vertex.

• **Exercise 6.82** Tabulate the distances between each pair of vertices in the directed graphs defined in Figure 6.18.

It is clear that the strong components always form a further subdivision of the connected components of the underlying undirected graph. We call this a *refinement* of a partition. The sort of situation in which the strong components are important is exemplified by the following.

Example 6.83 We have some sort of process which can be in one of a finite number of states $S_1, \ldots, S_n$. Perhaps these are the states a certain calculation could be in, or the line of a certain program which is currently being executed, or the binary state of a computer carrying out a calculation. Anyway, whichever interpretation we take, we know that transitions can occur at sporadic intervals from one state to another. A calculation progresses, or a program branches, or the timer in a computer ticks on, and a register in the processor is loaded.

We can draw a digraph in which the states are the vertices, and the possible transitions are the edges. We can designate one state as the initial state, and one or more other states as the final states, and then put our program or computer into its initial state, and watch it progress. We can see that we require the final state(s) to be reachable from the initial state, else the calculation will never terminate.

There is something else we should watch for as well. Suppose that our digraph possesses a strong component which does not contain a final vertex, and such that no final vertex is reachable from that strong component. The calculation can get stuck in an infinite loop, which it will never leave.

In general, there is a partial ordering of strong components, determined by whether one component is reachable from another. A calculation will progress, either within one strong component, where it might loop forever, or from one strong component to another, in an irreversible transition. Analysis of these components, and of the transitions within and between them, is one step towards verifying that a computation will terminate correctly.

7

Graph algorithms

7.1 Introduction

In this chapter, we will be putting the results we proved in Chapter 6 to work. We will develop algorithms to solve a variety of optimization problems, all important in their own right.

The first is to minimize the cost of a network joining together several nodes. This can always be achieved by using what is called a 'greedy algorithm'.

Another problem is to find the distance between any two nodes along a given network, say a road network. Two simple iterative algorithms exist for this problem. A related problem is to find the path of *longest* length between two vertices of an acyclic directed graph. This arises in certain types of sequencing problems, where the edges represent elapsed times. We shall see that one of our algorithms for shortest paths can easily be adapted to solve this problem.

A different type of problem is exemplified by the construction of a timetable, given simple compatibility constraints. We can model this by colouring the vertices of a graph, but the best we can achieve is a heuristic algorithm, not optimal but just reasonably efficient.

We should note that Warshall's algorithm can also be interpreted as a graphical algorithm to calculate strong components, but that was treated when we studied transitive closures.

Implementations of these algorithms in *Modula-2* can be found in the appendices.

7.2 Kruskal's minimal spanning tree algorithm

Let us recall a result from Chapter 6, namely, that every connected graph possesses a spanning tree. We showed that this tree could be constructed by removing edges from the graph until no cycles remained, and the resulting acyclic graph would then be a spanning tree.

There are certain circumstances in which we require a spanning tree which is *optimal* in some sense. There is usually a *cost* or *weight* associated with each edge in the graph, and we wish to minimize this cost over all possible spanning trees.

Example 7.1 The University of Networkham wishes to link its 30 computer sites together. It has calculated the cost of linking any two sites together, and this information is stored in a file with 435 lines, each line containing two site numbers and a cost. It can complete its network by choosing 29 of those links, but which 29?

Example 7.2 The kingdom of Outgland has decided that it can no longer afford to maintain all of its road network. It still wishes to link the 50 main cities of the kingdom by retaining improved links between them. The other roads will just have to degenerate. Anyone who wishes to travel from Entiter to Kidneypool will have to travel via Lags and Shower if there is no other route, and there probably will be no other route, because the bureaucrats have costed the improvement of every section of road in the kingdom, and are intent upon minimizing their total costs.

The criterion for deciding between two spanning trees need not be a real cost in pounds or dollars; it could be any numerical quantity at all, such as lengths of wire or tons of cement.

Definition Let S be a set. A **cost** or **weight** function on S is a mapping $w : S \to \mathbb{R}$. A **length** function is a weight function the range of which is a subset of $\mathbb{R}^+$, the set of non-negative reals. The cost, length or weight of any subset $U \subseteq S$ is defined as

$$w(U) = \sum_{x \in U} w(x),$$

where $w(\emptyset) = 0$ by convention.

Notice that we have bent the rules a bit in defining $w(U)$. Really, what we should be doing is defining a new weight function $w'(U)$ defined on the power set $\mathcal{P}(S)$ of S. There is no chance of confusion in our notation, since if the argument of w is an element of S, we mean the initial weight function, and if it is a subset of S we mean the derived function w'.

The weight function we are interested in is defined on the edges of an undirected graph.

Definition Let $G = (V, E)$ be a connected graph, and let $w : E \to \mathbb{R}$ be a weight function on E. A **minimal spanning tree** is a spanning tree of G such that the weight of its edge set is minimal.

Since a graph is finite, and so possesses only finitely many spanning trees, an exhaustive search of all those trees would reveal the optimal solution to our problem. For the graph K_{10}, there are 45 edges, and a spanning tree would have 9 edges. Thus the possible candidates for a spanning tree would number $\binom{45}{9} = 886{,}163{,}135$. Each of these would have to be examined to see if it is a tree!

An exhaustive search, even for a modest number of vertices, is thus out of the question. Fortunately, there is an algorithm which will find a minimal spanning tree in a reasonable time. This is *Kruskal's algorithm*. In outline, the algorithm is very simple. We first sort the edges into ascending order of weight. It is well known that the optimal time required for sorting n objects is of order $n \log n$. Even a naïve sorting algorithm would not take much more than $n^2/2$ units of time. We could find the smallest object in time n, by examining every object. This could be swapped to the front of the list, and then the second largest object could be found in time $n - 1$, and so on, giving a running time of

$$n + (n - 1) + (n - 2) + \cdots + 2 = \frac{1}{2}(n - 1)(n + 2) \approx \frac{1}{2}n^2.$$

After the edges have been sorted, we run through the list of edges, and we include an edge in the tree we are constructing if and only if its addition to the edges previously selected does not produce any cycles. When $|V| - 1$ edges have been selected, the tree is complete. The algorithm is given in outline in Figure 7.1.

Fig. 7.1 **Kruskal's algorithm**
Sort edges $\{e_1, \ldots, e_m\}$ **so that** $w(e_1) \leqslant w(e_2) \leqslant \cdots \leqslant w(e_m)$;
$T := (V, \varnothing)$;
$i := 0$;
REPEAT
    $i := i + 1$;
    IF $T + e_i$ **is acyclic THEN** $T := T + e_i$ **END;**
UNTIL $|E(T)| = |V(T)| - 1$;

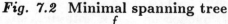

Fig. 7.2 **Minimal spanning tree**

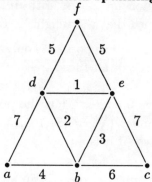

Example 7.3 Consider the graph in Figure 7.2. Our first job is to sort the edges into ascending order of weight, which is easily done, as in the first line of the following table.

Edges	de	bd	be	ab	df	ef	bc	ce	ad
Tree	✓	✓		✓	✓		✓		

We then trace along the list of edges, inserting them in the minimal spanning tree only if insertion does not produce a cycle. Thus, *de* and *bd* are inserted immediately, but *be* is then banned, since addition of *be* would result in a cycle *edbe*. Similarly, *ef* cannot be added, because then the cycle *edfe* would be formed. We stop when we have $6 - 1 = 5$ edges, because then we have an acyclic graph on 6 vertices with 5 edges, and this has to be a spanning tree. It has weight 18.

We note that if our sorting had placed *ef* ahead of *df*, then *ef* would have entered the tree. This would not have altered the weight of the constructed tree.

Having seen an Example of Kruskal's algorithm, we had better verify that it does what it is supposed to do. First, though, let us prove a property that all minimal spanning trees have.

Theorem 7.1 Let $G = (V, E)$ be a graph, and let $w : E \to \mathbb{R}$ be a weight function on E. Let $T = (V, E')$ be a minimal spanning tree, and suppose that $e \in E \setminus E'$. The fundamental cycle of e with respect to T consists of e and edges $e' \in E'$ with $w(e') \leqslant w(e)$.

Proof Otherwise, we could take $T - e' + e$ instead of T, and obtain a tree of smaller weight than T, because the net change would be $w(e) - w(e') < 0$. The fact that $T - e' + e$ is a spanning tree follows from the facts that its edges still link all the vertices of G, and it has the correct number of edges to be a tree, namely, $|V| - 1$. □

Let us define a tree as being a *Kruskal tree* if it would be possible to produce that tree by an application of Kruskal's algorithm to G. We note that there might be several Kruskal trees, since the equality of the weights of two edges would imply that there were two different sortings of the edges into ascending order of weights.

Theorem 7.2 Any Kruskal tree is a minimal spanning tree.

Proof Let $G = (V, E)$, and let $T = (V, F)$ be a Kruskal tree, with
$$F = \{ e_1, \ldots, e_n \}, \qquad w(e_1) \leqslant w(e_2) \leqslant \cdots \leqslant w(e_n).$$
Suppose that we assume that T is not minimal, so that there is a minimal spanning tree $M = (V, H)$ with $w(H) < w(F)$. Of all such possible minimal spanning trees, choose one with the maximum number of edges in common with T, that is, with $F \cap H$ as large as possible, but with $F \neq H$.

Both T and M are spanning trees on the vertex set V, so they have the same number of edges, that is, $|F| = |H|$. However, $F \neq H$, and so there exists an edge e_p with $e_p \in F$, $e_p \notin H$. Let e_p be the first such edge of T which is not in M. Thus $e_1, \ldots, e_{p-1} \in H$, but $e_p \notin H$.

Consider the fundamental cycle of e_p with respect to M. This consists of edges
$$e_p, h_1, \ldots, h_k, \qquad h_i \in H, \quad 1 \leqslant i \leqslant k.$$
By Theorem 7.1, each of $h_1, \ldots, h_k$ has weight no larger than that of e_p. We also note that $h_1, \ldots, h_k$ cannot all be edges of T, because then this fundamental cycle would be a cycle contained in the acyclic tree T. There must therefore exist an edge h_r such that $h_r \notin F$.

If $w(h_r) < w(e_p)$, then h_r should have been chosen instead of e_p when the Kruskal tree T was being constructed. After all, we know that $e_1, \ldots, e_{p-1}$ were chosen in sequence in building T, and the next choice should have been an edge of smallest possible weight which did not form a cycle with $e_1, \ldots, e_{p-1}$. The edge h_r does not form a cycle with $e_1, \ldots, e_{p-1}$, since $\{ e_1, \ldots, e_{p-1}, h_r \} \subseteq H$. Also, $w(h_r) < w(e_p)$ by assumption, so the edge e_p was chosen wrongly.

We must conclude that $w(h_r) \geqslant w(e_p)$. By Theorem 7.1, $w(h_r) \leqslant w(e_p)$, and so $w(h_r) = w(e_p)$. Modify M into $M' = M - h_r + e_p$. Then M' has the same weight as M, and so is minimal. However, M' has one extra edge e_p in common with T, and so we have a contradiction of the assumption that M and T had the maximum number of edges in common. It is thus impossible to assume that M and T are different, so T is indeed minimal! (Phew!)   □

• **Exercise 7.4** Use Kruskal's algorithm to find a minimal spanning tree for each of the graphs in Figure 7.3. Draw in your spanning tree, and state its weight.

• **Exercise 7.5** Find minimal spanning trees for the connected graphs with the following edges, where the subscript on an edge indicates its weight. What is the weight of the minimal spanning tree?

(i) ab_1, ac_3, ad_3, ag_5, bc_2, be_4, bi_2, bj_2, cf_3, cg_6, de_2, df_4, dg_1, dh_6, dj_1, ef_2, ei_1, fg_2, fh_4, fk_6, gi_6, hk_7.

(ii) ab_3, ac_2, ad_7, ae_2, bd_4, bf_8, bk_6, bl_1, cf_2, ck_5, de_1, df_6, dg_9, dh_1, dl_2, ef_1, ej_2, fg_5, fh_4, fj_3, gh_2, hi_3.

(iii) ab_3, ac_2, ad_7, ae_2, bd_4, bf_8, bk_6, bl_1, cf_2, ck_5, de_1, df_6, dg_9, dh_6, dj_1, ef_2, ei_1, fg_2, fh_4, fk_6, gi_6, hk_7.

• **Exercise 7.6** Repeat Exercise 7.5 on the following graphs.

(i) ab_5, ac_9, ad_9, ag_5, bc_2, be_8, bi_2, bj_2, cf_9, cg_6, de_2, df_8, dg_5, dh_1, dj_5, ef_2, ei_5, fg_2, fh_8, fk_1, gi_1, hk_1.

(ii) ab_9, ac_7, ad_1, ae_7, bd_8, bf_8, bk_1, bl_5, cf_7, ck_5, de_5, df_1, dg_9, dh_5, dl_7, ef_5, ej_7, fg_5, fh_4, fj_9, gh_7, hi_9.

(iii) ab_9, ac_7, ad_1, ae_7, bd_4, bf_8, bk_1, bl_5, cf_7, ck_5, de_5, df_1, dg_9, dh_6, dj_5, ef_7, ei_5, fg_7, fh_4, fk_6, gi_6, hk_1.

7.3   Prim's minimal spanning tree algorithm

There is just one thing wrong with Kruskal's algorithm. It is that apart from in very simple cases, it is difficult to determine whether the addition of an edge will create a cycle. If we cannot decide this then we cannot hope to be able to program the algorithm. There *are* ways of deciding whether a cycle will be created, relying on a way of representing the edges of G as *vectors*, and applying some matrix theory, but an easier solution exists.

What we do is to grow the minimal tree from a selected vertex, gradually linking more and more vertices to that vertex. Instead of choosing the edge with smallest possible weight which does not produce a cycle at each stage, we restrict the search only to edges with one

Fig. 7.3 **Exercises on Kruskal's algorithm**

(i)

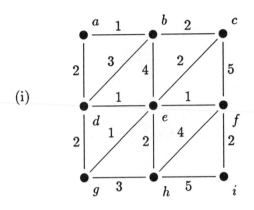

(ii)

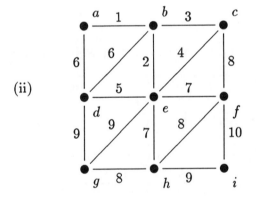

vertex amongst those already linked to the initial vertex, and the other vertex a new vertex which is about to be linked. We choose the edge of minimal weight which does this. The algorithm is known as *Prim's algorithm*, and it is described in more detail in Figure 7.4. We see that, unlike Kruskal's algorithm, Prim's algorithm contains a double loop.

Example 7.7 Let us rework the graph in Figure 7.1, but this time use Prim's algorithm. We shall find that the edges are added to the tree in a different order. This order depends on which vertex we start from. The tree grows from that vertex. Suppose we start from

Fig. 7.4 **Prim's algorithm**

Sort edges $\{e_1, \ldots, e_m\}$ **so that** $w(e_1) \leqslant w(e_2) \leqslant \cdots \leqslant$ $w(e_m)$;

Choose $w \in V$;

$T := (\{w\}, \emptyset)$;

REPEAT

   $i := 0$; *added* := *FALSE*;

   REPEAT

      $i := i + 1$;

      IF $e_i = uv$ **AND** $u \in V(T)$ **AND** $v \notin V(T)$ **THEN**

         $V(T) := V(T) \cup \{v\}$;

         $E(T) := E(T) \cup \{e_i\}$;

         added := *TRUE*;

      END;

   UNTIL *added*;

   UNTIL $V(T) = V(G)$;

vertex a. The table below indicates the order in which edges are added to the tree.

Edges	de	bd	be	ab	df	ef	bc	ce	ad
Tree	3	2		1	4		5		

If, on the other hand, we start with c, the tree grows in a different order.

Edges	de	bd	be	ab	df	ef	bc	ce	ad
Tree	3	2		4	5			1	

We see that the order of addition of the edges bears little relation to the weights on those edges, and an edge which might have been chosen very early by Kruskal's algorithm could be chosen late by Prim's algorithm.

Let us call a tree a *Prim tree* if some choice of initial vertex and order of edges could cause that tree to be produced by Prim's algorithm.

Theorem 7.3 Any Prim tree is a minimal spanning tree.

Proof Let $G = (V, E)$ and let $T = (V, F)$ be a Prim tree, with $F = \{e_1, \ldots, e_n\}$, the edges being sorted in the order in which they were selected into T. Suppose that we assume that T is not minimal, so that there is a minimal spanning tree $M = (V, H)$ with $w(H) < w(F)$. Of all such possible minimal spanning trees, choose one with the maximum number of edges in common with T, that is, with $F \cap H$ as large as possible, but with $F \neq H$.

Both T and M are spanning trees on the vertex set V, so they have the same number of edges, that is, $|F| = |H|$. However, $F \neq H$, and so there exists an edge e_p with $e_p \in F$, $e_p \notin H$. Let e_p be the first such edge of T which is not in M. Thus $e_1, \ldots, e_{p-1} \in H$, but $e_p \notin H$.

Consider the fundamental cycle of e_p with respect to M. This consists of edges

$$e_p, h_1, \ldots, h_k, \qquad h_i \in H, \quad 1 \leqslant i \leqslant k.$$

Each of $h_1, \ldots, h_k$ has weight no larger than that of e_p, by Theorem 7.1. Let X denote the vertex set of the edges $e_1, \ldots, e_{p-1}$. We know that one vertex of e_p lies in X, and the other in $V \setminus X$. Choose an edge h_r such that one of its vertices lies in X, and the other lies in $V \setminus X$.

If $w(h_r) < w(e_p)$, then h_r should have been chosen instead of e_p when the Prim tree T was being constructed. For, we know that $e_1, \ldots, e_{p-1}$ were chosen in sequence in building T, and the next choice should have been an edge of smallest possible weight which linked a new vertex into the existing tree. The edge h_r does not form a cycle with $e_1, \ldots, e_{p-1}$, since $\{ e_1, \ldots, e_{p-1}, h_r \} \subseteq H$. The connected graph with edges $\{ e_1, \ldots, e_{p-1}, h_r \}$ is thus acyclic, and so is a tree. Also, $w(h_r) < w(e_p)$ by assumption, so the edge e_p was chosen wrongly.

We must conclude that $w(h_r) \geqslant w(e_p)$. By Theorem 7.1, $w(h_r) \leqslant w(e_p)$, and so $w(h_r) = w(e_p)$. Modify M into $M' = M - h_r + e_p$. Then M' has the same weight as M, and so is minimal. However, M' has one extra edge e_p in common with T, and so we have a contradiction of the assumption that M and T had the maximum number of edges in common. It is thus impossible to assume that M and T are different, so T is indeed minimal! $\qquad \square$

Many authors regard Kruskal's and Prim's algorithms as one and the same. The first algorithm should only be used if there is an effective way of deciding whether or not a graph is acyclic. If the graph is specified as a list of cycles, then that would be a good reason for using Kruskal's algorithm.

• **Exercise 7.8** Use Prim's algorithm to find a minimal spanning tree for each of the graphs in Figure 7.3, starting from the given vertex. At each stage of the algorithm, indicate the vertices linked into the current tree, and the next edge to be added.

(i)   *e.*   (ii)   *d.*

• **Exercise 7.9** Use Prim's algorithm to solve Exercises 7.5 and 7.6.

• **Exercise 7.10** Explain how Prim's algorithm and Kruskal's algorithm may be adapted to find a *spanning tree* of a graph.

• **Exercise 7.11** Use a variant of Prim's algorithm to find the *maximal spanning tree* for each graph in Exercises 7.4 to 7.6, defined as the tree for which the sum of the weights is a *maximum*.

7.4 Dijkstra's shortest path algorithms

If the weight function on the edges of a connected graph is a length function, it would be useful to determine, for each vertex v, its distance from every other vertex, and also the path which must be traversed to attain this minimal distance.

> **Definition** Let $l : E \to \mathbb{R}$ be a length function on the edges of a connected graph $G = (V, E)$. A **shortest path** from u to v in G is a path P with edge set E', such that $l(E')$ is as small as possible.

It turns out that given a fixed vertex u, there will always exist a spanning tree T rooted at u in the graph G, such that, for any $v \in V$, there will be a minimal path in G from u to v which lies entirely in T.

> **Definition** A **rooted tree** is a tree with a distinguished vertex.

> **Example 7.12** There is a route planning map for the city of Yoik. The shortest routes to all other cities in Oingland are indicated in red on this map, and the red lines form a rooted tree on Yoik. It was felt unnecessary to give alternative routes, so there are no cycles in the graph composed of the red lines.

> **Example 7.13** The computer typesetting language TEX uses a shortest path algorithm to break each paragraph into lines so that the distance from beginning to end is as short as possible, when measured in terms of the badness of each line produced.

The definition of a shortest path can be extended easily to a directed graph in which every vertex is reachable from u. In this case, what we can say is that the underlying undirected graph of the shortest paths will form a spanning tree. We should notice that if we form paths *to* u rather than *from* u, we will generally get different results.

The first algorithm we shall present constructs the nearest vertex to u, then the second nearest, third nearest, and so on, until all the vertices have been linked to u. We shall give the algorithm for an undirected graph, but stated in such a way that it easily adapts to a directed graph.

We form a set of vertices U such that the maximum distance from u to any vertex of U is less than or equal to the minimum distance from u to any $v \notin U$. If $|U| = k$, then U consists of the k nearest vertices of G to u. Our only problem is to decide how we can progress from $|U| = k$ to $|U| = k + 1$.

To see how to solve this problem, suppose that we take a vertex $v \in V \setminus U$, and a minimal path from u to v, say $uv_1v_2v_3 \cdots v_pv$. Suppose also that v is as close to u as any other vertex of $V \setminus U$. We must conclude that if $v_i \notin U$ for some $1 \leqslant i \leqslant p$, we could have chosen v_i rather than v as the next nearest vertex to u. We must therefore assume that v is adjacent to some vertex of U, and as near to u as possible.

Fig. 7.5 Dijkstra's algorithm

$d(u) := 0$;
$d(v) := \infty$ **for all** $v \neq u$;
$U := \varnothing$;
REPEAT
   Find $v \in V \setminus U$ **with** $d(v)$ **a minimum**;
   $U := U \cup \{v\}$;
   FOR each edge $vx \in E$ **DO**
      $d(x) := \text{MIN}(d(x), d(v) + l(vx))$;
   END;
UNTIL $U = V$;

Dijkstra's algorithm is presented in Figure 7.5. We mark each vertex other than u with a *sentinel* value, notionally infinite, but in practice just a very large number. Such a vertex will never be chosen as the next nearest vertex, because the algorithm always marks at least one vertex not in U with a finite value, equal to the length of a path from u to that vertex. Generally, several vertices will be so marked, and we choose the vertex with the smallest marking as the next vertex to add to U. If this vertex is v, we update all the markings of vertices adjacent from v accordingly. The *finite* markings on vertices equal the lengths of shortest paths to those vertices, using *only* vertices of U along the path. Since the next nearest vertex will always be at the end of such a path, as we showed above, it is the vertex chosen by Dijkstra's algorithm at the next stage. The algorithm therefore correctly calculates the minimum distances.

It should be noted that the first stage of the above algorithm automatically chooses u, and marks all vertices adjacent *from* u with finite values.

If it is required to find the minimal spanning tree as well as the minimal distances, all we need do is store, with each vertex, the edge which was last used to update its value, before it entered U. This edge will be in the tree of shortest paths.

Example 7.14 We shall find the shortest paths from b to every other vertex of the graph in Figure 7.6. The markings on the vertices

Fig. 7.6 Shortest paths

```
 i        j        k        l
 •————————•————————•————————•
 |   2    |   1    |   2    |
 |        |        |        |
8|      15|       3|       6|
 |        |        |        |
 e        |        |        h
 •————————•————————•————————•
 |   3    f  18  g |   3    |
 |        |        |        |
2|       1|      15|      14|
 |        |        |        |
 •————————•————————•————————•
 a   7    b   5    c   4    d
```

are as indicated in the table in Figure 7.7. The next vertex to be added to the tree is indicated by enclosing it in a box. The following line will then indicate an updating of the markings of some of the vertices adjacent to that vertex.

The final tree of shortest paths is indicated in Figure 7.8.

•**Exercise 7.15** In each of the graphs in Figure 7.9, find the distance of each vertex from the distinguished one by means of Dijkstra's algorithm. Mark each vertex with the distance from the distinguished vertex.

•**Exercise 7.16** Suppose that in the following, the number next to each edge refers to its length. Find the distance of each vertex from a.

Fig. 7.7 Successive markings in Dijkstra's algorithm

a	b	c	d	e	f	g	h	i	j	k	l
∞	[0]	∞	∞	∞	∞	∞	∞	∞	∞	∞	∞
7	0	5	∞	∞	[1]	∞	∞	∞	∞	∞	∞
7	0	5	∞	[4]	1	19	∞	∞	16	∞	∞
6	0	[5]	∞	4	1	19	∞	12	16	∞	∞
[6]	0	5	9	4	1	19	∞	12	16	∞	∞
6	0	5	[9]	4	1	19	∞	12	16	∞	∞
6	0	5	9	4	1	19	23	[12]	16	∞	∞
6	0	5	9	4	1	19	23	12	[14]	∞	∞
6	0	5	9	4	1	19	23	12	14	[15]	∞
6	0	5	9	4	1	18	23	12	14	15	[17]
6	0	5	9	4	1	[18]	23	12	14	15	17
6	0	5	9	4	1	18	[21]	12	14	15	17

Fig. 7.8 The tree

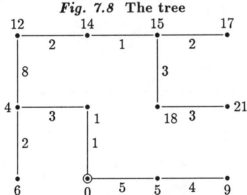

(i) ab_5, ac_3, ae_2, ag_1, bc_2, be_6, bi_2, bj_1, cf_2, cg_1, de_4, df_7, dg_3, dh_2, dj_4, ef_5, ei_6, fg_2, fh_1, fk_2, gi_7, hk_6.

(ii) ab_2, ac_1, ad_1, ae_3, bd_5, bf_8, bk_5, bl_3, cf_9, ck_1, de_5, df_2, dg_8, dh_2, dl_4, ef_5, ej_1, fg_9, fh_7, fj_7, gh_4, hi_3, hk_1, hl_3, ij_2, il_1, jk_1, jl_2, kl_1.

(iii) ab_1, ac_3, ad_2, ae_4, bd_5, bf_6, bk_7, bl_8, cf_9, ck_8, de_7, df_6, dg_4, dh_5, dj_2, ef_4, ei_2, fg_1, fh_3, fk_5, gi_7, hk_9, hl_1, ij_8, ik_2, jk_2, jl_1, kl_3.

•*Exercise 7.17* Repeat Exercise 7.16, but with each of the other vertices as base point; this gives over 30 problems to tackle!

Fig. 7.9 Exercises on Dijkstra's algorithm

(i)

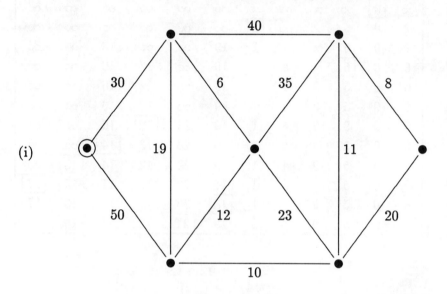

(ii)

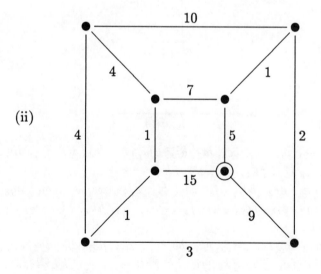

• **Exercise 7.18** Rework Exercise 7.16, but this time regard the edges as *directed*. Find minimal routes from a to every other accessible vertex.

Fig. 7.10 Dijkstra's algorithm—iterative form

$d(u) := 0;$

$d(v) := \infty$ for all $v \neq u;$

REPEAT

  $finished := TRUE;$

  FOR each edge $vx \in E$ **DO**

    IF $d(x) > d(v) + l(vx)$ **THEN**

      $d(x) := d(v) + l(vx);$

      $finished := FALSE;$

    END;

  END;

UNTIL $finished;$

There is a second, iterative form of Dijkstra's algorithm, which works by marking every vertex with a number at least as large as the correct marking, and then gradually reducing these markings to the correct values. It is represented in Figure 7.10. Generally, the edges will be scanned in a fixed order, to see if any of them force an update of a marking. Any edge may cause one of its endpoints to be updated on several occasions as the algorithm progresses. However, we can easily see that after one scan of the edges, the nearest vertex will have been marked correctly, and after two scans the second nearest will have been marked correctly, and so on, so that the repeat loop will only be executed a maximum of $|V| - 1$ times.

Example 7.19 Let us rework the graph in Figure 7.6, using the iterative form of the algorithm. The edges will be scanned in order of increasing length, namely, in order

$jk, bf, ae, ij, kl, gh, ef, gk, cd, bc, hl, ab, ei, dh, cg, fj, fg.$

Initially, all vertices are marked with ∞ apart from b, which is marked with 0, as in Figure 7.11. On the first scan, we have the following updates:

• $d(f) := d(b) + l(bf) = 0 + 1 = 1;$

Fig. 7.11 Minimal path by Dijkstra's iterative algorithm

a	b	c	d	e	f	g	h	i	j	k	l
∞	0	∞	∞	∞	∞	∞	∞	∞	∞	∞	∞
7	0	5	∞	4	1	19	∞	12	16	∞	∞
6	0	5	9	4	1	19	22	12	14	17	19
6	0	5	9	4	1	18	22	12	14	15	17
6	0	5	9	4	1	18	21	12	14	15	17

- $d(e) := d(f) + l(fe) = 1 + 3 = 4;$
- $d(c) := d(b) + l(bc) = 0 + 5 = 5;$
- $d(a) := d(b) + l(ba) = 0 + 7 = 7;$
- $d(i) := d(e) + l(ei) = 4 + 8 = 12;$
- $d(g) := d(c) + l(cg) = 5 + 15 = 20;$
- $d(j) := d(f) + l(fj) = 1 + 15 = 16;$
- $d(g) := d(f) + l(fg) = 1 + 18 = 19.$

The second scan updates vertices as follows:

- $d(k) := d(j) + l(jk) = 16 + 1 = 17;$
- $d(a) := d(e) + l(ea) = 4 + 2 = 6;$
- $d(j) := d(i) + l(ij) = 12 + 2 = 14;$
- $d(l) := d(k) + l(kl) = 17 + 2 = 19;$
- $d(h) := d(g) + l(gh) = 19 + 3 = 22;$
- $d(d) := d(c) + l(cd) = 5 + 4 = 9.$

We notice that the value $d(j) = 16$ is used before it is updated to 14 two steps further on. The third scan gives:

- $d(k) := d(j) + l(jk) = 14 + 1 = 15;$
- $d(l) := d(k) + l(kl) = 15 + 2 = 17;$
- $d(g) := d(k) + l(kg) = 15 + 3 = 18.$

The fourth scan updates h using the new value of $d(g)$, and the fifth scan produces no changes, and so the algorithm is finished.

●**Exercise 7.20** Rework Exercise 7.16 and its successors using the second form of Dijkstra's algorithm.

7.5   Dijkstra's longest path algorithm

There is a type of scheduling problem which gives rise to a directed graph in which we require the longest path between two vertices.

Example 7.21 A computer has to carry out the following computations:

```
a:=1.0;    b:=SIN(2.0);    c:=EXP(3.0);
a:=2.0*a+3.0*b;    c:=b+c;    a:=a-b+c;
```

If the computer is sequential, there is no problem, but if it can operate concurrently, we see that there is a natural directed graph associated with the computations. We can represent each assignment by a vertex, drawing an edge from v to w if assignment v must precede assignment w. The graph is as in Figure 7.12, where we have added extra vertices S and F to mark the start and finish of the computations. The number against each edge represents the time taken for

Fig. 7.12 Parallel computations

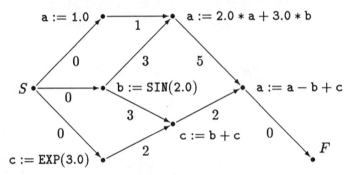

the computation at the beginning of the edge.

It is clear that the delay between S and F must be at least 8 units of time, and this number represents the longest path which can be drawn from S to F.

It is perhaps surprising that the first form of Dijkstra's shortest path algorithm is not adaptable to longest paths. We cannot find the most distant vertex from a given vertex u by examining only those vertices adjacent to u. The iterative form does work, and is presented in Figure 7.13. We should be careful to verify that there really is a solution to the problem of finding a longest path. This will be the case if every vertex is reachable from u, and also the graph is acyclic. Without the acyclic condition, there might be walks of arbitrary length in the graph, but the condition is really a reflection of the condition of consistency of the prerequisites of a scheduling problem. We should also ignore edges incident *to* the initial vertex u.

Fig. 7.13 Dijkstra's longest path algorithm
$d(v) := 0$ for all v;
REPEAT
  finished := *TRUE*;
  FOR each edge $vx \in E$ **with** $x \neq u$ **DO**
    IF $d(x) < d(v) + l(vx)$ **THEN**
      $d(x) := d(v) + l(vx)$;
      finished := *FALSE*;
    END;
  END;
UNTIL *finished*;

Example 7.22 Consider the graph in Figure 7.14. We are trying to find longest paths from the vertex b. The edges have been sorted into

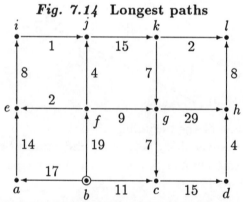

Fig. 7.14 Longest paths

descending order of length, although this is not absolutely necessary:
$$gh, bf, ba, cd, jk, ae, bc, fg, hl, ei, kg, gc, fj, dh, fe, kl, ij.$$
Figure 7.15 shows the progress of the labelling of the vertices. The algorithm works in a similar way to the shortest path version, so there is no need to go into this labelling in great detail. The first phase of relabelling starts:

- $d(h) := d(g) + l(gh) = 0 + 29 = 29$;
- $d(f) := d(b) + l(bf) = 0 + 19 = 19$;
- $d(a) := d(b) + l(ba) = 0 + 17 = 17$;

$\vdots$

Fig. 7.15 Longest paths by Dijkstra's algorithm

a	b	c	d	e	f	g	h	i	j	k	l
0	0	0	0	0	0	0	0	0	0	0	0
17	0	35	15	31	19	28	29	39	40	15	37
17	0	69	50	31	19	62	57	39	40	55	65
17	0	69	84	31	19	62	91	39	40	55	99

- $d(j) := d(i) + l(ij) = 39 + 1 = 40.$

We again see a tree structure representing the longest paths out of b, as seen in Figure 7.16. In this tree, for any vertex v, there is a unique

Fig. 7.16 Longest paths forming a tree

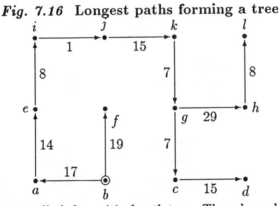

path from b to v, called the *critical path* to v. The edges along this path determine the length of the critical path—99 in the case of vertex l— and any attempt to reduce this longest path must concentrate on these edges. In Figure 7.12, if we want to reduce the running time of our calculation, there is no point in concentrating on making the calculation of the exponential function more efficient.

- **Exercise 7.23** In the directed, acyclic graph of Figure 7.17, each directed edge represents a process, and the number against it represents the time in μseconds that the process needs. At any vertex, all processes entering the vertex must terminate before any process leaving the vertex can start, but otherwise processes can run concurrently. The vertices S and F represent the start and finish of the computations respectively. How long will it take for the whole computation to run to completion? Mark each vertex with the time at which processes leaving that vertex can commence, assuming that S is labelled 0.

Fig. 7.17 A critical path problem

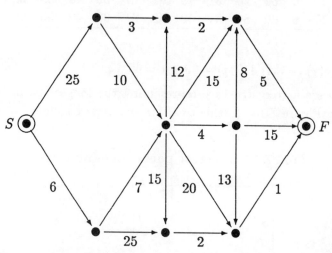

• **Exercise 7.24** Using the edges in Exercise 7.16, now regarded as directed edges, and starting with vertex a at time zero, mark every other vertex with an earliest possible time. The edge xy_n represents the fact that the time at y must be at least n more than the time at x.

• **Exercise 7.25** Solve the following problems, the context being as in the last Exercise.

(i) ab_2, ad_7, af_4, ah_6, bd_4, bf_9, bi_1, bk_3, cd_3, ce_4, de_5, df_2, dg_8, di_5, dl_6, eg_3, eh_4, fg_3, fh_6, fl_2, gh_4, ik_6.

(ii) ab_3, ac_2, ad_6, ag_3, bc_7, bd_4, bi_8, bm_2, cf_9, cl_8, cm_2, de_8, df_3, dj_4, dk_2, eg_4, ei_3, fg_2, fh_8, fm_4, gk_4, hj_2, hk_4, hl_5, hm_5, ik_3, jk_4, jl_3, kl_4, lm_6.

(iii) ab_1, ac_3, ad_2, ae_4, af_7, ag_9, ah_2, ai_3, aj_4, ak_7, al_{10}, be_3, bg_8, bh_3, bl_3, cd_9, cf_8, de_9, df_2, dg_8, dh_7, di_5, eh_6, ei_3, fg_6, fi_9, fj_7, gh_8, hk_2, hi_4, ij_8, ik_4, jk_6, jl_8, kl_9.

7.6 Vertex colouring

We saw in Chapter 6 that we can colour the vertices of a graph by sorting the vertices, and then colouring each vertex with the first available colour, taking account of the colours used to colour previous vertices. We only need decide which order to put the vertices in. One option is to order them in descending order of vertex degrees. This gives the algorithm in Figure 7.18. Of course, the given sorting is not essential to the

Fig. 7.18 **Graph colouring—a greedy algorithm**
Sort vertices $v_1, \ldots, v_n$ **so that** $\deg v_1 \geqslant \deg v_2 \geqslant \cdots \geqslant \deg v_n$;
$c(v_1) := 1$;
FOR $i := 2$ **TO** n **DO**
$\quad U := \{ c(v_j) : v_i v_j \in E, j < i \}$; $\quad c(v_i) := \min \mathbb{N} \setminus U$;
END;

algorithm, nor does the algorithm necessarily give the best colouring of the vertices. It is a base from which to explore other algorithms, and works fairly well in practice.

Fig. 7.19 **Graph colouring**

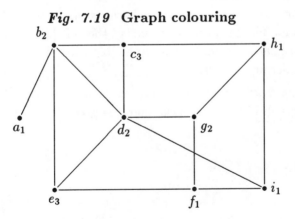

Example 7.26 We shall colour the graph in Figure 7.19. First, the vertices are sorted into the order
$$d, b, c, i, e, f, g, h, a,$$
and colour 1 is assigned to d. Next, b is given colour 2, because colour 1 is impossible, as db is an edge of G. After this, c is given

colour 3, i colour 2, e colour 3, and so on, and the final colouring is indicated in Figure 7.19, as a subscript to the vertex.

• **Exercise 7.27** Use the greedy algorithm to colour the graphs with the following sets of edges.

(i) ab, ac, ae, ag, bc, be, bi, bj, cf, cg, de, df, dg, dh, dj, ef, ei, fg, fh, fk, gi, hk.

(ii) ab, ac, ad, ae, bd, bf, bk, bl, cf, ck, de, df, dg, dh, dl, ef, ej, fg, fh, fj, gh, hi, hk, hl, ij, il, jk, jl, kl.

(iii) ab, ac, ad, ae, bd, bf, bk, bl, cf, ck, de, df, dg, dh, dj, ef, ei, fg, fh, fk, gi, hk, hl, ij, ik, jk, jl, kl.

• **Exercise 7.28** Colour the graphs with the following edges.

(i) ab, ad, af, ah, bd, bf, bi, bk, cd, ce, de, df, dg, di, dl, eg, eh, fg, fh, fl, gh, ik.

(ii) ab, ac, ad, ag, bc, bd, bi, bm, cf, cl, cm, de, df, dj, dk, eg, ei, fg, fh, fm, gk, hj, hk, hl, hm, ik, jk, jl, kl, lm.

(iii) ab, ac, ad, ae, af, ag, ah, ai, aj, ak, al, be, bg, bh, bl, cd, cf, de, df, dg, dh, di, eh, ei, fg, fi, fj, gh, hk, hi, ij, ik, jk, jl, kl.

One way of improving the algorithm is to run it, but to remember which vertices needed the highest numbered colour. The algorithm is then run again, but with these vertices placed at the head of the queue. This process of reordering is repeated, until no improvement has been made to the number of colours used over several iterations. There is no justification for this procedure, except that of the following Exercise. There is no guarantee that an optimal colouring will ever be achieved by this reordering process.

• **Exercise 7.29** Show that there exists an ordering of the vertices of the graph G which is such that the greedy algorithm uses $\chi(G)$ colours.

8

Abstract algebra

8.1 Introduction

The types of mappings we have met in Chapter 5 have mostly been the sort where the domain has been simple, that is, not a cartesian product of sets. There is a type of mapping which arises frequently in applications, and it is exemplified by the function $f : \mathbb{R}^2 \to \mathbb{R}$ given by $f(x, y) = x + y$. Such mappings are called *binary operations*, and much effort has been expended during the last two centuries on studying their properties.

A seemingly unrelated problem is that of finding a mathematical specification for *strings* in programming languages. Strings and binary operations are not all that different when we look at their formalism, and the theory we shall develop will also be able to model *stacks*, *queues*, and other related structures.

Finally, we shall look at the way in which programming languages are specified, and shall develop a notation for working with their syntax. We shall investigate the way we can simplify the structure of a language, and how to write a program to recognize valid statements in the language.

The pace of this chapter will be brisker than previous ones. We shall leave more details for the student to fill in. It is hoped that by now the student has acquired enough mathematical confidence to be able to do this.

8.2 Binary operations

We saw in Chapter 5 that a mapping was a relation f on $A \times B$ which was such that, to each $a \in A$ there existed a unique $b \in B$ with $(a, b) \in f$, that is, $a \, f \, b$. We then wrote $b = f(a)$ to denote this unique result of the mapping. We also noted that the set A itself could possibly be a product set, and so the mapping could be a function of several variables.

One case occurs so often that we single it out. This is where we have a mapping from A^2 to A.

Example 8.1 Let $A = \mathbf{Z}$. The mappings $(a, b) \mapsto a + b$, $(a, b) \mapsto a - b$ and $(a, b) \mapsto ab$ are all of this type, for $a, b \in A$.

Most of modern mathematics is built around such mappings. They represent a way of combining two objects in a set to obtain a third object of the same set, and are called *laws of composition* or *binary operations* on the set.

The usual way of representing such a binary operation is with a symbol ∘ placed between the two arguments of the function. The general symbol ∘, which we call 'circle', could, in some particular situation, be the symbol $+$, $-$, $\times$, $/$, or any others we wish to define. It can even be nothing at all, as in the notation ab for $a \times b$. The expression ab is called the *concatenation* of a and b.

Before we formulate a definition of such an operation, we shall introduce more generality into the discussion.

Definition Let A and B be two sets. A **binary mapping** on A and B is a mapping f from $A \times B$ to some third set C. We choose some symbol such as ∘ to represent such a mapping, and write $f(a, b)$ as $a \circ b$. The symbol ∘ is then called an **infix operator**.

We have removed the restriction that A, B and C should be the same set. Let us put this restriction back.

Definition Let A be a set. A **binary operation** or **law of composition** on A is a binary mapping $(a, b) \mapsto a \circ b$ from A^2 to A.

The essential property of a binary operation is that it is defined for all $a, b \in A$, and that $a \circ b \in A$ also.

8.3   Commutative and associative operations

The whole point of the infix notation $a \circ b$ is to make us think of the mapping as if it were a product or sum, similar to the ordinary arithmetic operations defined on $\mathbf{Z}$ or $\mathbf{R}$. This notation will mislead us if it suggests properties for ∘ which it does not have.

Example 8.2 Let us define an operation ∘ on $\mathbf{R}$, which takes the average of two numbers. We have $a \circ b = \frac{1}{2}(a + b)$. Then $a \circ b = b \circ a$ is certainly true. Consider $1 \circ (2 \circ 10) = 1 \circ 6 = 3.5$, whilst

$(1 \circ 2) \circ 10 = 1.5 \circ 10 = 5.75$. We get different answers depending on the order in which we group the operations. This is completely different to addition and multiplication operations on $\mathbb{R}$. If we look at subtraction on $\mathbb{R}$, we find the same sort of behaviour—in fact, even worse! For $a - b$ and $b - a$ are different whenever $a \neq b$, and also $1 - (2 - 10) = 9$ but $(1 - 2) - 10 = -11$.

Even in ordinary arithmetic, there are properties which are possessed by some binary operations and not by others.

Definition The binary operation $\circ$ on A is said to be **commutative** if $a \circ b = b \circ a$ for all $a, b \in A$. It is **associative** if $(a \circ b) \circ c = a \circ (b \circ c)$ for all $a, b, c \in A$.

The commutative property lets us change the order of terms in $(a \circ b) \circ c$, and write it as $(b \circ a) \circ c$, or $c \circ (a \circ b)$, or even $c \circ (b \circ a)$. We see that these are all different from the operations which we get when we have an associative property; the latter *never* changes the order of a, b and c, but it does permit a change in the order of the calculations. Thus one property is concerned with variables, whilst the other is concerned with operations.

Although the associative property seems to apply only to a three-term combination, it applies to any bracketing whatsoever, as we can see in the following Example.

Example 8.3 Let $\circ$ be an associative operation on A. We show that

$$((a \circ (b \circ c)) \circ d) \circ e = a \circ (b \circ (c \circ (d \circ e))).$$

We apply the associative property several times over in the following.

$$
\begin{aligned}
((a \circ (b \circ c)) \circ d) \circ e &= (a \circ (b \circ c)) \circ (d \circ e) \\
&= ((a \circ b) \circ c) \circ (d \circ e) \\
&= (a \circ b) \circ (c \circ (d \circ e)) \\
&= a \circ (b \circ (c \circ (d \circ e))).
\end{aligned}
$$

The same sort of transformation can be done on any bracketing whatsoever, into a form in which the evaluation starts with the last $\circ$ and proceeds through to the first. The details of proof are messy, and are left as an Exercise. It follows that any two bracketings for an associative operation are equivalent, and so brackets are dropped, with $(a \circ b) \circ c$ becoming $a \circ b \circ c$. We must, however, religiously respect the order of the variables, unless we also have commutativity.

•*Exercise 8.4* Prove by induction on the number of variables appearing that any bracketing of $a_1 \circ a_2 \circ \cdots \circ a_n$ with an associative operation $\circ$ equals any other bracketing.

8.4   Neutrality and invertibility

The number 1 is very special as far as multiplication on $\mathbb{R}$ is concerned. It satisfies the relationships $1 \times a = a \times 1 = a$, for any $a \in \mathbb{R}$. It is said to be *neutral* with respect to multiplication. Multiplication by 1 does not modify a number.

The number 0 has the same property as regards addition, that $0+a = a + 0 = a$ for all $a \in \mathbb{R}$. It is neutral with respect to addition.

Consider the following proof by contradiction.

Example 8.5 Let our set be $\mathbb{R}$, and our operation be $-$. We shall show that nothing is neutral for this operation. Thus suppose $a - e = e - a = a$ for all $a \in \mathbb{R}$. If $a = 0$, we obtain $-e = e = 0$, so $e = 0$. However, $1 - 0$ and $0 - 1$ are definitely different, so we deduce that there is a contradiction in assuming that any such e exists.

Again, we have a property which may or may not be true.

Definition Let $\circ$ be a binary operation on A. We say that $e \in A$ is a **neutral element**, **identity element** or **unit element** for $\circ$ if $a \circ e = e \circ a = a$ for all $a \in A$.

The expressions $a \circ e$ and $e \circ a$ have both been included just in case $\circ$ happens not to be commutative; if it is, only one of them is needed.

Our definition of neutrality implies that several elements might be neutral for the same operation. This is not the case.

Theorem 8.1 Let $\circ$ be a binary operation on A, and suppose that e and f are both neutral with respect to $\circ$. Then $e = f$.

Proof Consider $e \circ f$. Since e is neutral, this equals f. Since f is neutral, it also equals e, so $e = f$ as required.   □

Note that 0 and 1 are both neutral in $\mathbb{R}$, but with respect to *different* operations. Thus we do not have $0 = 1$, thankfully, because the deduction $0 = 1$ is the basis of many proofs by contradiction.

If we have a set A with a binary operation $\circ$, and there is no neutral element in A, then we can use a little trick to make one. The idea is that we choose some object e not in A, and extend A to $B = A \cup \{ e \}$, at the same time *defining* $e \circ x = x \circ e = x$ for all $x \in B$. The new element e will then, of course, be neutral by definition.

Example 8.6 Starting with the natural numbers, and their addition as binary operation, we note that the set has no neutral element, as $m + e > m$ for all $e \in \mathbb{N}$. The extension, by adding a neutral element 0, gives us the set $\mathbb{Z}^+$.

•Exercise 8.7 What happens if the above extension is applied to a set A which *does* have a neutral element. Do we get two neutral elements?

In $\mathbb{R}$ with the binary operation $\times$ and neutral element 1, the numbers 2 and 0.5 combine to produce the product $2 \times 0.5 = 1$. Similarly, 4 and 0.25 combine to produce 1. We say that these are *inverses* of one another with respect to this operation.

If we change the operation to addition, then 2 and -2, 4 and -4 and so on similarly combine to produce the neutral element $2 + (-2) = 4 + (-4) = 0$. We have inverse pairs of elements.

Definition Let A be a set with a binary operation $\circ$, and let us assume that there is a neutral element $e \in A$ with respect to this operation. Let $a, b \in A$ be such that $a \circ b = b \circ a = e$. We say that b is an **inverse** of a with respect to $\circ$ on A, and we say that a is **invertible**.

We include both $a \circ b$ and $b \circ a$ in the definition in case $\circ$ is not commutative.

Example 8.8 Let S be a set. Let A be the set of all mappings $f : S \to S$. Let $f \circ g$ denote the ordinary composition of mappings. Our definition of invertible matches that of Chapter 5—the invertible mappings are the bijections.

8.5 Semigroups and monoids

We have enough properties of binary operations to be able to recognize some patterns of properties which occur quite regularly. The idea is that we should examine any new example, and see how many of the properties it possesses. Then, we should have a store of knowledge about sets with this combination of properties. The common properties of such sets will presumably illuminate the example we have in mind. This course is known as the *abstract approach*. The properties possessed by a model are called the *axioms* for that model. Here is one such model.

Definition Let A be a set with an associative binary operation o. We say that A with this operation o is a **semigroup**, sometimes written as (A, o).

This is a model for the arithmetic operations $+$ and $\times$ on $\mathbb{R}$, and also for composition of mappings $f : S \to S$.

The associative property is the minimum requirement for us to be able to define *powers* of an element. There is never any problem with defining $a^2 = a \circ a$, but when we come to a^3, there are two possible interpretations, namely $(a \circ a) \circ a$ and $a \circ (a \circ a)$. If our operation happens to be commutative, then these are equal; we then meet problems with a^4, as no amount of commutativity by itself will ensure that $(a \circ a) \circ (a \circ a)$ and $a \circ (a \circ (a \circ a))$ are equal.

Example 8.9 Suppose that we define an operation o on $\mathbb{R}$, by the rule $x \circ y = (x + y)/3$. This operation is commutative. However, $1 \circ 1 = 2/3$ so $(1 \circ 1) \circ (1 \circ 1) = 4/9$, while $1 \circ (1 \circ 1) = 5/9$, so $1 \circ (1 \circ (1 \circ 1)) = 14/27$.

We can easily define positive powers of an element of a semigroup.

Definition Let A be a semigroup under o, and suppose $a \in A$. We define a^n for $n \in \mathbb{N}$ by $a^1 = a$, $a^2 = a \circ a$, and, for $n > 2$, $a^n = a \circ a^{n-1}$. The expression a^n is called the n-th **power** of a.

If our binary operation is written as a sum $a + b$, then we must change our notation, and refer to the n-*th multiple* of a, or na.

Given that we are using the notation a^n, we could expect certain properties to be possessed by these powers, coinciding with the properties of powers of integers or real numbers.

Theorem 8.2 Let a be an element of a semigroup, and let $m, n \in \mathbb{N}$. Then $a^m \circ a^n = a^{m+n}$ and $(a^m)^n = a^{mn}$.

Proof These can both be proved rigorously by induction on n. However, the first is just an identity for a bracketing of $m + n$ as, and the second similarly for mn as. ◻

We do *not* have the result $(a \circ b)^n = a^n \circ b^n$. For instance, when $n = 2$, the expressions $a \circ b \circ a \circ b$ and $a \circ a \circ b \circ b$ will usually not be equal. They will be equal if the semigroup is commutative.

Our next axiom system places a restriction on a semigroup.

Definition A **monoid** is a semigroup which possesses a neutral element.

Any semigroup can easily be converted into a monoid by adding a neutral element.

Theorem 8.3 Let A be a semigroup under the binary operation $\circ$. Suppose $e \notin A$. Put $B = A \cup \{e\}$, and define $e \circ b = b \circ e = b$ for all $b \in B$. Then B is a monoid.

Proof The element e is neutral. We must show that $\circ$ is still associative. If e does not appear in any compositions, then we are still working in A, and associativity is true by assumption. Consider a composition such as $e \circ (a_1 \circ a_2)$ with $a_1, a_2 \in A$:
$$e \circ (a_1 \circ a_2) = a_1 \circ a_2 = (e \circ a_1) \circ a_2,$$
by the assumed neutrality of e. The proofs of $e \circ (e \circ e) = (e \circ e) \circ e$, $e \circ (a \circ e) = (e \circ a) \circ e$ and other cases are similar. $\square$

Thus there is no loss in generality in studying only monoids. For this reason, a semigroup is sometimes defined as having a neutral element.

• **Exercise 8.10** Let S be a semigroup, and let $T \subseteq S$. We say that T is a *subsemigroup* of S if it is a semigroup in its own right, with the same binary operation as that on S.

Show that a subset T of S with the property that
$$a, b \in T \implies a \circ b \in T$$
is a subsemigroup of S. There is a similar definition for *submonoids*, but the above characterization is no longer true.

• **Exercise 8.11** The set $\mathbb{Z}$ is a semigroup under multiplication. Which of the following sets are subsemigroups of $\mathbb{Z}$, and which are submonoids?
(i) $\mathbb{N}$. (ii) $\mathbb{Z}^+$. (iii) $\mathbb{Z} \setminus \mathbb{Z}^+$.
(iv) The set of all even integers.
(v) The set of all odd integers. (vi) $H = \{2^n : n \in \mathbb{N}\}$.

• **Exercise 8.12** An *isomorphism* $f : G \to H$ between two monoids G and H is a bijection such that $f(g_1 \circ g_2) = f(g_1) \circ f(g_2)$ for all $g_1, g_2 \in G$. Show that if the neutral element of G is e, then $f(e)$ is neutral in H. Show by counter-example that this result is false if 'bijection' is replaced by 'mapping'.

• **Exercise 8.13** Let $f : G \to H$ be a monoid *homomorphism*, that is, a mapping with the property that $f(a \circ b) = f(a) \circ f(b)$ for all

$a, b \in G$, and such that it maps the neutral element e of G to the neutral element e' of H. Define
$$K = \{\, g \in G : f(g) = e' \,\}.$$
Show that K is a submonoid of G.

For a monoid, we can use the notation $a^0 = a$ to extend the powers of any element to all cardinals n. We cannot define negative powers unless a is invertible. If it exists, however, an inverse is unique.

Theorem 8.4 Let A be a monoid with neutral element e. Suppose that $a, b, c \in A$ satisfy $c \circ a = a \circ b = e$. Then $b = c$. An element can therefore have at most one inverse in a monoid.

Proof Consider the simplification
$$c \circ a \circ b = c \circ (a \circ b) = c \circ e = c.$$
Using associativity to re-bracket in a different way, we obtain
$$c \circ a \circ b = (c \circ a) \circ b = e \circ b = b,$$
and so $b = c$.

An inverse b of a would satisfy $b \circ a = a \circ b = e$. A second inverse c would satisfy $c \circ a = a \circ c = e$. Thus $c \circ a = a \circ b = e$, forcing $b = c$. ☐

This uniqueness allows us to use the notation a^{-1} for the inverse of an element a of a monoid which happens to be invertible.

Definition Let a be an invertible element of a monoid. The **unique inverse** of a is written a^{-1}, and $a \circ a^{-1} = a^{-1} \circ a = e$.

Once a^{-1} exists, then so do all the negative powers of a.

Definition If a is an invertible element of a monoid, then we define $a^{-2} = a^{-1} \circ a^{-1}$, and $a^{-n} = a^{-1} \circ a^{-n+1}$ for $n \geqslant 3$.

We have the following properties of these powers.

Theorem 8.5 Let a be an invertible element of a monoid. For any $m, n \in \mathbb{Z}$ we have $a^m \circ a^n = a^{m+n}$ and $(a^m)^n = a^{mn}$.

Proof The proof works by considering various cases, since there are three different definitions of a^m, depending on whether m is positive, zero or negative. The details are trivial but tiresome. ☐

Finally, we have a result for the calculation of inverses of products.

Theorem 8.6 Let a and b be invertible elements of a monoid. Then $a \circ b$ is invertible, and $(a \circ b)^{-1} = b^{-1} \circ a^{-1}$.

Proof To prove this, we merely need to check the definition of an inverse:
$$(a \circ b) \circ (b^{-1} \circ a^{-1}) = a \circ (b \circ b^{-1}) \circ a^{-1} = a \circ e \circ a^{-1} = a \circ a^{-1} = e.$$
The other identity is similar. Thus $a \circ b$ is invertible, and has the unique inverse $b^{-1} \circ a^{-1}$. $\qquad\qquad\qquad\qquad\qquad\qquad\qquad\qquad\qquad\qquad \Box$

8.6 Groups

In some monoids, every element is invertible.

Definition A **group** is a set G with an associative binary operation and a neutral element, in which a^{-1} exists for all $a \in G$.

Example 8.14 $\mathbb{R}$ is a group under the operation $+$, since the inverse of a is $-a$.

Example 8.15 Binary addition gives a group structure on $\{0, 1\}$. We have $0 + 0 = 1 + 1 = 0$, $0 + 1 = 1 + 0 = 1$. Thus, 0 has inverse 0, and 1 has inverse 1.

•**Exercise 8.16** Which of the following sets are *groups* under the given binary operations? Justify your answers.

(i) $(\mathbb{Z}, +)$. (ii) $(\mathbb{R}, \times)$. (iii) $(\mathbb{R} \setminus \{0\}, \times)$.

(iv) $(\mathbb{Z} \setminus \{0\}, \times)$. (v) $(\mathbb{Q} \setminus \{0\}, \times)$.

The most important group structures from our point of view are those which arise from the operation m MOD n of most programming languages. Suppose that we fix the natural number n. We can equivalence two integers p and q if $p - q$ is a multiple of n, that is

$$p \equiv q \iff p - q = kn, \qquad \text{for some } k \in \mathbb{Z}.$$

This relation on $\mathbb{Z}$ is an equivalence relation, as we have seen. There are n equivalence classes, one containing each of the numbers from 0 to $(n-1)$. Let $\mathbb{Z}_n$ denote the set of these equivalence classes. It is perhaps simpler to think of $\mathbb{Z}_n$ as the set $\{0, 1, \ldots, n-1\}$. We define a binary operation on $\mathbb{Z}_n$ by taking $a \oplus b$ to be (a+b)MOD n, that is, the remainder on dividing $a + b$ by n. This remainder is the unique element $c \in \mathbb{Z}_n$ such that $a + b - c$ is a multiple of n. With this operation, $\mathbb{Z}_n$ is called the set of *integers modulo n*. We show that this operation is a group operation.

Theorem 8.7 The integers modulo n form a commutative group under addition.

Proof **Associativity:** Suppose that $a, b, c \in \mathbb{Z}_n$. We have $b \oplus c = b + c - kn$ for some $k \in \mathbb{Z}$. Thus

$$a \oplus (b \oplus c) = a + (b \oplus c) - ln = a + b + c - (k + l)n,$$

for some $l \in \mathbb{Z}$. A similar calculation shows that $(a \oplus b) \oplus c$ and $a + b + c$ also differ by a multiple of n, and so

$$a \oplus (b \oplus c) - (a \oplus b) \oplus c$$

is a multiple of n. This is impossible unless it is 0, as both numbers lie in $\mathbb{Z}_n$, so their difference is less than $n - 1$ in absolute value. Thus we have associativity.

Neutral Element: 0 is neutral.

Inverses: 0 has inverse 0, and m has inverse $n - m$ for $1 \leqslant m \leqslant n - 1$.

Commutativity: This is obvious.

Thus the set $\mathbb{Z}_n$ is a commutative group under $\oplus$. $\qquad \square$

A commutative group is also described as *abelian*, named after the mathematician Abel.

In our notation, the integers modulo 2 are called $\mathbb{Z}_2$.

The mathematical way of expressing the MOD operation of programming is in the form $a \equiv b \pmod{n}$, meaning that a and b differ by a multiple of n.

• *Exercise 8.17* Show that $\mathbb{Z}_n$ is a commutative monoid under the operation *multiplication modulo* n, where $a \otimes b$ is the remainder on dividing ab by n. Show that $\mathbb{Z}_n$ is *not* generally a group under $\otimes$.

• *Exercise 8.18* Find the invertible elements of $\mathbb{Z}_5$ under multiplication.

• *Exercise 8.19* Find all the invertible elements of $\mathbb{Z}_6$ under $\otimes$.

• *Exercise 8.20* Find all the invertible elements of $\mathbb{Z}_7$ under $\otimes$.

• *Exercise 8.21* Find all the invertible elements of $\mathbb{Z}_{12}$ under $\otimes$.

• *Exercise 8.22* Prove the *cancellation law* for groups, that if G is a group and $a, b, c \in G$, then $a \circ b = a \circ c$ implies $b = c$. Give an example to show that this law is false in some semigroups.

• *Exercise 8.23*   (i) Define $\circ$ on $\mathbb{R}$ by $a \circ b = a + b + ab$. Show that the binary operation $\circ$ makes $\mathbb{R}$ into a monoid. Find the invertible elements of $\mathbb{R}$ under $\circ$.

(ii) Define $\circ$ on $G = \mathbb{R} \setminus \{-1\}$ by $a \circ b = a + b + ab$. Show that $\circ$ is a binary operation on G, and that G forms a group under this operation.

• **Exercise 8.24** Let c be the speed of light. Put $S = \{v \in \mathbb{R} : -c < v < c\}$, and

$$u \circ v = \frac{u + v}{1 + uv/c^2}, \qquad \forall u, v \in S.$$

(i) Show that

$$((c^2 - u^2) > 0) \wedge ((c^2 - v^2) > 0) \implies (c^2 - (u \circ v)^2) > 0,$$

and so $\circ$ is a binary operation on S.

(ii) Show that $(S, \circ)$ is an abelian group, the *Lorentz velocity transformation group* of Einstein's theory of relativity.

• **Exercise 8.25** Let G be a group, and let H be a *subgroup* of G, that is, a subset which is itself a group under the same binary operation. Define a relation $\sim$ on G by taking $a \sim b \iff ab^{-1} \in H$. Show that this is an equivalence relation on G. The equivalence classes are called *cosets* of H in G.

• **Exercise 8.26** Let G be a finite group. Show that the equivalence classes of the above equivalence relation all have the same cardinality. Hence show that $|H|$ divides $|G|$ exactly. This is known as *Lagrange's Theorem*.

• **Exercise 8.27** Let $f : G \to H$ be a *homomorphism* between the groups G and H, that is, such that $f(a \circ b) = f(a) \circ f(b)$ for all $a, b \in G$. Show that if e and e' are the neutral elements of G and H respectively then $f(e) = e'$.

• **Exercise 8.28** Show that if $f : G \to H$ is a homomorphism between two groups G and H, then $f(g^{-1}) = f(g)^{-1}$ for every $g \in G$.

• **Exercise 8.29** Let $f : G \to H$ be a group homomorphism, and define $K = \{g \in G : f(g) = e'\}$, where e' is the neutral element of H. Show that K is a subgroup of G. It is called the *kernel* of the homomorphism.

8.7 Alphabets and words

We shall next look at a concept which has found applications in the theory of computations and in the design of computing languages, as well as in the study of the grammar of natural languages. It also provides a model for *strings* in programming languages.

We start with a finite set $\mathcal{A}$, and call it the *alphabet*. This can be thought of as consisting of the letters **a** to **z**, although this need not be the case, and indeed, the interesting applications are to completely different situations.

Definition An **alphabet** is a finite set, and the elements of an alphabet are called **letters**.

We next form a new set from $\mathcal{A}$, consisting of all strings which are composed of one or more letters from $\mathcal{A}$.

Example 8.30 If $\mathcal{A} = \{\, a \,\}$ then our new set is $\{\, a, aa, aaa, \dots \,\}$.

Example 8.31 From $\mathcal{A} = \{\, a, b, c \,\}$ we obtain
$$\{\, a, b, c, aa, bb, cc, ab, ba, bc, cb, ac, ca, aaa, abc, \dots \,\}.$$

These strings are called *words*. The property they have is that they each consist of an ordered list of one or more letters. But such an object *aab* is called an *n*-tuple, when written as (a, a, b). We should also compare the notation *ab* to denote an edge in a digraph.

Example 8.32 If $\mathcal{A} = \{\, a, b \,\}$ then
$$\mathcal{A}^2 = \{\, (a, a), (a, b), (b, a), (b, b) \,\}.$$
If we write xy instead of (x, y) then $\mathcal{A}^2 = \{\, aa, ab, ba, bb \,\}$. Similarly
$$\mathcal{A}^3 = \{\, aaa, aab, aba, abb, baa, bab, bba, bbb \,\}.$$

Definition Let $\mathcal{A}$ be an alphabet. We put
$$\mathcal{A}^+ = \mathcal{A} \cup \mathcal{A}^2 \cup \mathcal{A}^3 \cup \dots = \bigcup_{n=1}^{\infty} \mathcal{A}^n.$$
The **positive closure** $\mathcal{A}^+$ is said to be obtained from $\mathcal{A}$ by **concatenation**. Its elements are called **words** over the alphabet $\mathcal{A}$.

Thus each element w of $\mathcal{A}^+$, which is read as '$\mathcal{A}$ plus', consists of an ordered *n*-tuple of elements of $\mathcal{A}$, $w = a_1 a_2 \cdots a_n$, for some n. We define the *length* $|w|$ of w to be n.

There is a natural binary operation which we can perform on $\mathcal{A}^+$. From *abaac* and *bcccbab* we can form *abaacbcccbab*.

Definition Given two words $w_1 = a_1 a_2 \cdots a_p$ and $w_2 = b_1 b_2 \cdots b_q$ over the alphabet $\mathcal{A}$, the word $a_1 a_2 \cdots a_p b_1 b_2 \cdots b_q$ is called the **concatenation** $w_1 w_2$ of w_1 and w_2.

In programming languages where words or strings are written 'abaac', the concatenation is written as
$$\mathtt{'abaac'} + \mathtt{'bcccbab'} = \mathtt{'abaacbcccbab'},$$
with an explicit binary operation + for concatenation.

Since we are not interested in the bracketing of the letters in a word, only in their order, we have the following.

Theorem 8.8 The set $\mathcal{A}^+$ together with the binary operation of concatenation forms a semigroup.

A concatenation will always be longer than its constituent words, and so there is initially no neutral element for concatenation. However, we know that we can adjoin a neutral element, by Theorem 8.3. This neutral element we shall write as ε, and call it the *empty word*.

It is all very well to define ε in this way, but what is it like in terms of strings? It would be written as something like $''$ in programming languages. Being as we are not using quotes to enclose our strings, we would have to write the empty word as , which does not show up very clearly! Thus we choose the ε symbol to make it visible. We have $|\varepsilon| = 0$ by convention. This makes $|w_1 w_2| = |w_1|\,|w_2|$ for any two words w_1 and w_2.

Definition The set $\mathcal{A}^* = \{\varepsilon\} \cup \mathcal{A}^+$ is called the **closure** of the alphabet $\mathcal{A}$ under concatenation.

The notation $\mathcal{A}^*$ is read as '$\mathcal{A}$ star'. We can also define $\mathcal{A}^0 = \{\varepsilon\}$, and then

$$\mathcal{A}^* = \bigcup_{n=0}^{\infty} \mathcal{A}^n.$$

We see that $\varepsilon w = w \varepsilon = w$ for any $w \in \mathcal{A}^+$. Thus

Theorem 8.9 The set $\mathcal{A}^*$ forms a monoid under the operation of concatenation. Its neutral element is ε.

•*Exercise 8.33* Which elements of $\mathcal{A}^*$ are invertible?

We can define the *powers* of a word in the obvious way, in terms of the concatenation operation.

•*Exercise 8.34* Let $\mathcal{A}$ be an alphabet. If X and Y are sets of words in $\mathcal{A}$, put

$$XY = \{xy : x \in X, y \in Y\}, \quad X|Y = X \cup Y,$$

$$X^{\#} = \{\varepsilon\} \cup \left\{ z : z = x^n = \underbrace{xx \cdots x}_{n \text{ times}}, \quad x \in X \right\}.$$

Describe the following sets of words, giving enough examples to illustrate the general pattern for each set, where $\mathcal{A} = \{a, b, c, \ldots\}$.

(i) $(\{a\}|\{b\})^{\#}$.   (ii) $(\{a\}\{b,c\})^{\#}$.
(iii) $(\{b\}^{\#}\{c\}\{b\}^{\#})|(\{c\}^{\#}\{b\}\{c\}^{\#})$.
(iv) $\{ab\}^{\#}\{ba\}^{\#}$.

•**Exercise 8.35** Let $A = \{a\}, B = \{b\}$. Describe the set of words formed by the following expressions.

(i) $A^{*}B^{+}$.   (ii) $(A \cup B)^{+}A$.
(iii) $(A \cup B)^{+}(\{\varepsilon\} \cup A)$.   (iv) $B^{*}B^{+}$.
(v) $AAB^{+}AB$.

8.8   Stacks

Abstract words or strings provide a simple model of the objects called *stacks*. A stack is a list of objects, all of the same type, such that we are allowed only limited access to objects in the list. We can add an object to the end of the list and remove an object from the end. We can also examine the end object. Think of this as a stack of plates. You can only add a plate to the top, or remove one from the top. The only plate you can see is the top one.

This kind of object arises in any situation in which a sequence of events happen, each one needing attention, and where each event is of more urgency than the ones which have gone before.

Example 8.36 Let `Proc_1`, `Proc_2` and `Proc_3` be three procedures in a programming language. If `Proc_1` calls `Proc_2`, which calls `Proc_3`, then a computer will stack the return address to `Proc_1`, and will commence `Proc_2`. Later, it will stack the return address to `Proc_2` and call `Proc_3`. When `Proc_3` finishes, the computer retrieves the `Proc_2` return address and carries on where it left off. When `Proc_2` is finished, the return address for `Proc_1` is retrieved, and processing continues in `Proc_1`.

The local variables of procedures are also stored on a stack.

Example 8.37 When a compiler reads an expression such as $a \times (b + c) - d$, it generates code to carry out the arithmetic operations. When it meets the '$\times$', it is ready to generate a *multiply* instruction. It then encounters a '(', which makes it suspend operation on the multiplication. It generates code to stack the multiplication and its first argument a, and starts generating code for the addition. The ')' indicates the end of the more urgent addition, so it generates code for the addition, and retrieves a from the stack, together with the multiplication instruction (really, just a return address from a subroutine call). It then carries on with the multiplication, and finally the subtraction.

The operations are not done in the order in which they appear in the given expression.

Let us produce a mathematical model for such a stack. The stack itself is not a problem, that is just a string or word of objects, be they return addresses, plates, record files or whatever. What makes these into a stack is the *operations* we perform on them.

Definition Let $\mathcal{A}$ be an alphabet. We define three operations on words over $\mathcal{A}$. The **top** operation is the mapping $T : \mathcal{A}^+ \to \mathcal{A}$. If $w = a_1 a_2 \cdots a_n$ then $T(w) = a_n$. Next we have the **rest** mapping $R : \mathcal{A}^+ \to \mathcal{A}^*$, $R(w) = a_1 a_2 \cdots a_{n-1}$, with w as given above. We have the **stack** or **push** mapping $S : \mathcal{A} \times \mathcal{A}^* \to \mathcal{A}^+$, where $S(a_n, a_1 a_2 \cdots a_{n-1}) = a_1 a_2 \cdots a_n$.

An alphabet subjected to these operations is called a **stack**.

There is also a *pop* operation, defined by a mapping $P : \mathcal{A}^+ \to \mathcal{A} \times \mathcal{A}^*$, given by $P(w) = (T(w), R(w))$. We have treated this separately because it returns two objects, the top and the rest of a word, that is, an ordered pair of objects. It is thus more complicated to manipulate.

Example 8.38 If $w = abc$ then $T(w) = c$ and $R(w) = ab$. We also have $S(d, w) = abcd$.

These operations can be combined with one another to any depth we like. We have some basic identities which are always true.

Theorem 8.10 With the above stack operations, we always have $R(S(x, w)) = w$ for any $x \in \mathcal{A}$ and $w \in \mathcal{A}^*$, and also $S(T(w), R(w)) = w$ for any $w \in \mathcal{A}^+$.

Proof These are immediate consequences of the definitions. $\quad\square$

•**Exercise 8.39** Find the values of the following expressions, where $w = abc$ and $v = xyz$.

(i) $S(T(w), w)$. (ii) $R(S(T(v), w))$.

(iii) $S(T(R(v)), R(R(S(T(v), R(w)))))$.

•**Exercise 8.40** Formulate a model for a *queue*. Define the mappings J, H and R to indicate the effect of an object joining a queue, the object at the head of the queue, and the rest of the queue.

Assume that objects join at the right and leave at the left of a word.
Thus $J(x, abc) = abcx$, $H(abc) = a$ and $R(abc) = bc$.

Calculate the following, when $w = abc$ and $v = xyz$.

(i) $J(H(w), R(v))$.

(ii) $J(H(J(H(v), R(w))), R(R(v)))$.

8.9   Preorder and postorder traversal

Although usually encountered as a branch of graph theory, the following
application is more natural here, since it is merely the transformation
of one word into another. The idea is that of representing an expression
unambiguously without the need for any brackets.

Example 8.41 Consider the expression $a \times (b + c)$. On dropping
brackets, this becomes $a \times b + c$, which could easily have come from
$(a \times b) + c$. However, we can rewrite the expression in *postorder*
or *postfix* form, with only one interpretation. The idea is to write
$A \times B$ as $AB\times$, and $A + B$ as $AB+$, no matter what A and B might
be. This presents us with a minor problem, in that we might have
transformed a part of an expression but not the whole, and so postfix
and ordinary *infix* or *inorder* may be mixed together. We agree to
enclose postfix expressions within curly braces {} to avoid ambiguity.
Thus
$$a \times (b + c) = a \times \{bc+\} = \{a\{bc+\}\times\} = \{abc + \times\}.$$
On the other hand,
$$(a \times b) + c = \{ab\times\} + c = \{ab \times c+\},$$
and so the two expressions are distinguishable. Of course, we can
drop the braces from the complete postfix expression.

We note that the operators and variables have been *stacked*, ready
for evaluation of the expression from right to left.

There is also a *preorder* or *prefix* form in which the operators come first.

Example 8.42 We have
$$a \times (b + c) = \times a + bc$$
in prefix, and
$$(a \times b) + c = + \times abc.$$

● **Exercise 8.43** Put each of the following into preorder form. Insert
brackets if necessary to give the normal priority to the arithmetic
operations.

(i) $(a \times b) + (c/d)$.   (ii) $a \times b/(c + d)$.

(iii) $a/b + c/d$.   (iv) $a - b + c/d$.

(v) $a \times (b - c/d)$.

• *Exercise 8.44* Put each expression in Exercise 8.43 into postorder form.

• *Exercise 8.45* Put each of the following expressions into postorder. Assume the usual precedence rules for arithmetical operators, ie, $\times$ and / have higher precedence than $+$ and $-$, otherwise work from left to right.

(i) $a + (bc - d)(b + cf)$.   (ii) $(a + b)(b + c)(c + a)$.

(iii) $(a - bc + d)(b + c(a - d))$.

(iv) $A \cup ((B \cup C) \cap (A \cup B))$.

• *Exercise 8.46* Rework Exercise 8.45, but putting the expressions into preorder.

8.10   Formal languages

If you look at the specification of the *syntax* or *grammar* of a language such as *Pascal*, *Modula-2* or *Ada*, you will see either a set of diagrams or a set of definitions which specify how each syntactic class of objects is defined in terms of other syntactic classes, or of the letters and symbols which occur in programs.

Example 8.47 An *identifier* is usually defined as a string of letters and digits, of length at least one, and starting with a letter.

Example 8.48 A *program* is defined as a *program heading* followed by a *block* in *Pascal*.

Example 8.49 A *program module* in *Modula-2* is defined as the string MODULE, followed by an *identifier*, then optionally a priority, then a semicolon, then any number of *import* statements, then a *block*, and finally an *identifier* followed by a period.

We see that in each case, we can regard a syntactic class as a set of words over the ASCII characters, and these definitions are telling us which words are valid members of that class. Thus

␣␣␣program␣a;␣begin␣end.

is a valid program in *Pascal*, but

␣␣␣program␣1:␣end;

is not. This is because the definition of a *program heading* starts
program, then *identifier*, and the numeral 1 does not qualify as an
identifier. There are, of course, other reasons why the second fragment
is not a program.

In reality, the specification is more complex than this. First, in *Pascal* we can write PROGRAM, or Program, or even PrOgRaM if the urge takes
us. Also, the string which is the whole program *must* contain spaces
at certain places. We cannot say programa;, but {Program␣␣a␣;} is
alright; spaces before the semicolon are optional; those between program
and a are mandatory. It is important to distinguish these *mandatory*
and *optional* spaces. We have a method already at our disposal. If ␣
represents a space, then {␣}* represents optional spaces, and {␣}+ represents mandatory spaces. The rules governing spaces are usually very
simple for programming languages, but in TEX they are quite complicated, and have to be carefully stated.

In the definition of a language, then, we find that certain sets of
strings are defined in terms of other sets of strings. Any set of strings
is as much a language as any other set, so the definition we give is
extremely egalitarian.

Definition Let $\mathcal{A}$ be an alphabet. A subset of $\mathcal{A}^*$ is called a **language** or **formal language** over $\mathcal{A}$.

Example 8.50 Taking $\mathcal{A} = \{a, b, c\}$, the set $\{\varepsilon, a, abc, aabba\}$ is a
language—though not a very exciting one!

Let us look at the ways in which we can combine languages together.

Definition Given two languages L_1 and L_2 over $\mathcal{A}$, we can define
their **product** or **concatenation** as
$$L_1 L_2 = \{w : w = w_1 w_2 \text{ for some } w_1 \in L_1, w_2 \in L_2\}.$$

Example 8.51 If $\mathcal{A} = \{a, b, c, \ldots, z, 0, 1, 2, 3, \ldots, 9\}$,
$L_1 = \{a, b, c \ldots, z\}$ and $L_2 = \mathcal{A}^*$, then $L_1 L_2$ is the language
consisting of all words which consist of a lower case letter followed
by a string of letters and digits.

• **Exercise 8.52** Define the class of *identifiers* in *Modula-2*.

We note, but do not need, the fact that the set of all languages over
$\mathcal{A}$ forms a monoid under this concatenation, with neutral element $\{\varepsilon\}$.
Next, we form the powers of a language.

Definition Given a language L over $\mathcal{A}$, the **powers** of L are defined by $L^0 = \{\varepsilon\}$, $L^1 = L$, and $L^n = LL^{n-1}$ for $n \geqslant 2$.

Example 8.53 If we take $\mathcal{A} = \{0, 1, \ldots, 9\}$ and $L = \{00, 11, 22, 33, \ldots, 99\}$, then
$$L^2 = \{0000, 0011, 0022, \ldots, 9988, 9999\}.$$

From the powers of a language, it is possible to form the closures.

Definition Let L be a language over $\mathcal{A}$. The **positive closure** of L is
$$L^+ = \bigcup_{n=1}^{\infty} L^n,$$
and the **closure** of L is
$$L^* = \bigcup_{n=0}^{\infty} L^n.$$

We note that $L^+ = LL^*$, and so $\mathcal{A}^+ = \mathcal{A}\mathcal{A}^*$. These definitions are merely extensions of those already given for the alphabet $\mathcal{A}$. The words in the language L are regarded as though they were letters in a higher order language, and the closure is formed in the natural way.

Example 8.54 If $\mathcal{A} = \{0, 1\}$ and $L = \{0, 11\}$, then L^+ is the language of all words from $\mathcal{A}$ which consist of either a string of one or more 0s, or a string of 0s with an arbitrary number of 11s inserted in it, or a string of an even number of 1s, containing at least two. Some elements are 0, 00, 000, 0110, 11011000, 11, 1111, and so on.

Example 8.55 Let N be the set of all English nouns; V the set of transitive verbs; S the set $\{\sqcup\}$; F the set $\{\,.\,\}$; and finally T the set $\{$ the $\}$. Apart from the *case* of the letters, the following would represent a class of English sentences:
$$TS^+NS^+VS^+TS^+NF.$$
One element of this would be
$$\texttt{the}_\sqcup\texttt{cauliflower}_{\sqcup\sqcup\sqcup\sqcup}\texttt{ate}_\sqcup\texttt{the}_{\sqcup\sqcup\sqcup\sqcup}\texttt{cook.}$$

• **Exercise 8.56** How would you modify the above Example to permit an optional adjective in front of each noun?

• **Exercise 8.57** Repeat the previous Exercise, but this time permit a as an alternative to the.

• **Exercise 8.58** What do we need if we are to permit any number, possibly zero, of adjectives, separated by commas?

● **Exercise 8.59** Extend the definition of sentences to allow them to be optionally linked by , and and , but, and then try to include as much complexity into your grammar as you possibly can. If you are not English, then use your native language.

● **Exercise 8.60** Prove or disprove each of the following results for languages L, M and N.

(i) $(L^*)^* = L^*$.   (ii) $(L \cup M)^* = L^* \cup M^*$.

(iii) $L(M \cap N) = (LM) \cap (LN)$.

(iv) $L(M \cup N) = (LM) \cup (LN)$.

8.11   Backus-Naur form and context-free languages

When we try to formulate rules for the description of languages such as *Modula-2*, we find that if we are to avoid a great deal of repetition then we will need to define various subsidiary languages on the way. The set of all *Modula-2* statements is such a subsidiary language, as is the set of all REPEAT...UNTIL... loops. The set of all valid programs is then defined in terms of these subsidiary languages. Usually, the number of intermediate languages is fairly modest. *Pascal* is defined in 110 steps, and *Modula-2* in just over 70.

Often, a language is described in such a way that it refers back recursively to its own definition.

Example 8.61 The fragment

```
REPEAT
    WHILE x<0 DO x:=f(x); END;
    IF x>1 THEN y:=f(x) ELSE y:=0; END;
UNTIL y<0;
```

is a statement in *Modula-2*. The language of statements includes REPEAT...UNTIL... statements, and there must be a sequence of statements between REPEAT and UNTIL. Each of these statements can itself be almost as complicated as the outer one. We have a *recursive* definition of statements.

If S represents the set of valid statements, we shall use $\langle S \rangle$ to represent this set in our formulae. This new symbol will be treated as a single letter, but it is no ordinary letter; we cannot really have $\langle S \rangle$ in a *Modula-2* statement. For this reason, we distinguish carefully between the elements of our original alphabet $\mathcal{A}$, called the *terminals*, and these new symbols, called the *nonterminals*. We assume that the set $\mathcal{N}$ of nonterminals is disjoint from $\mathcal{A}$. We need a way of transforming nonterminals into terminals.

> **Definition** Let $\mathcal{A}$ be an alphabet, called the **terminal** alphabet, and let $\mathcal{N}$ be a disjoint alphabet called the **nonterminal** alphabet. A **rewriting system** is a finite relation between $\mathcal{N}$ and $(\mathcal{A} \cup \mathcal{N})^*$, that is, a finite subset of $\mathcal{N} \times (\mathcal{A} \cup \mathcal{N})^*$. A **production** is one element of this relation, that is, an ordered pair $(\langle N \rangle, w)$, where w is a word consisting of a string of zero or more terminal and nonterminal letters. The relation is written $\langle N \rangle \to w$, and we interpret this as '$\langle N \rangle$ can be replaced by w'.

The full generality of a relation is needed here, since each production represents a different possible substitution for the nonterminal on its left. Strictly, the above definition is of a *context-free production*; the more general *phrase structure productions* are binary relations on $\mathcal{A} \cup \mathcal{N}$. They are not needed in this book.

Example 8.62 We could write down a production for a *Pascal* program:
$$\langle program \rangle \to \langle programheading \rangle \langle block \rangle.$$
in this notation.

Example 8.63 The definition of a statement in *Modula-2* could be split into several productions. The first would be
$$\langle statement \rangle \to \varepsilon$$
and the definition in terms of a REPEAT loop would be
$$\langle statement \rangle \quad \to \quad \text{REPEAT} \langle statsequence \rangle \text{UNTIL} \langle expression \rangle$$
$$\langle statsequence \rangle \quad \to \quad \langle statement \rangle$$
$$\langle statsequence \rangle \quad \to \quad \langle statement \rangle ; \langle statsequence \rangle$$
with similar productions for each of the other types of statement which can occur.

The pair of productions
$$\langle N \rangle \quad \to \quad uv$$
$$\langle N \rangle \quad \to \quad uwv,$$
for some word w over $\mathcal{A} \cup \mathcal{N}$ occurs so commonly that it is denoted by the compound production
$$\langle N \rangle \to u[w]v,$$

indicating an *optional occurrence* of w in a production.

Example 8.64 In *Pascal*, we have
$$\langle \mathit{ifstatement} \rangle \rightarrow \mathtt{if} \langle \mathit{expression} \rangle \mathtt{then} \langle \mathit{statement} \rangle [\mathtt{else} \langle \mathit{statement} \rangle].$$
The corresponding concept is more complex in *Modula-2*.

Similarly, we often meet the combination
$$\langle N \rangle \ \rightarrow \ u \langle A \rangle v$$
$$\langle A \rangle \ \rightarrow \ \varepsilon$$
$$\langle A \rangle \ \rightarrow \ w \langle A \rangle$$

with $\langle A \rangle$ not occurring in any other productions. This generates a string of zero or more ws, and we write
$$\langle N \rangle \rightarrow u \{ w \} v$$
to indicate this *arbitrary repetition*.

Example 8.65 In *Modula-2*, we have
$$\langle \mathit{repeatstat} \rangle \rightarrow \mathtt{REPEAT} \langle \mathit{statement} \rangle \{ ; \langle \mathit{statement} \rangle \} \mathtt{UNTIL} \langle \mathit{exprn} \rangle.$$

Another possibility is that we have a sequence of productions
$$\langle N \rangle \ \rightarrow \ u w_1 v$$
$$\langle N \rangle \ \rightarrow \ u w_2 v$$
$$\vdots$$
$$\langle N \rangle \ \rightarrow \ u w_m v$$

We write this *alternative expression* as
$$\langle n \rangle \rightarrow u (w_1 | w_2 | \cdots | w_m) v.$$

Example 8.66 In *Modula-2*, we have
$$\langle \mathit{hexDigit} \rangle \rightarrow \langle \mathit{digit} \rangle | \mathtt{A} | \mathtt{B} | \mathtt{C} | \mathtt{D} | \mathtt{E} | \mathtt{F}.$$

A rewriting system which uses these notations is said to be in *extended Backus-Naur form*, *BNF* or *EBNF* for short. This, or a graphical version of it, is the standard way of specifying the syntax of programming languages. Round parentheses (and) may be used to group combinations together. The symbols (,), {, }, [,], | and $\rightarrow$ are not part of the alphabet $\mathcal{A} \cup \mathcal{N}$; they are so-called *meta-symbols*, and are part of our mathematical formalism. When handwriting, it is common to write strings of terminals between quotation marks, so terminal (would be written $"("$. Most of the time, we shall avoid using these special symbols as terminals.

We have yet to discuss the way a set of rewriting rules yields the set of all programs in *Modula-2*. Let us look at one stage of this substitution process.

Definition Let $\mathcal{A}$ and $\mathcal{N}$ be the terminal and nonterminal alphabets of a rewriting system, and let $\langle X \rangle \to w$ be a production. Let x be a word over $\mathcal{A} \cup \mathcal{N}$, with $x = u\langle X \rangle v$, for some words u and v over $\mathcal{A} \cup \mathcal{N}$. We say that x **directly yields** uwv, and write $x \Rightarrow uwv$. The operation $\Rightarrow$ is a binary operation on the set of words over $\mathcal{A} \cup \mathcal{N}$.

Example 8.67 Suppose that we have a production $\langle C \rangle \to \text{ab}\langle C \rangle \text{a}\langle D \rangle$. Then
$$\langle D \rangle \langle C \rangle \text{f}\langle C \rangle \Rightarrow \langle D \rangle \text{ab}\langle C \rangle \text{a}\langle D \rangle \text{f}\langle C \rangle.$$
Here, we have substituted for one occurrence of $\langle C \rangle$, but we could equally well substitute for the other, to directly yield
$$\langle D \rangle \langle C \rangle \text{fab}\langle C \rangle \text{a}\langle D \rangle.$$
Having done one substitution, there is no need to stop there. We can do no substitution, one, two, or any finite number. What we get is the reflexive transitive closure $\Rightarrow^*$ of $\Rightarrow$. This gives us the set of words which can be obtained from a given word by an arbitrary number of substitutions, using any of the productions.

Definition With the context as in the last definition, suppose that x and y are words over $\mathcal{A} \cup \mathcal{N}$. We say that x **yields** y if $x = y$ or there exists a sequence of words $w_1, \ldots, w_n$ such that $x = w_1$, $y = w_n$, and $w_i \Rightarrow w_{i+1}$ for $1 \leqslant i \leqslant n - 1$. We then write $x \Rightarrow^* y$.

This defines the operations of transforming one grammatical string into another, but we are only interested in final strings which are composed entirely of terminal symbols, that is, in words over $\mathcal{A}$. These are the only things that could be programs, or procedures, or repeat loops. We finally have a definition of what a formal grammar is. There will be a nonterminal letter which specifies the start of all yielding operations.

Definition A **context-free grammar** G consists of a terminal alphabet $\mathcal{A}$, a nonterminal alphabet $\mathcal{N}$, a start symbol $\langle S \rangle \in \mathcal{N}$, and a rewriting system $\to$. The **context-free language** generated by this grammar consists of the set of all $w \in \mathcal{A}^*$ such that $\langle S \rangle$ yields w, $L(G) = \{ w \in \mathcal{A}^* : \langle S \rangle \Rightarrow^* w \}$.

•**Exercise 8.68** Give a context-free grammar for the *well-formed formulae* W of logic, consisting of propositional variables $a, b, c, \ldots$, together with ¬, ∨ and ∧, and possibly a few brackets.

•**Exercise 8.69** Here is a grammar for arithmetic expressions. For
simplicity, capital letters represent nonterminals, and the other symbols are all terminals, apart from → and ε.

$$
\begin{aligned}
E &\rightarrow TE' \\
E' &\rightarrow +TE' \\
E' &\rightarrow -TE' \\
E' &\rightarrow \varepsilon \\
T &\rightarrow FT' \\
T' &\rightarrow \times FT' \\
T' &\rightarrow /FT' \\
T' &\rightarrow \varepsilon \\
F &\rightarrow -F \\
F &\rightarrow (E) \\
F &\rightarrow DF' \\
F' &\rightarrow DF' \\
F' &\rightarrow \varepsilon \\
D &\rightarrow 0 \\
&\vdots \\
D &\rightarrow 9
\end{aligned}
$$

Show that the following are valid expressions, by demonstrating how
the grammar yields them.

(i)   1.   (ii) $1 \times 1 - 2$.   (iii) $-(1)$.
(iv) $((-1))$.   (v) $--1$.

•**Exercise 8.70** There is a more general sort of grammar than the
context-free grammar, called a *phrase structure grammar*. In it,
productions take the form $v \rightarrow w$, where v is any word contain-
ing at least one nonterminal. If $a\langle A\rangle \rightarrow \langle B\rangle b$ is a production, then
$\langle C\rangle\langle B\rangle a\langle A\rangle\langle A\rangle a \Rightarrow \langle C\rangle\langle B\rangle\langle B\rangle b\langle A\rangle a$.

The following phrase-structure grammar generates all 'abacus'
identities such as $1 + 1 = 11$ and $111 + 11 = 11111$. Capital letters
are nonterminals.

$$S \rightarrow 1X + 1X = 11$$

$$X \;\to\; 1RX$$
$$X \;\to\; \varepsilon$$
$$R1 \;\to\; 1R$$
$$R+ \;\to\; +R$$
$$R= \;\to\; =1.$$

Convince yourself that this grammar works by looking at some examples, such as $S \Rightarrow 1X+1X = 11 \Rightarrow 11RX+1X = 11 \Rightarrow 11R+1X = 11 \Rightarrow 11R+1 = 11 \Rightarrow 11+R1 = 11 \Rightarrow 11+1R = 11 \Rightarrow 11+1 = 111$.

Modify the above grammar so that it produces the following types of equations.

(i) All sums of two equal summands, such as $111 + 111 = 111111$.

(ii) All sums of an arbitrary number of summands, such as $11 + 111 + 1 = 111111$.

(iii) All equations such as $11 + 1111 = 111 + 11 + 1$.

(iv) All products, such as $111 \times 11 = 111111$.

8.12 Regular grammars

We saw above that there is an inherent circularity in the definition of statements in programming languages which is not present in the definition of integers or identifiers. The latter can be defined in terms of productions of a very specialized kind. These sorts of productions are such that the whole righthand side consists of terminals.

Example 8.71 The definition of an identifier in most languages is

$$\langle letter \rangle \;\to\; \mathsf{a|b|} \cdots \mathsf{|z}$$
$$\langle digit \rangle \;\to\; \mathsf{0|1|} \cdots \mathsf{|9}$$
$$\langle identifier \rangle \;\to\; \langle letter \rangle \{ \langle letter \rangle | \langle digit \rangle \}$$

in EBNF.

The first two productions are in terms of terminals. Using the third, we find that we can expand the whole definition of $\langle identifier \rangle$ as

$$\langle identifier \rangle \to (\mathsf{a|b|} \cdots \mathsf{|z})\{\mathsf{a|b|} \cdots \mathsf{|z|0|1|} \cdots \mathsf{|9}\}.$$

We have ignored the complication of upper and lower case letters, but that does not affect our argument.

Definition A **regular grammar** is a grammar in which the EBNF productions can be combined into a single production, with the start symbol on the left, and only terminals on the right. A **regular language** is the language of a regular grammar.

The sort of expression that can appear on the right, involving combinations of operations $\{w\}$, w_1w_2, $[w]$ and $w_1|w_2$, on words over $\mathcal{A}$, is called a *regular expression*.

Example 8.72 The grammar $\langle S \rangle \to \{ab\}[c]$ generates the language of an arbitrary number of abs, optionally terminated by a c. Some elements are ε, c, ab, abc, abab, ababc, and so on.

•**Exercise 8.73** Show that there is a regular grammar for the following, by giving an EBNF production in terms of D =digits.

(i) unsigned real constants, without an exponent, eg, 34.29.

(ii) signed or unsigned real constants, without an exponent.

(iii) real constants, possibly with an exponent.

The regular languages are closed under the usual operations on languages.

Theorem 8.11 Let L and M be regular languages. The following are also regular:

(i) L^*;   (ii) L^+;   (iii) LM;   (iv) $L \cup M$.

Proof   (i) Suppose that we have an EBNF production $\langle S \rangle \to w$ for L. Then $\langle S \rangle \to \{w\}$ will generate L^*.

(ii) Take $\langle S \rangle \to w\{w\}$.

(iii) If $\langle S \rangle \to v$ generates M, take $\langle S \rangle \to wv$ to generate LM.

(iv) Take $\langle S \rangle \to w|v$.

□

It is essential for many programs to be able to recognize whether their input contains a valid identifier. The simpler we can make the productions, the easier it will be to write a program to do the recognition.

Theorem 8.12 Given a regular language L, there exists a grammar for L in which the productions are all of the two kinds

(i) $\langle X \rangle \to a\langle Y \rangle$;   (ii) $\langle X \rangle \to \varepsilon$.

This grammar can be chosen so that $\langle S \rangle$ never appears on the righthand side of a production.

It is instructive to see what we could do with the grammar of some simple regular language first, before starting a general proof.

Example 8.74 Consider the language defined by
$$\langle S \rangle \to ab\{ac\}\{d\}.$$

We can easily split off the initial ab, in two stages:

$$\langle S \rangle \rightarrow a\langle T \rangle \tag{1}$$

$$\langle T \rangle \rightarrow b\langle U \rangle \tag{2}$$

$$\langle U \rangle \rightarrow \{ac\}\{d\},$$

but what can we do with the remaining concatenation? Well, it can be handled in terms of the productions

$$\langle U \rangle \rightarrow a\langle V \rangle \tag{3}$$

$$\langle V \rangle \rightarrow c\langle U \rangle \tag{4}$$

$$\langle U \rangle \rightarrow \{d\}$$

where the last production can be handled as

$$\langle U \rangle \rightarrow \varepsilon \tag{5}$$

$$\langle U \rangle \rightarrow d\langle U \rangle. \tag{6}$$

We have achieved our aim in a total of six productions of this very simple form.

Proof Suppose that the regular grammar is expressed by the EBNF production

$$\langle S \rangle \rightarrow w,$$

where w only involves terminals. Our proof is an induction on the complexity of w, which can be measured by the number of symbols in w. If w is just one symbol, then it must be a single terminal a, and we can write

$$\langle S \rangle \rightarrow a\langle T \rangle$$

$$\langle T \rangle \rightarrow \varepsilon$$

to reduce the grammar to our simple operations. Suppose, for our induction, that w is longer than one symbol. Suppose we look at the outermost level of w, and look at the EBNF operation that is being performed there. If this is an alternative expression using | then there is no problem, as

$$\langle S \rangle \rightarrow w_1|w_2|\cdots|w_n$$

can be replaced by

$$\langle S \rangle \rightarrow w_1$$

$$\langle S \rangle \rightarrow w_2$$

$$\vdots$$

$$\langle S \rangle \;\;\rightarrow\;\; w_n$$

and we can then tackle these new simpler productions separately. We produce a grammar of the desired type for each, and then take all the resulting productions together, taking care to use different intermediate nonterminals in each subsidiary grammar.

If the outermost level is an optional occurrence

$$\langle S \rangle \rightarrow [v]$$

we can replace it by

$$\langle S \rangle \;\;\rightarrow\;\; v$$
$$\langle S \rangle \;\;\rightarrow\;\; \varepsilon,$$

and then expand the first production by induction.

Suppose the outermost operation is a concatenation $\langle S \rangle \rightarrow w_1 w_2$. We assume by induction that we can generate a grammar of the required type for

$$\langle S \rangle \rightarrow w_1$$

and also for

$$\langle T \rangle \rightarrow w_2.$$

We need to modify the first grammar so that it always produces a $\langle T \rangle$ at the end of each word generated by it. We notice that the simple productions always yield a string of terminals, possibly terminated by a nonterminal, and that the only productions which yield an element of $\mathcal{A}^*$ are those in which this final nonterminal is eventually eliminated. Modify all productions in the grammar for $\langle S \rangle \rightarrow w_1$ so that any production $\langle X \rangle \rightarrow \varepsilon$ is replaced by $\langle X \rangle \rightarrow w$, whenever $\langle T \rangle \rightarrow w$ was a production in the second grammar, and we are done!

Finally, if the outermost level is an arbitrary repetition $\langle S \rangle \rightarrow \{v\}$, we generate a grammar for $\langle S \rangle \rightarrow v$ and then modify it in the following way. First, we add the production $\langle S \rangle \rightarrow \varepsilon$. Next, we look at any production $\langle X \rangle \rightarrow \varepsilon$ in the grammar, with $\langle X \rangle \neq \langle S \rangle$. The nonterminal $\langle X \rangle$ is being eliminated. We find all productions $\langle S \rangle \rightarrow a\langle Y \rangle$, and add the production $\langle X \rangle \rightarrow a\langle Y \rangle$ to the original set. Whenever an original production is on the point of eliminating its nonterminal, it is either allowed to do so, or to behave as though that nonterminal were $\langle S \rangle$. This completes our discussion of cases.   □

We shall refer to the grammar constructed in the above Theorem as in *normal form*. In the normal form of a regular grammar, each production relates a nonterminal either to ε, or to a terminal followed by a nonterminal. It can also be shown that the productions can be chosen in such a way that there are never two different productions $\langle X \rangle \to a\langle Y \rangle$ and $\langle X \rangle \to a\langle Z \rangle$ using the same terminal on the right, but different nonterminals. We shall demonstrate this in Section 8.13.

Example 8.75 We simplify the grammar
$$\langle S \rangle \to (\{a\}|[b])\{c\}.$$
Our first stage is to write down a grammar for
$$\langle S \rangle \to \{a\}|[b],$$
which is equivalent to

$$\langle S \rangle \quad \to \quad \{a\}$$
$$\langle S \rangle \quad \to \quad [b],$$

and so to

$$\langle S \rangle \quad \to \quad a\langle Y \rangle$$
$$\langle Y \rangle \quad \to \quad a\langle Y \rangle$$
$$\langle S \rangle \quad \to \quad \varepsilon$$
$$\langle Y \rangle \quad \to \quad \varepsilon$$
$$\langle S \rangle \quad \to \quad b\langle X \rangle$$
$$\langle X \rangle \quad \to \quad \varepsilon.$$

Then we produce the grammar

$$\langle T \rangle \quad \to \quad c\langle Z \rangle$$
$$\langle Z \rangle \quad \to \quad c\langle Z \rangle$$
$$\langle T \rangle \quad \to \quad \varepsilon$$
$$\langle Z \rangle \quad \to \quad \varepsilon$$

for $\langle T \rangle \to \{c\}$. Replacing every righthand ε in the first grammar by the righthand of a production from $\langle T \rangle$ in the second grammar, we arrive at

$$\langle S \rangle \quad \to \quad a\langle Y \rangle$$
$$\langle Y \rangle \quad \to \quad a\langle Y \rangle$$
$$\langle S \rangle \quad \to \quad c\langle Z \rangle$$
$$\langle S \rangle \quad \to \quad \varepsilon$$
$$\langle Y \rangle \quad \to \quad c\langle Z \rangle$$
$$\langle Y \rangle \quad \to \quad \varepsilon$$
$$\langle S \rangle \quad \to \quad b\langle X \rangle$$
$$\langle X \rangle \quad \to \quad c\langle Z \rangle$$

$$\langle X \rangle \;\rightarrow\; \varepsilon$$
$$\langle Z \rangle \;\rightarrow\; \mathsf{c}\langle Z \rangle$$
$$\langle Z \rangle \;\rightarrow\; \varepsilon.$$

•**Exercise 8.76** It is required to put the regular grammar $\langle S \rangle \rightarrow$ a|{b} into normal form. A grammar for $\langle S \rangle \rightarrow$ a is

$$\langle S \rangle \;\rightarrow\; \mathsf{a}\langle X \rangle$$
$$\langle X \rangle \;\rightarrow\; \varepsilon,$$

and for $\langle S \rangle \rightarrow$ {b} we have

$$\langle S \rangle \;\rightarrow\; \mathsf{b}\langle S \rangle$$
$$\langle S \rangle \;\rightarrow\; \varepsilon.$$

What is wrong with taking

$$\langle S \rangle \;\rightarrow\; \mathsf{a}\langle X \rangle$$
$$\langle X \rangle \;\rightarrow\; \varepsilon$$
$$\langle S \rangle \;\rightarrow\; \mathsf{b}\langle S \rangle$$
$$\langle S \rangle \;\rightarrow\; \varepsilon$$

for the full grammar?

•**Exercise 8.77** Put the following regular grammars into normal form, with all productions either $\langle X \rangle \rightarrow$ x$\langle Y \rangle$ or $\langle X \rangle \rightarrow \varepsilon$.
(i) $\langle S \rangle \rightarrow$ [ab].   (ii) $\langle S \rangle \rightarrow$ [a][b].
(iii) $\langle S \rangle \rightarrow$ [a]|{bc}.   (iv) $\langle S \rangle \rightarrow$ {a}{b}{ab}.
(v) $\langle S \rangle \rightarrow$ {{a}{bb}}.
(vi) $\langle S \rangle \rightarrow$ ((a{b})|(b{c}))({a}|[d]).

8.13   Finite state machines

The simplification we carried out in the last section would be of only academic interest if it were not for a link between regular expressions and their recognition, and the capabilities of computers. This link is based upon a model for a computer which regards it as a machine which can be in one of a finite number of *states*, and of changing its state as it reads each character in its input stream. Every computer proceeds from a starting state to one of a collection of finishing states when doing a calculation, unless caught in an infinite loop.

This simple type of machine is what we shall model now.

Definition Let A be an alphabet, called the **input alphabet**. Let S be a set called the **set of states**. Suppose we are given a **starting**

state i and a subset $\mathcal{F} \subseteq \mathcal{S}$ of **finishing states**. Suppose that we also have a mapping $t : \mathcal{A} \times \mathcal{S} \to \mathcal{S}$. This combination is called a **finite state machine**. The state $t(\mathsf{a}, s)$ is meant to represent the state resulting one time unit later when the machine is in state s and reads the letter a, and t is called the **transition mapping**.

The machine starts in state i and reads the first letter a_1. It moves to state $t(\mathsf{a}_1, i)$ and reads a_2, moving to state $t(\mathsf{a}_2, t(\mathsf{a}_1, i))$, and so on, and if it reaches $\mathcal{F}$, it has finished its calculation. We have a property of strings over $\mathcal{A}$, that they do or do not result in the state being in $\mathcal{F}$.

Definition The string $\mathsf{a}_1 \mathsf{a}_2 \cdots \mathsf{a}_n$ is said to be **recognized** or **accepted** by the above finite state machine if $s_1 = t(\mathsf{a}_1, i)$, $s_2 = t(\mathsf{a}_2, s_1)$, ..., $s_n = t(\mathsf{a}_n, s_{n-1})$, and $s_n \in \mathcal{F}$.

A similar thing happens with a procedure in a compiler which is looking for the next *token* in a program. A token is something like a reserved word `BEGIN` or `FOR`; an identifier `recnumber`; an assignment symbol `:=`; a relation symbol `<=`; an arithmetic operator `+`; or anything else the programming language makes legal. The procedure which extracts the next token is called the *lexical analyser*. Its job is to distinguish between `END` and `ENDOWMENT`, between `<` and `<=`, or `:` and `:=`, or `12`, `12..20` and `12.782E9`. It does not check the meaningfulness of what it is reading, it just blindly picks out tokens, and passes them back to the calling procedure.

Since the permissible tokens are defined in terms of some regular expression, we need some way of translating a regular expression back into a form that a finite state machine can digest. The regular expression should determine a set of states, and a transition mapping between these states, so that we can construct a machine to do the recognition. Let us look at some Examples.

Example 8.78 Suppose that the machine is to recognize the strings which consist of a letter followed by a string of letters and digits. The regular expression is
$$\langle letter \rangle \{ \langle letter \rangle | \langle digit \rangle \}.$$
We can model our machine with three states i, f and x, the start, finish and fail states. The transitions are as follows. First,
$$t(\mathsf{a}, i) = \begin{cases} f & \text{if } \mathsf{a} \text{ is a letter,} \\ x & \text{otherwise.} \end{cases}$$

Second,
$$t(\text{a}, f) = \begin{cases} f & \text{if a is a letter or digit,} \\ x & \text{otherwise.} \end{cases}$$
Finally, $t(\text{a}, x) = x$ for all a.

Example 8.79 Our next machine is capable of recognizing both integers $dddd$ and reals $dddd.ddddd$. The regular expression is
$$\langle D\rangle\{\langle D\rangle\}[.\langle D\rangle\{\langle D\rangle\}],$$
where $\langle D\rangle$ represents a digit. Thus 123, 123.4 and 123.45 are numbers. The problem is, how to exclude things like 1.2.3 or 123. as numbers. We can manage with five states i, f_i, f_r, t and x. The finishing states f_i and f_r represent finishing with an integer or real. We can simplify our discussion by saying that any transition not explicitly mentioned is to x. A digit causes a transition from i to f_i. A digit causes a transition from f_i to f_i. A full stop causes a transition from f_i to t. A digit causes a transition from t to f_r, or from f_r to f_r.

Example 8.80 Suppose that we want to recognize numbers as above, except that we allow 123. and .123 as valid real numbers, and we also accept a sequence of two dots, as used in subranges. A real must involve at least one digit. The regular expression we are working with is
$$(\langle D\rangle\{\langle D\rangle\}[.\{\langle D\rangle\}])|(\{\langle D\rangle\}.\langle D\rangle\{\langle D\rangle\})|(..).$$
If the input starts with a digit, then we know that we are reading a number. If it starts with . then we could be reading .. or a number. We can specify the states i, f_i, f_r, t and x as before, but we also need a state u to represent an initial dot, and f_d to represent a double dot. The details are left to the reader.

We see in these Examples that there is an interference between the various parts of the regular expression, in that we cannot simply design a machine to do each part of the recognition, and then piece them together. For instance, when we meet a digit, we do not know whether it starts an integer or a real. When we meet a dot, we are not sure if this is a real or a repeated dot. The 'state of mind' of the machine is given by specifying the set of possibilities it is deciding between. We could think of the machine as having an area of its memory set aside as an array of boolean values, the setting of one of which indicates that it is considering that possibility at the moment.

At this stage, our simplification of regular grammars will be of a considerable help. This simplification shows that we only ever need to consider productions of the form $\langle X \rangle \to \mathsf{a}\langle Y \rangle$ or $\langle X \rangle \to \varepsilon$. Suppose that we start with a word that we might be able to recognize, and that this word is $w = \mathsf{a}_1 \mathsf{a}_2 \cdots \mathsf{a}_n$. Start with an array of boolean values, one for each nonterminal, and set all boolean values false, except that the one for $\langle S \rangle$ is set true. Suppose that in the productions, there was only one production $\langle S \rangle \to \mathsf{a}_1 \langle Y \rangle$. Then w must have been formed from this production. We read a_1 from w, set the boolean for $\langle S \rangle$ false, and that for $\langle Y \rangle$ true. On the other hand, if a production $\langle S \rangle \to \mathsf{a}_1 \langle Z \rangle$ had also existed, we would have set the boolean for $\langle Z \rangle$ true as well, to indicate a 'mixed state', where we have not decided between $\langle Y \rangle$ and $\langle Z \rangle$.

At the next stage, the letter a_2 must be produced, from a production of the form $\langle Y \rangle \to \mathsf{a}_2 \langle V \rangle$ or $\langle Z \rangle \to \mathsf{a}_2 \langle W \rangle$. For each of the nonterminals set true at stage one, we look for all productions from those nonterminals using a_2 and another nonterminal on the right, then set the new nonterminals true.

This process continues until we meet a_n, which will set certain nonterminals true. It is only possible to form this word w from these productions if one of the nonterminals set true has a production yielding ε. Thus this must be our definition of a final state for our machine, namely that one of the nonterminals defining the state yields ε.

We see our way to designing a recognizer for a regular grammar. We write the regular grammar in simplified form. The states $\mathcal{S}$ of our machine correspond to subsets of the nonterminals, $\mathcal{S} = \mathcal{P}(\mathcal{N})$, and the starting state is the set $\{\langle S \rangle\}$ with single element the start letter. A state corresponds to the set of possibilities being considered at the moment. If s is a state, and a is a letter, we define $t(\mathsf{a}, s)$ by

$$t(\mathsf{a}, s) = \bigcup_{\langle U \rangle \in s} \{\langle V \rangle : \langle U \rangle \to \mathsf{a}\langle V \rangle\}.$$

Whenever there is a production $\langle U \rangle \to \mathsf{a}\langle V \rangle$ with $\langle U \rangle \in s$, we put $\langle V \rangle$ in $t(\mathsf{a}, s)$. A finishing state is a state f such that there exists a $\langle U \rangle \in f$ with $\langle U \rangle \to \varepsilon$.

We have proved the following theorem.

Theorem 8.13 Given any regular language, there exists a finite state machine which recognizes only the words in that regular language.

The converse of this result is also true, and is left for the reader to verify.

We have incidentally proved the result we described on page 225

for the normal form of a grammar, where we said that the productions
could be chosen in such a way that in any production the nonterminal
on the left and the terminal on the right determined the nonterminal on
the right. The method is to replace our original nonterminals by sets of
nonterminals, as above.

This has done the bulk of the work on our lexical analyser. The above
ideas can be translated directly into a procedure to identify and return
the next token of a language. An example is given in the appendices.
The ideas are also of use in sophisticated text editors, which have the
ability to search for a regular expression, rather than just a string of
ASCII characters. This sort of search is useful when we want to find
the next REPEAT or WHILE in a program, or we want to find the next
occurrence of a[$\cdots$], where the dots indicate an arbitrary string.

8.14   Simplifying context-free grammars

Having found a normal form for regular grammars, our next task is to do
the same for general context-free grammars. Our first query might be,
whether we really have anything more general in context-free grammars
than we have in regular grammars. The answer to this question is a
definite *yes*, as we now show.

> **Example 8.81** Let $L = \{0, 1\}$. The set of words
> $$L = \{ w \in \mathcal{A}^* : w = 1^n 0^n \text{ for some } n \in \mathbb{Z}^+ \}$$
> is the language of a context-free grammar. For example, the following
> productions will generate it:
> $$\langle S \rangle \;\rightarrow\; 1\langle S \rangle 0$$
> $$\langle S \rangle \;\rightarrow\; \varepsilon.$$
> It is not regular, as we prove by contradiction. For, suppose we had
> a language in normal form which would generate L. This language
> would have to be capable of yielding arbitrarily long strings of the
> form $1^p \langle X \rangle$ when generating $1^p 0^p$, with $\langle X \rangle \Rightarrow^* 0^p$. There would
> only be a finite number of possibilities for $\langle X \rangle$, for varying p, as
> the nonterminal alphabet is finite. It would therefore be possible
> to find $p < q$ with $\langle S \rangle \Rightarrow^* 1^p \langle X \rangle$ and $\langle S \rangle \Rightarrow^* 1^q \langle X \rangle$, and also
> $\langle X \rangle \Rightarrow^* (0^p | 0^q)$. Thus $\langle S \rangle \Rightarrow^* 1^q 0^p$, a contradiction.

The above result seems more natural when we recall that a finite state
machine which recognized the above language would have to be capable

of remembering how many 1s there were at the beginning of the string, so that it could count them off at the end, and make sure the counts were equal. However, it would not be capable of remembering numbers larger than the total number of its states.

The above Example might seem artificial. Consider the far more complex examples which occur in real programming languages.

Example 8.82 In a *Modula-2* program, the variable declarations contain

```
VAR abcdxyz:REAL;
    pqrw:mytype;
```

and a bit further on the statement

```
abcdxyz:=pqrw;
```

is encountered. A compiler must note that the identifiers match, and then emit an error message if `mytype` and `REAL` are not compatible types. It is not just two words of the same length that are being matched here, but two arbitrary words.

It is beyond the capabilities of even context-free grammars to generate programs in which identifier names match in different parts of the program, but phrase structure grammars are adequate.

•*Exercise 8.83* Show that the language $L = \{\, 1^p 0^q 1^p : p, q \in \mathbb{N} \,\}$ over $\{\, 0, 1 \,\}$ is context-free, but not regular.

General context-free grammars are thus truly more powerful than regular languages. Let us examine the productions for context-free grammars, and see how we can simplify them. The techniques of simplification are very similar to those we used for regular grammars, except that we can never dispense with productions of the form $\langle X \rangle \to \langle Y \rangle \langle Z \rangle$.

Theorem 8.14 Any context-free grammar can be simplified by adding new nonterminals so that all productions are of one of the forms

$$\langle X \rangle \;\; \to \;\; \langle Y \rangle \langle Z \rangle$$
$$\langle X \rangle \;\; \to \;\; \mathbf{x}$$
$$\langle X \rangle \;\; \to \;\; \langle Y \rangle$$
$$\langle X \rangle \;\; \to \;\; \varepsilon,$$

with $\mathbf{x}$ a terminal letter.

Proof Any productions resulting in ε or a single terminal or nonterminal are covered. Suppose we have a production of the form $\langle X \rangle \to uv$, with u a terminal or nonterminal letter and v a word of length at least

one consisting possibly of both terminals and nonterminals. We can
replace this production by three productions $\langle X \rangle \to \langle U \rangle \langle V \rangle$, $\langle U \rangle \to u$
and $\langle V \rangle \to v$, where $\langle U \rangle$ and $\langle V \rangle$ are two new nonterminals. If u or v
is a nonterminal, then $\langle U \rangle$ or $\langle V \rangle$ is unnecessary. We can thus decom-
pose our complex productions gradually so that they are all of length at
most two on the righthand side, and so the result follows.   □

The proof is similar to the trick we use in regular languages to handle
a production containing a string of terminals.

Example 8.84 We simplify the grammar with productions

$$\begin{aligned}
\langle S \rangle &\to \langle A \rangle \langle B \rangle \langle A \rangle \\
\langle A \rangle &\to \mathsf{a} \langle S \rangle \mathsf{a} \\
\langle B \rangle &\to \mathsf{b} \\
\langle A \rangle &\to \mathsf{ccc.}
\end{aligned}$$

We replace the first production by the two productions
$\langle S \rangle \to \langle A \rangle \langle X \rangle$ and $\langle X \rangle \to \langle B \rangle \langle A \rangle$. The second production is
replaced by $\langle A \rangle \to \langle Y \rangle \langle Z \rangle$, $\langle Y \rangle \to \mathsf{a}$ and $\langle Z \rangle \to \langle S \rangle \langle Y \rangle$. The third
production can be left as it is. The fourth becomes $\langle A \rangle \to \langle C \rangle \langle D \rangle$,
$\langle C \rangle \to \mathsf{c}$ and $\langle D \rangle \to \langle C \rangle \langle C \rangle$. The simplified grammar is

$$\begin{aligned}
\langle S \rangle &\to \langle A \rangle \langle X \rangle \\
\langle X \rangle &\to \langle B \rangle \langle A \rangle \\
\langle A \rangle &\to \langle Y \rangle \langle Z \rangle \\
\langle Z \rangle &\to \langle S \rangle \langle Y \rangle \\
\langle A \rangle &\to \langle C \rangle \langle D \rangle \\
\langle D \rangle &\to \langle C \rangle \langle C \rangle \\
\langle Y \rangle &\to \mathsf{a} \\
\langle B \rangle &\to \mathsf{b} \\
\langle C \rangle &\to \mathsf{c.}
\end{aligned}$$

• *Exercise 8.85* Simplify the following grammars.
    (i) This models begin...end blocks in *Pascal*.

$$\begin{aligned}
\langle S \rangle &\to \mathsf{b} \langle Q \rangle \mathsf{e} \\
\langle Q \rangle &\to \langle S \rangle ; \langle Q \rangle \\
\langle Q \rangle &\to \langle S \rangle \\
\langle S \rangle &\to \varepsilon \\
\langle S \rangle &\to \mathsf{s}
\end{aligned}$$

(ii) A simple model for declarations.

$$\langle S \rangle \;\; \rightarrow \;\; \mathtt{d} \langle Q \rangle$$
$$\langle Q \rangle \;\; \rightarrow \;\; \langle D \rangle$$
$$\langle Q \rangle \;\; \rightarrow \;\; \langle D \rangle ; \langle Q \rangle$$
$$\langle D \rangle \;\; \rightarrow \;\; \mathtt{i:t}$$

8.15 Left recursion

There is a type of production which is undesirable in a grammar, the sort where the lefthand nonterminal immediately reappears as the first letter on the righthand side.

Definition A production of the form $\langle X \rangle \rightarrow \langle X \rangle u$ is called a **left recursive production**.

This kind of production can always be eliminated from a grammar, at the expense of introducing *right recursive* productions. Let us see how this is done for just one nonterminal.

Theorem 8.15 Given any context-free grammar, and a nonterminal $\langle X \rangle$, there is an equivalent context-free grammar which does not contain any left recursive productions from $\langle X \rangle$, and containing no new left recursive productions for any other nonterminals.

Proof Any productions of the form $\langle X \rangle \rightarrow \langle X \rangle$ can immediately be dropped from the grammar.

The original productions from $\langle X \rangle$ can be classified into two types, those that are left recursive, $\langle X \rangle \rightarrow \langle X \rangle u_i$ for $1 \leqslant i \leqslant n$, and those that are not, $\langle X \rangle \rightarrow v_j$ for $1 \leqslant j \leqslant m$. The use of the recursive productions for $\langle X \rangle$ will always result in a word which leads with $\langle X \rangle$ again, and so eventually one of the nonrecursive productions must be used before this $\langle X \rangle$ can be eliminated. Any yielding operation from $\langle X \rangle$ must produce either a v_j immediately, or must yield something of the form

$$\langle X \rangle \Rightarrow^* \langle X \rangle u_{i_k} \cdots u_{i_1} \Rightarrow v_j u_{i_k} \cdots u_{i_1}.$$

We can achieve this result in a different way. Choose a nonterminal $\langle U \rangle$ different from any others in the grammar, and use the productions

$$\langle X \rangle \;\; \rightarrow \;\; v_j$$
$$\langle X \rangle \;\; \rightarrow \;\; v_j \langle U \rangle$$
$$\langle U \rangle \;\; \rightarrow \;\; u_i$$

$$\langle U \rangle \;\to\; u_i \langle U \rangle$$

instead. We see that some of these are right recursive, but none are left recursive.   □

Example 8.86 Let us remove left recursion on $\langle S \rangle$ from the grammar

$$\langle S \rangle \;\to\; \langle S \rangle + \langle T \rangle$$
$$\langle S \rangle \;\to\; \langle T \rangle$$
$$\langle T \rangle \;\to\; \langle T \rangle * \langle F \rangle$$
$$\langle T \rangle \;\to\; \langle F \rangle$$
$$\langle F \rangle \;\to\; (\langle S \rangle)$$
$$\langle F \rangle \;\to\; 1$$

which is a very much simplified grammar for arithmetic expressions. The round brackets are terminals.

The recursive $\langle S \rangle$ production is

$$\langle S \rangle \to \langle S \rangle + \langle T \rangle,$$

and the nonrecursive one is

$$\langle S \rangle \to \langle T \rangle.$$

We introduce $\langle U \rangle$, and replace the grammar by

$$\langle S \rangle \;\to\; \langle T \rangle$$
$$\langle S \rangle \;\to\; \langle T \rangle \langle U \rangle$$
$$\langle U \rangle \;\to\; + \langle T \rangle$$
$$\langle U \rangle \;\to\; + \langle T \rangle \langle U \rangle$$
$$\langle T \rangle \;\to\; \langle T \rangle * \langle F \rangle$$
$$\langle T \rangle \;\to\; \langle F \rangle$$
$$\langle F \rangle \;\to\; (\langle S \rangle)$$
$$\langle F \rangle \;\to\; 1.$$

By repeatedly removing left recursion for each variable, we arrive at the result we want.

Theorem 8.16 Every context-free grammar has an equivalent non-left recursive grammar.

Example 8.87 We continue with Example 8.86. We next eliminate left recursion on $\langle T \rangle$, of which there is one instance, by introducing a new nonterminal $\langle V \rangle$:

$$\langle S \rangle \;\to\; \langle T \rangle$$

$$\langle S \rangle \;\; \rightarrow \;\; \langle T \rangle \langle U \rangle$$
$$\langle U \rangle \;\; \rightarrow \;\; + \langle T \rangle$$
$$\langle U \rangle \;\; \rightarrow \;\; + \langle T \rangle \langle U \rangle$$
$$\langle T \rangle \;\; \rightarrow \;\; \langle F \rangle$$
$$\langle T \rangle \;\; \rightarrow \;\; \langle F \rangle \langle V \rangle$$
$$\langle V \rangle \;\; \rightarrow \;\; * \langle F \rangle$$
$$\langle V \rangle \;\; \rightarrow \;\; * \langle F \rangle \langle V \rangle$$
$$\langle F \rangle \;\; \rightarrow \;\; (\langle S \rangle)$$
$$\langle F \rangle \;\; \rightarrow \;\; 1.$$

The removal of left recursion is useful when a program is using procedure calls to recognize each nonterminal. Left recursion would lead to an infinite recursive chain.

8.16 Greibach normal form

The reader who is familiar with recursion will know that there is more than one variety of this beast. The simple sort is where a procedure calls itself, and this is analogous to the left recursion we have met above. The more general case is where we have a chain of procedure calls which eventually lead to a recursive call. In the case of our grammars, this is no less disastrous than a direct recursive call. Thus if $\langle A \rangle \rightarrow \langle B \rangle u$ and $\langle B \rangle \rightarrow \langle A \rangle v$ are two productions, then any recognizer for the nonterminal $\langle A \rangle$ might call the recognizer for $\langle B \rangle$, and that might immediately call the recognizer for $\langle A \rangle$ again without any progress being made.

It is clear that if the righthand side of each production starts with a terminal letter then this situation cannot arise, and that is the basis of *Greibach normal form*. This form is the usual one in which to present a grammar to a compiler, or to a procedure in any other program which is parsing its input, be it in a database, editor, operating system or whatever.

Before we prove that any context-free grammar can be so transformed, we need a preliminary result of interest in its own right.

Theorem 8.17 Suppose a grammar has a production $\langle X \rangle \rightarrow \langle Y \rangle u$, with $\langle X \rangle \neq \langle Y \rangle$, and that the full list of productions for $\langle Y \rangle$ consists of $\langle Y \rangle \rightarrow v_i$ for $1 \leqslant i \leqslant n$. We obtain the same language if we replace the production from $\langle X \rangle$ by the productions $\langle X \rangle \rightarrow v_i u$ for $1 \leqslant i \leqslant n$.

Proof In any yielding operation which used that production, the $\langle Y \rangle$ which was introduced would eventually be replaced by some v_i. We replace it immediately in the new grammar.   □

Example 8.88 We replace the fourth production in

$$\langle S \rangle \;\rightarrow\; \langle A \rangle \langle B \rangle$$
$$\langle A \rangle \;\rightarrow\; \langle S \rangle \langle B \rangle$$
$$\langle A \rangle \;\rightarrow\; \langle A \rangle \langle C \rangle$$
$$\langle C \rangle \;\rightarrow\; \langle B \rangle \langle C \rangle$$
$$\langle B \rangle \;\rightarrow\; \langle B \rangle \langle S \rangle$$
$$\langle A \rangle \;\rightarrow\; \mathsf{a}$$
$$\langle B \rangle \;\rightarrow\; \mathsf{b}$$
$$\langle C \rangle \;\rightarrow\; \mathsf{c}$$

to obtain

$$\langle S \rangle \;\rightarrow\; \langle A \rangle \langle B \rangle$$
$$\langle A \rangle \;\rightarrow\; \langle S \rangle \langle B \rangle$$
$$\langle A \rangle \;\rightarrow\; \langle A \rangle \langle C \rangle$$
$$\langle C \rangle \;\rightarrow\; \langle B \rangle \langle S \rangle \langle C \rangle$$
$$\langle C \rangle \;\rightarrow\; \mathsf{b} \langle C \rangle$$
$$\langle B \rangle \;\rightarrow\; \langle B \rangle \langle S \rangle$$
$$\langle A \rangle \;\rightarrow\; \mathsf{a}$$
$$\langle B \rangle \;\rightarrow\; \mathsf{b}$$
$$\langle C \rangle \;\rightarrow\; \mathsf{c}.$$

Armed with this result, and those on the elimination of left recursion, let us show how we can make every production lead with a terminal. The following is a somewhat restricted version of Greibach's Theorem. The most obvious restriction is that none of the original productions are permitted to be of the form $\langle X \rangle \rightarrow \varepsilon$. As a consequence, it follows that the grammar cannot yield ε either. It is rare in programming language grammars to find instances where a production does end in an empty string, and usually it is possible to slightly change the productions so that this does not occur. Removal of this restriction leads to some complications which are beyond the scope of this book.

Theorem 8.18 (Greibach normal form) Any context-free language with no productions of the form $\langle X \rangle \rightarrow \varepsilon$ has a grammar i . which every production is of the form $\langle X \rangle \to \mathbf{x}u$, with $\mathbf{x}$ a terminal letter.

Proof Suppose that the nonterminals are $\langle A_1 \rangle$, $\langle A_2 \rangle$, ..., $\langle A_n \rangle$. We first remove left recursion on $\langle A_n \rangle$, which possibly produces a new nonterminal, of higher subscript than n. Nonterminals from $\langle A_n \rangle$ upwards will only have productions to words starting either with a terminal or with a nonterminal of lower subscript.

Next, we remove any productions of the form $\langle A_{n-1} \rangle \to \langle A_k \rangle u$, with $k \geqslant n$, using Theorem 8.17. Since there is no left recursion on $\langle A_i \rangle$ for $i \geqslant n$, it follows that no new productions of the kind we are eliminating will be produced. After this, we eliminate left recursion on $\langle A_{n-1} \rangle$, adding any new nonterminal to the end of our list.

We continue with $\langle A_{n-2} \rangle$. Any productions $\langle A_{n-2} \rangle \to \langle A_k \rangle u$ with $k \geqslant n-1$ are eliminated. This will possibly introduce some more productions of the same sort, but the values of k will strictly decrease in this process. Finally, left recursion on $\langle A_{n-2} \rangle$ is removed.

This process continues all the way down to $\langle A_1 \rangle$.

Consider the productions from $\langle A_1 \rangle$. These cannot lead with a nonterminal, and so are of the desired form. Any productions $\langle A_2 \rangle \to \langle A_1 \rangle u$ can be eliminated using Theorem 8.17, so that all productions from $\langle A_2 \rangle$ also conform to Greibach normal form. And so this process continues all the way up to the nonterminal of highest index. Essentially, this last phase is one of substitution.   □

A suitable choice of the ordering of the nonterminals will ease the burden of this reduction.

Example 8.89 Consider the grammar

$$\begin{aligned}
\langle E \rangle &\to \langle T \rangle \\
\langle E \rangle &\to \langle T \rangle + \langle E \rangle \\
\langle T \rangle &\to \langle F \rangle \\
\langle T \rangle &\to \langle F \rangle * \langle T \rangle \\
\langle F \rangle &\to \mathtt{i} \\
\langle F \rangle &\to (\langle E \rangle)
\end{aligned}$$

for simple expressions. The round brackets are terminals. In this case, the grammar has been so chosen that most of the elimination is unnecessary, provided we take the nonterminals in the order $\langle F \rangle$, $\langle T \rangle$, $\langle E \rangle$. Only the very last stage is needed. The productions from $\langle F \rangle$ are already in Greibach form, but those from $\langle T \rangle$ are not. We replace these by

$$\langle T \rangle \;\rightarrow\; \texttt{i}$$
$$\langle T \rangle \;\rightarrow\; (\langle E \rangle)$$
$$\langle T \rangle \;\rightarrow\; \texttt{i}*\langle T \rangle$$
$$\langle T \rangle \;\rightarrow\; (\langle E \rangle)*\langle T \rangle.$$

Next we look at the productions from $\langle E \rangle$, and replace these in the same way by

$$\langle E \rangle \;\rightarrow\; \texttt{i}$$
$$\langle E \rangle \;\rightarrow\; (\langle E \rangle)$$
$$\langle E \rangle \;\rightarrow\; \texttt{i}*\langle T \rangle$$
$$\langle E \rangle \;\rightarrow\; (\langle E \rangle)*\langle T \rangle.$$
$$\langle E \rangle \;\rightarrow\; \texttt{i}+\langle E \rangle$$
$$\langle E \rangle \;\rightarrow\; (\langle E \rangle)+\langle E \rangle$$
$$\langle E \rangle \;\rightarrow\; \texttt{i}*\langle T \rangle+\langle E \rangle$$
$$\langle E \rangle \;\rightarrow\; (\langle E \rangle)*\langle T \rangle+\langle E \rangle.$$

These eight productions for $\langle E \rangle$, four for $\langle T \rangle$ and two for $\langle F \rangle$ constitute the Greibach normal form of the grammar.

Example 8.90 We look at a somewhat unsatisfactory grammar for expressions

$$\langle E \rangle \;\rightarrow\; \langle E \rangle+\langle E \rangle$$
$$\langle E \rangle \;\rightarrow\; \langle E \rangle*\langle E \rangle$$
$$\langle E \rangle \;\rightarrow\; \texttt{i}$$
$$\langle E \rangle \;\rightarrow\; (\langle E \rangle),$$

in which the brackets in the last production are terminal brackets. There is only one nonterminal, and so we only need to remove left recursion. For this, we need to introduce a new nonterminal $\langle F \rangle$, and replace the first two left recursive rules. This gives

$$\langle E \rangle \;\rightarrow\; \texttt{i}\langle F \rangle$$
$$\langle E \rangle \;\rightarrow\; (\langle E \rangle)\langle F \rangle$$
$$\langle F \rangle \;\rightarrow\; +\langle E \rangle\langle F \rangle$$
$$\langle F \rangle \;\rightarrow\; *\langle E \rangle\langle F \rangle$$
$$\langle F \rangle \;\rightarrow\; *\langle E \rangle$$
$$\langle F \rangle \;\rightarrow\; +\langle E \rangle$$

$$\langle E \rangle \;\rightarrow\; \texttt{i}$$
$$\langle E \rangle \;\rightarrow\; (\langle E \rangle).$$

The second phase is unnecessary, since this is in Griebach normal form.

•*Exercise 8.91* Why did we assume that no productions lead to ε?

•*Exercise 8.92* Put the following grammar into Greibach normal form. The nonterminal $\langle S \rangle$ is meant to represent a statement, $\langle L \rangle$ a loop, $\langle A \rangle$ an assignment and $\langle X \rangle$ a statement sequence.

$$\langle S \rangle \;\rightarrow\; \langle L \rangle$$
$$\langle S \rangle \;\rightarrow\; \langle A \rangle$$
$$\langle A \rangle \;\rightarrow\; \texttt{i := i}$$
$$\langle L \rangle \;\rightarrow\; \texttt{l}\langle X \rangle\texttt{e}$$
$$\langle X \rangle \;\rightarrow\; \varepsilon$$
$$\langle X \rangle \;\rightarrow\; \langle S \rangle$$
$$\langle X \rangle \;\rightarrow\; \langle S \rangle;\langle X \rangle.$$

Appendix A

Solutions to selected exercises

1. Introduction

1.1 The first is proved by the following argument. Having decided what to place first, in n possible ways, there remain $n - 1$ choices of what to put next, then $n - 2$ for the third object, and so on. The independence of all these choices means that we multiply all these numbers together.

Secondly, suppose we choose r objects from n. We can list these objects in $r!$ different ways, and the remaining objects can be listed after them in $(n - r)!$ ways. When we do all of these listings, we obtain all of the $n!$ listings of all n objects. Thus the number of choices satisfies

$$\binom{n}{r} \times r! \times (n - r)! = n!.$$

1.3 (Hint) $9^{m+1} = 9 \times 9^m = 9 \times (9^m + 7) - 9 \times 7.$

1.5 Certainly true for $n = l = 1$. Assume true for $n \leqslant m$. Then
$$s_{m+1} = s_m + (m + 1) = \frac{1}{2}m(m + 1) + (m + 1) = \frac{1}{2}(m + 1)([m + 1] + 1),$$
and so the result is true for $n = m + 1$. Thus true for all n by induction.

2. Logic

2.8   (i) Yes. False.

(ii) Yes. False.

(iii) Yes. False, I suppose. There is presumably someone out there with only one ear

(iv) Yes. True.

(v) Yes. True.

(vi) This sort of statement presents philosophical problems. It appears to be a simple proposition like the last one, but when we look closely at it there are difficulties. If it is true, then what it says is that it is false, so we have a contradiction. If it is false, then what

it says, namely that it is false, is false, so it is true, and we again
have a contradiction. Thus it is certainly not a proposition!

The difficulty lies in deciding when a statement *is* a proposition, if
this one is excluded. How can we ever know, for a very complicated
statement, that it is not of this type? The essential property
this particular sentence has is that of being *self-referential*: the
statement says something about itself. Thus we should perhaps
exclude such sentences as propositions. But then what about 'This
sentence is in Appendix A', which is blatantly self-referential, yet
perfectly innocent? Also, there are pairs of sentences which refer
to one another. Thus suppose we have two sentences A and B,
where A is 'Sentence B is false', and B is 'Sentence A is true'?

Such difficulties will not affect us in this book. The statements
we make in mathematics are rarely of the type that present such
difficulties. The only nagging doubt in the author's mind is, was
the last sentence self-referential? Or even the one previous to this
one...?

2.10 In *Modula-2*, the loop terminates when $a \neq b$ but $c = d$, whereas
in most *BASIC*s it terminates when $a = b$ but $c \neq d$.

2.13 Perhaps '$x < y < z$' or 'x gave a y to z'.

2.14 (Hint) If you cannot think of one, wait until you have finished
Chapter 2, and that should suggest a way of constructing predicates
with arbitrarily many places.

2.16 (i) $Parent(x, y)$.
  (ii) $Real(x)$.
 (iii) $Twothirds(x, y)$.
 (iv) $Order(x, y, z)$. More literally handled when we have covered connectives.
  (v) $Mean(m, x, y)$.
 (vi) $Jobpriority(x, y)$ Again, better handled using connectives.
(vii) $Leq(x, x)$, where $Leq(x, y)$ means $x \leqslant y$.
(viii) $Type(x, t)$.

2.17

P	P
T	T
F	F

. Does it need two columns?

2.18 If the universe of discourse were finite, we could make a list of all of the elements in this universe, and list the truth value of the predicate. This course would be impractical for a large universe, and impossible for an infinite one. Such a table is rarely used in practice, unless there is some sort of property which we want to express, but which we are unable to find any finite expression for.

	P	Q	R	$\neg W$
	T	T	T	F
	T	T	F	T
	T	F	T	T
2.19	T	F	F	T
	F	T	T	T
	F	T	F	F
	F	F	T	F
	F	F	F	T

2.20 Whereas in mathematics we always put 'not' in front of our proposition, in English we would absorb the word into the middle of a sentence. The negation of 'I can solve this problem' is 'I cannot solve this problem', not 'not I can solve this problem. From 'I managed to solve this problem' we obtain 'I did not manage to solve this problem'.

The mathematical notation is designed to strip away the inessential details of grammar, and to concentrate on the meaning of the proposition. This simplification will become more and more profound as we add more basic constructions to our simple mathematical grammar.

2.21 (i) Yes.

  (ii) No.

 (iii) Ambiguous second statement. With the interpretation that it means 'all sheep are some colour other than white', it is not the negation of 'all sheep are white'. But if we interpret it as 'not every sheep is white', it *is* the negation. Natural language has failed to be specific enough.

 (iv) Yes.

2.23 Notice how clumsily some of these translate back into ordinary language. The precision of the mathematical notation has been completely lost. Add a tiny bit more complexity, and natural language will have difficulty expressing anything at all!

(i) I slowly solved this problem.

(ii) I gave a sensible answer, and I got some marks for it.

(iii) I solved the problem, and I didn't give a quick, correct solution, but it was not a silly answer which I got no marks for.

2.24 The first four are given in the following.

P	$P \wedge P$	$\neg P$	$P \wedge \neg P$	$\neg(P \wedge P)$	$\neg(P \wedge \neg P)$
T	T	F	F	F	T
F	F	T	F	T	T

The last has truth table

P	Q	R	$(P \wedge Q) \wedge R$
T	T	T	T
T	T	F	F
T	F	T	F
T	F	F	F
F	T	T	F
F	T	F	F
F	F	T	F
F	F	F	F

2.25   (i) $Real(x) \wedge Greaterthan(x, \pi)$.

(ii) $File(f) \wedge Copy(f) \wedge Del(f) \wedge \neg Arch(f)$.

(iii) $Lessthan(x, y) \wedge Lessthan(y, z)$.

(iv) $Anc(x, y) \wedge Anc(x, z)$.

(v) $Term(x) \wedge Term(y) \wedge Comp(c) \wedge Direct(x, c) \wedge \neg Direct(y, c)$.

2.27   (i) I either write a cheque or use a credit card.

(ii) I bank with Floyds Bank and if I am in credit I write a cheque.

(iii) I use a cheque or credit card.

(iv) If I am not in credit I do not pay a bill.

(v) If I pay a bill, I pay by cheque if I am in credit, or by credit card otherwise.

P	Q	R	$P \wedge Q$	$(P \wedge Q) \vee R$
T	T	T	T	T
T	T	F	T	T
T	F	T	F	T
T	F	F	F	F
F	T	T	F	T
F	T	F	F	F
F	F	F	F	T
F	F	F	F	F

2.29 (i)

(ii)

P	Q	R	$P \vee R$	$Q \vee R$	$(P \vee R) \wedge (Q \vee R)$
T	T	T	T	T	T
T	T	F	T	T	T
T	F	T	T	T	T
T	F	F	T	F	F
F	T	T	T	T	T
F	T	F	F	T	F
F	F	T	T	T	T
F	F	F	F	F	F

2.30 (i) $\neg Userfile(f) \vee \neg(Copy(f) \wedge Write(f))$.

(ii) $\neg(File(x) \wedge File(y) \wedge Samename(x,y)) \vee Identical(x,y)$.

(iii) $Term(x) \wedge (Direct(x) \vee Net(x))$.

(iv) $Message(m) \wedge (From(x,m) \vee From(y,m))$.

2.33 (i) $Integer(x) \rightarrow Real(x)$.

(ii) $Userfile(f) \rightarrow (Write(f) \vee Copy(f))$.

(iii) $Divisor(x,y) \rightarrow Lessthanorequal(x,y)$.

(iv) $Priority(x,6) \rightarrow Access(x,f)$. Should $Male(x)$ figure somewhere in this?

2.34 (i) $Access(x,f) \leftrightarrow Priority(x,7)$.

(ii) $Chrgd(x) \leftrightarrow [(Ordry(x) \wedge Over(x,0)) \vee (Special(x) \wedge Over(x,y))]$.

(iii) $Runs(c) \leftrightarrow \neg Overrevved(c)$.

(iv) $Puffin(b) \leftrightarrow (Seagoing(b) \wedge (Parrotbill(b) \vee Whitefacialpatch(b)))$.

2.36 (i) `(a<b) AND (b<=c)`.

(ii) `(a>b) AND ((a>c) OR ((b-a)>c))`.

(iii) `(a<>b) AND (b<>c) AND (a<>c)`.

(iv) `(a>=0)=(b>=0)`.

(v) (a>0)=(b<c) looks convincing, but it will fail if $a < 0$ but $b = c$; the loop will end prematurely. The condition ((a>0) AND (b<c)) OR ((a<0) AND (b>c)) will work, as will a(b-c)<0.

2.44 (Hint) To prove $P \iff \neg\neg P$, we calculate the truth table of $P \leftrightarrow \neg\neg P$.

2.45 (Hint) In (iv), we look at $(P \wedge \neg P) \to Q$.

2.50 x is an African elephant. To get a computer to make this deduction would be an elephantine task. The reasoning can be done by means of *modus ponens* and the use of a few tautologies. For instance, A_1 is of the form $(L \wedge M) \to (A \vee E)$. Axioms A_7 and A_9 assert L and M, so we can deduce $A \vee E$, that is, that x is either an ant-eater or elephant. Axioms A_2 and A_3 state $E \to H$, and $A \to \neg H$, and we use the tautology
$$[(A \vee E) \wedge (E \to H) \wedge (A \to \neg H) \wedge H] \to E$$
of Exercise 2.46 to deduce that x is an elephant, by means of A_{10}. The rest is left to the reader.

2.51 (Hint) The most obvious advantage would be that one could input the description 'medium-sized, black' and instantly have the names of all the birds fitting this description. But then, suppose one had seen a bird, and knew it was either brown or black, did not have a red bill, but did have a long curved bill, and it was either medium or large in size. This sort of information could be handled in just the same way, if Sylvia's program understood logical operations.

On the other hand, ornithologists are generally squeamish about carrying a pair of binoculars weighing more than a kilogram, so a portable computer as well might not be that popular!

2.54 Suppose the loop terminates. There exist integers i, j and k satisfying the conditions. From $i > (j+k)$ we deduce that $i^2 > j^2 + k^2 + 2jk$, and we also have $i^2 = k^2 - j^2$, so $k^2 - j^2 > j^2 + k^2 + 2jk$, giving $0 > j(j+k)$. But if $0 > j > i > j+k$ then both j and $j+k$ are negative, so their product is positive, a contradiction. We deduce that the loop could not terminate.

2.55 (Hint) The ones involving **T** and **F** are the only ones which may present problems. Regard **T** and **F** as propositional constants, taking

246   *Appendix A. Solutions to selected exercises*

only one value. Thus the truth table of $P \wedge \mathbf{T}$ is

P	$\mathbf{T}$	$P \wedge \mathbf{T}$
T	T	T
F	T	F

The number of rows in the truth table of a wff in n propositional variables is *still* equal to 2^n, even when it involves the propositional constants $\mathbf{T}$ and $\mathbf{F}$.

2.56 (i) $P!P \iff \neg(P \vee P) \iff \neg P$.

(ii) $(P!P)!P \iff (\neg P)!P \iff \neg(\neg P \vee P) \iff \neg\mathbf{T} \iff \mathbf{F}$.

(iii) This is equivalent to $\mathbf{F}!\mathbf{F} \iff \neg(\mathbf{F} \vee \mathbf{F}) \iff \neg\mathbf{F} \iff \mathbf{T}$.

(iv) $W!W \iff \neg W$, so this one is $\neg(P!Q) \iff \neg\neg(P \vee Q) \iff (P \vee Q)$.

(v) We have $(\neg P)!(\neg Q) \iff \neg(\neg P \vee \neg Q) \iff P \wedge Q$.

(vi) This time, we have $\neg[(\neg P)!Q] \iff \neg\neg[\neg P \vee Q] \iff \neg P \vee Q \iff P \to Q$.

2.58 We could rewrite $W_1 \wedge W_2$ as $\neg(\neg W_1 \vee \neg W_2)$.

2.60 (i) $\neg[(\neg P \vee Q) \wedge (\neg Q \vee R)] \vee [(P \wedge R) \vee (\neg P \wedge \neg R)]$.

(ii) $\neg[(P \vee Q) \wedge \neg(P \wedge Q)] \vee [(Q \wedge \neg R) \vee (\neg Q \wedge R)]$.

(iii) $\neg[(\neg(P \wedge Q)) \wedge [(P \vee (\neg Q \vee P)) \wedge \neg(P \wedge (\neg Q \vee P))]]$.

Did we claim we were *simplifying* the expressions?

2.63 (i) $\neg P \vee \neg Q \vee \neg R$.

(ii) $(\neg P \vee \neg Q) \wedge (\neg Q \vee \neg R)$.

(iii) $(P \wedge Q) \vee (\neg Q \wedge R \wedge P)$.

These are now looking simpler!

2.66 $(P \wedge Q) \vee (P \wedge R) \vee (P \wedge \neg S \wedge T) \vee (P \wedge \neg S \wedge U)$.

2.69 The answers are not necessarily unique.

(i) $(P \wedge \neg P) \vee (P \wedge \neg Q) \iff P \wedge \neg Q$.

(ii) $(P \wedge \neg Q) \vee (Q \wedge \neg R) \vee \neg P \vee R$.

(iii) $P \wedge R \wedge \neg P \wedge \neg Q \iff \mathbf{F}$.

(iv) $P \wedge \neg Q$, after dropping two terms.

(v) $(\neg P \wedge Q) \vee (P \wedge \neg Q) \vee (\neg P \wedge \neg Q)$. This expression is equivalent to P nand Q, since the factor $\neg(P \operatorname{xor} Q)$ adds no extra restriction. A simpler disjunctive form is $\neg P \vee \neg Q$.

2.74 The DNFs are as follows.

(i) $P \wedge \neg Q$. (ii) $\mathbf{T}$. (iii) $\mathbf{F}$. (iv) $P \wedge \neg Q$.

(v) $(\neg P \wedge Q) \vee (P \wedge \neg Q) \vee (\neg P \wedge \neg Q)$.

2.76 $P \to Q \iff \neg P \vee Q$ is represented by Figure A.1.

Fig. A.1 **Implication**

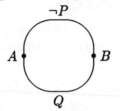

2.78 (i) $(P \vee Q) \leftrightarrow R \iff [(P \vee Q) \wedge R] \vee [\neg P \wedge \neg Q \wedge \neg R]$, yielding Figure A.2.

Fig. A.2 $(P \vee Q) \leftrightarrow R$

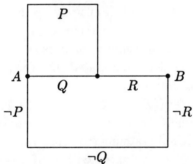

(ii) $(\neg P \vee Q) \vee [R \wedge (\neg P \vee \neg R)] \iff \neg P \vee Q$. The result is in Figure A.1.

(iii) The wff first simplifies to $\neg(P \operatorname{xor} Q) \vee \neg R$. But $\neg(P \operatorname{xor} Q) \iff P \leftrightarrow Q$, and so we obtain Figure A.3.

Fig. A.3 $(P \operatorname{xor} Q)$ nand R

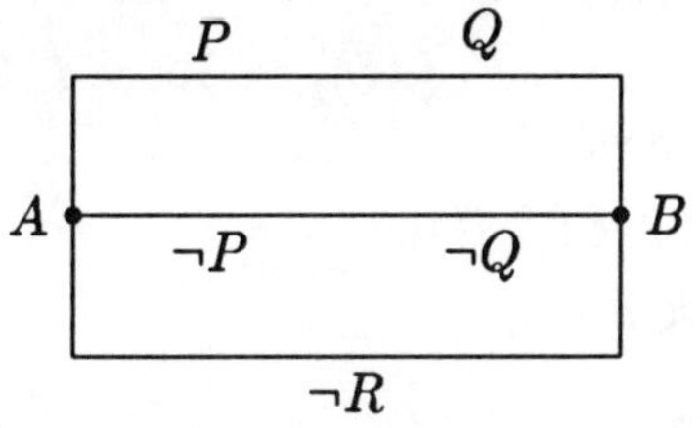

2.87 (i) If the universe of discourse is all customers then take
$$\forall c \, In\,Credit(c).$$

Alternatively, with the universe consisting of all people, use
$$\forall c \; Customer(c) \rightarrow InCredit(c).$$

(ii) The universe of discourse is natural numbers:
$$\forall n \; ((Prime(n) \wedge Unequal(n,2)) \rightarrow Odd(n)).$$

(iii) The universe of discourse includes suppliers, parts and towns:
$$\forall s \; (Supplies(p,s) \rightarrow Resides(s, \text{Birmingham})).$$

(iv) We could use something like
$$\forall k \; ((SS(k) \wedge K(k) \wedge Made(k, \text{Sheffield})) \rightarrow LTG(k).$$

(v) $\forall n \; (\neg \forall m \; Le(m,n))$. This one is tricky. If we said that $\forall m \; Le(m,n)$, then this would be a property of n which would make it the largest integer. The negation is the property of not being the largest integer. Thus this property has to be possessed by every n.

(vi) This time, we shall go into a bit more detail in our specification. How much detail to include is entirely up to us. Let r be a request and d a delay in handling a request. Let $P(r)$ be a predicate indicating that r is a request for personal records. Let $D(r,d)$ indicate that d is a delay associated with the request r. Let $L(x,y)$ mean $x \leqslant y$. We could say
$$\forall r \; ((P(r) \wedge D(r,d)) \rightarrow L(d,14)),$$
but there is something wrong here. We have a predicate in d, whereas the original statement did not involve d. We want d to be the *unique* delay associated with r. If d is *not* this delay, then there is no problem, as we are saying nothing in this case. We can therefore quantify d out of our expression, to obtain
$$\forall r,d \; ((P(r) \wedge D(r,d)) \rightarrow L(d,14)).$$
If $D(r,d)$ is false, the implication is automatically true, so there is no problem.

2.94 (i) $\forall f \exists u \; A(f,u)$.

(ii) $\forall f,d,d' \; ((R(f,d,d') \wedge E(f,d')) \rightarrow W(f,d,d'))$. The existential quantifier is not needed.

(iii) $\neg \exists f, f' \; (N(f,f') \wedge E(f,f'))$.

(iv) $\forall c \; (C(c) \rightarrow \exists r \; (R(c,r)))$.

2.96 *Algol68* and *Ada*.

2.99 $\forall a,b \; \exists h \; Hcf(h,a,b)$, where Hcf is as defined in the Example.

3. Set theory

3.13 (i) $\{-2, 2\}$.
(ii) $\{-1, -2\}$.
(iii) $\{-1\}$.
(iv) $\{(-1)^k(k - \frac{1}{2}) : k \in \mathbb{N}\} = \{\frac{1}{2}, -\frac{3}{2}, \frac{5}{2}, -\frac{7}{2}, \ldots\}$.
(v) Suppose that x is rational and $x = p/q$, with $p \in \mathbb{Z}$ and $q \in \mathbb{N}$. Remove any common factors, so that x is in its lowest terms; for example, $84/108 = 7/9$. If $x^2 = 2$ we have $p^2 = 2q^2$. The square of an odd integer is odd, so p has to be even, say $p = 2m$. Hence $p^2 = 4m^2 = 2q^2$, and so $q^2 = 2m^2$, and thus q is even. But we should have removed that common factor of 2 between p and q already, so we have a contradiction. It is *impossible* for a rational to square to 2; $\sqrt{2}$ is *irrational*. The answer is $\varnothing$.
(vi) $n^n - 2n = n(n^{n-1} - 2) = 0$ gives $n^{n-1} = 2$, because $n \neq 0$. Since n^{n-1} increases with n, and equals 2 when $n = 2$, we deduce the answer $\{2\}$.

3.15 (Hint) Can sets still be compared for equality?

3.20 (Hint) Look at a previous Exercise!

3.21 (i) If $|x| < 1$ then $|x|^2 = x^2 < 1$, and also $x < 1$, so $|x|^2 + 2x < 1 + 2 = 3$. Strict inclusion, because -2 is in the larger set.
(ii) If $x^2 + y^2 \leqslant 1$ then $x^2 \leqslant 1 - y^2 \leqslant 1$, so $|x| \leqslant 1$, and similarly for $|y|$. Strict inclusion, as $(1, 1)$ lies in one set but not the other.

3.22 (Hint) Consider $|x| \leqslant |y|$ and $|y| < |x|$ separately. A diagram might help.

3.24 (Hint) Show that the number of subsets of size k is $\binom{|S|}{k}$, and expand $(1 + (-1))^{|S|}$ by the binomial theorem $(a + b)^n = \sum_{k=0}^{n} \binom{n}{k} a^k b^{n-k}$.

3.27 The expressions evaluate as follows.
(i) $\{3\}$. (ii) $\{4, 5, 6\}$. (iii) $\{3\}$.
(iv) $\{1, 2, 3\}$. (v) $\{1, 2, 4, 5, 6\}$.

3.32 The expressions evaluate as follows.
(i) $\{1, 2\}$. (ii) $\{4, 5, 6\}$. (iii) $\{1, 2, 4, 5\}$.
(iv) $\{1, 2, 3\}$. (v) $\{5\}$. (vi) $\varnothing$.
(vii) $\{1, 4, 5, 6\}$.

3.36 In $A_b \cup A_e = \{a, f, g\}$.

3.38 $\{c, d, g\}$. See also Chapter 6.

3.40 The union equals $\varnothing$, since if $x \in \bigcup_{i \in \varnothing} A_i$ then there exists an $i \in \varnothing$ such that $x \in A_i$, which is impossible.

On the other hand, if $x \notin \bigcap_{i \in \varnothing} A_i$ then there exists some $i \in \varnothing$ with $x \notin A_i$, again impossible. Thus the intersection equals E, which is quite a shock!

3.41 The union is A_1, and the intersection is $\varnothing$.

3.42 The set of prime numbers.

3.45   (i) $(A \cap C) \cup (A \cap D) \cup (B \cap C) \cup (B \cap D)$.

(ii) $(A \cap D) \cup (A \cap E) \cup (B \cap D) \cup (B \cap E) \cup (C \cap D) \cup (C \cap E)$.

(iii) $(A \cap B \cap C) \cup (A \cap B \cap A) \cup \cdots$. There are 8 terms, but some are duplicated, and some are subsets of other terms. One minimal representation is $(A \cap B) \cup (B \cap C) \cup (C \cap A)$.

(iv) Similar to the third part. It simplifies back into that part.

3.46 (Hint) $A \cup B \cup C = A \cup (B \cup C)$. Use the result for two sets, and the distributive law.

3.51 (Hint) First write $A \setminus (B \cup C) = A \cap (B \cup C)'$, and similar on the righthand side, then use de Morgan's laws.

3.52 Take $E = \{1\}$, $A = B = \varnothing$ and $C = D = E$.

3.53 Well, it isn't really a counter-example, as they don't just use a couple of sets of data, but a common way of testing a compiler is to run it on a validation suite of programs to see that it gives the right results, as regards successful compilation or rejection. Even a suite of several thousand programs will not ensure that the compiler is correct!

3.57 The normal forms are as follows.

(i) $(A \cap B) \cup (A \cap B')$.   (ii) $A' \cap B' \cap C$.

(iii) $(A \cap B) \cup (A \cap B') \cup (A' \cap B)$.

(iv) $\varnothing$; like **F** in logic.

(v) $(A' \cap B \cap C) \cup (A' \cap B \cap C') \cup (A' \cap B' \cap C)$.

3.61 (Hint) First prove the identity $B = (A \cap B) \cup ((A \cup B) \setminus A)$.

3.68 There are 32 elements. Two of them are $(\mathbf{F}, \mathbf{T}, \mathbf{F}, \mathbf{T}, \mathbf{T})$ and $(\mathbf{T}, \mathbf{T}, \mathbf{T}, \mathbf{T}, \mathbf{T})$.

3.69 Just (x) with $x \in E$. These are usually regarded as the same as the elements of E, that is, we ignore the left and right bracket.

3.72 $A \times B = \{(1,2),(2,2),(3,2),(1,4),(2,4),(3,4)\}$.
$B \times A = \{(2,1),(2,2),(2,3),(4,1),(4,2),(4,3)\}$.
The intersection is $\{(2,2)\}$.

4. Relations

4.6 See Figure A.4.

Fig. A.4 $\leqslant$

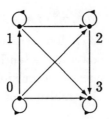

4.7 See Figure A.5.

Fig. A.5 Proper divisors

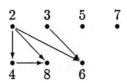

4.11 The domain and range both equal A.

4.12 The domain is $\{2,3,4\}$ and the range is $\{4,6,8\}$.

4.15 In terms of the relation of Example 4.14, what is being said is that $2\,R\,4$ and $-2\,R\,4$, so $2 = -2$, which is nonsense. The argument uses the square root notation in a bogus way, as first it uses it in the sense 'this number is a square root of that', and then in the sense 'this number is the only square root of that'.

4.18 $S \circ R = \{(a,h),(a,k),(b,h),(b,k),(c,h),(c,k),(d,j),(d,k)\}$.

4.19 $\{(a^8, a) : a \in \mathbb{Z}\}$.

4.20 $(4, 2) \in S$ and $(2, 16) \in R$, so $(4, 16) \in R \circ S$. However, $(4, 16) \notin S \circ R$, since then there would exist y with $(4, y) \in R$ and $(y, 16) \in S$. The latter implies that $y = 256$, and this contradicts the former, since $4^2 + 256^2 \neq 20$.

4.24 Put $S = R^2$. If $(p, q) \in S$, we must be able to find $r \in \mathbb{Z}$ with $(p, r), (r, q) \in R$. Thus $(p, r) = (m^2, m^4)$ for some $m \in \mathbb{Z}^+$, and $(r, q) = (n^2, n^4)$ for some $n \in \mathbb{Z}^+$. It follows that $r = m^4 = n^2$, and so $n = \pm m^2$. However, $n = -m^2$ is excluded, unless $m = 0$. Hence $(p, q) = (m^2, m^8)$, so

$$S = \{(m^2, m^8) : m \in \mathbb{Z}^+\}.$$

4.25 $R^2 = \{(k^{18}, k^{50} : k \in \mathbb{Z}^+\}$. The reason is that, if $(p, r), (r, q) \in R$, then r must be both a sixth power and a tenth power of an integer. Thus each of its prime factors is repeated a multiple of 6 times, and similarly a multiple of 10 times, hence a multiple of 30 times, and $r = k^{30}$ for some $k \in \mathbb{Z}^+$.

4.30 $a^2 + a^3$ is always even, so $a\,R\,a$ for all a.

4.34 $a\,R\,b$ if and only if both are even or both are odd. Thus the symmetry follows.

4.39 Suppose $a\,R\,b$ and $b\,R\,a$. Then $a = b^2$ and $b = a^2$, so $a = a^4$, forcing $a = 0$ or $a = 1$. In either case $a = b$, so the relation is anti-symmetric.

4.47 $(7, 2) \in R$, $(2, 13) \in R$, but $(7, 13) \notin R$.

4.48 If $\underline{B} = \emptyset$ then $\overline{\emptyset} = A$, so the result is trivial. Otherwise, every $x \in \underline{B}$ did at most as well as every $b \in B$ on every exam, so every $b \in B$ did at least as well on every exam as every $x \in \underline{B}$. This means that $b \in \overline{(\underline{B})}$ for every $b \in B$, as required.

4.57 The symmetric closure of R is the relation $R \cup R^{-1}$.

4.58 $(R \cup R^{-1})^*$. The parent relation is transformed into the '*is related or identical to*' relation.

4.59 This cannot be defined since anti-symmetry implies the *mutual exclusion* of (a, b) and (b, a) for $a \neq b$. If the original relation R includes both, it can never become anti-symmetric by extending it.

If R starts as an anti-symmetric relation, we still have problems. For instance, suppose $A = \{a, b, c\}$, and $R = \{(a, b), (b, c), (c, a)\}$. Any attempt to impose transitivity would contradict anti-symmetry.

4.66 The situation is not possible in *Pascal*, unless we include pointer variables. After the fragment

```
TYPE realptr=^real;
VAR  a,b:realptr;
BEGIN
    new(a); b:=a; a^:=3.142;
```

the variables a^ and b^ will both have the value 3.142.

Modula-2 lets a pointer to a real point to the same space as an actual real variable, a feat which is impossible in *Pascal*. This is achieved through an ADR function, which returns the address of a variable as its result.

It is also possible to have two real variables accessing the same space, provided you are prepared to specify the address of this space, and risk corrupting the operating system if you get it wrong! Thus

```
VAR a[1024]:BYTE;
    b[1024]:BYTE;
BEGIN
    a:=BYTE(0);
```

will simultaneously zero b as well.

Fortran provides an EQUIVALENCE statement which does the same sort of job of making variables address the same storage locations.

4.70 We see that
$$ac - bd = ac - ad + ad - bd = a(c - d) + d(a - b),$$
and so the right hand side is the sum of two multiples of n.

4.71 Let $\equiv$ denote equivalence modulo 3. We notice that $2^2 = 4 \equiv 1$. Thus $(2^2)^k \equiv 1$ for any integer k, and we only need write $2^{55555} = 2(2^2)^{27777}$ to see that this differs from 2 by a multiple of 3.

4.72 Some of these use Exercise 4.70 heavily.

  (i)   7   (ii) 1   (iii) 0   (iv) 11   (v) 5

4.73 The solutions are $1 + 11k$ and $10 + 11k$, $k \in \mathbb{Z}$.

4.75 (Hint) Replace 3333 by 3, using Exercise 4.70.

4.80 Statements are partitioned into

  (i)   Assignments   (ii)   Procedure calls
 (iii) IF statements (iv) CASE statements
  (v) WHILE statements (vi) REPEAT statements
 (vii) LOOP statements (viii) FOR statements

(ix)   **WITH** statements   (x)   **EXIT** statements
(xi)   **RETURN** statements   (xii)   Null statements

4.84 Suppose $\bar{a} \cap \bar{b} \neq \emptyset$. Thus $x \in \bar{a}$ and $x \in \bar{b}$, for some x. This means that $a \sim x$ and $x \sim b$, thus $a \sim b$. But then $b \in \bar{a}$. If y is any element of $\bar{b}$, then $b \sim y$, so $a \sim b \sim y$, implying $a \sim y$. Thus $y \in \bar{a}$. Similarly, any element of $\bar{a}$ is in $\bar{b}$, and so $\bar{a} = \bar{b}$ whenever they overlap. It thus follows finally that two such sets are either disjoint or identical, as required.

4.86 Any wff has several disjunctive forms, and it is not clear how we would decide that two such forms were equivalent, apart from resorting to the *normal* form again. How could we provide guidelines which would indicate immediately whether or not $(P \wedge Q) \vee (\neg P \wedge Q \wedge R)$ and $(P \wedge Q \wedge \neg R) \vee (Q \wedge R)$ were logically equivalent?

4.88 We verify that $\equiv$ is
Reflexive $a_1 a_2 = a_1 a_2$ so $a \equiv a$.
Symmetric $a \equiv b$ and $b \equiv a$ lead to the same condition $a_1 b_2 = b_1 a_2$.
Transitive If $a \equiv b$ and $b \equiv c$, then
$$a_1 b_2 = b_1 a_2, \qquad b_1 c_2 = c_1 b_2$$
so
$$a_1 b_2 b_1 c_2 = b_1 a_2 c_1 b_2$$
or
$$b_1 b_2 (a_1 c_2 - c_1 a_2) = 0.$$
Since $b_2 \in \mathbb{N}$, it is non-zero, and so may be cancelled, giving
$$b_1 (a_1 c_2 - c_1 a_2) = 0.$$
If $b_1 \neq 0$, we can cancel b_1 and obtain $a \equiv c$. But if $b_1 = 0$, then the original relationships imply $a_1 b_2 = c_1 b_2 = 0$, and since $b_2 \neq 0$, $a_1 = c_1 = 0$, so again $a \equiv c$.
The equivalence classes can be thought of as rational numbers, where $\overline{(a_1, a_2)}$ represents a_1/a_2. The equivalence relation has been chosen in such a way that
$$(a, b) \equiv (c, d) \iff a/b = c/d.$$

4.90 Yes. All sets below are subsets of E.
Reflexive $A \subseteq A$ for all A.
Anti-symmetric If $A \subseteq B$ and $B \subseteq A$ then $A = B$.
Transitive If $A \subseteq B$ and $B \subseteq C$ then $A \subseteq C$.
The order is not total except when $|E| \leqslant 1$, since if $a, b \in E$ and $a \neq b$ then $\{a\}$ and $\{b\}$ are unrelated in either direction.

4.91 No; see Exercise 4.59.

4.93 $b \prec a \prec c \prec j \prec i \prec d \prec e \prec f \prec g \prec h$. The order is not unique.

4.98 Let N, D, Q and P be sets from which part numbers, descriptions, quantities and prices are taken. The first database is a ternary relation R which is a subset of $N \times Q \times P$, and the second is a relation S which is a subset of $N \times D$. For each triple (n, q, p) and pair (n, d) we form a 4-tuple (n, d, q, p) in the obvious way.

This new 4-ary relation contains all the information we require, but it also has a field N which is not requested. This can be eliminated by the so-called *projection* operation, which painlessly converts a 4-tuple to a triple by eliminating the field N. Given the 4-ary relation $T \subseteq N \times D \times Q \times P$, we can project it onto $D \times Q \times P$ by taking

$$\{ (d, q, p) : \exists n \in N \ [(n, d, q, p) \in T] \}.$$

Another way to achieve the desired result is to think of R as a relation between N and $Q \times P$ and S as a relation between N and D. We then form the composition $R \circ S^{-1}$.

5. Mappings

5.7 It *is* a partial mapping, though an explicit formula is hard to come by. If $m < n$ then $e^m < e^n$, so $e^m + m < e^n + n$. Thus the ordered pairs corresponding to m and n have different first components.

5.9 (Hint) What happens if the number input is negative? Too large to be represented as an integer? Such that n^2 overflows? Suppose that only error messages generated by the program are acceptable output, rather than system messages such as overflow messages. Suppose the program is to print the number -1 if it cannot complete its calculation successfully. What if the user types '0' when asked to input a natural number? Or 'one'?

These considerations are vital to the correct functioning of the program, and are all related to a broad enough definition of A and B, and of ensuring that the program has domain A.

5.10 (Hint) We could take A to consist of ordered pairs (f, x); f would be the filename and x would represent the string of characters typed until the edit terminated with a `file` command. Alternatively, f could be the entire edited file, rather than just its name. Hopefully, the set B would consist of a pair (f, m) where f was the edited file, and m was some sort of status message for the termination of the edit. It would be extremely unkind to allow m to include a system-generated 'out of range' error, with the edit terminating with the file not updated.

Can you think of any good reasons why *any* information about f should be included in A and B?

What do you do if the user *never* types file or quit? Well, in this case, there is little you *can* do, since the program is interactive, and so you must put some restrictions on the valid inputs to it, otherwise most inputs will not result in termination. The *domain* of our partial mapping is restricted to input strings which end with a file or quit command.

5.11 (Hint) format command? The program will not terminate correctly unless it can execute file. There is now a restriction on the domain that the amount of disk space should exceed the size of the file being edited, so perhaps the disk should be included in the inputs too! Input terminating with a quit command will still work.

5.13 Let P be the set of people in Freedonia, and C the set of constituencies. Define

$$R = \{ (p, c) : p \text{ is a candidate in } c \}.$$

5.22 The mapping is from $B \times S$ to S.

If the body of the loop is translated as S and the expression as E then the translation of the loop might be into the single statement

```
continue
    E
    BEQ    end
    S
    BRA    continue
end
```

5.23 No, since 2 MOD 0 is not defined, so there is no mapping of $(2, 0)$ to an integer value.

There are more fundamental problems with this partial mapping, since a MOD b is defined by Wirth to be a-(a DIV b)*b, whilst a DIV b is defined as TRUNC(a/b), and finally TRUNC(x) is defined as x without its fractional part, that is, truncated towards zero. Taking $a = -5$ and $b = 2$, we would expect -5 MOD 2 to equal 1, but TRUNC(-5/2)=-2, so -5 DIV 2=-2, and so -5 MOD 2=-5-(-2)*2=-1! Beware, as this sort of discrepancy with usual mathematical conventions can lead to unexpected results. What do you think -5 MOD -2 should equal?

5.30 Yes. Take $A = \{a\}$, $B = \{b, c, d\}$, $C = \{e, f\}$, and
$$T = \{(a, b), (a, c)\}, S = \{(b, e), (c, e), (d, e), (d, f)\}.$$

5.44 The reasoning is that if $t_1 \neq t_2$ then $f(t_1) \neq f(t_2)$, so the pairs $(f(t_1), g(t_1))$ and $(f(t_2), g(t_2))$ have different first components. Thus R must be a partial mapping.

5.46 See Figure A.6.

Fig. A.6 Injective and surjective

	$\phi(a)$	$\phi(b)$	Injective	Surjective
ϕ_1	A	A	F	F
ϕ_2	A	B	T	F
ϕ_3	A	C	T	F
ϕ_4	B	A	T	F
ϕ_5	B	B	F	F
ϕ_6	B	C	T	F
ϕ_7	C	A	T	F
ϕ_8	C	B	T	F
ϕ_9	C	C	F	F

	$\psi(A)$	$\psi(B)$	$\psi(C)$	Injective	Surjective
ψ_1	a	a	a	F	F
ψ_2	a	a	b	F	T
ψ_3	a	b	a	F	T
ψ_4	a	b	b	F	T
ψ_5	b	a	a	F	T
ψ_6	b	a	b	F	T
ψ_7	b	b	a	F	T
ψ_8	b	b	b	F	F

5.47 f is injective, since if $m < n$ then $f(m) = f(n)$ only if $\log_2 m!$ and $\log_2 n!$ differ by less than 1. This difference will always be at least $\log_2(m + 1) \geqslant \log_2 2 = 1$. This also shows that f is an increasing function. Thus no two values of n give the same running time.

Mapping f is not surjective, since to be so and also increasing, it would have to be $\imath_{\mathrm{N}}$, but it is not, since $f(4) = 5$.

5.48 Let C be the range of f. Define $h(c) = c$ for all $c \in C$, and $g(a) = f(a)$ for all $a \in A$.

5.49 (Hint) Try $n = 10$.

5.50 Take $f(m,n) = 2^m 3^n$. Suppose $m \geqslant p$ and $2^m 3^n = 2^p 3^q$. Then $2^{m-p} = 3^{q-n}$, and this number is both odd and even simultaneously unless $m - p = q - n = 0$.

5.56 Let us show first that f is injective. Suppose
$$f(i_1, j_1) = n(i_1 - 1) + j_1 - 1 = f(i_2, j_2) = n(i_2 - 1) + j_2 - 1.$$
Then $n(i_1 - i_2) = j_2 - j_1$. But $-n < j_2 - j_1 < n$, since two j indices can differ by at most $n - 1$. It follows that $(j_2 - j_1) = 0 = (i_2 - i_1)$, so $(i_1, j_1) = (i_2, j_2)$.

We verify that f is surjective. If $t \in T$, let us take the equation
$$n(i - 1) + j - 1 = t,$$
and try to solve for i and j. First, take $j - 1 \equiv t \pmod{n}$, and $1 \leqslant j \leqslant n$. This would be expressed by the statement j:=1 + (t MOD n) in most computing languages. Given this value of j, take $i = 1 + (t - j + 1)/n$ or in other words i=1 + (t DIV n). We see that as t is at most $mn - 1$, therefore $(t - j + 1)/n$ is at most $(mn - 1 - 1 + 1)/n < m$, and so i is at most m. Thus $(i, j) \in M \times N$ and $f(m, n) = t$ so f is surjective. See also Exercise 5.40.

5.61 None mathematically, but there is the electronic reason that numbers are stored as binary numbers, with a fixed number of binary digits. If electronic devices were ternary, that is, worked to base 3, and we used four ternary digits to represent an integer, then we could represent all numbers in the range $-40, \ldots, 40$, and -1 would have the representation 2222, 40 would be 1111 and -40 would be 1112. There would not, of course, be a 'sign bit'; the sign bit in binary form is only incidental to the representation.

5.62 The sixteen bit representations are as follows.

   (i)   0000000000001100.   (ii)   1111111111110101.
 (iii)   1111111111110100.   (iv)   1111111111110011.
  (v)   0000001111101000.   (vi)   1101100011110000.

5.66 $f^{-1}(x) = \sinh^{-1}(\sqrt[3]{x} - 1)$.

5.67 We assume that the set of customers and the set of their addresses are the relevant domain and codomain. The first assertion states that each customer has only one address. The second states that each address has only one customer, that is, no two customers live at the same address.

5.69 First note that f really is a mapping as described! This follows since it is impossible for $\frac{1}{1-x}$ to equal either 0 or 1. Now

$$f \circ f(x) \;=\; \cfrac{1}{1 - \frac{1}{1-x}}$$
$$=\; \frac{x-1}{x}$$

so

$$f \circ f \circ f(x) \;=\; \cfrac{1}{1 - \left(\frac{x-1}{x}\right)}$$
$$=\; x$$

as required. Thus $f \circ f$ must be the inverse of f.

5.70 We have

$$g(f(x)) = 4 + f(x)g(f(f(x))) = 4 + \frac{1}{1-x}g(f(f(x)))$$

and

$$g(f(f(x))) = 4 + f(f(x))g(f(f(f(x)))) = 4 + \frac{x-1}{x}g(x).$$

This gives us three equations in $g(x)$, $g(f(x))$ and $g(f(f(x)))$, and we solve for $g(x)$:

$$
\begin{aligned}
g(x) \quad - \quad xg(f(x)) \qquad\qquad\qquad &= \; 4 \\
g(f(x)) \quad - \quad \tfrac{1}{1-x}g(f(f(x))) &= \; 4 \;. \\
\tfrac{1-x}{x}g(x) \qquad\qquad + \qquad g(f(f(x))) &= \; 4
\end{aligned}
$$

We multiply by 1, x and $\frac{x}{1-x}$ respectively, and add, to obtain

$$2g(x) = 4 + 4x + \frac{4x}{1-x},$$

and the result follows. [Check it in the original identity!]

5.72 If $f : A \to B$ and $g : B \to C$ are both injective, then suppose we put $h = g \circ f$, and suppose $h(x_1) = h(x_2)$ for some $x_1, x_2 \in A$. Then $g(f(x_1)) = g(f(x_2))$, so because g is injective, it follows that $f(x_1) = f(x_2)$. But then $x_1 = x_2$, so h is injective.

The other result is also true.

5.73 The definitions given previously work without change. A partial mapping is invertible if and only if it is injective.

5.80 (12 15 3 13 6 11 4 5 9 2).

5.82 We omit trivial cycles (x).

   (i)   (1 3 5)(2 8)(4 6).   (ii)   (1 9 6 3 2 8 4 7 5).

5.85 (1 8 5 2 10 7 4)(3 9 6).

5.87 (1 10)(10 8)(2 5)(5 3)(3 6)(6 9)(9 4).

5.92 We know by Example 2.52 that it is an infinite subset of $\mathbf{N}$. Thus it is countable.

5.93 1, 2, 1/2, 3, 1/3, 4, 3/2, 2/3, 1/4, 5, 1/5, 6, ...

This is not an obvious sequence! It is based on the ordering used in Theorem 5.9.

5.95 We know, from Theorem 5.9 that $\mathbf{N}^2$ is countable. We also have a mapping $(m, n) \mapsto s_{m,n}$, where $s_{m,n}$ is the n-th element of S_m. Thus we can find a surjection of $\mathbf{N}$ onto $\bigcup_{m \in \mathbf{N}} S_m$, and by deleting duplicated copies of any element, we can make this into a bijection.

The other result follows more easily by forming the sequence consisting of the elements of S_1, followed by the elements of S_2, and so on.

5.96 Any *Pascal* program consists of a sequence of ASCII characters, and there are only 128 such characters, some of which are not valid anyway in a *Pascal* program. The number of programs which are n characters long is at most 128^n. The set of all *Pascal* programs is the union of all the finite sets of programs with n characters in them, so is a countable union of finite sets. It can easily be seen to be infinite, just by including arbitrary repetitions of some assignment such as x:=0.

5.101 We assume there are only countably many such mappings, and obtain a contradiction. Suppose we have enumerated all such mappings, in the sequence $f_1, f_2, f_3, \ldots$; define f by

$$f(n) = \begin{cases} 1 & \text{if } f_n(n) = 0 \\ 0 & \text{if } f_n(n) = 1 \end{cases}.$$

Then $f(n) \neq f_n(n)$ for any $n \in \mathbf{N}$, so $f \neq f_n$ for any n. But this means that f has been omitted from the enumeration, a contradiction.

5.102 Consider the mapping $A \mapsto f_A$ from subsets of $\mathbf{N}$ to mappings as in Exercise 5.101, where

$$f_A(n) = \begin{cases} 1 & \text{if } n \in A \\ 0 & \text{if } n \notin A \end{cases}.$$

This is a bijection, and so the power set is uncountable.

A more direct way to prove the same result is to suppose that all the subsets of $\mathbf{N}$ have been enumerated in the sequence $A_1, A_2, A_3, \ldots$; define the subset $A \subseteq \mathbf{N}$ by

$$A = \{ n \in \mathbf{N} : n \notin A_n \}.$$

For any $n \in \mathbf{N}$, either $n \in A_n$ or $n \in A$, but not both. Hence $A \neq A_n$ for any n, so A has been left out of the enumeration, a contradiction.

5.115 (Hint)   (i) The publisher's address should be kept in a separate file, listing publishers' names and addresses. If a publisher changed addresses, thousands of entries would need changing.

(ii) Only one of the prices should be retained, and a separate file kept with a list of sterling and dollar values for conversion. A more sensible solution would be to give a conversion formula.

6. Graphs

6.3 See Figure A.7.

Fig. A.7 Tetrahedron and cube

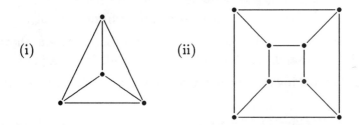

(i)   (ii)

6.4 (Hint) Octahedron, dodecahedron, icosahedron.

6.7 An edge is not just a pair of vertices, since then any two edges between the same vertices would be mathematically identical. Define G by taking two disjoint sets V and E, with V and V_2 also disjoint, and also a mapping $f : E \rightarrow (V \cup V_2)$, such that $f(e)$ gives the set of vertices incident to the edge e. We could have $f(e_1) = f(e_2) = \{u, v\}$ without e_1 and e_2 being identical. We are just defining a multigraph in terms of its incidence matrix.

6.11 There might be some collapsing of the first graph when it is embedded in the second. For instance, suppose
$$G = (\{a, b, c, d, e\}, \{ab, bc, cd, ad\})$$
and
$$G' = (\{p, q, r, s\}, \{pq, rs\}).$$
We could have
$$f(a) = f(c) = p, \quad f(b) = f(d) = f(e) = q.$$

6.14 (Hint) There are 13 different subgraphs, if you include $G|_\emptyset = (\emptyset, \emptyset)$.

6.16 $2^{|V|}$.

6.18 If there are two edges from u to v, then these will contribute two to the first definition, but only one to the second.

Neither definition is satisfactory for a multigraph; for each vertex v, count one for every edge to a different vertex, and *two* for each edge from v to itself. Draw a diagram!

6.22 (Hint) Regard the people as vertices of a graph G, with two people adjacent if they know one another.

6.23 Yes. Take $m = |V|$.

6.29 (Hint) Consider u, uv, v, vu, u.

6.31 The concatenation of two paths is a *walk*, and not necessarily a path. However, it always contains at least one path from v_1 to w_n.

6.32 (Hint) One direction of proof is easy. In the other direction, show by induction on $|E|$ that E can be broken into edge-disjoint circuits.

6.33 (Hint) Try making such a walk into a circuit by adding an extra edge to G.

6.38 (Hint) Try looking at $G|_X$ with $|X| = 2$.

6.39 (Hint) Prove the existence of a path of length q by induction. Clearly a path of length 1 exists. As induction hypothesis, suppose a path of length $k - 1$ exists, $k \leqslant q$, say $v_1 v_2 \cdots v_k$. Consider the vertex degree of v_k.

6.40

$$\sum_{k=0}^{n-2} \binom{n-2}{k} k! = \sum_{k=0}^{n-2} \frac{(n-2)!}{(n-2-k)!}$$

$$= (n-2)! \sum_{i=0}^{n-2} \frac{1}{i!} \qquad (i = n - 2 - k)$$

$$\leqslant (n-2)!\, e,$$

since $e = \sum_{i=0}^{\infty} \frac{1}{i!}$.

6.45 (Hint) In any connected graph $G = (V, E)$ we have $\Delta(G) \leqslant (|V| - 1)$. Assume that G has more than one connected component, and obtain a contradiction.

6.47 (Hint) Regard the papers as vertices and join two vertices when they have different examiners.

A different approach is given elsewhere, based on graph colouring.

6.50 (Hint) Use an argument similar to that used in the proof of Theorem 6.10.

6.52 (Hint) Gradually increment $\Delta(G)$.

6.55 (Hint) K_1, K_2 have 1, 2 centres respectively. Suppose T is a tree with more than two vertices, and let u be a vertex of T. First prove that if the eccentricity $\epsilon(u) = r$, then any vertex v with $d(u,v) = r$ is pendant, by considering a path from u to v. Then show that a centre cannot be pendant.

Finally form T' from T by deleting all pendant vertices, and show that any centre of T is a centre of T'.

6.58 (Hint) Use Theorem 6.1 and the result of this section.

6.59 (Hint) Consider the minimum vertex degree $\delta(G)$, and the result in Exercise 6.58.

6.60 (Hint) Use the fact that a tree always possesses pendant vertices. Choose e to be an edge with a pendant vertex at one end.

6.63 (Hint) $\sum_i d_i = |V|$.

6.67 The graph contains K_4 as a subgraph.

6.68 (Hint) For K_n, if fewer than n colours are used then $c : V \rightarrow C$ is not injective.

6.69 (Hint) Select a vertex u with $\deg u < \Delta$. Choose any spanning tree for G, and order the vertices by first listing u, then all vertices at distance 1 from u, then all vertices at distance 2, and so on. Colour the vertices in the reverse of this order. The vertex u is adjacent to fewer than Δ of its predecessors in this reverse order, and every other vertex also has this property, by the way the vertices were listed, since every other vertex is adjacent to at least one vertex *before* itself in the original order, or *after* itself in the reverse order.

6.71 (i)

	a	b	c	d	e	f	g
a	0	1	0	0	0	0	0
b	1	1	0	1	0	0	0
c	0	1	0	0	0	0	0
d	0	0	1	0	0	0	0
e	0	0	1	0	0	0	0
f	0	0	0	0	0	0	1
g	0	0	0	0	0	0	0

(ii)

	ab	ba	bb	bd	dc	cb	ec	fg
a	−1	+1	0	0	0	0	0	0
b	+1	−1	+1	−1	0	+1	0	0
c	0	0	0	0	+1	−1	+1	0
d	0	0	0	+1	−1	0	0	0
e	0	0	0	0	0	0	−1	0
f	0	0	0	0	0	0	0	−1
g	0	0	0	0	0	0	0	+1

6.73 n^2.

6.75 (Hint) Use induction on the number of vertices of G.

6.82 (Hint) You may find it easier to calculate the distances on the *strong components* of the graphs first.

7. Graph algorithms

7.5 (i) ab, dg, dj, ei, bc, bi, bj, ef, fh, fk; 22.

  (ii) bl, de, dh, ef, ac, ae, dl, ej, gh, hi, ck; 22.

  (iii) bl, de, dj, ei, ac, ae, cf, fg, ab, fh, ck; 24.

7.10 (Hint) Give every edge weight 1. Tidy up the algorithms.

7.16

	a	b	c	d	e	f	g	h	i	j	k	l
(i)	0	4	2	4	2	3	1	4	6	5	5	
(ii)	0	2	1	1	3	3	7	3	4	3	2	3
(iii)	0	1	3	2	4	7	6	6	6	4	6	5

7.18

	a	b	c	d	e	f	g	h	i	j	k	l
(i)	0	5	3		2	5	1	6	7	6	7	
(ii)	0	2	1	1	3	3	9	3	6	4	2	3
(iii)	0	1	3	2	4	7	6	7	6	4	6	5

7.24

	a	b	c	d	e	f	g	h	i	j	k	l
(i)	0	5	7	0	11	16	18	17	25	6	23	
(ii)	0	2	1	7	12	17	26	30	33	35	36	37
(iii)	0	1	3	6	13	17	18	20	25	33	35	38

Note that in the first problem, d can start immediately since it is not constrained by a.

7.27 The colouring depends upon the order in which the vertices were taken. Here are some solutions. The notation x_n means that vertex x was given colour n.

  (i) $f_1, b_1, g_2, d_3, e_2, a_3, c_4, h_2, i_3, j_2, k_3$.

  (ii) $f_1, d_2, l_1, h_3, b_3, k_2, j_3, e_4, a_1, g_4, i_2, c_3$.

  (iii) $f_1, d_2, k_2, b_3, e_3, a_1, l_1, h_3, i_1, j_3, c_3, g_3$.

7.29 (Hint) Take any colouring of G in $\chi(G)$ colours. Order the vertices so that all those of colour i precede those of colour $i + 1$.

8. Abstract algebra

8.4 (Hint) If $n \leqslant 3$ the result is obvious. We assume that the result is true for any $k < n$ terms, and show that it is true for n terms. Consider a bracketing in which the outermost brackets look like

$$(\ldots a_1 \ldots a_p \ldots) \circ (\ldots a_{p+1} \ldots a_n \ldots),$$

with $1 \leqslant p \leqslant n - 1$. The idea is to transform the first part, by the inductive hypothesis, into

$$((\cdots((a_1 \circ a_2) \circ a_3) \cdots) \circ a_p)$$

and the last part into

$$(a_{p+1} \circ (a_{p+2} \circ (\cdots (a_{n-1} \circ a_n)) \cdots)).$$

This allows a_p to be peeled from the first expression into the second, then a_{p-1}, and so on down to a_2 by associativity, as in Example 8.3.

The same transformation on any other bracketing transforms it into the same form, whence it follows that any two bracketings are equivalent. The author did warn that the details were messy!

8.7 No. If the old neutral element was f, and the new one is e, then $e \circ f = f \circ e = f$. Thus e is neutral in the bigger set B, but f is no longer neutral.

8.10 Since the binary operation is associative on S, it is associative when restricted to T. The only thing we need to check is that $\circ$ is a binary operation on T. But the assumed condition assures us of this, that is, that $\circ : T^2 \to T$.

8.17 **Associativity:** Suppose that $a, b, c \in \mathbb{Z}_n$. We have $b \otimes c = bc - kn$ for some $k \in \mathbb{Z}$. Thus
$$a \otimes (b \otimes c) = a(bc - kn) - ln = abc - (ak + l)n,$$
for some $l \in \mathbb{Z}$. A similar calculation shows that $(a \otimes b) \otimes c$ and abc also differ by a multiple of n, and so
$$a \otimes (b \otimes c) - (a \otimes b) \otimes c$$
is a multiple of n. This is impossible unless it is 0. Thus we have associativity.

Neutral Element: 1 is neutral.

Commutativity: This is obvious.

Thus $\mathbb{Z}_n$ is a commutative monoid. It is not a group, since $0 \otimes a = 1$ is impossible—0 and 1 do not differ by a multiple of n. It might appear that 0 is exceptional, and that $\mathbb{Z}_n \setminus \{0\}$ might be a group. Even $\mathbb{Z}_4 \setminus \{0\} = \{1, 2, 3\}$ fails to be a group, since $\otimes$ is not even a binary operation on this set!

8.18 1 has inverse 1. 2 and 3 are inverses of one another. 4 is its own inverse. 0 does not have an inverse.

8.22 $a^{-1} \circ a \circ b = a^{-1} \circ a \circ c$, so $e \circ b = e \circ c$, giving $b = c$.

The law is false in the semigroup of integers under multiplication, if we take $a = 0$.

8.23   (i) We check associativity.
$$
\begin{aligned}
a \circ (b \circ c) &= a \circ (b + c + bc) \\
&= a + (b + c + bc) + a(b + c + bc) \\
&= a + b + c + ab + ac + bc + abc \\
&= (a \circ b) \circ c,
\end{aligned}
$$
so associativity is true. Thus $\mathbb{R}$ is a semigroup. Next, any neutral element satisfies $e \circ a = a \circ e = a$, $\forall a \in \mathbb{R}$. Thus
$$a + e + ae = a \implies e(1 + a) = 0 \implies e = 0$$
when $a = 0$. It is easy to check that 0 is neutral, so $\mathbb{R}$ is a monoid.

If a is invertible, with inverse b, then $a \circ b = 0$, so $a + b + ab = 0$, and $b(1 + a) = -a$. But this gives $b = -a/(1 + a)$ if $a \neq -1$, and has no solution if $a = -1$. So, only -1 has no inverse.

(ii) Firstly, $a \circ b \in \mathbb{R}$, so we only need check that $a \circ b \neq -1$. If $a + b + ab = -1$ then $(a + 1)(b + 1) = 0$ so $a = -1$ or $b = -1$, a contradiction. Thus $\circ$ is a binary operation on $\mathbb{R} \setminus \{-1\}$.

The associativity of $\circ$ and the neutrality of 0 follow as in the first part. We need to demonstrate the existence of inverses in the given set. Since $a \neq -1$ by assumption, we can form $b = -a/(1 + a)$, and $b \circ a = 0$. The complication is that b might not be in G. Assume $b \notin G$, so $b = -1$, and we obtain $-a/(1 + a) = -1$, giving $-a = -1 - a$, or $0 = -1$, a clear contradiction. Thus b is indeed in G, and G is a group.

8.25 Reflexivity: $aa^{-1} = e \in H$, so $a \sim a$.

Symmetry: If $a \sim b$, so $ab^{-1} \in H$, then $\left(ab^{-1}\right)^{-1} = \left(b^{-1}\right)^{-1}a^{-1} = ba^{-1} \in H$. Thus $b \sim a$.

Transitivity: If $a \sim b$ and $b \sim c$ then $ab^{-1}, bc^{-1} \in H$. Thus $ab^{-1}bc^{-1} = ac^{-1} \in H$, so $a \sim c$.

8.27 (Hint) Consider $f(e \circ e)$.

8.33 (Hint) Look at the length of $w_1 w_2$.

8.43 The preorder forms are as follows.

(i) $+ \times ab/cd$.   (ii) $(a \times b)/(c + d) = / \times ab + cd$.

(iii) $+/ab/cd$.   (iv) $+ - ab/cd$.   (v) $\times a - b/cd$.

8.44 The postorder forms are as follows.

(i) $ab \times cd/+$.   (ii) $ab \times cd + /$.   (iii) $ab/cd/+$.

(iv) $ab - cd/+$.   (v) $abcd/ - \times$.

8.56 Let A be the set of adjectives, and put $B = \{\varepsilon\} \cup AS^+$. A selection from B means no adjective, or one adjective followed by spaces. One solution is

$$TS^+BNS^+VS^+TS^+BNF.$$

8.70 (Hint) The last part is tricky! Here is a sketch of the way it is done.

(i) Generate words such as $1R1R1R \times 11 =$.

(ii) Let each R migrate right but change it to a T when it passes the $\times$. Thus we have productions such as $R1 \to 1R$ and $R\times \to \times T$.

(iii) Let $T1$ become $1WT$, and let W migrate right, past $=$, to become 1.

(iv) Let T annihilate itself when it hits $=$.

Each R replicates the second multiplicand as a sequence of Ws as it scans it, and these Ws produce 1s on the righthand side.

8.76 In the new grammar $\langle S \rangle \Rightarrow \mathsf{b}\langle S \rangle \Rightarrow \mathsf{ba}\langle X \rangle \Rightarrow \mathsf{ba}$, which is a different regular language.

8.91 The process would have failed in the last stage if one of the productions had given ε, since, for instance, the combination of $\langle A_5 \rangle \rightarrow \langle A_3 \rangle \langle A_7 \rangle \mathsf{ab} \langle A_4 \rangle$ with $\langle A_3 \rangle \rightarrow \varepsilon$ would have given $\langle A_5 \rangle \rightarrow \langle A_7 \rangle \mathsf{ab} \langle A_4 \rangle$, destroying the non-increasing property we had so carefully created.

8.92 *(Hint)* First replace the fourth production by $\langle L \rangle \rightarrow \mathsf{le}$ and the new production $\langle L \rangle \rightarrow \mathsf{l}\langle Y \rangle \mathsf{e}$, where $\langle Y \rangle$ *only* generates *nonempty* statement sequences.

Appendix B

Example programs

The following programs implement some of the algorithms in previous chapters. They are in *Modula-2*, but so written that a translation into *Pascal* or *Ada* would not be too arduous. None of the special features of *Modula-2* have been used; there are no separate modules, pointers have only been used once, and sets have been avoided because of the difficulties associated with the size of the universal set.

The typography of the programs has been improved to make them more readable. The grotesqueness of <> or # instead of $\neq$, and similar infelicities, have been removed.

B.1   Equivalence classes

Here is a program to compute equivalence classes, given a list of ordered pairs.

```
MODULE EquivClass;
FROM InOut IMPORT OpenInput, ReadCard, WriteCard,
  CloseInput, WriteLn, WriteString;
CONST
  minvertex=1; maxvertex=1000;
TYPE
  vertices=CARDINAL[minvertex .. maxvertex];
  componentarrays=ARRAY vertices OF vertices;
  graphs=RECORD  (* graph type *)
    nrfvertices:vertices;
    component:componentarrays; (* connected component *)
  END;
VAR
  graph:graphs;
PROCEDURE Process(VAR g:graphs);
VAR
  i,j,nrfpairs,k:CARDINAL;
  v,a1,a2:vertices;
```

```
PROCEDURE Initialise(VAR g:graphs);
VAR
 v:vertices;
BEGIN
 WITH g DO
  FOR v:=minvertex TO nrfvertices DO
   component[v]:=v;
  END;
 END;
END Initialise;
PROCEDURE ancestor(v:vertices; VAR c:componentarrays):vertices;
 BEGIN
  WHILE c[v]≠v DO
   v:=c[v];
  END;
  RETURN v;
 END ancestor;
BEGIN
 WITH g DO
  OpenInput('DAT');
  ReadCard(i);nrfvertices:=vertices(i);
  ReadCard(nrfpairs);
  Initialise(g);
  FOR k:=1 TO nrfpairs DO
   ReadCard(i);ReadCard(j);
   a1:=ancestor(vertices(i),component);
   a2:=ancestor(vertices(j),component);
   IF a1<a2 THEN
    component[a2]:=a1;
   ELSE
    component[a1]:=a2;
   END;
  END;
  CloseInput; WriteLn;
  FOR v:=minvertex TO nrfvertices DO
   IF component[v]≠component[component[v]] THEN
    component[v]:=component[component[v]];
   END;
  END;
 END;
END Process;
PROCEDURE WriteData(VAR g:graphs);
VAR
 v:vertices;
```

```
BEGIN
 WITH g DO
  FOR v:=minvertex TO nrfvertices DO
   WriteCard(CARDINAL(component[v]),5);
  END;
  WriteLn;
 END;
END WriteData;
BEGIN
 Process(graph); WriteData(graph);
END EquivClass.
```

The program reads from a file giving the number of elements in the set, the number of ordered pairs, and a list of ordered pairs specifying which elements are related. This list can be a minimal one, in that the reflexive, symmetric, transitive closure of the given relation is calculated. Here is an example datafile.

```
12  9
1 2      1 3      2 5      5 9      4 6
4 12     3 9      11 7     6 11
```

B.2 Warshall's algorithm and strong components

We can use the following program to compute either the transitive closure of a relation, or the strong components of a graph.

```
MODULE Warshall;
FROM InOut IMPORT OpenInput, ReadCard, WriteCard,
 CloseInput, WriteLn, WriteString;
CONST
 minelt=1; maxelt=100;
TYPE
 elts=CARDINAL[minelt .. maxelt];
 relnarrays=ARRAY elts OF ARRAY elts OF BOOLEAN;
 componentarrays=ARRAY elts OF elts;
 relations=RECORD  (* relation type *)
  nrfelts:elts;
  reln:relnarrays;
  component:componentarrays;
 END;
VAR
 R:relations;
PROCEDURE WriteRelation(VAR r:relations);
VAR
 i,j:elts;
```

```
BEGIN
 WITH r DO
  FOR i:=minelt TO nrfelts DO
   FOR j:=minelt TO nrfelts DO
    IF reln[i,j] THEN
      WriteCard(1,2);
    ELSE
      WriteCard(0,2);
    END;
   END;
   WriteLn;
  END;
 END; WriteLn;
END WriteRelation;
PROCEDURE ReadData(VAR r:relations);
VAR
 i,j,nrfpairs,k:CARDINAL;
 PROCEDURE Initialise(VAR r:relations);
 VAR
  i,j:elts;
 BEGIN
  WITH r DO
   FOR i:=minelt TO nrfelts DO
    component[i]:=i;
    FOR j:=minelt TO nrfelts DO
     reln[i,j]:=FALSE;
    END;
   END;
  END;
 END Initialise;
BEGIN
 WITH r DO
  OpenInput('DAT'); WriteLn;
  ReadCard(i);nrfelts:=elts(i);
  ReadCard(nrfpairs);
  Initialise(r);
  FOR k:=1 TO nrfpairs DO
   ReadCard(i);ReadCard(j);
   reln[elts(i),elts(j)]:=TRUE;
  END;
  CloseInput;
 END;
END ReadData;
PROCEDURE TClose(VAR r:relations);
    (* Warshall's algorithm to take the transitive closure *)
VAR
 i,j,k:elts;
```

```
BEGIN
 WITH r DO
  FOR k:=minelt TO nrfelts DO
   FOR i:=minelt TO nrfelts DO
    IF reln[i,k] THEN
      FOR j:=minelt TO nrfelts DO
       IF reln[k,j] THEN
        reln[i,j]:=TRUE;
       END;
      END;
     END;
    END;
   END;
  END;
END TClose;
PROCEDURE CalcComponents(VAR r:relations);
    (* calculate strong components *)
VAR
 i,j,k,l:elts;
 PROCEDURE ancestor(i:elts; VAR c:componentarrays):elts;
  BEGIN
   WHILE c[i]≠i DO
    i:=c[i];
   END;
  RETURN i;
 END ancestor;
BEGIN
 WITH r DO
  FOR i:=minelt TO nrfelts DO
   FOR j:=i TO nrfelts DO
    IF reln[i,j]&reln[j,i] THEN
     k:=ancestor(i,component);l:=ancestor(j,component);
     IF k<l THEN
      component[l]:=k;
     ELSE
      component[k]:=l;
     END;
    END;
   END;
  END;
  FOR i:=minelt TO nrfelts DO
   IF component[i]≠component[component[i]] THEN
    component[i]:=component[component[i]];
   END;
  END;
 END;
END CalcComponents;
PROCEDURE WriteComponents(VAR r:relations);
VAR
 i:elts;
```

```
BEGIN
  WITH r DO
    FOR i:=minelt TO nrfelts DO
      WriteCard(CARDINAL(component[i]),5);
    END;
    WriteLn;
  END;
END WriteComponents;
BEGIN
  ReadData(R);WriteRelation(R);
  TClose(R);WriteRelation(R);
  CalcComponents(R);WriteComponents(R);
END Warshall.
```

The program needs to be provided with a representation of the relation in a file, giving the number of elements and pairs, and a list of ordered pairs. An example is the following.

```
12  15
1 2    1 3    2 5    5 9    4 6    4 12   3 9    11 7
6 11   10 8   9 1    8 4    5 6    8 7    12 10
```

B.3 Total ordering

We here sequence a list of processes, given a partial ordering of them.

```
MODULE TotalOrder;
FROM InOut IMPORT OpenInput, ReadCard, WriteCard,
  CloseInput, WriteLn, WriteString;
CONST
  minelt=1; maxelt=100; zelt=minelt-1;
TYPE
  elts=CARDINAL[minelt..maxelt]; zelts=CARDINAL[zelt..maxelt];
  successors=ARRAY elts OF BOOLEAN;
  relnarrays=ARRAY elts OF successors;
  posets=RECORD  (* poset type *)
    nrfelts:elts;
    reln:relnarrays;
  END;
VAR
  R:posets;
PROCEDURE ReadData(VAR r:posets);
VAR
  i,j,nrfpairs,k:CARDINAL;
  PROCEDURE Initialise(VAR r:posets);
  VAR
    i,j:elts;
```

```
BEGIN
  WITH r DO
   FOR i:=minelt TO nrfelts DO
    FOR j:=minelt TO nrfelts DO
      reln[i,j]:=FALSE;
    END;
   END;
  END;
 END Initialise;
BEGIN
  WITH r DO
   OpenInput('DAT'); WriteLn;
   ReadCard(i); nrfelts:=elts(i);
   ReadCard(nrfpairs);
   Initialise(r);
   FOR k:=1 TO nrfpairs DO
    ReadCard(i); ReadCard(j);
    reln[elts(i),elts(j)]:=TRUE;
   END;
   CloseInput;
  END;
 END ReadData;
PROCEDURE TClose(VAR r:posets);
    (* take transitive closure *)
VAR
 i,j,k:elts;
BEGIN
  WITH r DO
   FOR k:=minelt TO nrfelts DO
    FOR i:=minelt TO nrfelts DO
     IF reln[i,k] THEN
       FOR j:=minelt TO nrfelts DO
        IF reln[k,j] THEN
          reln[i,j]:=TRUE;
        END;
       END;
      END;
     END;
    END;
  END;
 END TClose;
PROCEDURE CalcSequence(VAR r:posets);
    (* total order *)
VAR
 i:zelts;
 PROCEDURE minimalelt(VAR r:posets):zelts;
 VAR
  i,j:zelts;
  found:BOOLEAN;
```

```
BEGIN
 WITH r DO
  i:=zelt; found:=FALSE;
  REPEAT
   INC(i); j:=zelt;
   REPEAT
    INC(j); found:=reln[i,j];
   UNTIL found OR (j=nrfelts);
  UNTIL found OR (i=nrfelts);
  IF found THEN
   j:=zelt;
   REPEAT
    INC(j);
    IF reln[j,i] THEN
     i:=j; j:=zelt;
    END;
   UNTIL (j=nrfelts);
   FOR j:=minelt TO nrfelts DO
    reln[i,j]:=FALSE; reln[j,i]:=FALSE;
   END;
   RETURN i;
  ELSE RETURN zelt;
  END;
 END;
END minimalelt;
BEGIN
 WITH r DO
  REPEAT
   i:=minimalelt(r);
   IF i≠zelt THEN
    WriteCard(i,4);
   END;
  UNTIL i=zelt;
 END;
END CalcSequence;
BEGIN
 ReadData(R); TClose(R);
 CalcSequence(R);WriteLn;
END TotalOrder.
```

The data file consists of the number of processes and constraints, and a list of ordered pairs, giving the order of precedence of the various processes. An example is as follows.

```
12   7
1 7      2 1      3 8      2 5      5 9      9 11     8 11
```

The output gives only the sequencing of the earliest of the processes; the order of all remaining processes is arbitrary.

B.4   Minimal spanning tree—Prim's Algorithm

This program illustrates the application of transpositions to the problem of sorting a list of edges into ascending order of weight. The algorithm chosen is known as *quicksort*.

```
MODULE Prim;
FROM InOut IMPORT OpenInput, CloseInput, ReadCard, WriteCard, ReadInt,
    WriteInt, WriteLn, WriteString;
CONST
  minvertex=1; maxvertex=100;
  minedge=1; maxedge=1000;
TYPE
  weights=INTEGER;  (* for weight function *)
  vertices=CARDINAL[minvertex .. maxvertex];  (* single vertex *)
  zvertices=CARDINAL[minvertex-1 .. maxvertex];
  edges=CARDINAL[minedge .. maxedge];
  zedges=CARDINAL[minedge-1 .. maxedge];
  vertsets=ARRAY vertices OF BOOLEAN;
  edgerecord=RECORD   (* single weighted edge *)
    start,finish:vertices;
    weight:weights;
  END;
  edgearray=ARRAY edges OF edgerecord;
  graphs=RECORD  (* graph type *)
    nrfvertices:vertices;
    nrfedges:edges;
    initial:vertices;  (* Prim's algorithm needs a start vertex *)
    edge:edgearray;
    marked:vertsets;  (* used for vertices of spanning tree *)
  END;
VAR
  graph:graphs;
PROCEDURE Readdata(VAR graph:graphs);
VAR
  i,j:CARDINAL;
  d:INTEGER;
  v:vertices;  k:edges;
BEGIN
  WITH graph DO
    OpenInput('DAT');
    ReadCard(i); nrfvertices:=vertices(i);
    ReadCard(i); nrfedges:=edges(i);
    ReadCard(i); initial:=vertices(i);
    FOR k:=minedge TO nrfedges DO
      ReadCard(i);ReadCard(j);ReadInt(d);
      WITH edge[k] DO
        start:=vertices(i);finish:=vertices(j);weight:=weights(d);
      END;
    END;
```

```
  CloseInput; WriteLn;
END;
END Readdata;
PROCEDURE sort(VAR graph:graphs);
   (* sorting algorithm chosen is called quicksort *)
   PROCEDURE quicksort(VAR graph:graphs; low,high:zedges);
   VAR
    i,j:zedges;
    comp:weights;
    PROCEDURE exchange(VAR e1,e2:edgerecord);  (* transposition *)
    VAR
     temp:edgerecord;
    BEGIN
     temp:=e1; e1:=e2; e2:=temp;
    END exchange;
   BEGIN
     WITH graph DO
      IF low<high THEN
       i:=low; j:=high; comp:=edge[j].weight;
       REPEAT
         WHILE (i<j) & (edge[i].weight≤comp) DO INC(i); END;
         WHILE (i<j) & (edge[j].weight≥comp) DO DEC(j); END;
         IF i<j THEN exchange(edge[i],edge[j]); END;
       UNTIL i≥j;
       IF i≠high THEN exchange(edge[i],edge[high]); END;
       (* edge i is now correct *)
       IF (i-low)<(high-i) THEN
         quicksort(graph,low,i-1); quicksort(graph,i+1,high);
       ELSE  (* for variety *)
         quicksort(graph,i+1,high); quicksort(graph,low,i-1);
       END;
      END;
     END;
   END quicksort;
   PROCEDURE displaysort(VAR graph:graphs);
   VAR
    e:edges;
   BEGIN
     WITH graph DO
      FOR e:=minedge TO nrfedges DO
       WITH edge[e] DO
         WriteCard(CARDINAL(start),8); WriteCard(CARDINAL(finish),8);
         WriteInt(INTEGER(weight),8); WriteLn;
       END;
      END;
     END;
   END displaysort;
```

```
BEGIN
 WITH graph DO
  quicksort(graph,minedge,nrfedges); displaysort(graph);
 END;
END sort;
PROCEDURE Initialise(VAR graph:graphs);
VAR
 v:vertices;
BEGIN
 WITH graph DO
  FOR v:=minvertex TO nrfvertices DO marked[v]:=FALSE; END;
  marked[initial]:=TRUE; sort(graph);
 END;
END Initialise;
PROCEDURE Writeresults(VAR graph:graphs; e:edges);
VAR
 v:vertices;
BEGIN
 WITH graph DO WITH edge[e] DO
  WriteString('Edge␣('); WriteCard(CARDINAL(start),1);
  WriteString(','); WriteCard(CARDINAL(finish),1);
  WriteString(')␣has␣weight␣'); WriteInt(INTEGER(weight),1);
 END;END;
 WriteLn;
END Writeresults;
PROCEDURE Process(VAR graph:graphs);
   (* Prim's algorithm *)
VAR
 e:zedges;
 total:weights;
 nrmarked:zvertices;
 PROCEDURE next(VAR graph:graphs):edges;
 VAR
  e:zedges;
  ok:BOOLEAN;
 BEGIN
  WITH graph DO
   e:=minedge-1;
   REPEAT
    INC(e);
    WITH edge[e] DO
     ok:=marked[start]≠marked[finish];
    END;
   UNTIL ok;
   RETURN edges(e);
  END;
 END next;
BEGIN
 nrmarked:=minvertex;
 WITH graph DO
  total:=0;
```

```
REPEAT
  e:=next(graph);
  WITH edge[e] DO
    marked[start]:=TRUE; marked[finish]:=TRUE;
    total:=total+weight;
  END;
  INC(nrmarked); Writeresults(graph,e);
UNTIL nrmarked=nrfvertices;
WriteString('Total weight is '); WriteInt(total,1); WriteLn;
  END;
END Process;
BEGIN
  Readdata(graph);Initialise(graph);Process(graph);
END Prim.
```

A sample data file follows. The number of vertices and edges, and
initial vertex, are followed by a list of triples: two vertices and the weight
of that edge.

```
9  16   5
1 2 1      2 3 2     1 4 2     2 4 3     2 5 4     3 5 2     3 6 5
4 5 1      5 6 1     4 7 2     5 7 1     5 8 2     6 8 4     6 9 2
7 8 3      8 9 5
```

B.5   Shortest path

Dijkstra's algorithms both use a datafile like the following.

```
12    17 2
2 1 7      2 3 5     3 4 4     5 6 3     6 7 18    7 8 3      9 10 2
10 11 1    12 11 2   1 5 2     5 9 8     2 6 1     6 10 15   3 7 15
7 11 3     4 8 14    8 12 6
```

The number of vertices and edges, and the root vertex, are followed by
triples representing an edge list together with the length of each edge.
The user is prompted to indicate whether or not the graph is directed.

Dijkstra's algorithm—first form

```
MODULE Dijkstra1;
FROM InOut IMPORT OpenInput, CloseInput, ReadCard, WriteCard,
  WriteLn, WriteString;
    (* progressive form of minimal path algorithm *)
CONST
  minvertex=1; maxvertex=100;
  minedge=1; maxedge=1000;
```

TYPE
  distances=CARDINAL;
  vertices=CARDINAL[minvertex .. maxvertex];
  edges=CARDINAL[minedge .. maxedge];
  *vertsets=***ARRAY** *vertices* **OF** *BOOLEAN;*
  *markings=***ARRAY** *vertices* **OF** *distances;*
  *edgerecord=***RECORD**
    start,finish:vertices;
    length:distances;
  END;
  *edgearray=***ARRAY** *edges* **OF** *edgerecord;*
  *graphs=***RECORD**
    nrfvertices:vertices;
    nrfedges:edges;
    initial:vertices; (* measure distances from here *)
    directed:BOOLEAN; (* digraph? *)
    edge:edgearray;
    marking:markings; (* the distance marked at a certain vertex *)
    marked:vertsets; (* used for vertices known to be correctly labelled *)
  END;
VAR
  graph:graphs;
  infty:distances; (* set to largest value possible *)
PROCEDURE *Readdata(***VAR** *graph:graphs);*
VAR
  i,j,l:CARDINAL;
  v:vertices; k:edges;
BEGIN
  WITH *graph* **DO**
    OpenInput('DAT');
    ReadCard(i);nrfvertices:=vertices(i);
    ReadCard(i);nrfedges:=edges(i);
    ReadCard(i);initial:=vertices(i);
    FOR *k:=minedge* **TO** *nrfedges* **DO**
      ReadCard(i);ReadCard(j);ReadCard(l);
      WITH *edge[k]* **DO**
        start:=vertices(i);finish:=vertices(j);length:=l;
      END;
    END;
    CloseInput;
    WriteString('Input␣1␣for␣directed␣graph,␣0␣for␣undirected:␣');
    ReadCard(i);WriteLn; directed:=(i=1);
  END;
END *Readdata;*
PROCEDURE *Initialise(***VAR** *graph:graphs);*
VAR
  v:vertices;

```
BEGIN
 infty:=MAX(distances);
 WITH graph DO
  FOR v:=minvertex TO nrfvertices DO
   marking[v]:=infty; marked[v]:=FALSE;
  END;
  marking[initial]:=0;
 END;
END Initialise;
PROCEDURE Writeresults(VAR graph:graphs);
VAR
 v:vertices;
BEGIN
 WITH graph DO
  FOR v:=minvertex TO nrfvertices DO
   IF marking[v]=infty THEN
    WriteString('␣infty');
   ELSE
    WriteCard(marking[v],6);
   END;
  END;
 END;
 WriteLn;
END Writeresults;
PROCEDURE Process(VAR graph:graphs);
   (* first of Dijkstra's algorithms *)
VAR
 v:vertices;
 nrmarked:CARDINAL[minvertex−1 .. maxvertex];
 e:edges;
 success:BOOLEAN;
 PROCEDURE next(VAR graph:graphs;
          VAR success:BOOLEAN):vertices;
 (* find next nearest vertex *)
 VAR
  v,bestv:vertices;
  best:distances;
 BEGIN
  best:=infty;
  WITH graph DO
   FOR v:=minvertex TO nrfvertices DO
    IF NOT marked[v] THEN
     IF marking[v]<infty THEN
     IF marking[v]<best THEN
      bestv:=v;best:=marking[v];
     END;
    END;
   END;
  END;
 END;
```

```
    IF best<infty THEN
      success:=TRUE; RETURN bestv;
    ELSE
      success:=FALSE; RETURN minvertex;
    END;
  END next;
BEGIN
  nrmarked:=0;
  WriteString('These␣are␣the␣successive␣markings␣of␣vertices:');
  WriteLn;
  WITH graph DO
   REPEAT
     Writeresults(graph);
     v:=next(graph,success);
     IF success THEN
       marked[v]:=TRUE; INC(nrmarked);
       WriteString('Vertex␣'); WriteCard(v,1);
       WriteString('␣is␣at␣distance␣'); WriteCard(marking[v],1); WriteLn;
       FOR e:=minedge TO nrfedges DO
         WITH edge[e] DO
          IF (start=v) AND (marking[finish]>(marking[v]+length)) THEN
            marking[finish]:=marking[v]+length;
          END;
          IF ¬directed THEN
           IF (finish=v) AND (marking[start]>(marking[v]+length)) THEN
             marking[start]:=marking[v]+length;
           END;
          END;
         END;
       END;
     END;
   UNTIL ¬success OR (nrmarked=nrfvertices);
  END;
  Writeresults(graph);
END Process;
BEGIN
  Readdata(graph); Initialise(graph); Process(graph);
END Dijkstra1.
```

Dijkstra's algorithm—second form

```
MODULE Dijkstra2;
FROM InOut IMPORT OpenInput, CloseInput, ReadCard, WriteCard,
  WriteLn, WriteString;
    (* Iterative form of minimal path algorithm *)
CONST
  minvertex=1; maxvertex=100;
  minedge=1; maxedge=1000;
```

```
TYPE
  distances=CARDINAL;
  vertices=CARDINAL[minvertex .. maxvertex];
  edges=CARDINAL[minedge .. maxedge];
  zedges=CARDINAL[minedge−1 .. maxedge];
  markings=ARRAY vertices OF distances;
  edgerecord=RECORD
    start,finish:vertices;
    length:distances;
  END;
  edgearray=ARRAY edges OF edgerecord;
  graphs=RECORD
    nrfvertices:vertices;
    nrfedges:edges;
    initial:vertices;   (* distances measured from here *)
    directed:BOOLEAN;   (* is this a digraph? *)
    edge:edgearray;
    marking:markings;   (* vertices marked with distances *)
  END;
VAR
  graph:graphs;
  infty:distances;  (* set to maximum cardinal *)
PROCEDURE Readdata(VAR graph:graphs);
VAR
  i,j,l:CARDINAL;
  v:vertices;    k:edges;
BEGIN
  WITH graph DO
    OpenInput('DAT');
    ReadCard(i);nrfvertices:=vertices(i);
    ReadCard(i);nrfedges:=edges(i);
    ReadCard(i);initial:=vertices(i);
    FOR k:=minedge TO nrfedges DO
      ReadCard(i);ReadCard(j);ReadCard(l);
      WITH edge[k] DO
        start:=vertices(i);finish:=vertices(j);length:=l;
      END;
    END;
    CloseInput;
    WriteString('Input␣1␣for␣directed␣graph,␣0␣for␣undirected:␣');
    ReadCard(i);WriteLn; directed:=(i=1);
  END;
END Readdata;
PROCEDURE Initialise(VAR graph:graphs);
VAR
  v:vertices;
```

```
BEGIN
  infty:=MAX(distances);
  WITH graph DO
    FOR v:=minvertex TO nrfvertices DO
      marking[v]:=infty;
    END;
    marking[initial]:=0;
  END;
END Initialise;
PROCEDURE Writeresults(VAR graph:graphs);
VAR
  v:vertices;
BEGIN
  WITH graph DO
    FOR v:=minvertex TO nrfvertices DO
      IF marking[v]=infty THEN
        WriteString('␣infty');
      ELSE
        WriteCard(marking[v],6);
      END;
    END;
  END;
  WriteLn;
END Writeresults;
PROCEDURE Process(VAR graph:graphs);
  (* second of Dijkstra's algorithms *)
VAR
  done:BOOLEAN;
  e:edges;
  PROCEDURE echo(i,j:vertices; d:distances);
  BEGIN
    WriteString('Using␣edge␣('); WriteCard(i,1); WriteString(',');
    WriteCard(j,1); WriteString(')␣to␣update␣end␣to␣');
    WriteCard(d,1); WriteLn;
  END echo;
BEGIN
  WriteString('Here␣are␣the␣successive␣markings␣of␣vertices:');
  WriteLn;
  WITH graph DO
    REPEAT
      Writeresults(graph);
      done:=TRUE;
      FOR e:=minedge TO nrfedges DO
        WITH edge[e] DO
          IF marking[start]≠infty THEN
            IF marking[finish]>(marking[start]+length) THEN
              marking[finish]:=marking[start]+length;
              echo(start,finish,marking[finish]);
              done:=FALSE;
            END;
          END;
```

```
        IF ¬directed THEN (* take edge with opposite orientation *)
          IF marking[finish]≠infty THEN
            IF marking[start]>(marking[finish]+length) THEN
            marking[start]:=marking[finish]+length;
            echo(finish,start,marking[start]);
            done:=FALSE;
            END;
          END;
        END;
      END;
    END;
  UNTIL done;
 END;
END Process;
BEGIN
  Readdata(graph);Initialise(graph);Process(graph);
END Dijkstra2.
```

B.6   Critical path

We compute the earliest start times for interdependent processes.

```
MODULE Critical;
FROM InOut IMPORT OpenInput, CloseInput, ReadCard, WriteCard,
  WriteLn, WriteString;
    (* critical path algorithm *)
CONST
  minvertex=1; maxvertex=100;
  minedge=1; maxedge=1000;
TYPE
  distances=CARDINAL;
  vertices=CARDINAL[minvertex .. maxvertex];
  edges=CARDINAL[minedge .. maxedge];
  zedges=CARDINAL[minedge−1 .. maxedge];
  markings=ARRAY vertices OF distances;
  edgerecord=RECORD
    start,finish:vertices;
    length:distances;
  END;
  edgearray=ARRAY edges OF edgerecord;
  graphs=RECORD
    nrfvertices:vertices;
    nrfedges:edges;
    initial,terminal:vertices; (* start and finish of all processes *)
    edge:edgearray;
    marking:markings; (* vertices marked with maximum distance *)
  END;
VAR
  graph:graphs;
  success:BOOLEAN;
```

```
PROCEDURE Readdata(VAR graph:graphs);
VAR
  i,j,l:CARDINAL;
  v:vertices;    k:edges;
BEGIN
  WITH graph DO
    OpenInput('DAT');
    ReadCard(i);nrfvertices:=vertices(i);
    ReadCard(i);nrfedges:=edges(i);
    ReadCard(i);initial:=vertices(i);
    ReadCard(i);terminal:=vertices(i);
    FOR k:=minedge TO nrfedges DO
      ReadCard(i);ReadCard(j);ReadCard(l);
      WITH edge[k] DO
        start:=vertices(i); finish:=vertices(j); length:=l;
      END;
    END;
    CloseInput;
  END;
END Readdata;
PROCEDURE Initialise(VAR graph:graphs);
VAR
  v:vertices;
BEGIN
  WITH graph DO
    FOR v:=minvertex TO nrfvertices DO
      marking[v]:=0;
    END;
  END;
END Initialise;
PROCEDURE Writeresults(VAR graph:graphs);
VAR
  v:vertices;
BEGIN
  WITH graph DO
    FOR v:=minvertex TO nrfvertices DO
      WriteCard(marking[v],6);
    END;
  END;
  WriteLn;
END Writeresults;
PROCEDURE Process(VAR graph:graphs; VAR success:BOOLEAN);
    (* longest path form of Dijkstra's algorithms *)
VAR
  done:BOOLEAN;
  e:edges;
  iteration:CARDINAL;
BEGIN
  WriteString('Here are the successive markings of vertices'); WriteLn;
  iteration:=0;
```

```
WITH graph DO
  REPEAT
  INC(iteration); Writeresults(graph); done:=TRUE;
  FOR e:=minedge TO nrfedges DO
    WITH edge[e] DO
    IF marking[finish]<(marking[start]+length) THEN
      marking[finish]:=marking[start]+length;
      WriteString('Using⎵edge⎵('); WriteCard(start,1);
      WriteString(','); WriteCard(finish,1);
      WriteString(')⎵to⎵update⎵end⎵to⎵');
      WriteCard(marking[finish],1); WriteLn;
      done:=FALSE;
    END;
    END;
  END;
  UNTIL done OR (iteration>nrfvertices);
  success:=iteration≤nrfvertices;
  END;
END Process;
BEGIN
Readdata(graph);Initialise(graph);Process(graph,success);
IF success THEN
  WriteString('The⎵critical⎵path⎵has⎵length⎵');
  WITH graph DO
  WriteCard(marking[terminal],1); WriteLn;
  END;
ELSE
  WriteString('The⎵graph⎵is⎵not⎵acyclic!'); WriteLn;
END;
END Critical.
```

The input consists of the number of vertices and edges, the initial and terminal vertex, and an edge list, such as the following.

```
12     17   2 12
2  1 17    2 3 11    3 4 15    6 5 2    6 7 9    7 8 29   9 10 1
10 11 15 11 12 2   1 5 14    5 9 8    2 6 19   6 10 4   7 3 7
11 7 7    4 8 4    8 12 8
```

B.7 Graph colouring

The algorithm sorts the vertices in descending order of vertex degree, and colours successively with the earliest available colour.

```
MODULE Gcol;
FROM InOut IMPORT OpenInput, CloseInput, ReadCard, WriteCard,
  WriteLn, WriteString;
  (* greedy algorithm for graph colouring *)
```

```
CONST
  minvertex=1; maxvertex=100; zvertex=minvertex−1;
  minedge=1; maxedge=1000;
TYPE
  vertices=CARDINAL[minvertex .. maxvertex];
  degrees=CARDINAL[zvertex .. maxvertex−1];
  zvertices=degrees;
  colours=CARDINAL[zvertex .. maxvertex];
  edges=CARDINAL[minedge .. maxedge];
  zedges=CARDINAL[minedge−1 .. maxedge];
  vertsets=ARRAY vertices OF BOOLEAN;
  colsets=ARRAY colours OF BOOLEAN; (* sets of colours used *)
  edgerecord=RECORD
    start,finish:vertices;
  END;
  edgearray=ARRAY edges OF edgerecord;
  colourings=ARRAY vertices OF colours;
  degreearray=ARRAY vertices OF degrees;
  permutation=ARRAY vertices OF vertices;
  graphs=RECORD
    nrfvertices:vertices;
    nrfedges:edges;
    edge:edgearray;
    vert:permutation;   (* the permutation of vertices *)
    marked:vertsets;    (* vertices already coloured *)
    deg:degreearray;    (* degree of a vertex *)
    col:colourings;     (* colour of a vertex *)
    nrfcolours:colours; (* total number of colours used *)
  END;
VAR
  graph:graphs;
PROCEDURE Readdata(VAR graph:graphs);
    (* and calculate vertex degrees *)
VAR
  i,j:CARDINAL;
  v:vertices;  k:edges;
BEGIN
  WITH graph DO
    OpenInput('DAT');
    ReadCard(i);nrfvertices:=vertices(i);
    ReadCard(i);nrfedges:=edges(i);
    FOR v:=minvertex TO nrfvertices DO
      vert[v]:=v;deg[v]:=zvertex
    END; (* identity permutation *)
```

```
    FOR k:=minedge TO nrfedges DO
      ReadCard(i);ReadCard(j);
      WITH edge[k] DO
        start:=vertices(i);finish:=vertices(j);
        INC(deg[start]);INC(deg[finish]);
      END;
    END;
    CloseInput;WriteLn;
  END;
END Readdata;
PROCEDURE sort(VAR graph:graphs);
  (* sorting by quicksort into descending order of degrees *)
  PROCEDURE quicksort(VAR graph:graphs; low,high:zvertices);
  VAR
    i,j:zvertices;
    comp:degrees;
    PROCEDURE exchange(VAR v1,v2:vertices);
    VAR
      temp:vertices;
    BEGIN
      temp:=v1; v1:=v2; v2:=temp;
    END exchange;
  BEGIN
    WITH graph DO
      IF low<high THEN
        i:=low; j:=high; comp:=deg[vert[j]];
        REPEAT
          WHILE (i<j) & (deg[vert[i]]≥comp) DO INC(i); END;
          WHILE (i<j) & (deg[vert[j]]≤comp) DO DEC(j); END;
          IF i<j THEN exchange(vert[i],vert[j]); END;
        UNTIL i≥j;
        IF i≠high THEN exchange(vert[i],vert[high]); END;
        (* vertex i is now correctly sorted *)
        IF (i-low)<(high-i) THEN
          quicksort(graph,low,i-1); quicksort(graph,i+1,high);
        ELSE
          quicksort(graph,i+1,high); quicksort(graph,low,i-1);
        END;
      END;
    END;
  END quicksort;
BEGIN
  WITH graph DO
    quicksort(graph,minvertex,nrfvertices);
  END;
END sort;
PROCEDURE Initialise(VAR graph:graphs);
VAR
  v:vertices;
```

```
BEGIN
 WITH graph DO
  FOR v:=minvertex TO nrfvertices DO marked[v]:=FALSE; END;
  sort(graph); nrfcolours:=zvertex;
 END;
END Initialise;
PROCEDURE Writeresults(VAR graph:graphs; v:vertices);
BEGIN
 WITH graph DO
  WriteString('Vertex␣'); WriteCard(CARDINAL(vert[v]),1);
  WriteString('␣has␣colour␣'); WriteCard(CARDINAL(col[vert[v]]),1);
 END;
 WriteLn;
END Writeresults;
PROCEDURE Process(VAR graph:graphs);
    (* the greedy algorithm *)
VAR
 v:vertices;
 c:colours;
 PROCEDURE next(VAR graph:graphs; v:vertices):colours;
 VAR
  e:edges;
  colset:colsets;
  c:colours;
 BEGIN
  WITH graph DO
   FOR c:=minvertex TO nrfvertices DO colset[c]:=FALSE; END;
   FOR e:=minedge TO nrfedges DO
    WITH edge[e] DO
    IF (start=v) AND marked[finish] THEN
      colset[col[finish]]:=TRUE;
    ELSIF (finish=v) AND marked[start] THEN
      colset[col[start]]:=TRUE;
    END;
    END;
   END;
   c:=zvertex;
   REPEAT
    INC(c);
   UNTIL ¬colset[c];
   RETURN c; (* first available colour *)
  END;
 END next;
```

```
BEGIN
  WITH graph DO
    FOR v:=minvertex TO nrfvertices DO
      c:=next(graph,vert[v]); col[vert[v]]:=c;
      IF c>nrfcolours THEN nrfcolours:=c; END;
      marked[vert[v]]:=TRUE;
      Writeresults(graph,v);
    END;
  END;
END Process;
BEGIN
  Readdata(graph);Initialise(graph);Process(graph);
  WITH graph DO
    WriteString('Number␣of␣colours␣used␣was␣');
    WriteCard(CARDINAL(nrfcolours),1); WriteLn;
  END;
END Gcol.
```

The datafile consists of the number of vertices and edges, and then
an edge list.

```
9   14
1 2      2 3      2 4      2 5      3 4      4 5      5 6
6 9      4 7      7 6      4 9      7 8      3 8      8 9
```

B.8   Preorder and postorder traversal

This program implements preorder and postorder traversal by constructing a *binary tree* from an expression and then visiting each vertex in turn
according to either algorithm.

```
MODULE Traverse;
FROM InOut IMPORT ReadString, WriteLn, WriteString, Read, Write;
FROM Storage IMPORT ALLOCATE;
CONST
  lbrace='(';
  minindex=0; maxindex=200;
TYPE
  atoms=CHAR;
  expressions=POINTER TO node;
  node=RECORD   (* for a binary operation *)
    left,right:expressions;
    atom:atoms;
  END;
  indices=[minindex .. maxindex];
  stringarrays=ARRAY indices OF atoms;
  strings=RECORD
    chr:stringarrays;
    posn:indices;
  END;
```

VAR
  s:strings;
  e:expressions;
PROCEDURE *grow*(**VAR** *s:strings*; **VAR** *e:expressions*);
BEGIN;
  NEW(*e*);
  WITH *s* **DO WITH** *e↑* **DO**
    left:=*NIL*;*right*:=*NIL*;
    IF *chr*[*posn*]=*lbrace* **THEN**
      INC(*posn*);(*skip lbrace*)
      grow(*s,left*); *atom*:=*chr*[*posn*];
      INC(*posn*);(* operator*)
      grow(*s,right*); *INC*(*posn*);(*skip rbrace*)
    ELSE(*assume a variable*)
      atom:=*chr*[*posn*]; *INC*(*posn*);
    END;
  END;**END**;
END *grow*;
PROCEDURE *preorder*(*e:expressions*);
    (* traverse in preorder or prefix form *)
BEGIN
  WITH *e↑* **DO**
    Write(*atom*);
    IF *left*≠*NIL* **THEN** *preorder*(*left*); **END**;
    IF *right*≠*NIL* **THEN** *preorder*(*right*); **END**;
  END;
END *preorder*;
PROCEDURE *postorder*(*e:expressions*);
    (* traverse in postorder or postfix form *)
BEGIN
  WITH *e↑* **DO**
    IF *left*≠*NIL* **THEN** *postorder*(*left*); **END**;
    IF *right*≠*NIL* **THEN** *postorder*(*right*); **END**;
    Write(*atom*);
  END;
END *postorder*;
BEGIN
  WriteString('Type␣in␣an␣expression,␣');
  WriteString('fully␣bracketed,␣with␣enclosing␣brackets'); *WriteLn*;
  ReadString(*s.chr*); *s.posn*:=*minindex*; *WriteLn*;*grow*(*s,e*);
  WriteString('Preorder␣is␣');*preorder*(*e*); *WriteLn*;
  WriteString('Postorder␣is␣');*postorder*(*e*); *WriteLn*;
END *Traverse*.

Note that the expression to be processed must be fully bracketed, with enclosing brackets, such as (a*(b+c)). No error checking is done. This is merely an illustration.

B.9   A recognizer for a regular expression

Consider the regular expression

$$\langle S \rangle \to [\mathbf{1}](\{\mathbf{01}\}|\{\mathbf{0}\}),$$

with normal form as follows.

$$
\begin{aligned}
\langle S \rangle &\to \varepsilon \\
\langle S \rangle &\to \mathbf{0}\langle U \rangle \\
\langle S \rangle &\to \mathbf{0}\langle W \rangle \\
\langle S \rangle &\to \mathbf{1}\langle T \rangle \\
\langle T \rangle &\to \varepsilon \\
\langle T \rangle &\to \mathbf{0}\langle U \rangle \\
\langle T \rangle &\to \mathbf{0}\langle W \rangle \\
\langle U \rangle &\to \mathbf{1}\langle V \rangle \\
\langle V \rangle &\to \varepsilon \\
\langle V \rangle &\to \mathbf{0}\langle U \rangle \\
\langle W \rangle &\to \varepsilon \\
\langle W \rangle &\to \mathbf{0}\langle W \rangle
\end{aligned}
$$

These productions translate directly into a program to recognize the words in the regular grammar.

MODULE *Regular*;
FROM *InOut* **IMPORT** *ReadString, WriteString, WriteLn*;
    (∗ A recognizer for the expression
                    $\langle S \rangle \to [\mathbf{1}](\{\mathbf{01}\}|\{\mathbf{0}\})$.
∗)
CONST
  minindex=0; *maxindex*=1000;
  zero='0'; *one*='1'; *space*='␣';
TYPE
  nonterminals=(S,T,U,V,W,F); (∗ nonterminals in normal form ∗)
  terminals=CHAR;   (∗ terminals are ASCII characters ∗)
  states=**ARRAY** *nonterminals* **OF** *BOOLEAN*; (∗ state is a set of nonterminals
∗)
  indices=CARDINAL[*minindex* .. *maxindex*];
  stringarrays=**ARRAY** *indices* **OF** *terminals*;
  strings=**RECORD**
   chr:stringarrays;
   posn:indices;
  END;

```
VAR
  expression:strings;
  state:states;
PROCEDURE ReadExpression(VAR e:strings);
BEGIN
  WriteString('Type⎵in⎵a⎵sequence⎵of⎵digits,⎵terminated⎵by⎵a⎵space');
  WriteLn;
  WITH e DO
    ReadString(chr); WriteLn;
  END;
END ReadExpression;
PROCEDURE Clear(VAR s:states);
VAR
  n:nonterminals;
BEGIN
  FOR n:=MIN(nonterminals) TO MAX(nonterminals) DO
    s[n]:=FALSE;
  END;
  s[F]:=TRUE;
END Clear;
PROCEDURE Initialise(VAR e:strings; VAR state:states);
BEGIN
  e.posn:=minindex; state[S]:=TRUE;
END Initialise;
PROCEDURE MakeTransition(VAR state:states; term:terminals);
  (* one transition of the finite state machine *)
VAR
  newstate:states;
  n:nonterminals;
BEGIN
  Clear(newstate);
  FOR n:=MIN(nonterminals) TO MAX(nonterminals) DO
    IF state[n] THEN  (* the transition mapping *)
    CASE n OF
      S:
        IF term=zero THEN
          newstate[U]:=TRUE; newstate[W]:=TRUE;
        ELSIF term=one THEN
          newstate[T]:=TRUE;
        END; |
      T:
        IF term=zero THEN
          newstate[U]:=TRUE; newstate[W]:=TRUE;
        END; |
      U:
        IF term=one THEN
          newstate[V]:=TRUE;
        END; |
```

```
        V:
         IF term=zero THEN
           newstate[U]:=TRUE
         END;|
        W:
         IF term=zero THEN
           newstate[W]:=TRUE;
         END;|
        F:
       END;
      END;
     END;
    state:=newstate;
    END MakeTransition;
    PROCEDURE Process(e:strings; VAR s:states);
       (* accept or reject *)
    BEGIN
     WITH e DO
       WHILE chr[posn]>space DO
         MakeTransition(s,chr[posn]); INC(posn);
       END;
     END;
    END Process;
    PROCEDURE Check(st:states);
    VAR
     accepted:BOOLEAN;
    BEGIN
     accepted:=st[S] OR st[T] OR st[V] OR st[W];
     IF accepted THEN
       WriteString('String␣accepted');
     ELSE
       WriteString('String␣not␣accepted');
     END;
     WriteLn;
    END Check;
    BEGIN
     WriteString('This␣program␣only␣accepts␣');
     WriteString('strings␣of␣the␣form␣[1]({01}|{0})');
     WriteLn; WriteString('Press␣"Q"␣as␣your␣final␣string'); WriteLn;
     REPEAT
       ReadExpression(expression); Initialise(expression,state);
       Process(expression,state); Check(state);
     UNTIL CAP(expression.chr[minindex])='Q';
    END Regular.
```

B.10 A lexical analyser

This program is only a minor step away from the previous one. The *tokens* or *lexemes* accepted in *Modula-2* are specified in terms of a regular grammar. We have

$$\langle integer \rangle \quad \rightarrow \quad \langle digit \rangle \{ \langle digit \rangle \}$$
$$\langle octal \rangle \quad \rightarrow \quad \langle octaldigit \rangle \{ \langle octaldigit \rangle \}(\text{B}|\text{b}|\text{C}|\text{c})$$
$$\langle hexadecimal \rangle \quad \rightarrow \quad \langle hexdigit \rangle \{ \langle hexdigit \rangle \}(\text{H}|\text{h})$$

and so on, representing the different kinds of numeric constants. The identifiers are given by

$$\langle identifier \rangle \rightarrow \langle letter \rangle \{ \langle letter \rangle | \langle digit \rangle \},$$

and there are also special combinations such as (* and :=, which are regarded as indivisible items. Nesting of comments is not detected, since it is a non-regular feature, easily implemented as a recursive procedure.

The rule followed in picking up a token is always to take the longest token permissible in the regular grammar. It is necessary to look ahead one character to see whether a token can be extended. The only troublesome case is a string of digits followed by a dot, which could start either a subrange or a real number.

```
MODULE Lex;
FROM InOut IMPORT OpenInput, CloseInput, WriteCard,
  EOL, Read, Write, WriteLn, WriteString, Done;
    (* A finite state machine to accept lexemes of Modula-2 *)
CONST
  minindex=0; maxindex=1000;
  zero='0'; seven='7'; nine='9'; A='A'; Z='Z'; F='F';
  equal='='; squote='''''; dquote='"'; less='<';
  greater='>'; space='␣';
  hatch='#'; period='.'; E='E'; C='C'; B='B'; H='H';
  plus='+'; minus='-';
  star='*'; colonch=':'; lpar='('; rpar=')'; tab=11C;
TYPE
  nonterminals=(Next,integernum,realnum,realexpt,
    octno,charno,hexno,dot,dots,becomes,colon,
    identifier,lt,leq,gt,geq,neq,
    leftpar,starcom,bcomment,ecomment,other,strg,spaces,
    realp,realdots,
    (* the rest are transients *)
    Fail,reale,realepm,oct,hex,sqstring,dqstring);
    (* these are the nonterminals that need special action *)
  terminals=CHAR; (* terminals are ASCII characters *)
  states=ARRAY nonterminals OF BOOLEAN;
```

```
  indices=CARDINAL[minindex .. maxindex];
  stringarrays=ARRAY indices OF terminals;
  strings=RECORD
    chr:stringarrays;
    start,posn:indices;
  END;
VAR
  expression:strings;
  EOF:BOOLEAN;  (* end of file *)
  lineno:CARDINAL;
PROCEDURE ReadLine(VAR s:ARRAY OF CHAR);
CONST Ignorech=12C;
VAR i:CARDINAL; ch:CHAR;
BEGIN
  s[0]:=0C; EOF:=FALSE; i:=0;
  LOOP
    IF i>(HIGH(s)-1) THEN EXIT END;
    Read(ch);
    IF ch≠Ignorech THEN
      IF ch=EOL THEN EXIT END;
      IF ¬Done THEN EOF:=TRUE;EXIT END;
      IF ch=tab THEN ch:=space; END;
      s[i]:=ch; INC(i);
    END;
  END;
  s[i]:=0C;
END ReadLine;
PROCEDURE Clear(VAR s:states);
VAR
  n:nonterminals;
BEGIN
  FOR n:=MIN(nonterminals) TO MAX(nonterminals) DO
    s[n]:=FALSE;
  END;
END Clear;
PROCEDURE Initialise(VAR e:strings);
BEGIN
  WITH e DO
    posn:=minindex; start:=minindex;
  END;
END Initialise;
PROCEDURE MakeTransition(VAR state:states; t:terminals;
  VAR made:BOOLEAN;VAR nt:nonterminals);
    (* This is the finite state machine driving Lex *)
VAR
  newstate:states;
  n:nonterminals;
  PROCEDURE digit(t:terminals):BOOLEAN;
  BEGIN
    RETURN (t≥zero) & (t≤nine);
  END digit;
```

```
PROCEDURE octal(t:terminals):BOOLEAN;
BEGIN
  RETURN (t⩾zero) & (t⩽seven);
END octal;
PROCEDURE hexadecimal(t:terminals):BOOLEAN;
BEGIN
  t:=CAP(t);
  RETURN ((t⩾zero) & (t⩽nine)) OR ((t⩾A) & (t⩽F));;
END hexadecimal;
PROCEDURE letter(t:terminals):BOOLEAN;
BEGIN
  t:=CAP(t);RETURN(t⩾A) & (t⩽Z);
END letter;
PROCEDURE setstate(t:nonterminals);
BEGIN
  newstate[t]:=TRUE;made:=TRUE;nt:=t;
END setstate;
BEGIN
  Clear(newstate); made:=FALSE;
  FOR n:=MIN(nonterminals) TO MAX(nonterminals) DO
  IF state[n] THEN  (* transition mapping *)
    CASE n OF
      Next:
      IF digit(t) THEN
        setstate(integernum); setstate(hex);
        IF octal(t) THEN setstate(oct); END;
      ELSIF letter(t) THEN setstate(identifier);
      ELSIF t=less THEN setstate(lt);
      ELSIF t=greater THEN setstate(gt);
      ELSIF t=hatch THEN setstate(neq);
      ELSIF t=lpar THEN setstate(leftpar);
      ELSIF t=star THEN setstate(starcom);
      ELSIF t=period THEN setstate(dot);
      ELSIF t=squote THEN setstate(sqstring);
      ELSIF t=dquote THEN setstate(dqstring);
      ELSIF t=space THEN setstate(spaces);
      ELSIF t=colonch THEN setstate(colon);
      ELSE setstate(other);
      END;|
      integernum:
      IF digit(t) THEN setstate(integernum);
      ELSIF t=period THEN setstate(realp);
      END;|
      realp:
      IF t=period THEN setstate(realdots);
      ELSIF digit(t) THEN setstate(realnum);
      ELSIF t=E THEN setstate(reale);
      END;|
```

oct:
  IF *octal(t)* **THEN** *setstate(oct)*;
  ELSIF *CAP(t)=B* **THEN** *setstate(octno)*;
  ELSIF *CAP(t)=C* **THEN** *setstate(charno)*;
  END;|
hex:
  IF *hexadecimal(t)* **THEN** *setstate(hex)*;
  ELSIF *CAP(t)=H* **THEN** *setstate(hexno)*;
  END;|
realnum:
  IF *digit(t)* **THEN** *setstate(realnum)*;
  ELSIF *t=E* **THEN** *setstate(reale)*;
  END;|
reale:
  IF *digit(t)* **THEN** *setstate(realexpt)*;
  ELSIF *(t=plus)* **OR** *(t=minus)* **THEN** *setstate(realepm)*;
  END;|
realepm:
  IF *digit(t)* **THEN** *setstate(realexpt)*; **END**;|
realexpt:
  IF *digit(t)* **THEN** *setstate(realexpt)*; **END**;|
dot:
  IF *t=period* **THEN** *setstate(dots)*; **END**;|
identifier:
  IF *digit(t)* **OR** *letter(t)* **THEN** *setstate(identifier)*; **END**;|
lt:
  IF *t=equal* **THEN** *setstate(leq)*;
  ELSIF *t=greater* **THEN** *setstate(neq)*;
  END;|
gt:
  IF *t=equal* **THEN** *setstate(geq)*; **END**;|
leftpar:
  IF *t=star* **THEN** *setstate(bcomment)*; **END**;|
starcom:
  IF *t=rpar* **THEN** *setstate(ecomment)*; **END**;|
sqstring:
  IF *t=squote* **THEN**
    setstate(strg);
  ELSE
    setstate(sqstring);
  END;|
dqstring:
  IF *t=dquote* **THEN**
    setstate(strg);
  ELSE
    setstate(dqstring);
  END;|
spaces:
  IF *t=space* **THEN** *setstate(spaces)*; **END**;|

```
      colon:
        IF t=equal THEN setstate(becomes); END;
      END;
    END;
  END;
  state:=newstate;
END MakeTransition;
PROCEDURE ProcessNextLexeme(VAR e:strings);
VAR
  s:states;
  made:BOOLEAN;
  nt:nonterminals;
  PROCEDURE WriteLexeme(VAR s:strings);
  VAR i:indices;
  BEGIN
    WITH s DO
      FOR i:=start TO (posn-1) DO Write(chr[i]);END;WriteLn;
    END;
  END WriteLexeme;
BEGIN
  WITH e DO
    Clear(s); s[Next]:=TRUE; start:=posn; made:=TRUE;
    WHILE made DO
      MakeTransition(s,chr[posn],made,nt);
      IF made THEN INC(posn); END;
    END; (* ends in a rejecting state *)
    IF nt=realdots THEN DEC(posn,2); nt:=realnum; END;
    WriteLexeme(e);
  END;
END ProcessNextLexeme;
BEGIN
  OpenInput('DAT'); WriteLn;
  WITH expression DO
    lineno:=0;
    REPEAT
      INC(lineno); ReadLine(chr);
      IF ¬EOF THEN
        WriteCard(lineno,8); WriteString(':␣');
        WriteString(chr); WriteLn;
        Initialise(expression);
        WHILE chr[posn]≠0C DO
          ProcessNextLexeme(expression);
        END;
      END;
    UNTIL EOF;
  END;
  CloseInput; WriteLn;
END Lex.
```

B.11   A parser for wffs

A simple grammar for wffs can be specified by taking the following.

$$
\begin{aligned}
\langle expr \rangle &\rightarrow \langle term \rangle \\
\langle expr \rangle &\rightarrow \langle term \rangle \langle endexpr \rangle \\
\langle expr \rangle &\rightarrow \langle or \rangle \langle expr \rangle \\
\langle or \rangle &\rightarrow \ | \\
\langle term \rangle &\rightarrow \langle factor \rangle \\
\langle term \rangle &\rightarrow \langle factor \rangle \langle endterm \rangle \\
\langle endterm \rangle &\rightarrow \langle and \rangle \langle term \rangle \\
\langle and \rangle &\rightarrow \ \& \\
\langle factor \rangle &\rightarrow \langle negation \rangle \\
\langle negation \rangle &\rightarrow \langle not \rangle \langle factor \rangle \\
\langle not \rangle &\rightarrow \\
\langle factor \rangle &\rightarrow \langle group \rangle \\
\langle group \rangle &\rightarrow \langle leftpar \rangle \langle endgroup \rangle \\
\langle endgroup \rangle &\rightarrow \langle expr \rangle \langle rightpar \rangle \\
\langle leftpar \rangle &\rightarrow \ (\\
\langle rightpar \rangle &\rightarrow \ ) \\
\langle factor \rangle &\rightarrow \langle atom \rangle \\
\langle atom \rangle &\rightarrow \ \mathsf{a} | \cdots | \mathsf{z}
\end{aligned}
$$

There is some redundancy in the above, but it will serve our purpose.

The grammar leads directly to the following parser, which checks that a formula is well-formed. A product of nonterminals coincides with a call of two procedures. The successful execution of both means that the parse was successful. Since the grammar is *recursive*, that is, not regular, it follows that the program is also recursive. It is capable of backtracking when it runs, through incorrectly parsing bits of the expression, and so most of the procedures need local variables to keep a copy of the current position in the parse. In fact, the whole expression is copied each time, but we could get away with only copying the variable **posn**.

MODULE *Parse*;
FROM *InOut* **IMPORT** *ReadString, WriteLn, WriteString*;

(∗ This module only accepts valid logical expressions such as

$$a\&b\&\tilde{\ }c|(b|\tilde{\ }\tilde{\ }c)\&x\&\tilde{\ }((b|\tilde{\ }c\&d)\&a)$$

not containing any spaces, where **&** means ∧, **|** means ∨, and ⁻ means ¬. The priorities chosen are ⁻, **&**, **|**, from high to low. ∗)

CONST
  minindex=0; *maxindex*=200;
  lpar='(' ; *rpar*=')'; *andch*='**&**'; *orch*='|';   *notch*='⁻';
TYPE
  terminals=*CHAR*;
  indices=*CARDINAL*[*minindex* .. *maxindex*];
  stringarrays=**ARRAY** *indices* **OF** *terminals*;
  strings=**RECORD**
    chr:*stringarrays*;
    posn:*indices*;
  END;
VAR
  expression:*strings*;
  success,null:*BOOLEAN*;
PROCEDURE *ReadExpression*(**VAR** *e*:*strings*);
BEGIN
  WriteString('Type␣in␣an␣expression,␣terminated␣by␣a␣return');
  WriteLn;
  WITH *e* **DO**
    ReadString(*chr*); *WriteLn*;
    posn:=*minindex*;
  END;
END *ReadExpression*;
  (∗ Put these in if yours is a single pass compiler:
PROCEDURE *Expr*(**VAR** *e*:*strings*; **VAR** *success*:*BOOLEAN*);
  FORWARD;
PROCEDURE *Term*(**VAR** *e*:*strings*; **VAR** *success*:*BOOLEAN*);
  FORWARD;
PROCEDURE *Factor*(**VAR** *e*:*strings*; **VAR** *success*:*BOOLEAN*);
  FORWARD;
  Next we have a procedure for each nonterminal ∗)
PROCEDURE *Expr*(**VAR** *e*:*strings*; **VAR** *success*:*BOOLEAN*);
VAR *ecopy*:*strings*;*succ*:*BOOLEAN*;
  PROCEDURE *endExpr*(**VAR** *e*:*strings*; **VAR** *success*:*BOOLEAN*);
  VAR *ecopy*:*strings*;
    PROCEDURE *Orop*(**VAR** *e*:*strings*; **VAR** *success*:*BOOLEAN*);
    BEGIN
      WITH *e* **DO**
        success:=(*chr*[*posn*]=*orch*); **IF** *success* **THEN** *INC*(*posn*); **END**;
      END;
    END *Orop*;
  BEGIN
    ecopy:=*e*; *Orop*(*ecopy,success*);
    IF *success* **THEN** *Expr*(*ecopy,success*); **END**;
    IF *success* **THEN** *e*:=*ecopy*; **END**;
  END *endExpr*;

```
BEGIN
  ecopy:=e; Term(ecopy,success);
  IF success THEN
  e:=ecopy; endExpr(ecopy,succ);
  IF succ THEN e:=ecopy; END;
  END;
END Expr;
PROCEDURE Term(VAR e:strings; VAR success:BOOLEAN);
VAR ecopy:strings; succ:BOOLEAN;
  PROCEDURE endTerm(VAR e:strings; VAR success:BOOLEAN);
  VAR ecopy:strings;
    PROCEDURE Andop(VAR e:strings; VAR success:BOOLEAN);
    BEGIN
      WITH e DO
      success:=(chr[posn]=andch); IF success THEN INC(posn); END;
      END;
    END Andop;
  BEGIN
    ecopy:=e; Andop(ecopy,success);
    IF success THEN
      Term(ecopy,success); IF success THEN e:=ecopy; END;
    END;
  END endTerm;
BEGIN
  ecopy:=e; Factor(ecopy,success);
  IF success THEN
  e:=ecopy; endTerm(ecopy,succ);
  IF succ THEN e:=ecopy; END;
  END;
END Term;
PROCEDURE Factor(VAR e:strings; VAR success:BOOLEAN);
VAR ecopy:strings;
  PROCEDURE Group(VAR e:strings; VAR success:BOOLEAN);
  VAR ecopy:strings;
    PROCEDURE Leftpar(VAR e:strings; VAR success:BOOLEAN);
    BEGIN
      WITH e DO
      success:=(chr[posn]=lpar); IF success THEN INC(posn); END;
      END;
    END Leftpar;
    PROCEDURE endGroup(VAR e:strings; VAR success:BOOLEAN);
    VAR ecopy:strings;
      PROCEDURE Rightpar(VAR e:strings; VAR success:BOOLEAN);
      BEGIN
        WITH e DO
        success:=(chr[posn]=rpar); IF success THEN INC(posn); END;
        END;
      END Rightpar;
```

```
BEGIN
  ecopy:=e; Expr(ecopy,success);
  IF success THEN
    Rightpar(ecopy,success); IF success THEN e:=ecopy; END;
  END;
END endGroup;
BEGIN
  ecopy:=e; Leftpar(ecopy,success);
  IF success THEN
    endGroup(ecopy,success); IF success THEN e:=ecopy; END;
  END;
END Group;
PROCEDURE Negations(VAR e:strings; VAR success:BOOLEAN);
VAR ecopy:strings;
  PROCEDURE Notop(VAR e:strings; VAR success:BOOLEAN);
  BEGIN
    WITH e DO
    success:=(chr[posn]=notch); IF success THEN INC(posn); END;
    END;
  END Notop;
BEGIN
  ecopy:=e; Notop(ecopy,success);
  IF success THEN
    Factor(ecopy,success); IF success THEN e:=ecopy; END;
  END;
END Negations;
PROCEDURE Atom(VAR e:strings; VAR success:BOOLEAN);
BEGIN
  WITH e DO
  success:=((CAP(chr[posn])≥'A')AND(CAP(chr[posn])≤'Z'));
  IF success THEN INC(posn); END;
  END;
END Atom;
BEGIN
  ecopy:=e; Negations(ecopy,success);
  IF ¬success THEN Group(ecopy,success); END;
  IF ¬success THEN Atom(ecopy,success); END;
  IF success THEN e:=ecopy; END;
END Factor;
BEGIN
  WriteString('This␣program␣only␣accepts␣valid␣logical␣expressions');
  WriteLn; WriteString('Press␣"!"␣to␣finish'); WriteLn;
  WriteString('Propositional␣variables␣are␣single␣letters'); WriteLn;
  WriteString("'~'␣is␣NOT,␣'&'␣is␣AND,␣'|'␣is␣OR;");
  WriteString("␣use␣'('␣and ch␣')'␣as␣brackets"); WriteLn;
  WITH expression DO
  REPEAT
    ReadExpression(expression); null:=chr[minindex]='!';
    IF ¬null THEN
      Expr(expression,success);
      success:=success & (chr[posn]≤'␣');
```

```
    IF success THEN
        WriteString('Expression␣valid'); WriteLn;
    ELSE
        WriteString('Expression␣'); WriteString(chr);
        WriteString('␣invalid'); WriteLn;
    END;
   END;
  UNTIL null;
 END;
END Parse.
```

Appendix C

Further reading

A leisurely introduction to the applications of the material in Chapters 2–5, together with an introduction to the specification language Z, may be found in the following. Z is a cross between mathematics and a programming language, and uses horizontal and vertical lines extensively to try to make the mathematics more palatable.

An Introduction to Discrete Mathematics and Formal System Specification, *D. C. Ince,* Oxford University Press, 1988.

An account of the theory of how programs, data and computers are modelled, including an excellently readable introduction to program verification, may be found in the next book.

Fundamental Structures of Computer Science, *William A. Wulf, Mary Shaw, Paul N. Hilfinger, and Lawrence Flon,* Addison-Wesley Publishing Company, 1981.

Database design is covered extensively in the following two books. The second is probably more readable, though sometimes inaccurate.

An Introduction to Database Systems, *C. J. Date,* Addison-Wesley Publishing Company, 1986.

A Pascal Database Book, *Julian R. Ullmann,* Oxford University Press, 1985.

The subject matter of Chapter 8 is considerably extended in the following excellently readable book.

Theory of Finite Automata, with an Introduction to Formal Languages, *John Carroll and Darrell Long,* Prentice-Hall International, Inc., 1989.

The following is only for the mathematically mature. It covers formal languages, automata, the theory of computation, complexity theory, cryptography and Petri nets.

Computation and Automata, *Arto Salomaa,* Cambridge
University Press, 1985.

The details of how a grammar is turned into a recognizer, and then
a code generator, are covered in the following.

Compilers, Their Design and Construction Using Pascal,
Robin Hunter, John Wiley & Sons, 1985.

INDEX

309

odd 89, 121
omega (Ω, ω)
omicron (O, o)
one-to-one correspondence 112
open path 150
open trail 150
open walk 150
operating system 235
operator 87
    infix 198
optional occurrence 218, 224
ordered pair 61
Ore's Theorem 158
outdegree 170

parallel computations 191
parser **B.11**
parsing 159
partial mapping **5.2**, 102, 109–110,
    117, 131–132, 256
partial order **4.12**, 136, 173, 274
partially ordered set 92
partition **4.11**, 121, 148, 157, 171
    block 88
    class 88
    refinement 173
path **6.7**, 170
    closed path 150
    critical path **7.5**
    longest path **7.5**
    nontrivial path 150
    open path 150
    shortest path **7.4**, 149
    trivial path 150
pendant 146, 263
permutation **5.8**, 2, 289
    cycle 118
    cyclic permutation 119
    even 121
    identity permutation 289
    odd 121
    product of permutations 117
phi (Φ, ϕ, φ)
phrase structure grammar 220,
    231

phrase structure production 217
pi (Π, π, ϖ)
place 8
police 4
pop 211
poset **4.12**, **B.3**, 135, 274
    total ordering 93
positive closure 208, 215
positive definite 155
postcondition 40
postfix 212, 292–293
postorder **B.8**, 212, 293
power 202, 204, 209, 215
power of a set 62
power set 49, 62, 101, 126, 136, 176
precondition 40
    weakest precondition 41
predicate **2.4**, **2.20**, 43–44, 48–50,
    55, 61, 74, 94, 129
predicate calculus 38
prefix 39, 212, 292–293
preorder **B.8**, 212, 293
Prim's algorithm **7.3**, **B.4**, 181,
    279
primes 250
primes, infinitely many 24
priority 28
product 130, 214
    unordered 139
product of permutations 117
production 217
    context-free production 217
    left recursive production **8.15**
    phrase structure production
    217
programs **B.**
projection 128, 133, 255
proof by contradiction (**see contradiction**)
proper subset 48
proper superset 48
proposition **2.2**, 6, 8
propositional variable **2.3**
pseudograph 139, 142, 144